DIONYSIUS OF HALICARNASSUS AND AUGUSTAN ROME

The Greek author Dionysius of Halicarnassus came to Rome in 30/29 BC. He learnt Latin, developed a network of students, patrons and colleagues, and started to teach rhetoric. He published a history of early Rome (*Roman Antiquities*), and essays on rhetoric and literary criticism, including *On the Ancient Orators, On Composition*, and several letters. This volume examines how Dionysius' critical and rhetorical works are connected with his history of Rome, and the complex ways in which both components of this dual project – rhetorical criticism and historiography – fit into the social, intellectual, literary, cultural and political world of Rome under Augustus. How does Dionysius' interpretation of the earliest Romans resonate with the political reality of the Principate? And how do his views relate to those of Cicero, Livy and Horace? This volume casts new light on ancient rhetoric, literary criticism, historiography and the literary culture of Augustan Rome.

RICHARD HUNTER is Regius Professor of Greek in the University of Cambridge and a Fellow of Trinity College. He has published extensively in the fields of Greek and Latin literature; his most recent books include *Plato and the Traditions of Ancient Literature: The Silent Stream* (Cambridge 2012), *Hesiodic Voices* (Cambridge 2014), *Apollonius of Rhodes, Argonautica Book IV* (Cambridge 2015) and *The Measure of Homer* (Cambridge 2018). Many of his essays have been collected in the two-volume *On Coming After: Studies in Post-Classical Greek Literature and Its Reception* (2008).

CASPER C. DE JONGE is Lecturer of Ancient Greek Language and Literature at Leiden University. His research focuses on ancient rhetoric and literary criticism, the history of grammar and scholarship, and Greek intellectuals in Rome. His publications include *Between Grammar and Rhetoric: Dionysius of Halicarnassus on Language, Linguistics and Literature* (2008). He has received a grant from the Netherlands Organisation for Scientific Research (NWO) for a research project on 'Greek Criticism and Latin Literature'.

GREEK CULTURE IN THE ROMAN WORLD

Editors

SUSAN E. ALCOCK,
University of Michigan

JAŚ ELSNER,
Corpus Christi College, Oxford

SIMON GOLDHILL,
University of Cambridge

MICHAEL SQUIRE,
King's College London

The Greek culture of the Roman Empire offers a rich field of study. Extraordinary insights can be gained into processes of multicultural contact and exchange, political and ideological conflict, and the creativity of a changing, polyglot empire. During this period, many fundamental elements of Western society were being set in place: from the rise of Christianity, to an influential system of education, to long-lived artistic canons. This series is the first to focus on the response of Greek culture to its Roman imperial setting as a significant phenomenon in its own right. To this end, it will publish original and innovative research in the art, archaeology, epigraphy, history, philosophy, religion and literature of the empire, with an emphasis on Greek material.

Recent titles in the series:

Reading Fiction with Lucian: Fakes, Freaks and Hyperreality
KAREN NÍ MHEALLAIGH

Greek Narratives of the Roman Empire under the Severans:
Cassius Dio, Philostratus and Herodian
ADAM M. KEMEZIS

The End of Greek Athletics
SOFIE REMIJSEN

Roman Festivals in the Greek East:
From the Early Empire to the Middle Byzantine Era
FRITZ GRAF

Greek Myths in Roman Art and Culture:
Imagery, Values and Identity in Italy, 50 BC-AD 250
ZAHRA NEWBY

Visual Style and Constructing Identity in the Hellenistic World:
Nemrud Dağ and Commagene under Antiochos I
MIGUEL JOHN VERSLUYS

DIONYSIUS OF HALICARNASSUS AND AUGUSTAN ROME

Rhetoric, Criticism and Historiography

EDITED BY

RICHARD HUNTER
University of Cambridge

CASPER C. DE JONGE
Universiteit Leiden

CAMBRIDGE
UNIVERSITY PRESS

Shaftesbury Road, Cambridge CB2 8EA, United Kingdom

One Liberty Plaza, 20th Floor, New York, NY 10006, USA

477 Williamstown Road, Port Melbourne, VIC 3207, Australia

314–321, 3rd Floor, Plot 3, Splendor Forum, Jasola District Centre, New Delhi – 110025, India

103 Penang Road, #05–06/07, Visioncrest Commercial, Singapore 238467

Cambridge University Press is part of Cambridge University Press & Assessment, a department of the University of Cambridge.

We share the University's mission to contribute to society through the pursuit of education, learning and research at the highest international levels of excellence.

www.cambridge.org
Information on this title: www.cambridge.org/9781108465588

DOI: 10.1017/9781108647632

© Cambridge University Press & Assessment 2019

This publication is in copyright. Subject to statutory exception and to the provisions of relevant collective licensing agreements, no reproduction of any part may take place without the written permission of Cambridge University Press & Assessment.

First published 2019
First paperback edition 2024

A catalogue record for this publication is available from the British Library

Library of Congress Cataloging-in-Publication data
NAMES: Hunter, R. L. (Richard L.), editor. | Jonge, Casper Constantijn de, 1977– editor.
TITLE: Dionysius of Halicarnassus and Augustan Rome : rhetoric, criticism and historiography / edited by Richard Hunter, Casper C. de Jonge.
OTHER TITLES: Greek culture in the Roman world.
DESCRIPTION: Cambridge : Cambridge University Press, 2018. | Series: Greek culture in the Roman world
IDENTIFIERS: LCCN 2018022948 | ISBN 9781108474900
SUBJECTS: LCSH: Dionysius, of Halicarnassus – Criticism and interpretation. | Rhetoric, Ancient. | Rome – Historiography.
CLASSIFICATION: LCC PA3967.Z4 D56 2018 | DDC 880.9/001–dc23
LC record available at https://lccn.loc.gov/2018022948

ISBN 978-1-108-47490-0 Hardback
ISBN 978-1-108-46558-8 Paperback

Cambridge University Press & Assessment has no responsibility for the persistence or accuracy of URLs for external or third-party internet websites referred to in this publication and does not guarantee that any content on such websites is, or will remain, accurate or appropriate.

Contents

List of contributors	*page* vii
Acknowledgements	viii
A note on editions, translations and abbreviations	ix

    Introduction   1
    Casper C. de Jonge and Richard Hunter

PART 1: DIONYSIUS AND AUGUSTAN RHETORIC AND LITERARY CRITICISM   35

1 Dionysius of Halicarnassus and the Idea of the Critic   37
   Richard Hunter

2 Experiencing the Past: Language, Time and Historical Consciousness in Dionysian Criticism   56
   Nicolas Wiater

3 Dionysius' Demosthenes and Augustan Atticism   83
   Harvey Yunis

4 Dionysius and Lysias' Charm   106
   Laura Viidebaum

PART 2: DIONYSIUS AND AUGUSTAN HISTORIOGRAPHY   125

5 The Expansive Scale of the *Roman Antiquities*   127
   S. P. Oakley

6 Ways of Killing Women: Dionysius on the Deaths of Horatia and Lucretia   161
   Clemence Schultze

7	The Prehistory of the Roman *polis* in Dionysius *Matthew Fox*	180

PART 3: DIONYSIUS AND AUGUSTAN ROME   201

8	Dionysius on Regime Change *Christopher Pelling*	203
9	How Roman Are the *Antiquities*? The Decemvirate according to Dionysius *Daniel Hogg*	221
10	Dionysius and Horace: Composition in Augustan Rome *Casper C. de Jonge*	242
	Envoi: Migrancy *Joy Connolly*	267

Bibliography   278
Index of Passages Discussed   297
General Index   299

Contributors

JOY CONNOLLY is Provost and Distinguished Professor of Classics at The Graduate Center, City University of New York.

MATTHEW FOX is Professor of Classics at the University of Glasgow.

DANIEL HOGG is Head of Classics and Senior Tutor at Cranleigh School, UK.

RICHARD HUNTER is Regius Professor of Greek at the University of Cambridge and a Fellow of Trinity College.

CASPER C. DE JONGE is Lecturer in Ancient Greek at Leiden University.

STEPHEN OAKLEY is Kennedy Professor of Latin at the University of Cambridge and a Fellow of Emmanuel College.

CHRISTOPHER PELLING is Emeritus Regius Professor of Greek at Oxford University.

CLEMENCE SCHULTZE, retired from Durham University, still works on ancient historiography and classical reception.

LAURA VIIDEBAUM is Assistant Professor of Classics at New York University.

NICOLAS WIATER is Senior Lecturer in Classics at the University of St Andrews.

HARVEY YUNIS is the Andrew W. Mellon Professor of Humanities and Professor of Classics at Rice University.

Acknowledgements

The ten chapters in this volume are based on papers delivered at a conference on 'Dionysius of Halicarnassus and Augustan Rome', organised at Leiden University on 31 May and 1 June 2012. Joy Connolly, who attended the conference, kindly agreed to our invitation to write an 'envoi'. Casper de Jonge would like to thank the Netherlands Organisation for Scientific Research (NWO) for their generous funding of the conference and the Vidi research project 'Greek Criticism and Latin Literature: Classicism and Cultural Interaction in Late Republican and Early Imperial Rome' (Leiden University, 2013–2018). We are grateful to Steven Ooms, Marianne Schippers and Ineke Sluiter for their critical reading of the introduction, and we thank Stephen Oakley and Clemence Schultze for their support in the early stages of the publication process. We also wish to thank the anonymous readers for their helpful suggestions. Particular thanks are due to Michael Sharp at Cambridge University Press for his unflagging support.

A note on editions, translations and abbreviations

All references to the rhetorical-critical works of Dionysius of Halicarnassus indicate the numbers of the chapters and paragraphs in the edition by Aujac (1978–1992, five volumes). References to the *Roman Antiquities* follow Cary's Loeb edition (1937–1950, seven volumes). Some contributors to this volume have provided their own translations of passages from Dionysius' works; some authors indicate that they cite or adapt Spelman 1758 or the Loeb translations by Cary (1937–1950) and Usher (1974–1985). Abbreviations follow those of *The Oxford Classical Dictionary* (4th edition), ed. S. Hornblower, A. Spawforth and E. Eidinow, Oxford 2012. Abbreviations of the works of Dionysius (Dion. Hal.) are as follows:

Amm. 1	*Epistula ad Ammaeum I*	*First Letter to Ammaeus*
Amm. 2	*Epistula ad Ammaeum II*	*Second Letter to Ammaeus*
Ant. Rom.	*Antiquitates Romanae*	*Roman Antiquities*
Comp.	*De compositione verborum*	*On Composition*
Dem.	*De Demosthene*	*On Demosthenes*
Din.	*De Dinarcho*	*On Dinarchus*
Imit.	*De imitatione*	*On Imitation*
Is.	*De Isaeo*	*On Isaeus*
Isoc.	*De Isocrate*	*On Isocrates*
Lys.	*De Lysia*	*On Lysias*
Orat. Vett.	*De oratoribus veteribus*	Preface to *On the Ancient Orators*
Pomp.	*Epistula ad Pompeium*	*Letter to Pompeius*
Thuc.	*De Thucydide*	*On Thucydides*

Introduction
Casper C. de Jonge and Richard Hunter

Dionysius of Halicarnassus: A Greek Historian and Rhetorician in Rome

Dionysius, son of Alexander, was born in Halicarnassus, before 55 BC.[1] He came to Rome in 30/29 BC, 'at the very time that Augustus Caesar put an end to the civil war'.[2] Having settled in the capital of the Roman world, he learnt Latin, developed an extensive network of colleagues, students and patrons, and wrote several Greek treatises on rhetoric and literary criticism. In 8/7 BC he published the first part of his monumental history of early Rome.[3] He probably lived on in Rome well beyond that date, while he was working on the remaining part of the *Roman Antiquities*, the complete edition of which was to be published in twenty books, covering the history of Rome down to the year 264 BC. The first eleven books plus some excerpts have been preserved. We do not know when and where Dionysius died.

Apart from the *Roman Antiquities*, ten of his works have survived, the chronological order of which can be partly established.[4] The early essays are *On Imitation* (which partially survives in fragments and an epitome) and the first part of his *On the Ancient Orators*, including the treatises *On Lysias, On Isocrates* and *On Isaeus*. The works of the middle period are *On Demosthenes, On Composition* (or *On the Arrangement of Words*), the *Letter to Pompeius* and the *First Letter to Ammaeus*. The later essays are *On Thucydides* along with its appendix, the *Second Letter to Ammaeus*, and

---

[1] See Dion. Hal. *Ant. Rom.* 2.6.4: Licinius Crassus led his army against the Parthians 'in my time' (κατὰ τὴν ἐμὴν ἡλικίαν); cf. Hidber 1996, 2; Fromentin 1998, xiii.
[2] *Ant. Rom.* 1.7.2: 'in the middle of the 187th Olympiad'. [3] *Ant. Rom.* 1.3.4 and 7.70.2.
[4] On the relative order of the rhetorical-critical works, see Bonner 1939, 25–38; Aujac 1978, 22–8; De Jonge 2008, 20–3.

I

On Dinarchus. Nothing survives of the treatises *On Figures* and *On Political Philosophy*.[5]

The extensive oeuvre of Dionysius of Halicarnassus is characterized by a dual tension between cultures and between genres. These two themes determine the agenda of this volume, which seeks to understand Dionysius as a writer positioned between Greece and Rome and between rhetoric and historiography. More specifically, the current volume examines how Dionysius' rhetorical and critical works are connected and intertwined with his history of early Rome, and the complex ways in which both components of this dual project – rhetorical criticism and historiography – fit into the social, intellectual, literary, cultural and political world of Rome under Augustus.

Rhetoric and Historiography

One of the most striking aspects of modern scholarship on Dionysius is its division, with a few exceptions, into two separate halves. Although it is often rightly asserted that Dionysius' rhetoric and historiography are really inseparable, it is still largely true that one group of scholars work on the *Roman Antiquities* and another group on the rhetorical-critical works. More problematic is the fact that specialists focusing on one genre have not always taken (the scholarship on) the other genre sufficiently into account.[6] One important aim of this volume is to bridge the gap between the two genres (and between the two groups of scholars), by interpreting Dionysius' rhetorical criticism and historiography as two closely connected components of one overarching intellectual and educational project.

Readers of the twenty-first century might be surprised by the fact that one ancient author devoted his life to both rhetoric and historiography, as these disciplines are nowadays sometimes thought to be hardly compatible. But ancient authors and readers were well aware that the two genres are naturally related, as any historical text inevitably starts from invention (selection of material), disposition and style, which are the basic tools of

---

[5] *On Political Philosophy*: Dion Hal. *Thuc*. 2.3. Cf. Aujac 1991, 46 n. 2. *On Figures*: Quint. *Inst*. 9.3.89. We may doubt that Dionysius ever wrote the treatise *On the Selection of Words*, which he hoped to present as a sequel to *On Composition* (see *Comp*. 1.10). The *Ars Rhetorica* attributed to Dionysius is not his work.

[6] Important exceptions include Goudriaan 1989; Gabba 1991; Fox 1993; Wiater 2011a (esp. 120–225). For the idea that the historical and rhetorical works are closely connected and inseparable, see, e.g., Gabba 1991, 4; De Jonge 2008, 19; Wiater 2011a, 123.

rhetoric.⁷ The historian constructs the past, just as the rhetorician carefully shapes the narration in a forensic speech. The very close connection in antiquity between rhetoric and historiography has even been suggested to anticipate – in one sense – the theories of the historian Hayden White. In his influential *Metahistory* (1973), White pointed out that historical writing mirrors literary writing, since both genres rely on narrative, which implies selecting, omitting and structuring material: the historian constructs a version of the past and moulds it into a coherent story.⁸ Such an understanding of historical writing sits well with Dionysius' criticism of Herodotus and Thucydides, but also with his own practice in the *Roman Antiquities*.

This volume will suggest various ways in which Dionysius' two fields of interest are related and intertwined. From a general perspective one could distinguish three levels where Dionysius' rhetorical-critical works are connected with his *Roman Antiquities*. One level is that of theory and practice.⁹ Dionysius' choices in writing his own history of Rome can be understood as reflecting the theories in his rhetorical-critical works. Three of his essays are obviously of essential importance here: the *Letter to Pompeius*, which contains an extensive comparison of Herodotus and Thucydides; the treatise *On Thucydides*, a critical discussion of the content and style of Thucydides' *Histories*; and the *Second Letter to Ammaeus*, an analysis of Thucydides' often obscure language.¹⁰ In the *Letter to Pompeius*, Dionysius explains how historians should proceed when choosing their topic, determining the beginning and end of the narrative, selecting the events, arranging the material and adopting the right attitude towards the events described (*Pomp.* 3.2–15). All such theoretical instructions can be compared with Dionysius' own practice as a historian.¹¹ Several authors in this volume indeed demonstrate that Dionysius' literary criticism helps us to

---

⁷ On rhetoric and historiography, see esp. the seminal work of Woodman 1988, who focuses on Cicero and Latin historians. Fox and Livingstone 2010 discuss Greek rhetoric and historiography.
⁸ White 1973. On Dionysius and Hayden White, see Wiater 2011a, 123–6, 160–1. He rightly warns (p. 123), however, that Dionysius should not be called a 'Hayden White of antiquity'. On White, see also Fox in this volume.
⁹ Schwartz 1903, 936 summarizes the *Roman Antiquities* as 'ein genauer Commentar zu seinen theoretischen Ausführungen über Historiographie'. For Schwartz, however, this is purely negative: the *Roman Antiquities* confirm that Dionysius did not understand anything of ancient historiography ('dass D. von dem, was die antike Historiographie wollte und konnte, auch nicht die ersten Elemente begriffen hat').
¹⁰ For Dionysius' theory of historiography in the rhetorical works, see Halbfas 1910, Pavano 1936, Grube 1950, Sacks 1983, De Jonge 2017. See further Pavano 1958, Pritchett 1975, Aujac 1991, Hunter in this volume on *Thuc.*; Aujac 1992; Fornaro 1997; Wiater 2011a, 132–54 on *Pomp.*; Aujac 1992, De Jonge 2011 on *Amm.* 2.
¹¹ Such comparisons have been presented by Halbfas 1910; Heath 1989, 71–89; Wiater 2011a, 132–54.

understand specific passages of the *Roman Antiquities*, but also the other way around – that his own history of Rome casts light on his criticism of Herodotus and Thucydides.

A second level at which rhetoric and historiography come together is that of 'imitation' (μίμησις), the central concept that may be said to encapsulate the intentions of all of Dionysius' works.[12] In the *Roman Antiquities*, Dionysius aims not only to inform his readers about the obscure origins of Rome, but also to provide models of imitation:

> (...) Rome from the very beginning, immediately after its founding, produced infinite examples of virtue in men whose superiors, whether for piety or for justice or for life-long self-control or for warlike valor, no city, either Greek or barbarian, has ever produced. (*Ant. Rom.* 1.5.3)[13]

The moral conduct of the early Romans should instruct and inspire the (Roman) readers of the *Roman Antiquities*:

> And again, both the present and future descendants of those godlike men will choose, not the pleasantest and easiest of lives, but rather the noblest and most ambitious, when they consider that all who are sprung from an illustrious origin ought to set a high value on themselves and indulge in no pursuit unworthy of their ancestors (μηδὲν ἀνάξιον ἐπιτηδεύειν τῶν προγόνων). (*Ant. Rom.* 1.6.4)

For Dionysius it is an essential function of historiography to provide inspiring models for the present and the future – *exempla*, as the Romans would say. In the *Letter to Pompeius* he argues that Herodotus did and Thucydides did not understand this central purpose of historical writing: Herodotus' Greeks accomplished 'wonderful deeds', whereas Thucydides describes a war that was 'neither glorious nor fortunate' and should have been forgotten altogether (*Pomp.* 3.2–4).

The idea of μίμησις is also central to the rhetorical works. Dionysius scrutinizes the writings of ancient poets, orators and historians, whose best qualities he feels should be carefully studied by his students. The concept of imitation was of such importance to Dionysius that he published a separate work on μίμησις, its aims, methods and techniques, as well as the literary models to be imitated and emulated. Unfortunately, his work *On Imitation* is largely lost, but apart from a few fragments and an epitome, we also have a long passage of the work

---

[12] See Delcourt 2005, 43–7; De Jonge 2008, 19–20. On the role of mimesis in Greek imperial literature, see esp. Whitmarsh 2001, 46–57.

[13] Translations of the *Roman Antiquities* in this introduction are borrowed or adapted from Cary 1937–1950.

that Dionysius cites in the *Letter to Pompeius*.¹⁴ Even if we did not have these precious remains, the importance of μίμησις to both sides of Dionysius' project would still be abundantly clear, as it is such a dominant theme in all of his works. In the preface to *On the Ancient Orators*, often seen as a 'manifesto of classicism', Dionysius emphatically presents the rhetorical culture of classical Athens as the model of rhetorical and literary writing in Rome under Augustus.¹⁵ The Attic Muse, which had been driven away by an Asian harlot after the death of Alexander the Great, had recently been restored thanks to Rome and 'its leaders' (δυναστεύοντες); as a result, Dionysius claims, many historical, political and philosophical treatises are published in his own time by 'both Romans and Greeks' (καὶ Ῥωμαίοις καὶ Ἕλλησιν, *Orat. Vett.* 3.2). After a period of decline, which Dionysius associates with 'Asian' influence and which modern readers in the wake of Gustav Droysen label the 'Hellenistic period', Rome becomes the new Athens, resulting in a revival of Attic eloquence.¹⁶ This revival is grounded, of course, in the concept of μίμησις, the creative and eclectic imitation and emulation of classical Greek models, not only of oratory, but also of morality and lifestyle, as becomes clear from Dionysius' programmatic questions:¹⁷

> Who are the most important of the ancient orators and historians? What manner of life and style of writing did they adopt? Which characteristic of each of them should we take over, or which should we avoid? (*Orat. Vett.* 4.2)

The formulation of these questions, juxtaposing lifestyle and writing style, suggests a third level at which the genres of rhetoric and historiography are connected. One important ideal underlying all of Dionysius' works is that of moral education and civilization, closely connected with Isocratean παιδεία.¹⁸ Readers of the *Roman Antiquities* will become better citizens if they look carefully at the early Romans; readers of the rhetorical works, like the young student Metilius Rufus, the addressee of *On Composition*, are likewise trained to become good citizens, who are both verbally and

---

¹⁴ For *On Imitation*, see the editions by Aujac 1992 and Battisti 1997; see also Hunter 2009. On the citation of *Imit.* in *Pomp.* 3, see Weaire 2002.
¹⁵ On the preface to *Orat. Vett.*, see Hidber 1996, who labels this text 'das klassizistische Manifest'. See also De Jonge 2014a.
¹⁶ On Augustan Rome as the revival of classical Athens, see Hidber 1996, 75–81.
¹⁷ See Hidber 1996, 56–75. Translations of the critical essays in this introduction are adapted from Usher 1974–1985.
¹⁸ On this important theme, see Goudriaan 1989; Hidber 1996, 44–75.

morally ready to play an active part in Roman society. In his treatise *On Isocrates*, Dionysius poses a series of rhetorical questions, which eloquently bring out the moral connotations of his program:

> Who could fail to become a patriotic supporter of democracy and a student of civic virtue after reading Isocrates' *Panegyricus*? (...) What greater exhortation could there be, for individuals singly and collectively for whole communities, than the discourse *On the Peace*? (...) Who would not become a more responsible citizen after reading the *Areopagiticus* (...)? (*Isoc.* 5.1, 7.1, 8.1)

Throughout his works, Dionysius is a patient and passionate teacher, whose lessons are not only concerned with rhetorical theory, literary criticism and the history of Rome, but also with virtue, civic life and human civilization. His program of moral education, as we will see, in many ways resonates with the concerns of Rome at the end of the first century BC.

Greece and Rome

Dionysius' works bear witness to the complex dialogue between Greek and Roman identities at the end of the first century BC.[19] This is a second main theme of this volume. The subject of Greek identity in the Roman Empire has been at the heart of recent research on the Second Sophistic (very roughly 50–250 AD): authors such as Plutarch, Dio of Prusa, Lucian and Philostratus show a very wide range of diverse attitudes towards Hellenic and Roman identity, depending on such factors as location (within the Empire), genre (history, rhetoric, biography, novel, etc.) and literary context.[20] Authors of Greek texts may emphasize continuity between the glorious Greek past and their own time, but they may also applaud the transformation of the world affected by the Roman Empire and the new opportunities that it offers to them. There was not one Greek identity: literary texts adopt a variety of strategies by which identities are constructed and re-constructed in differing and dynamic ways. A similar variety of perspectives on Greek and Roman identities was available to the Greek authors of the Augustan period (27 BC–AD 14), who witnessed the gradual emergence and early development of the Roman Empire. As a substantial

---

[19] See esp. Luraghi 2003, Peirano 2010.
[20] Cf., e.g., Swain 1996, Goldhill 2001, Whitmarsh 2001. See also Whitmarsh 2013 with further bibliography. Barchiesi 2009 examines Roman responses to Greece, Whitmarsh 2009 Greek responses to Rome.

amount of Greek literature of the Augustan Age is either lost or survives in excerpts or fragments only (e.g., the works of Caecilius of Caleacte, Nicolaus of Damascus, Timagenes of Alexandria), Dionysius of Halicarnassus is – with Strabo of Amasia and Antipater of Thessalonica – our principal literary witness for Greek perspectives on Rome in the Augustan period.[21]

On the one hand, Dionysius is thoroughly Greek. He comes from Greek-speaking Asia Minor; he consistently writes in the Greek language; and he teaches about the literature of (what we call) archaic and classical Greece, from Homer to Demosthenes. He is especially interested in the styles of the Attic orators and historians, which are to be imitated and emulated by his students and readers; but he is also more generally intrigued by what he identifies as the highlights of classical Greek culture: Pindar, Plato, Polyclitus and all the great representatives of Greek poetry, music, sculpture, painting and philosophy. Furthermore, as a literary critic he self-consciously presents himself as working in the Greek tradition of learning and scholarship, represented in his works by such celebrated names as Isocrates, Aristotle, Theophrastus, Aristoxenus and Chrysippus.

On the other hand, Dionysius is very Roman. He arrived in Rome at a very significant moment in Roman history and became bilingual, after 'learning the language of the Romans and acquiring knowledge of their writings' (*Ant. Rom.* 1.7.2). Some of the sources of Roman history that he studied were in Greek, like those of Quintus Fabius Pictor and Lucius Cincius Alimentus (*Ant. Rom.* 1.6.3), but Dionysius also read the works of historians who wrote in Latin: 'Porcius Cato, Quintus Fabius Maximus, Valerius Antias, Licinius Macer, the Aelii, Gellii and Calpurnii, and many others of note' (*Ant. Rom.* 1.7.3); elsewhere, Dionysius mentions his older contemporary Varro (*Ant. Rom.* 1.14.1) and several other Roman historians.[22] Furthermore, Dionysius was personally in direct contact with Romans and Greeks who lived at Rome: 'Some information I received orally from men of the greatest learning, with whom I associated' (οἷς εἰς ὁμιλίαν ἦλθον, *Ant. Rom.* 1.6.3).

---

[21] On Greek identity in the Augustan Age, see esp. the volume edited by Schmitz and Wiater 2011a, with contributions on Dionysius by Fox 2011 and Wiater 2011b. Bowersock 1965, 122–39 and Hidber 2011, 122–3 provide overviews of Greek literature under Augustus. On Strabo, Nicolaus and Antipater, see below, pp. 11–13.

[22] On Dionysius' knowledge of Latin, see Marin 1969; Rochette 1997, 231–3; Delcourt 2005, 28–30; De Jonge 2008, 60–5; Nesselrath 2013. On Dionysius and Varro, see De Jonge forthcoming. On Dionysius' sources in *Ant. Rom.*, see Schwartz 1903; Oakley in this volume. 'Aelii' (*Ant. Rom.* 1.7.3) refers to Quintus Aelius Tubero (and possibly his father): see below.

We know the names of several members of Dionysius' intriguing network in Rome.[23] Some of them were Greek, like Demetrius, the addressee of *On Imitation* (otherwise unknown), and Caecilius of Caleacte, the famous historian and rhetorician.[24] Some of them were Roman, like Metilius Rufus, the student who received his *On Composition* as a birthday present. Dionysius describes the father of this young boy as his 'most esteemed friend' (*Comp.* 1.4), which may imply that he acted as his patron; an additional argument for a relationship of patronage is the fact that Dionysius includes the family of the Metilii in his list of Alban *principes* (*Ant. Rom.* 3.29.7).[25] In introducing Metilius Rufus to the secrets of stylistic composition, Dionysius seems to have made a useful contribution to the political career of his Roman pupil: Metilius was to become governor of the province of Achaea, where he had ample opportunity to put his teacher's theories into practice.[26] Another important Roman connection was Quintus Aelius Tubero, the addressee of Dionysius' treatise *On Thucydides*. Aelius Tubero himself wrote a history of Rome (one of Dionysius' sources: see below), possibly in the Thucydidean style, but he was also a lawyer from an influential family, known to us through Cicero's *Pro Ligario* (20–9): Quintus Aelius Tubero's father was a legate in Asia; his sons were consuls in 11 and 4 BC.[27] Dionysius also mentions the names of Ammaeus, addressee of *On the Ancient Orators* and two letters, and Cn. Pompeius Geminus, the addressee of one letter, who was also in touch with Dionysius' friend Zeno.[28] We do not know whether Ammaeus and Pompeius Geminus considered themselves to be Greek or Roman. What is clear, however, is that Dionysius was well connected in Rome, not only with scholars, teachers and students, who stimulated his ideas and intellectual development, but also with influential families who seem to have supported his project.[29] Dionysius' Greek works have a social,

---

[23] On Dionysius' 'literary circle' or 'network of intellectuals' in Rome, see Roberts 1900; Wisse 1995, 78–80; Hidber 1996, 5–7; De Jonge 2008, 25–34. Applying social identity theory, Wiater 2011a, 22–9 interprets Dionysius' network of colleagues and friends as an 'elite community of classicists'.

[24] *Pomp.* 3.1, 3.20. For the fragments of Caecilius, see Woerther 2015.

[25] See Bowersock 1965, 132 n. 2.

[26] Bonner 1939, 2 n. 4; Bowersock 1965, 132; De Jonge in this volume. On Dionysius' strategies as the Greek teacher of a Roman student, see Weaire 2012.

[27] Quintus Aelius Tubero: *Thuc.* 1.1, 55.5. See also *Ant. Rom.* 1.80.1 on Aelius Tubero's history of Rome as one of Dionysius' sources. Cf. Bowersock 1965, 130; Bowersock 1979, 68–70; Fromentin 1998, xiv–xviii. Dionysius may have been familiar with Strabo (who mentions him in *Geogr.* 14.2.16) via the Tuberones.

[28] *Orat. Vett.* 1.1; *Amm.* 1 1.1; *Amm.* 2 1.1; *Pomp.* 1.1.

[29] The Tuberones were among the more prominent families in Rome, as Fromentin 1998, xiv–xv points out: 'une grande famille aristocratique qui comptait plusieurs personnages illustres et qui tenait, semble-t-il, une place de premier plan dans la Rome d'Auguste'. Cf. Bowersock 1979, 68 and

intellectual and cultural context in Rome; Dionysius himself, moreover, explicitly reflects on the complex relationship between Greece and Rome, both in his rhetorical criticism and in his historiography.

In the preface to *On the Ancient Orators*, as we have just seen, Dionysius praises Rome for the cultural revolution it had achieved, and, in particular, for the restitution of the Attic Muse, who stands for a morally serious oratory and literature of high standards. According to Dionysius' manifesto, Rome and its 'leaders' (plural) shaped the political circumstances that facilitated the production of great texts, both in Greek and in Latin. Dionysius' words of praise have been interpreted either as mere flattery, or as the sincere gratitude of a newcomer who enjoyed Roman hospitality. Whichever reading one prefers, the preface stimulates us to understand Dionysius' works within their Roman context, and to ask how precisely the classical Greek orators (and historians and poets) were to be relevant to the political and cultural situation of the city in which he himself was writing and teaching.

The complex relationship between Greece and Rome is the main theme of the *Roman Antiquities*. That work powerfully presents the – for modern readers somewhat remarkable – thesis that the earliest Romans were Greeks, who lived a Greek life, characterized by Greek virtues and organized in Greek institutions. The Greeks, as Dionysius tells us, came to Italy in five successive stages: (1) Arcadian Aborigines, (2) Thessalian Pelasgians (from the Peloponnese), (3) Arcadians from Pallantium who were led by Evander, (4) Peloponnesians who were guided by Hercules and (5) Aeneas with the Trojans (who were in fact also Greeks).[30] All these groups founded settlements in Italy and contributed to the gradual progress of civilization. Evander founded Pallantium, Aeneas and the Trojans (now Latins) built Lavinium and Alba. Sixteen generations after the fall of Troy, the Latins surrounded Pallantium with a wall, and 'this settlement they called Rome, after Romulus' (*Ant. Rom.* 1.45.3). Dionysius' extensive narrative of these earliest events in Roman history finds its climax in his emphatic presentation of Rome as a 'Greek city':

> Hence, from now on let the reader forever renounce the views of those who make Rome a retreat of barbarians, fugitives and vagabonds, and let him confidently affirm it to be a Greek city (Ἑλλάδα πόλιν), – which will be easy

---

contrast Schwartz 1903, 934, who thought that Dionysius' addressees were 'no distinguished people' ('keine vornehmen Leute').

[30] See *Ant. Rom.* 1.11.1–4, 17.1, 31.1, 34.1–2, 45.1, 61–2, 89.1–2. Important discussions include Gabba 1991, 98–118; Fromentin 1998, xxxi–xxxiv; Luraghi 2003, 277–81; Delcourt 2005; Fox in this volume.

when he shows that it is at once the most hospitable and friendly of all cities, and when he bears in mind that the Aborigines were Oenotrians, and these in turn Arcadians (...). (*Ant. Rom.* 1.89.1)

Dionysius' portrayal of Roman institutions as essentially Greek, most clearly articulated in the famous Constitution of Romulus (*Ant. Rom.* 2. 3–26), has been challenged and rejected by readers through the centuries; more recently, however, his account has also provoked more positive responses. Dionysius' interpretation of Roman antiquity has received partial support from those historians and archaeologists who have identified Greek elements in the material culture of early Rome. Two millennia after Dionysius published his *Roman Antiquities*, the question 'Was Rome a *polis*?' turns out to be highly topical.[31] Furthermore, Dionysius' understanding of Rome as a Greek city has – obviously in a strongly modified form – found serious approval in recent scholarship:

> Greek culture leaves its mark on Rome at every moment we can document, and the more we learn about archaic Rome, the more we are inclined to accept, even if in a rather different sense, the argument of the Augustan historian, Dionysius of Halicarnassus, that Rome was from the first a Greek city.[32]

This volume will not enter the debate on the historical (in)accuracy of Dionysius' portrayal of Rome as a Greek city. What matters here is the fact that the complex relationship between Greek and Roman identity deeply informs the *Roman Antiquities*, just as it informs Dionysius' rhetorical works. This raises numerous questions about Dionysius' project. How Roman are the *Roman Antiquities*? For whom does Dionysius write that work: for Greeks, Romans or both? And how would these readers feel about Rome as a Greek city? Does Dionysius' perspective belittle the Romans (whose civilization turns out to be Greek), or does it contribute to the harmony of the *Pax Augusta* by suggesting a peaceful continuity between Greece and Rome? Who is the intended audience of the rhetorical works?[33] Was a student like Metilius Rufus supposed to apply Dionysius' analysis of Greek stylistic composition to his own (first) language, or was he trained to make speeches for audiences in the Greek-speaking parts of the Empire? Can we in fact adequately distinguish between Greeks and Romans in a world that is thoroughly bilingual? How does Dionysius' version of Rome's history differ from the Latin *Ab Urbe Condita* written by

---

[31] Ando 1999.   [32] Wallace-Hadrill 2008, 25.   [33] On Dionysius' audience, see below.

his contemporary colleague Livy?[34] And to what extent do the critical essays and the history of Rome reflect the discourse of Greek and Roman debates on literature at the end of the first century BC? The authors of this volume address many of these questions and formulate their own answers. But before we can begin pondering these and related problems, one aspect of Dionysius' project must be examined more closely, namely its complex relationship to Augustan Rome and Augustus.

Greek Literature of the Augustan Age

When scholars speak of Augustan literature, they are usually thinking of the Latin poetry of Virgil, Horace, Propertius, Tibullus and Ovid.[35] In various different ways, the works of these Roman poets respond to the cultural and political reality of the Principate established by Augustus. To what extent might we consider Greek texts of the period to be 'Augustan' as well, and what would it mean for these texts to be called Augustan? In order further to contextualize the works of Dionysius, we single out three contemporary authors, who together with Dionysius may be considered characteristic of the Greek literature of the Augustan Age: Strabo of Amasia, Nicolaus of Damascus and Antipater of Thessalonica.

Strabo of Amasia (ca. 64 BC–AD 24) was born one year before Augustus; though an indefatigable traveler, he also spent many years in Rome.[36] His *Geography* includes detailed descriptions of Augustan monuments. Strabo's patron was Gaius Aelius Gallus, the second prefect of Egypt. In Rome he seems to have learnt at least some Latin, while establishing contacts with several members of the Roman elite. Throughout the *Geography* Strabo offers a positive appraisal of Augustus: the *princeps* is depicted as a pious, generous and educated man whose building projects greatly contributed to the beauty of Rome. Strabo also mentions 'Dionysius the historian' (Διονύσιος ὁ συγγραφεύς) as one of the famous men who 'in my time' came from Halicarnassus.[37]

Nicolaus of Damascus (also born around 64 BC) was a friend of king Herod the Great; as the king's diplomat Nicolaus traveled several times to Rome, where he met Augustus himself. This meeting had consequences,

---

[34] It is debated whether Dionysius knew Livy's work: see below and Oakley in this volume.
[35] The four chapters on 'Augustan Literature' in Galinsky 2005a focus on Latin poetry, although Galinsky 2005b, 341–4 includes some comments on Strabo and Nicolaus. Bowersock 1965, 122–39 discusses 'Greek literature under Augustus'.
[36] On Strabo and Augustan Rome, see Dueck 2000, 85–106.   [37] Strabo 14.2.16, 656C.

for apart from a universal history, an autobiography and a *Life of Herod*, Nicolaus also wrote a *Life of Augustus*.[38] The latter document, of which some fragments survive, appears to be based on Augustus' autobiography *De vita sua* – an intriguing example of the interaction between Latin and Greek texts in the Augustan Age. Nicolaus' affinity with classical Greek philosophy and literature appears from the fact that he composed a treatise *On Aristotle's Philosophy* as well as some Greek tragedies and comedies.[39] Nicolaus' projects thus covered a variety of genres dealing with both Greek and Roman topics – an intellectual and cultural versatility that he obviously shared with Dionysius. Just like the historian and rhetorician of Halicarnassus, Nicolaus of Damascus is mentioned in the work of their contemporary colleague Strabo.[40]

Antipater of Thessalonica was born around 40 BC.[41] He was a client of Lucius Calpurnius Piso Caesoninus (the Pontifex): this famous general and senator, who was consul in 15 BC, was a protégé of Augustus himself. Antipater dedicated several epigrams to his patron when Piso had put down the revolt of the Bessii in Thrace, a military success for which the Roman statesman was honored with a triumph.[42] Antipater accompanied his patron to Rome, where he settled to become a teacher of rhetoric, just like Dionysius, if we are allowed to infer this from one epigram in which Antipater refers to the 'endless discourses' of his pupils, for whom he has to leave his bed in the early morning.[43] Albin Lesky recognized 'Reflexe der augusteischen Kulturpolitik' in the epigrams of Antipater.[44] Two themes stand out in his poetry, one related to the Greek past, one rather to the Roman present. On the one hand, many of his epigrams deal with archaic and classical Greek poets like Homer, Hesiod, Archilochus, Sappho and Pindar, literary models who also figure prominently in Dionysius' *On Composition* and *On Imitation*. On the other hand, Tim Whitmarsh has demonstrated that patronage is a crucial theme in Antipater's poems, which reveals the close ties between the Greek poet and the Roman elite of the Augustan Age.[45]

In connection with Greek authors of the Augustan period, Bowersock has pointed out that '[i]t would be surprising if these men failed to

---

[38] Fragments in Parmentier and Barone 2011. On Nicolaus, see Bowersock 1965, 134–8.
[39] Drossaart Lulofs 1965.   [40] Strabo 15.1.73, 719C.
[41] A number of his poems have survived in the *Palatine Anthology*. See the edition with commentary by Gow and Page 1968. On Antipater, see Bowersock 1965, 132–3; Gow and Page 1968 vol. 2, 18–20; Whitmarsh 2011, 199–201.
[42] See esp. Antipater 1 = *Anth. Pal.* 9.428.   [43] Antipater 7 = *Anth. Pal.* 5.3.   [44] Lesky 1971, 907.
[45] Whitmarsh 2011, 199–201.

encounter one another at Rome'.⁴⁶ We simply do not know, however, whether Dionysius ever met Strabo, Nicolaus or Antipater. But Strabo's references to his colleagues (like Dionysius' reference to Caecilius of Caleacte, see above, p. 8) do make it clear that Greek authors of this period were familiar with works of their Greek colleagues. All these authors were thoroughly Greek, not only in their choice of language, but also in their attitudes towards the literary past. At the same time, they were involved in the social and political circles of Augustan Rome. Dionysius' Roman friends, Quintus Aelius Tubero and the father of Metilius Rufus, were perhaps not as famous as the patrons of Strabo, Nicolaus and Antipater, but they too were members of influential families, who occupied important administrative positions under Augustus. Like Strabo, Nicolaus and Antipater, Dionysius is an 'Augustan' author – not, to be sure, in the sense that he writes Augustan propaganda, but in the sense that his works reflect the political, cultural and intellectual climate of Augustan Rome.

Dionysius and Augustus

Octavian is mentioned only once in Dionysius' oeuvre: the Greek author traveled to Italy 'at the very time that Augustus Caesar put an end to the civil war' (ἅμα τῷ καταλυθῆναι τὸν ἐμφύλιον πόλεμον ὑπὸ τοῦ Σεβαστοῦ Καίσαρος, *Ant. Rom.* 1.7.2). He was not the only one: in the early years of the Principate many intellectuals came to Rome from Greek-speaking areas of the Mediterranean World.⁴⁷ Authors like Strabo, Antipater, Caecilius and Dionysius found employment in the flourishing capital of the Roman world, where there was great interest in the teaching and writings of learned Greek men. Coming from various parts of the Hellenized world, these authors could of course adopt different attitudes towards the political system that was gradually taking shape in the first years of the Principate. To put it very simply, some authors writing in Greek may have been enthusiastic, some critical, and some neutral, nuanced or without a strong opinion; in most cases we just do not know.⁴⁸

As far as serious attention has been given to Dionysius' Augustan context, the scholarly debate has indeed focused on his political orientation, that is, his supposed pro- or anti-Augustan sentiments. This debate

---

⁴⁶ Bowersock 1965, 124. ⁴⁷ See Hidber 1996, 2–4; De Jonge 2008, 29–33.
⁴⁸ One might compare the attitudes of Timagenes of Alexandria and Nicolaus of Damascus. Timagenes burnt his account of Augustus' deeds after a conflict with the emperor: Bowersock 1965, 125. Nicolaus of Damascus' presentation of Augustus substantially differed from the latter's official self-portrayal: Pausch 2011, 159.

has now a rather old-fashioned ring to it, as also do debates about pro- and anti-Augustan sentiment in Roman poetry, and it has always been conducted with a selective attitude to the evidence. Several passages from the rhetorical treatises and the *Roman Antiquities* have been cited as testimony to Dionysius' political views. On the one hand, Dionysius' praise of the Roman 'leaders' (δυναστεύοντες), who 'administer the state according to the highest principles' (ἀπὸ τοῦ κρατίστου τὰ κοινὰ διοικοῦντες, *Orat. Vett.* 3.1), has been interpreted as a pro-Augustan statement.[49] Even if we suppose that the 'leaders' are not Augustus himself but those influential Roman aristocrats (like the Tuberones and the Metilii) who acted as patrons of Greek culture, it seems undeniable that the preface to *On the Ancient Orators* presents a positive image of Roman administration, which is hailed for sponsoring and facilitating Greek and Latin literature. This appraisal of the Roman present is indeed very different from the pessimistic views that we find in the final chapter of Longinus' *On the Sublime*.[50] In the *Roman Antiquities*, there are no explicit statements on Augustus' policies, but there are many passages that could be and have been read as indirect comments on the *princeps*, like Dionysius' praise of the *gens Julia*:[51]

> This house became the greatest and at the same time the most illustrious of any we know of, and produced the most distinguished commanders, whose virtues were so many proofs of their nobility. (*Ant. Rom.* 1.70.4)

Other passages that have been interpreted as indirectly alluding to Augustus include Dionysius' narratives of Evander, Aeneas, Hercules and Romulus, role models who figured prominently in Octavian's discourse of images.[52] On a more general level, Dionysius' interest in the religious life and morality of the early Romans and his emphasis on virtues like piety, justice and moderation (εὐσέβεια, δικαιοσύνη, σωφροσύνη) have been understood as resonating with the Augustan program of moral reform.[53] Although it remains worthwhile to pursue such possible links between past and present, as several authors in this volume will indeed do, scholarship has rightly turned away from the once popular view, mainly based on the influential work of Eduard Schwartz, that Dionysius was

---

[49] Bonner 1939, 10: 'He found himself fully in sympathy with Augustus and his ministers'. See also, e.g., Wilamowitz 1900, 45; Kennedy 1972, 352; Luraghi 2003, 275.
[50] Cf. Heldmann 1982, 122–31, 286–93; De Jonge 2014a.
[51] Luraghi 2003, 275 reads in this passage a clear confirmation of Dionysius' pro-Augustan stance.
[52] Zanker 1987, 204–13 on Aeneas and Romulus.
[53] Luraghi 2003, 275: 'Die Anlehnung an Augustus' restauratorisches Programm ist unübersehbar'. On religious thought in Dionysius, see Mora 1995.

a slavish spokesman of Augustus' propaganda, who 'betrayed' his own Hellenic culture.⁵⁴

Some scholars have pointed to passages that might suggest a more critical stance towards Augustus' reign, on the basis of which Dionysius has even been accounted among the 'opposition' against the regime.⁵⁵ One much cited passage is a chapter of the *Roman Antiquities* in which Dionysius points out that 'the authority of the ancient kings (βασιλέων) was not self-willed (αὐθάδεις) and based on one single judgment (μονογνώμονες) as it is in our days' (οὐχ ὥσπερ ἐν τοῖς καθ' ἡμᾶς χρόνοις, 2.12.4). It seems doubtful that Dionysius would describe Augustus as a 'king' of his own time – he might rather be thinking of Mithridates of Pontus and other kings who were conquered by the Romans – but such passages do make it clear that the *Roman Antiquities* should not be read simply as a (very long) pamphlet of Augustan propaganda, as publications of the early twentieth century were inclined to do.

The rhetorical works further complicate the picture, as they clearly celebrate the democracy of classical Athens that produced the eloquence of the Attic orators: Demosthenes was Dionysius' preferred model of oratory,⁵⁶ not only because he was the master of all styles, but also because he was remembered as the fierce defender of Athenian democracy. In other words, when Dionysius expresses his gratitude for the return of the Attic muse in Augustan Rome, he must have hoped that this city would somehow adopt not only the moral and literary, but also the political values that he associated with the Athens of Pericles and Demosthenes. If this surprises us, we should realize that during the early Principate many 'Augustan' phenomena, including the form of government, 'were in a state of nascence and evolution':⁵⁷ Augustan culture was not homogeneous, but extremely dynamic and multifaceted. Dionysius lived and worked in a time of transition, even if we from our modern perspective sometimes tend to

---

⁵⁴ Schwartz 1903. One citation should be enough to characterize the tone and approach of this highly influential publication (p. 936): 'Sie [the Ἀρχαιολογία = *Roman Antiquities*] ist ein trauriges Dokument dafür, wie tief die geistige Potenz noch mehr als die Bildung der Griechen gesunken war, nachdem die hellenistischen Staaten verfallen waren und ehe der Weltfriede des Kaiserreichs neue Samen hatte reifen lassen'. The influence of Schwartz can still be seen in such publications as Lendle 1992, 242: 'Das Werk des Dionysios is geprägt von einer völlig unkritischen, auf Kosten des Griechenlands gehenden Bewunderung für Rom'. On Schwartz's position, see also Fox in this volume.
⁵⁵ Egger 1902, 12; Marin 1956, 183 (the latter wrongly attributes the treatise *On the Sublime* to Dion. Hal.); Hurst 1982, 855–6. See also Hill 1961, 131 n. 3, who argues that Dionysius opposes the regime by departing from the 'official' version of Rome's early history as represented by Virgil's *Aeneid*. For a comparison of Virgil and Dionysius on the origins of Rome, see Fox in this volume.
⁵⁶ Cf. Yunis in this volume.   ⁵⁷ Galinsky 1996, 8.

assume that 'Augustan Rome' had a clear-cut and stable character. Nor, of course, should we make the mistake of believing that Augustus himself directly or indirectly determined everything that was done or written in Rome.

Dionysius' perspective on Augustan Rome, in short, was necessarily complex and allusive.[58] What is certain is that Dionysius was deeply interested in Rome, its organization and its history; and it seems quite clear that upon his arrival in that city he was generally happy with the ways in which rhetorical and literary writing flourished under Roman administration. His focus on classical Athenian exempla of eloquence elegantly tied in with the Augustan interest in classical Greek culture (sculpture, architecture, literature) and also with what has been called Augustus' 're-Hellenisation' of the east.[59]

Several contributions in this volume are concerned with passages of the *Roman Antiquities* (on political organization, regime change, tyranny, the treatment of women) that seem to resonate with events in Rome during the first century BC.[60] Such readings exploit, whether explicitly or implicitly, the idea that Dionysius' contemporary readers in Rome may have drawn connections between the earliest stages of Roman history, as described by Dionysius, and their own time. A strong argument in favor of such interpretations is provided by Dionysius himself, who frequently invites his readers to connect the past and the present: he talks about sacrifices 'which the Romans performed even in my time' (*Ant. Rom.* 1.32.5), reports about 'the things that I myself know by having seen them' (1.68.1) and describes the hut of Romulus, which 'remained even to my day on the Palatine hill' (1.79.11). The connection between past and present is however not only one of continuity, but also one of contrast and development, as Dionysius makes clear when contrasting the village of Pallantium with the city of Rome into which it would evolve in the course of centuries:[61]

> Yet this village was ordained by fate to excel in the course of time all other cities, whether Greek or barbarian, not only in size, but also in the majesty of

---

[58] See Wiater 2011a, 8–18, who offers a nuanced approach to Dionysius as 'Augustan' author.
[59] Spawforth 2012.
[60] A similar approach in Luraghi 2003, 281, who argues that Dionysius' portrayal of the distant past contains a clear 'message' for the Romans of the Augustan Age: during the civil wars of the first century BC they have alienated themselves from their Hellenic identity. Dionysius tells his Roman readers to return to their virtuous Greek roots. See also Peirano 2010, who argues that the (fragmentary) concluding books of the *Roman Antiquities*, dealing with the Pyrrhic War, warn the readers that 'the moral supremacy the Romans have acquired by remaining true to their Greek heritage is under threat' (p. 51).
[61] Cf. Fox in this volume.

its empire and in every other form of prosperity, and to be celebrated above them all as long as mortality shall endure. (*Ant. Rom.* 1.31.3)

The opposition between Greek and barbarian evoked here draws our attention to Dionysius' Hellenocentrism: the world is still divided into Greeks and barbarians, as it was for Herodotus and Isocrates; the Romans are simply included among the Greeks. For Dionysius, Rome is in fact more Greek than any other city of his time, even if the moral Greekness of the Romans is at times under threat, as in the Pyrrhic War described in the concluding books of the *Roman Antiquities*.[62] All of Dionysius' works seek to demonstrate that the wonderful fruits of Greek civilization – rhetorical, literary, cultural and political – will continue to flourish, as long as Rome will continue to support the project of Dionysius and his community.

Dionysian Criticism

As a critic and theorist of poetry and rhetoric, Dionysius' stock has certainly fluctuated in the course of the last generations, despite (or perhaps because of) the very sizeable body of his criticism which survives.[63] At the beginning of the last century, W. Rhys Roberts, perhaps Dionysius' greatest champion, made plain that the virtues which he found in Dionysius were solid 'Victorian' ones, which might well be thought unfashionable in our postmodern age: Dionysius helps 'to confirm our belief in the essential continuity of critical principles – in the existence of a firm and permanent basis for the judgments of taste' and he is, moreover, 'no frivolous dabbler or dilettante (such as the many who have made literary criticism a byword for superficiality), but he believes in serious, prolonged, and fortifying literary-historical studies'.[64] Roberts (and he certainly was not alone) took at face value Dionysius' claims (notably in the preface to *On the Ancient Orators* and in *On Composition*) about 'the debased standards of the ages immediately preceding his own', standards which he wished to replace with 'a classic excellence'.[65] Although we now no longer share Dionysius'

---

[62] Peirano 2010.
[63] For a brief survey of his (poor) standing in nineteenth and early twentieth-century German scholarship, cf. De Jonge 2008, 4–5.
[64] Roberts 1901, 49; Roberts 1910, vii.
[65] Roberts 1910, vii. In the same preface Roberts has a (now) amusing reflection on the excitement being generated at that time by the papyrological revolution: if *On Composition* had 'lately been discovered in the sands of Egypt or in some buried house at Herculaneum', it is not just the citations of Sappho, Simonides, etc. which would have caused excitement; 'it would be gladly acknowledged that its skilful author had known how to enliven a difficult subject by means of eloquence, enthusiasm, humour, variety in vocabulary and in method of presentation generally (...)'.

classicizing and judgmental view of the history of Greek rhetoric, his confidence in a contemporary resurgence remains a matter of the greatest importance, as it offers a clear point of intersection between his criticism and the Augustan political and moral program,[66] a program which is crucial to an understanding, not just of the *Roman Antiquities*, but also of Dionysius' critical essays.

The current renewal of interest in Dionysius' criticism may be traced to several causes. In the first place, 'rhetoric' is no longer a dirty word. Some thirty years after Rhys Roberts, Stanley Bonner, in what was in some ways a groundbreaking study of the chronology and presuppositions of the critical treatises, was no less quick than Dionysius himself to award praise and blame, and for Bonner there was no doubt where the blame for what he perceived to be Dionysius' faults lay: Dionysius was a victim of 'the singular lack of mental elasticity which was so peculiar a product of the rhetorical training'.[67] Humane studies now approach the nature and purposes of systematized ancient rhetoric rather more sympathetically than did Bonner. The renaissance in the last decades of 'rhetoric' as an academic discipline has often been charted, and Dionysius has, to some extent, shared in this renewed interest. Various strands of this new attention may be teased out. First of all, an interest in the techniques and theorization of persuasion has naturally brought new focus on Dionysius' essays on the orators of classical Athens, for no comparable ancient comparative study exists. It is not simply that Dionysius' repeated concern with questions of authenticity – 'is this a genuine speech of Lysias or not?' – foreshadows a particular concern of modern philology, but rather that Dionysius is now seen as a kind of prism reflecting several important ancient debates. As a Greek critic writing in Rome under Augustus, Dionysius is, after Cicero, our best evidence for the form in which Greek rhetorical theory reached Rome; as, moreover, it is much more likely than not that Dionysius himself was familiar with some at least of Cicero's rhetorical works,[68] Dionysius is a key witness not just for the Greek side of the Augustan intellectual milieu, but for the two-way interchange between Greek and Latin theorizing and literature from the late Republic onwards which modern scholarship is coming more and more to appreciate.[69]

---

[66] Cf. already Bonner 1939, 10.   [67] Bonner 1939, 72.
[68] For the relevant texts and bibliography, cf., e.g., Calboli 1987, 47; Fromentin 1998, xix; De Jonge 2008, 14–15, 214–16; see further below pp. 25, 261–3. Steven Ooms (Leiden University) is currently preparing a PhD thesis on the connections between the stylistic theories of Cicero and Dionysius.
[69] On Dionysius and Horace, see De Jonge in this volume.

Dionysius and Cicero travel together in another way also, as they are respectively our best witnesses to the Greek and Roman 'Atticist' rhetorical movements, both of which, though to different degrees,[70] seem to have constructed an 'other', so-called 'Asian', rhetoric as a term for stylistic features of which they disapproved. Although the precise connection between the two movements remains unclear,[71] a shared stylistic terminology, shared admiration – more tempered in the case of the Greek Atticists – for the 'slender' qualities of Lysias, and a shared identification of Hegesias, a historian of Alexander and rhetorician of the late fourth / early third centuries, as the 'founder' and poster-boy of the hated 'Asianism' show the close connection between them.[72] In his *Brutus* and *Orator* (46 BC), Cicero was forced to defend himself against the attacks of C. Licinius Calvus and his fellow *Attici*, who aspired to write in the clear and unadorned style of Lysias and Hyperides. Dionysius likewise hails 'the Attic muse' in his preface to *On the Ancient Orators*, and devotes one treatise to Lysias. In these respects, his interests echo the concerns of the Roman *Attici* of the previous generation; his flexible version of Atticism, however, with separate treatises also on Isocrates, Isaeus and Demosthenes, reminds us rather of Cicero's inclusive openness to various Attic models with different styles, and his privileging of Demosthenes as the champion who masters all those registers. As with Livy and Dionysius, scholars are nowadays more ready than in the past to accept Ciceronian influence on Dionysius.

For Dionysius, Atticism also serves a larger agenda, namely that of a classicism which sees in the new world order established by Rome a revival of 'classical' Greek cultural values, and not merely rhetorical styles;[73] these values were to be found, above all, in the πολιτικοὶ λόγοι and φιλοσοφία of Isocrates. Rhetorical style and political ideology are always intertwined: Augustus himself, who was known for his clear and

---

[70] Passages such as Cicero, *Brutus* 325 show that Roman theorists could use 'Asian' to describe particular types of style, without that term being inherently pejorative.

[71] For a survey and bibliography, cf. Wisse 1995; De Jonge 2008, 11–14; Wiater 2011, 113–14; Lucarini 2015; Yunis in this volume.

[72] For Dionysius' distaste for Hegesias, cf. *Comp.* 4.11, 18.21–8; it is usually thought, and probably rightly so, that Dionysius also has Hegesias in mind in his attack on 'Asian' rhetoric in the Preface to *Orat. Vett.*; he traces its origins to the period after death of Alexander, and that would certainly fit Hegesias. Hegesias' style comes in for some strong criticism in our earliest witness, Agatharchides of Cnidus (probably late second century), cf. *FGrH* 142 T3, but there is no suggestion there of the language of Asianism which we encounter in Cicero (cf. *Brutus* 286–7, *Orator* 226), Dionysius and Strabo 14.1.41, though Lucarini 2015, 21–2 suggests that there is no other reason for this persistent and early interest in Hegesias. On Hegesias' style, cf. Norden 1898, vol. 1, 133–9; Russell 1964 on 'Longinus', *On the Sublime* 3.2; Calboli 1987.

[73] Wiater 2011a is the fullest exposition of Dionysius' classicism.

unadorned style of writing, seems to have affiliated himself with the supporters of Atticism – possibly under the influence of his teacher Apollodorus of Pergamon. According to Suetonius, Octavian reproached Marcus Antonius for his inconsistent style, which swung between the extremes of obscure archaism and 'the verbose and unmeaning fluency of the Asiatic orators' (*Asiaticorum oratorum inanis sententiis uerborum uolubilitas*): Suetonius' report of the polemic resonates with Dionysius' vivid portrayal of the contest between the Attic muse and the Asian harlot.[74]

One aspect of this classicism is the persistent manner in which Dionysius retrojects his own interests and indeed critical presuppositions back onto poets and prose-writers of the 'classical' age, that is, before the death of Alexander.[75] A striking illustration may be drawn from *On Composition*:

> Virtually all of the ancient writers (οἱ ἀρχαῖοι) gave considerable attention[76] to [word-order], so that their metres, their lyrics and their prose-works are things of beauty. With a few exceptions, the same is not true for their successors (οἱ μεταγενέστεροι), and as time passed it became completely neglected and no one thought that this matter was essential or that it contributed anything to the beauty of discourse. (*Comp.* 4.14)[77]

'Classical' writers, whether poets or prose-writers, philosophers or orators (*Comp.* 5.12), were in fact surprisingly like Dionysius himself: they had a τέχνη of good composition and followed rules (θεωρήματα) which meant that they left nothing to chance, whether at the level of the word, colon or period. Dionysius is therefore not imposing a system upon them, so much as simply, to the best of his ability (*Comp.* 5.13), describing their own system, one of which they were fully conscious. As for later writers, although Dionysius proceeds to a catalogue of those 'whom no one could bear to read to the very end', it is Chrysippus (*Comp.* 4.17–21), as (in part) a representative of a philosophical theorizing about language and (in part) a notoriously bad stylist, who is then singled out as offering, as it were, a reversed mirror-image of Dionysius, namely a theorist (though not

---

[74] Suet. *Aug.* 86. See De Jonge in this volume.
[75] One perhaps paradoxical result of this classicism is that Thucydides can be praised for following some of Dionysius' precepts and criticized for failing to follow others, cf. Hunter in this volume. Dionysius' assumptions about earlier writers are not, of course, unique to him; very many examples of this attitude could, for example, be selected from 'Demetrius', *On Style*.
[76] The transmitted ἐπίδοσις is (*pace* Wiater 2011, 236 n. 611) hard to understand; Sylburg's ἐπιτήδευσις gives excellent sense, though the corruption seems hard to explain. Dionysius' recapitulation in *Comp.* 5.12, which looks like a variation upon *Comp.* 4.14, suggests that the required word will have been a synonym for πρόνοια.
[77] Our translation. For further discussion of this passage, cf. Wiater 2011a, 235–9; Kim 2014, 363–4.

of the right theory)[78] and someone with no concern for the style of his own writings, and – of course – a figure of the postclassical age (third century BC).

It is easy to accuse Dionysius here of an ahistorical circularity, particularly as he is notoriously vague on the detail of the virtues of classical writers, frequently appealing to what should be obvious to any person of proper literary sensitivity;[79] thus, for example, anyone 'with a moderate literary sensibility' will accept his classification of the opening of one of Pindar's dithyrambs (fr. 75 Maehler = *Comp.* 22.12) as belonging to the 'austere' style and his description of the aesthetic effects of that passage, although the detailed analysis of the sound effects of the passage which follows is clearly also designed as a display of critical τέχνη which very few of Dionysius' contemporaries could match. To dissent from Dionysius, in other words, is to display one's own ignorance. In the case of what is perhaps his most famous citation, that of Sappho fr. 1 (*Comp.* 23.11–17), Dionysius offers an explicitly brief and incomplete account of the poem, which his young addressee and 'everyone else' will have 'ample opportunity and leisure' to expand upon by following Dionysius' outline analysis; Dionysius has no space for a full account, so he is content simply to set out his views 'sufficiently for those who will be able to follow me'. Throughout Dionysius' critical essays, these two voices – that of the teacher instructing his pupils and that of the educated πεπαιδευμένος speaking with his equals – mingle to create a very particular version of the rhetoric of community and shared values. As the critical ideas and doctrines are themselves manifestations of those values, which are assumed to be inherent in the class of people to whom Dionysius addresses himself, Dionysius cannot just offer 'instruction' in areas alleged to be unknown to his audience; rather, he must draw to the surface that which was already (at some level) familiar to his audience, or so that audience must believe. We may perhaps liken Dionysius' critical procedure to a version of Platonic ἀνάμνησις, however unlike Dionysius and the Platonic Socrates may be.

Many of Dionysius' attitudes, just as some of his characteristic metaphors and images for style, were not his alone, but were inherited or developed from a very long tradition. Thus, for example, his attitude to the 'ignoble and feminised' rhythms of a Hegesias (*Comp.* 4.11) lies in a line of descent from Attic comedy's mocking attitude to the 'broken and

---

[78] On Dionysius' actual debt to the Stoics, see esp. De Jonge 2008, esp. 36–7, 273–314.
[79] Cf., e.g., Damon 1991; Hunter in this volume.

feminised' rhythms of the 'New Music'; appropriately enough, elements of Dionysius' classicism do indeed go back to the 'classical' period, just as Aristophanes' *Frogs* has long been recognized as a central 'classicizing' text. Dionysius' criticism is in fact a remarkable blend of the traditional and what might seem very new indeed; Plato and Aristotle have both made major contributions, but so also have lesser names of whom we know much less and that only by chance.[80]

We are now in a better position than was W. Rhys Roberts to judge where Dionysius stands with regard to 'the debased standards of the ages immediately preceding his own'. Our evidence for Hellenistic oratory has to some extent increased since his day, thanks to the steady flow of new (often, of course, very fragmentary) epigraphic texts, and appreciation of what inscriptions have to teach us in these areas has grown significantly, as part of a more general (and very welcome) collapsing of boundaries in classical studies between types of textual evidence.[81] More striking than advances in the field of oratory is the very significant growth in knowledge of Hellenistic poetic and rhetorical criticism, both through the very detailed work which has been devoted to the Peripatetic and other sources of Horace's *Ars Poetica*,[82] and through the decipherment and publication of further significant texts from the critical works of Philodemus (110–35 BC), preserved on the charred papyrus rolls of Herculaneum. This material, which is very difficult to decipher and interpret, nevertheless offers a glimpse of critics of the third and perhaps also early second centuries, now standardly referred to as οἱ κριτικοί, from Philodemus' designation of them in several of these texts, who – in varying degrees and with varying nuances – placed high store on euphony in poetry and who shared with Dionysius later such fundamental frameworks of analysis as the opposition between diction (ἐκλογὴ ὀνομάτων) and word-arrangement (σύνθεσις ὀνομάτων) and techniques of analysis such as *metathesis*.[83] Dionysius' particular concerns in *On Composition* are now much more clearly contextualized for us, though new questions inevitably arise. Philodemus seems to owe his knowledge of this body of criticism to the work of the Stoic Crates of Mallos (mid-second century BC), and as Dionysius never

---

[80] A recent account of some of the central issues in Dionysius' criticism can be found in Porter 2016, 213–45.
[81] On Hellenistic oratory, see Kremmydas and Tempest 2013, with a contribution by Edwards 2013 on Dionysius' *On Isaeus*.
[82] The work of Brink 1963–1971 is obviously crucial here.
[83] Cf., e.g., Janko 2000, 227; Janko 2000 is fundamental to this whole area. For a brief survey and bibliography of the κριτικοί, cf. de Jonge 2008, 37–40, 193–6. See also below, pp. 25–6.

names any of the κριτικοί whose names we happen to know from Philodemus, it remains very difficult to interpret apparent parallels between this body of criticism and Dionysius' works. We can, however, see more clearly than ever before that there *is* a Hellenistic context for Dionysius' criticism (particularly for *On Composition*), although we still lack the evidence which would allow us to construct a coherent picture out of the fragmentary pieces which have survived. It is this tantalising interplay between this still shadowy Hellenistic background and the much better illuminated Augustan intellectual milieu which is central to the essays on Dionysius' criticism in this volume.

Dionysius makes another call on our attention as a critic, and this arises simply from the very number of passages, often surprisingly lengthy, of both prose and poetry which he cites and discusses. Modern attention tends, unsurprisingly, to focus on his citations of, in particular, Sappho and Pindar, which preserve for us poems (or parts of poems) which would otherwise be lost, but Dionysius' role as a critic of prose texts, discussed by several contributors to this volume, is in many ways more important when viewed within the longer history of critical practice. In particular, Dionysius' transference to the realm of prose of the comparative method of criticism (a practice explicitly defended in *Letter to Pompeius* 1), long familiar for poetry (cf., e.g., Aristophanes, *Frogs*), marks for us an important step forward in critical practice, though it will hardly have been original to him. When it comes, however, to the actual discussion of texts from the past – what we think of as 'literary criticism' – Dionysius' practice can sometimes surprise and, it must be admitted, disappoint. It is hard for us now to imagine that someone would feel, for example, that what really matters in Sappho fr. 1 is the number of conjunctions of semivowels with voiceless consonants (*Comp.* 23.10–17); in some of Dionysius' best known criticism, it may be felt that there is a remarkable divorce of any consideration of subject-matter from that of style, particularly in comparison to, say, the essay of 'Demetrius', *On Style*. In *On Composition*, however, Dionysius chooses to focus very exclusively upon (precisely) 'composition', σύνθεσις, in part as a result of his much heralded claim that the nature of this work is all but entirely novel (*Comp.* 4.19–23); to deviate into other areas would have been to diminish the novel achievement. The ancient practice of seeing 'composition' as separate from both diction and 'thought' here produces what might appear to us a strangely unbalanced form of criticism. It is clear, however, particularly from the rich imagery with which he describes the style of Plato and the fourth-century orators, that Dionysius was indeed well aware of the linkage between subject and style.[84] The very differences between the scope of *On Composition* and the individual treatises dedicated to the Attic orators and to Thucydides are instructive as to the frameworks within which rhetorical critics, both Greek and Latin, operated.

Dionysius and Augustan Rome: This Volume

The words 'Augustan Rome' in the title of this volume should be understood in their broadest sense. Augustan Rome here refers not just to the politics of Augustus, but also to the social, intellectual, literary and cultural reality in which Dionysius developed and presented his dual project of rhetorical criticism and historiography. In the past, many studies have ignored this important synchronic dimension of his works, looking at Dionysius' contributions from an exclusively diachronic (and Greek) perspective: such studies typically focus on Dionysius' relationship to earlier Greek scholars and critics, like Theophrastus, Aristoxenus and Chrysippus, and on his reception of earlier historians, like Herodotus, Polybius and Fabius Pictor, rather than on the connections with contemporary authors, patrons, politicians, students and readers in Rome.[85]

This volume takes the Roman context of Dionysius' project seriously and draws attention to the complex interactions of his history and rhetorical criticism with the political, historiographical, rhetorical and literary discourse at Rome.[86] The volume consists of three parts: (1) Dionysius and Augustan Rhetoric and Literary Criticism, (2) Dionysius and Augustan Historiography, and (3) Dionysius and Augustan Rome. Below, we will illuminate Dionysius' position within each of these three contexts and prepare the ground for the chapters of this volume. The close connections between the three parts will be clear from the chapters themselves, but also from the 'envoi' by Joy Connolly, who draws special attention to Dionysius' status as a 'migrant thinker' and how this impacts on the issues raised throughout the book.

1. Dionysius and Augustan Rhetoric and Literary Criticism

Rhetorical teaching flourished at Rome in the first century BC. The most famous Greek rhetoricians of the period were Apollonius Molon, the

---

[84] On the imagery of Dionysius' stylistic discussions, cf. Hunter 2012, 151–84; Worman 2015, 282–93.
[85] E.g., Bonner 1939, Pohl 1968, Fornaro 1997.
[86] Although some publications on Dionysius have 'Augustus' or 'Augustan Rome' in their title (e.g., Egger 1902, Hurst 1982), they hardly address the Roman context of Dionysius' works.

teacher of Caesar and Cicero, who visited Rome twice as an ambassador from Rhodes, Dionysius' friend Caecilius of Caleacte (mentioned above), Apollodorus of Pergamon, the teacher of Octavian, and Theodorus of Gadara, the teacher of Tiberius. Quintilian mentions in one breath these four names and that of Dionysius of Halicarnassus, which suggests that he thought of Dionysius as playing in the same league.[87] There were also Latin rhetoricians, the successors of Lucius Plotius Gallus, who had opened his school in 93 BC. All these rhetoricians taught in the shadow of the great Cicero (106–43 BC), who was soon 'to be regarded as the name, not of a person, but of eloquence itself',[88] and although Dionysius never mentions the name of Cicero, it seems almost unthinkable that one could teach students in Rome (like Metilius Rufus) without being familiar with the great Republican orator's contributions to the practice and theory of rhetoric.[89]

For Dionysius, the criticism of literature and rhetorical theory were inseparable aspects of one discipline: with his critical analyses of classical Greek prose and poetry (cf. above p. 17–24) he intended to guide his contemporary readers and students in the composition of new texts. In Rome, literary criticism was practiced by rhetoricians, but also by grammarians, philosophers and poets. In the Augustan Age, the interests of Caecilius of Caleacte were especially close to the concerns of Dionysius: Caecilius published many works, including *On the Style of the Ten Orators*, *On the Sublime*, an Atticizing pamphlet *Against the Phrygians* and a treatise *On Figures* that draws on the speeches of Demosthenes.[90] In this context (Pseudo-)Longinus should also be mentioned, as some scholars have argued that the extant treatise *On the Sublime*, attributed to 'Dionysius (or) Longinus', should be dated to the Augustan period.[91]

It is in many cases difficult to establish the precise connections between Greek literary criticism and contemporary Latin literature, but there is one important exception: the Epicurean philosopher, rhetorician, scholar and poet Philodemus (mentioned above), who came to Italy around 80 BC, embodies one link between Greek criticism and Latin poetry. In some respects, Philodemus' social and intellectual position foreshadows that of Dionysius, who would arrive in Rome fifty years later. A friend of Lucius

---

[87] Quint. *Inst.* 3.1.16–18. For the fragments of Apollodorus and Theodorus, see Woerther 2013.
[88] Quint. *Inst.* 10.1.112.
[89] Caecilius T6 Woerther (Plutarch, *Demosth.* 3.1–2) and Longinus, *Subl.* 12.4–5 compare Demosthenes and Cicero. On Cicero and Dionysius, see Fromentin 1998, xix; De Jonge 2008, 14–15, 214–16; above p. 18.
[90] Innes 2002, Woerther 2015.
[91] E.g., Mazzucchi 2010. On Dionysius and Longinus, see De Jonge 2012.

Calpurnius Piso Caesoninus, Philodemus was admired by Cicero, and connected to several famous writers of Latin poetry: Virgil, Plotius Tucca, Varius Rufus and Quintilius Varus were among the addressees of his works; and most probably he knew Horace as well (see De Jonge in this volume). The carbonized fragments of Philodemus' works, which survived in the library of the Villa dei Papiri at Herculaneum, continue to be examined, as new technologies provide access to the damaged papyrus scrolls. Recent scholarship has explored Philodemus' influence on the Augustan poets, especially on Virgil and Horace.[92] But the fragments of his *On Poems* also cast light on critical theories that were available and circulating in Rome in the first century BC,[93] and, as we have seen (above p. 22), this new material has greatly enriched our sense of the intellectual context of Dionysius' criticism. Several authors in this volume (Hunter, De Jonge, Viidebaum) reflect on the connections among Philodemus, the κριτικοί and Dionysius.

Richard Hunter, 'Dionysius of Halicarnassus and the Idea of the Critic' (chapter 1), offers an introduction to Dionysius as a literary critic, focusing on the treatise *On Thucydides*. Hunter examines the assumptions underlying Dionysian criticism, including the important concepts of προαίρεσις (an author's 'project') and δύναμις (his capacity); he shows that many of Dionysius' aesthetic categories have a moral flavor, which ties in with the ethical aspects of his project (for which cf. the contributions of Schultze and De Jonge). One defining aspect of Dionysian criticism, indeed, is a multifaceted continuity between classical Athens and Augustan Rome, which are presented as sharing similar ethical and aesthetic values.

This constructed continuity is also on show in Nicolas Wiater's 'Experiencing the Past: Language, Time and Historical Consciousness in Dionysian Criticism' (chapter 2). Classicism is often summarized simply as a nostalgic desire for the classical Greek past, but Wiater proposes a distinction between two versions of the past in Dionysius' thinking: on the one hand, the ideal past ('a structure of feelings'); on the other hand, the historical past. Dionysius is not so much interested in the latter version of the past, that is, the historical, cultural and political contexts in which Lysias, Demosthenes and Thucydides actually wrote and lived. His fascination is rather with the idealized past that he constructs in his reading of the classical texts and presents as the model for Augustan Rome. Dionysius wants his readers to have a direct, immediate experience of this idealized

---

[92] Armstrong, Fish, Johnston, Skinner 2004. See also De Jonge in this volume.
[93] Porter 1995, Janko 2000.

classical past. The speeches in the *Roman Antiquities* function as models for the political practice of his readers and students. The technique of rewriting texts (μετάθεσις), Wiater argues, enables Dionysius and his readers to engage directly with classical texts and thus to construct the idealized image of the past that is to inspire the present.

Two contributors to this volume ask how the rhetorical role models of Attic oratory discussed by Dionysius were relevant to the Roman context in which he was writing. Harvey Yunis, 'Dionysius' Demosthenes and Augustan Atticism' (chapter 3), examines the rhetorical and critical backgrounds of Dionysius' *On Demosthenes* and its celebration of Demosthenes as the champion of stylistic writing. He reviews what we know about Roman and Greek Atticism, examines some of the assumptions underlying postclassical stylistic theory and focuses on the theory of three styles, different versions of which appear in three rhetorical treatises of the first century BC: the *Rhetorica ad Herennium*, Cicero's *Orator* and Dionysius' *On Demosthenes*. In his analysis of Demosthenes' style, Dionysius applies the insights of his theory of composition, including the distinction of pleasure (ἡδονή) and beauty (καλόν), but Dionysius' *On Demosthenes* is especially successful, Yunis argues, in asserting the interdependence of stylistic, aesthetic and political values: Demosthenes stands not only for the limit of stylistic possibilities, but also for what active citizens can achieve within society. On this reading, *On Demosthenes* is a vital witness to the links between classical Greece and contemporary Rome.

Laura Viidebaum, 'Dionysius and Lysias' Charm' (chapter 4), examines why Dionysius and his audience felt so attracted to the 'simple' style of Lysias. Like the Roman Atticists before him, Dionysius obviously admired the linguistic purity and clarity of Lysias' speeches, as the early treatise *On Lysias* testifies, but the real secret of the Attic orator's style lay for him in the notion of χάρις (charm). Viidebaum investigates the connotations that this term had acquired through its use in classical poetry, and shows how the term was used before Dionysius in the criticism of poetry on show in Philodemus' *On Poems*. The concept of 'instinctive' (or 'irrational') feeling (ἄλογος αἴσθησις), which plays an important role in Dionysius' critical essays (see also Hunter in this volume), casts light on his admiration of Lysias' charm. Viidebaum argues that the elusive quality of χάρις, with its connotations of wit and enchanting simplicity, had a special appeal to young Roman students. In the speeches of Lysias one could find all the (stylistic and civic) virtues that a Roman audience of the time would appreciate. In devoting his first treatise to precisely this Attic orator,

Dionysius thus seems to have aimed to bridge the gap between classical Athens and Augustan Rome.

2. *Dionysius and Augustan Historiography*

Dionysius mentions several of his colleagues in historiography at Rome, including Varro (116–27 BC) and Quintus Aelius Tubero (see above, pp. 7–8). The one author whom he does not mention is his exact contemporary Titus Livius (59 BC–AD 17), who treated the early history of Rome in his *Arb Urbe Condita*. Of Livy's 142 books only 35 are extant (1–10 and 21–45). He probably started writing before 31 BC and published the first pentad, covering Roman history down to 390 BC, between 27 and 25 BC; the second pentad, covering the period up to 293 BC, was published before 23 BC.[94] It is chronologically possible, then, that Dionysius, whose history ran down to 264 BC, had read Livy's treatment of the origins of Rome when he published the first part of his *Roman Antiquities* in 8/7 BC – and this is indeed the view adopted by Oakley in this volume.[95] Whereas it was once assumed that everything is Greek before it becomes Roman, it is nowadays rightly accepted that the Greeks were also 'heirs' of the Romans.[96] Dionysius may have studied Livy, and he may have read Cicero, as well.[97]

Comparisons between Dionysius and Livy are not rare in previous scholarship, which has examined various differences between the two authors and their treatment of the same material.[98] But in the past such comparisons have too often started from the (implicit) assumption that Livy was a much better historian than Dionysius: differences between their historical narratives have in many cases been explained as confirming the superiority of the Latin historian.[99] A more valuable approach is to ask how the differences between the two versions of early Rome are related to the aims and methods of their authors, their intended audiences and their cultural backgrounds. One major difference between Dionysius and Livy, commented upon by several authors in this volume (Pelling, Oakley,

---

[94] Luce 1965.
[95] See the discussion in Schwartz 1903, 946. Cary 1937, xvii rules out Livy as one of Dionysius' sources.
[96] On the Greeks as heirs of the Romans, see Schubert, Ducrey, Derron 2013.
[97] Virgil's *Aeneid* offers yet another Augustan version of the origins of Rome: for a comparison between Virgil and Dionysius, see Fox in this volume.
[98] See, e.g., Schwartz 1903, 946–60. Fromentin 2003 and Oakley 2010 provide more recent case studies.
[99] See, e.g., Schwartz 1903, 946; Cary 1937, xix–xx: 'The dignified restraint shown by Livy in relating these same events is far more impressive'.

Schultze), is the extraordinary length and attention to detail that characterizes the Greek account. Earlier commentators and translators complained about Dionysius' 'tiresome speeches' and his 'cumulation of pathetic or gruesome details'.[100]

In this volume, Stephen Oakley, 'The Expansive Scale of the *Roman Antiquities*' (chapter 5), takes a fresh look at Dionysius' fondness for detail. He shows that Dionysius' theoretical observations on historiography in the rhetorical-critical essays help us to understand why Dionysius wished his history of Rome to be so lengthy and detailed; he argues that the expansiveness of the *Roman Antiquities* depended on the material that Dionysius found in the Roman annalistic tradition; and he demonstrates that the difference between Dionysius' expansiveness and Livy's relative brevity is closely related to the reception that the authors expected for their works.

Clemence Schultze, 'Ways of Killing Women: Dionysius on the Deaths of Horatia and Lucretia' (chapter 6), analyzes two stories of the *Roman Antiquities* that feature female characters. Horatia is killed by her brother, because she has disgraced her family by openly expressing grief for her beloved cousin, the slain Curiatius; Lucretia commits suicide after having been raped by Sextus Tarquinius. Schultze explains how Dionysius' framing of the narratives resonates with the moral legislation of Augustus (18 BC), which aimed at securing family morality. The connection between past and present becomes even more suggestive when we realize that Dionysius elsewhere presents the proper interaction with women as a central element of Romulus' legislation. Again, the emphasis on decent family values need not be Augustan in the sense that Dionysius 'presents' the views or the moral program of Augustus himself; but the prominence of such themes does suggest that Dionysius' text interacts with the contemporary discourse of civic morality, which leaves its marks in various texts and documents of the Augustan period. Schultze also shows how Dionysius' criticism of Herodotus and Thucydides in the rhetorical works helps us to understand the choices that he as a historian makes in narrating the stories of Horatia and Lucretia.

Matthew Fox, 'The Prehistory of the Roman *polis* in Dionysius' (chapter 7), asks what Dionysius' discussion of the earliest stages of Roman history tells us about his political orientation. He observes that Dionysius focuses on details, emphasizes the difficulties of the conflicting sources and keeps involving his readers in the evaluation of those sources. His examination of the source material and his insistence on variant versions, which reminds us

---

[100] Cary 1937, xix–xx.

of the method of his fellow-townsman Herodotus, show that Dionysius is a critical historian, who is indeed far removed from being a propagandist of either (classical) Greece or (Augustan) Rome. Dionysius' emphasis on the complexity of the source material mirrors the complexity of his own attitude towards Rome.

3. Dionysius and Augustan Rome

The third part of this volume further explores the ways in which both Dionysius' historiography and his critical essays relate to the Roman world of Augustus. Attention is drawn to those political and intellectual dimensions of his works that suggest connections and interactions with the Roman context in which they were written. Above we have suggested various different ways in which Dionysius' works may be seen to respond to the political reality of Augustan Rome. Turning away from simplified readings of Dionysius as either a spokesman of Augustus or a voice of the 'opposition', two contributors ask how different elements of Dionysius' history of early Rome might resonate with the events and developments of the late Republic and early Principate.

Christopher Pelling, 'Dionysius on Regime Change' (chapter 8), examines the interpretation of constitutional shifts in the *Roman Antiquities*, focusing on the transition from the regal period to the Republic. The continuity that Dionysius suggests between those periods, as Pelling observes, might well remind his audience of the Augustan claims for continuity between Republic and Principate. In Dionysius' descriptions of regime change Pelling detects various themes with an 'Augustan ring', but he also warns that such resonances can often be interpreted equally as criticism and as praise of the Principate. Furthermore, he raises the important question whether Dionysius' history of Rome as a whole suggested the same tripartite pattern that is characteristic of his history of rhetorical writing (presented in the preface to *On the Ancient Orators*), that is, a model of a glorious beginning, a period of decline and a revival in the (Augustan) present.

Daniel Hogg, 'How Roman Are the *Antiquities*? The Decemvirate according to Dionysius' (chapter 9), focuses on a fascinating episode in Roman history, which is narrated by both Dionysius and Livy (*Ant. Rom.* 10.54–11.44; Livy 3.33–49). The decemvirate was the board of ten Roman men who codified Roman law, but who turned tyrannical and were then expelled in 449 BC. Hogg's comparison of the two accounts, one in Greek and one in Latin, reveals what is typical and characteristic of Dionysian narrative: his treatment of the *decemviri* focuses on senatorial conflicts and procedural chaos, which, as Hogg suggests, resonate with the weak performance of the senate in the first century BC. Again, a woman must die in order to preserve her honor – this time her name is Verginia (cf. the stories of Horatia and Lucretia discussed by Schultze) – before the people finally get rid of the decemvirate. Whereas Livy emphasizes the connection between the decemvirate and the regal period, Dionysius seems to hint at a link with the Rome of the late Republic: Hogg argues that the decemvirate episode is really a story about the political chaos that is caused when a failing senate loses its control. Again, readers of Dionysius may draw different conclusions about the role that might be assigned to Augustus in this story – do the tyrannical *decemviri* foreshadow the reign of the *princeps*, or is he the one who, by reforming the senate, puts an end to the chaos and disorder?

The Augustan Age is commonly regarded as the Golden Age of Latin literature. Turning once more from historiography to literary criticism, the final chapter of this volume concentrates on Rome as a place where literary notions and concepts were constantly traded and exchanged. The Roman poet Horace (65–8 BC) was a direct contemporary of Dionysius in Rome, and his *Ars Poetica*, or *Epistle to the Pisones*, is one of the most influential texts in the history of literary criticism. The close relationship between Dionysius' criticism and Horace's *Odes* and *Satires* has been explored in recent scholarship, and this volume extends this research to the *Ars Poetica*.[101] Casper C. de Jonge, 'Dionysius and Horace: Composition in Augustan Rome' (chapter 10), explores the relationship between two major works of literary criticism of the Augustan Age: Dionysius' *On Composition* and Horace's *Ars Poetica*. De Jonge points to a number of shared traditional themes and more innovative ideas linked to the contemporary Roman world. The shared ideal of a 'clever arrangement' of commonplace words is anticipated by the views of the critics discussed in Philodemus' *On Poems*, but it was especially celebrated in Augustan poetry, rhetoric and literary criticism, and De Jonge reminds us that Virgil's style and artful syntax in the *Aeneid* is very much part of the same critical scene in which Dionysius wrote.

Dionysius' Audience

Did Dionysius write for Greeks or (also) for Romans? The rhetorical-critical works, as we have seen, are dedicated to both Greek and Roman

---

[101] For earlier contributions, cf. Freudenburg 1993 on the *Satires*; Hunter 2009, 124–7 on the *Odes*.

intellectuals, who were the members of Dionysius' circle or network: it seems clear that he intended his essays to be read by all cultured and civilized men – whether they thought of themselves as Greek or Roman – who were interested in questions of rhetorical theory and literary criticism. In the *Roman Antiquities*, Dionysius himself makes explicit statements on the relevance of that work to both Greek (*Ant. Rom.* 1.4.2) and Roman readers (1.6.4: cited above). Modern scholars, however, have questioned these statements, which has resulted in a fierce debate on the intended audience of Dionysius' history of early Rome.

Bowersock stated that Dionysius wrote the *Roman Antiquities* 'for upper-class Roman readers'.[102] Gabba, on the other hand, argued for a 'Greek readership', and many other scholars adopted the same view.[103] Schultze proposed a third option, claiming that Dionysius wrote for a 'mixed readership'.[104] Luraghi refueled the debate by making a refined distinction between a real and a fake audience.[105] According to this interpretation, the 'real' intended readers of the *Roman Antiquities* were Romans. In describing the gradual decline of Roman civilization, Dionysius had an implicit message for the Romans of his time: having become alienated from their Hellenic identity through the civil wars, they should go back to their Greek roots and look to the virtuous lives of their earliest ancestors. According to Luraghi, Dionysius' references to the Greek audience of his work would merely function as a disguise: being an outsider, he did not have the authority to convey his message directly to the Romans, since the elite of Augustan Rome would not be pleased with a Greek voice lecturing them on the importance of the *mos maiorum*.

Luraghi's contribution to the debate has been important, because it has rehabilitated the idea that Dionysius (also) aimed at Roman readers. That is not to say, however, that he did not hope to be read by Greeks: it is not necessary to assume that Dionysius' statements on the relevance of his narrative to a Greek audience are nothing more than a 'disguise' – and in fact, one might wonder whether such a camouflage would be very effective: Dionysius' admonition to the Romans to follow the example of their early predecessors (*Ant. Rom.* 1.6.4, cited above) is clear and explicit enough.

Several authors in this volume contribute to this ongoing debate on Dionysius' audience (in particular, Hogg and Schultze). The position adopted here is that Dionysius wrote both his rhetorical-critical and his

---

[102] Bowersock 1965, 131. [103] Gabba 1982, 79–80. See also Fox 1993, 34; Galinsky 1996, 340–1.
[104] Schultze 1986. See also Fromentin 1998, xxxv–xxxvii. Weaire 2005, 246 adopts a similar position on the audience of the critical essays.
[105] Luraghi 2003, 270–7.

historical works for all those readers who were trained and competent enough to read Greek: and this obviously includes a substantial number of (bilingual) Roman citizens, people like his addressees Quintus Aelius Tubero and Metilius Rufus, as well as their families. It seems that the debate on Dionysius' intended audience is one of many themes where Dionysian scholarship has been too much divided between the *Roman Antiquities* and the rhetorical treatises. If we accept that Dionysius hoped and expected both Greeks like Ammaeus and Romans like Aelius Tubero to read his contributions to rhetoric and criticism, as the names of his addressees put beyond any doubt, we should also feel encouraged to accept that he intended his history of early Rome to inspire a mixed audience.

One might actually wonder whether the sharp distinction between 'Greeks' and 'Romans' that modern readers tend to make in this debate was in any strict sense applicable to the world in which Dionysius worked. Many Greek-speaking men of the Roman Empire acquired Roman citizenship and adopted a Roman name: they acquired a Roman *praenomen* and *nomen*, while using their Greek name as a *cognomen* (e.g., Lucius Mestrius Plutarchus, Lucius Flavius Arrianus). It has been suggested that Dionysius' addressee Gnaeus Pompeius Geminus belonged to this group of Greek men, who carried Roman citizenship, a Roman name and a Roman identity.[106] Were these men Greeks or Romans? For Dionysius, Romans were Greeks anyway – and from that perspective we might say that the modern debate about his intended audience somehow misses the point of his project. If our interpretation of Dionysius' mixed readership is correct, it shows yet another dimension of his tireless efforts to unite Greece and Rome.

---

[106] See the discussion in Hidber 1996, 7 n. 50.

PART I

Dionysius and Augustan Rhetoric and Literary Criticism

CHAPTER I

Dionysius of Halicarnassus and the Idea of the Critic

Richard Hunter

Histories of the idea of the 'critic', the man who 'judges' literature, have often been written, but it is worth beginning from the fact that in recent years the familiar story has become more complicated and perhaps more interesting.[1] In particular, the decipherment of carbonized papyrus rolls from Herculaneum has taught us more and more about the κριτικοί of the Hellenistic period who preceded Dionysius, and we now have a slightly clearer, though still desperately fragmentary, view of the background to Dionysius' intellectual context in Augustan Rome;[2] rather, however, than offering another survey of 'where we are now',[3] I wish in this chapter to take one sounding in Dionysius' own practice to try to tease out some of the assumptions which underlie his critical practice. Dionysius' concern both with the overarching conceptions of classical literature and with how those conceptions play themselves out at the micro-level of language makes him a figure of the greatest importance in the history of what we think we are doing in studying literature and how the ancients perceived that task.

In his treatise *On Thucydides*, with which I will here largely be concerned, Dionysius marks a structural break in the essay by recapitulating its purpose to his addressee, Quintus Aelius Tubero:[4]

> [I shall discuss the matter] under broad headings and by subjects, offering examples of narration and rhetorical speeches and setting out the reasons for his successes and failures in both subject-matter and expression. I request

---

[1] This is the very lightly revised text of the closing lecture given to the Leiden conference; I have not sought to eliminate all marks of oral performance or to disguise the fact that it was expressly aimed at a 'wider' audience than most of the papers at the conference. I am indebted to Casper de Jonge for much helpful criticism.

[2] On the κριτικοί, see the introduction to the volume, and the chapters by Viidebaum and De Jonge this volume.

[3] For a brief account of Dionysius and contemporary criticism, cf. the introduction to this volume.

[4] On Quintus Aelius Tubero, see Wiater in this volume, p. 74 with further references. Quintus Aelius Tubero was one of the sources of Dionysius' *Roman Antiquities*: see Oakley in this volume, p. 154.

again of you and of all other scholars (φιλόλογοι) who will read my account to take note of my intention in choosing (προῄρημαι) this subject, namely to set forth all the features of his style which require comment, in the hope of being of assistance to those who wish to imitate this writer. (*Thuc.* 25.1–2)[5]

There is much here which is typical of Dionysius and his criticism – the appeal to a like-minded audience, the emphasis on the intention or purpose, the προαίρεσις, of a writer, ancient or modern (cf. *Orat. Vett.* 4.2, *Ant. Rom.* 1.1.2, 3.6), to say nothing of the language of success and failure, are hallmarks of how Dionysius approaches his critical task. The wording in fact takes us back to the very beginning of the treatise. In looking at the work of the ancients, there are, so Dionysius tells us through a description of his largely lost work *On Imitation*,[6] two broad areas to consider:

> In the essays I published on the subject of imitation, Quintus Aelius Tubero, I examined those poets and prose-writers whom I considered to be most illustrious, and I briefly indicated the virtues of each in both subject-matter and style; I also indicated where failures caused each most to fall short of his own standards, whether because his purpose (ἡ προαίρεσις) did not foresee every issue down to the finest detail or because his powers (ἡ δύναμις) were not up to the task throughout. My purpose was that those who undertake (οἱ προαιρούμενοι) to write and speak well should have excellent and tested standards (κανόνες) to employ in each of their own exercises; they should not imitate everything which they find in these writers, but rather take over their virtues and guard against their failings. (*Thuc.* 1.1–2)

The sentences pose more than one specific difficulty of interpretation, but the overall sense is clear: προαίρεσις, what a writer plans to do, what – as we might say – his project is, and δύναμις, how he actually carried it out, are the two concerns of the critic,[7] and it is around those two poles that Dionysius' analysis will hinge. As he says of Thucydides:

> When his purpose and his powers come together, the nature of his success is perfect, more than human; but when his powers fall short and the intensity (ὁ τόνος) is not maintained throughout, then his language becomes obscure because of the speed of his narration and this brings with it other unattractive blemishes. (*Thuc.* 24.12)

There are blemishes (κῆρες) on the Thucydidean body which are not pretty to look at, and we might remember Dionysius' comparison in

---

[5] Translations are my own.
[6] On this work see Battisti 1997; Hunter 2009, chapter 4; Wiater 2011a, 78–83.
[7] For a collection of passages involving this dichotomy, cf. Aujac 1991, 145.

On Imitation of a perfect work to that of a perfectly beautiful woman,[8] with no *menda* ('stain') anywhere in sight, as Ovid might have said (cf. *Am.* 1.5.18). Be that as it may, the language of προαίρεσις and δύναμις is not of course unique to Dionysius, but repetition makes it very particularly his; προαίρεσις, in particular, is a word with a strong resonance of ethical theorizing – the choices we make reveal moral character – and this is very relevant here also, not just because of the traditionally intimate link between ethical and rhetorical criticism,[9] but also because Thucydides' choices of what to write and what to write about are to reveal much about him, not all of it very pretty. The dichotomy of προαίρεσις and δύναμις is in fact part of Dionysius' rhetoric of being a critic – writers and orators can go wrong in any number of ways, and the ability to group successes and failures under different heads is one of the ways in which the critic establishes his authority. Modern critics used occasionally to compare Horace's *Ars Poetica*, and they were surely correct to do so:

> sumite materiam uestris, qui scribitis, aequam
> uiribus et uersate diu, quid ferre recusent,
> quid ualeant umeri. cui lecta potenter erit res,
> nec facundia deseret hunc nec lucidus ordo.
>
> You who write should choose a subject equal to your strength, and consider for a long time what your shoulders cannot carry and what they can. The writer whose choice of subject is in accordance with his powers,[10] will not find himself abandoned either by the flow of words or by clarity of order. (Hor. *Ars P.* 38–41)

As usual, Horace has expressed 'textbook ideas' in a strikingly novel and concrete fashion: he plays with the physical sense of *materia*, 'wood, the trunk of a tree' (cf. *OLD* s.v. 2, Greek ὕλη) to conjure a picture of the would-be poet struggling to test just how much his shoulders can actually carry.[11] Horace too, like Dionysius, claims to be giving practical instruction for young people who themselves want to write creatively: 'criticism' is in antiquity rooted in education and instruction, rather than, for example, in what we tend to think of as 'scholarship'.[12] There would, in fact, be much to be said by way of comparison between Horace and Dionysius,

---

[8] *On Imitation*, Epitome 1.4, cf. Hunter 2009, chapter 4. [9] Cf., e.g., Russell 1981, 11.
[10] The meaning is disputed, cf. Brink 1971 ad loc.
[11] We may compare 'Ps-Scymnus', *Periodos* 36–42 – the 'bundle of wood' image taken from Apollodorus of Athens.
[12] Cf., e.g., Russell 1981, 11.

contemporaries working in the same city,[13] but in this case it is the difference within similarity which attracts attention. Horace plays with contemporary critical ideas through image and metaphor, whereas – as we shall see – some of Dionysius' most interesting effects come through allusion and literary reminiscence, where the critic practises what he preaches. This is not, I think, the result of the difference between the Greek rhetorician and the Latin poet – we might, after all, have expected the techniques to be reversed – but rather of the fact that, whereas Dionysius is so immersed in 'classical' literature that he clothes his own essays in the language of that past, Horace creates a fresh critical discourse which is neither technical nor trite and which allows him to keep a distance, both didactic and ironical, from the poetic forms he discusses.

If we go back to the opening of the *On Thucydides*, we will find three different layers of προαίρεσις: that of the classical writers themselves, that (*Thuc.* 1.2) of the modern students who wish to write and orate in imitation of the ancient pattern, and finally the προαίρεσις (*Thuc.* 1.3) of Dionysius, the teacher and critic, himself. This verbal repetition is one small marker of something both very obvious and also very important: the modern student has in fact two guides along the way of his rhetorical and political career – the great classics themselves, and the contemporary critic's distillation of the virtues and failings of those classics; students are to approach the literature of the past in ways approved by teachers such as Dionysius – only the properly trained can really appreciate the emotional power of that literature. The pedagogical situation ought to make those of us who teach in universities smile with recognition. In another way, however, Dionysius' role as critic and teacher is very different from anything practised today. Let us go back to *On Thucydides* 25.2.

Dionysius tells us that his aim (σκοπός) is to give help (ὠφέλεια) to people who wish to imitate 'the man'. In the context (and cf. σκοπεῖν in Dionysius' text immediately before) it seems very hard not to sense here an echo of Thucydides' own most famous programmatic claim, one which Dionysius knew well, one which he evokes in other works (most notably, of course, in the opening sections of the *Roman Antiquities*)[14] and one which has in fact been explicitly cited earlier in the treatise (*Thuc.* 7.3):

καὶ ἐς μὲν ἀκρόασιν ἴσως τὸ μὴ μυθῶδες αὐτῶν ἀτερπέστερον φανεῖται· ὅσοι δὲ βουλήσονται τῶν τε γενομένων τὸ σαφὲς σκοπεῖν καὶ τῶν

---

[13] Cf. Hunter 2009, 124–7; De Jonge in this volume, pp. 242–66.
[14] Cf. esp. *Ant. Rom.* 1.1.2: see Oakley in this volume, pp. 130, 141–2.

μελλόντων ποτὲ αὖθις κατὰ τὸ ἀνθρώπινον τοιούτων καὶ παραπλησίων
ἔσεσθαι, ὠφέλιμα κρίνειν αὐτὰ ἀρκούντως ἕξει. κτῆμά τε ἐς αἰεὶ μᾶλλον ἢ
ἀγώνισμα ἐς τὸ παραχρῆμα ἀκούειν ξύγκειται.

The absence of the mythical will perhaps make my work less appealing when heard. But it will be sufficient for me if all who wish to receive a clear account of what happened and of what is likely at some future time to happen again in this and similar ways should judge this work useful. It has been written to be a possession for all time, rather than a display-piece for immediate hearing. (Thuc. 1.22.4)[15]

The echo points in a number of important directions, as well as affirming the structural parallelism of author and critic.[16] The implications of Thucydides' statement have been endlessly discussed, but Dionysius will certainly have understood him to be expressing the hope that his readers, 'those who wish to receive a clear account...', judge his work useful, particularly given the likelihood of similar events occurring again in the future. 'Repetition' is built into Thucydides' intellectual structure here, as it is also in Dionysius: 'imitation', which is a particular form of 'repetition' and one sanctioned by Isocrates, to whom Dionysius owes so much of his conception of both classical culture and historiography in particular,[17] is thus not just a classicizing exercise, but is in fact *the* classical practice, whether that be the affairs of states or the composition of creative literature, as, for example, Longinus' account in *On the Sublime* of all the great classical authors who were 'very Homeric' most famously sets forth (*Subl.* 13.4).

To return. Part in fact of where Thucydides went wrong, according to Dionysius elsewhere (*Pomp.* 3.6), was precisely that his pursuit of novelty led him to choose a disastrous subject, unlike Herodotus who was willing to do battle with his predecessors, as indeed Dionysius' students are being urged to do, and unlike Dionysius himself was to do, as he repeatedly stresses in the proem of the *Roman Antiquities* (1.1.2, 2.1); to put it very crudely indeed, Herodotus followed Dionysius' advice, whereas Thucydides did not.[18]

---

[15] On the significance of this passage to Dionysius' *Roman Antiquities*, see Oakley in this volume, pp. 141–2.
[16] Weaire 2005 is an important study of Dionysius' appropriation of a Thucydidean voice. See also De Jonge 2017.
[17] Cf. Isoc. *Paneg.* 7–10, with the remarks of Wiater 2011a, 146–7. There is, incidentally, much more to be done on Dionysius' creative imitation of Isocrates, which is one of the most powerful strains in his writing. The famous dedicatory opening of Dionysius' great work *On Composition*, for example, offers a virtuoso blend of Homer and Thucydides within a frame borrowed from the dedicatory opening of Isocrates' homily *To Demonicus* (cf. Hunter 2009, 123–4), and such cases could no doubt easily be multiplied.
[18] Cf. Wiater 2011a, 2011b.

The parallelism of the two sentences which I am pursuing, however, shows us that Thucydides did in fact understand crucial Dionysian principles – just not enough of them, as it turned out, unfortunately.

Dionysius returned to Thucydides' programmatic statement in the conclusion and summary of his work. Here he pleads once more that one must make distinctions within the *Histories* and separate those parts which are useful for modern imitators and students from those whose idiosyncrasy rules them out of court:

> Let me draw things together. There is no sense in considering equally worthy of imitation those passages of the historian which lack clarity (τὰ μὴ σαφῶς εἰρημένα) and those which combine clarity with his other virtues. We must admit that the more perfect is better than the less perfect and the clear than the unclear. Why on earth, then, do some of us praise the whole of the historian's language, being forced to claim that Thucydides wrote this for his contemporaries, to whom it was familiar and well known, whereas he gave no thought to us who would come after, while others throw out the whole of Thucydides' style as useless in court-rooms and public assemblies. Why do we not agree that the narrative part of it (τὸ διηγηματικὸν μέρος) is, with a few exceptions, marvellously well done and adapted for all kinds of uses, whereas the oratorical part (τὸ δημηγορικόν) is not all suitable for imitation, though it contains material which all men can easily understand, even if not all are capable of such composition. (*Thuc.* 55.3–4)

Thucydides claimed that the style of the *Histories* was determined by the needs of present and future readers: is it then likely, asks Dionysius, that he gave no thought (no λόγος) to 'us' who would come after? 'We' are, of course, those for whom Dionysius is writing, students of rhetoric who wish to imitate and use the historian in the composition of πολιτικοὶ λόγοι; whether or not Thucydides ever in his worst nightmares imagined the rise of such a group, we can hardly say, but Dionysius' argument grows from a structure within Thucydides' own expression and offers a reading of Thucydides' claims which itself claims to be self-evident. Only, in other words, by accepting Dionysius' analysis of Thucydides, which involves the identification of success and failure within Thucydides' history, can one be true to the meaning which Thucydides himself gave to his work: what critic could be truer to his subject than that? We know from Cicero that Dionysius is certainly not original in rejecting Thucydides' more elaborate stylistic turns within the speeches as material that the modern orator should not (or could not) imitate (cf. Cic. *Brut.* 287–8, *Orat.* 30–2),[19] but

---

[19] Cf. De Jonge 2008, 214–16.

to enlist Thucydides himself in support of the argument is a remarkable feat. When Dionysius ends the work with a close echo of what Thucydides reported Nicias to have written to the Athenians, we will therefore see more than just a final flourish:

> τούτων ἡδίω μὲν εἶχόν σοι περὶ Θουκυδίδου γράφειν, ὦ βέλτιστε Κόιντε Αἴλιε Τουβέρων, οὐ μὴν ἀληθέστερα.
>
> I could, my dear Quintus Aelius Tubero, have written you something about Thucydides which was more pleasant (ἡδίω), but it would not have been more true. (*Thuc.* 55.5)[20]

> τούτων ἐγὼ ἡδίω μὲν ἂν εἶχον ὑμῖν ἕτερα ἐπιστέλλειν, οὐ μέντοι χρησιμώτερά γε, εἰ δεῖ σαφῶς εἰδότας τὰ ἐνθάδε βουλεύσασθαι. καὶ ἅμα τὰς φύσεις ἐπιστάμενος ὑμῶν, βουλομένων μὲν τὰ ἥδιστα ἀκούειν, αἰτιωμένων δὲ ὕστερον, ἤν τι ὑμῖν ἀπ' αὐτῶν μὴ ὅμοιον ἐκβῇ, ἀσφαλέστερον ἡγησάμην τὸ ἀληθὲς δηλῶσαι.
>
> I could have sent you different, more pleasant news, but certainly not more useful, if you are to have clear knowledge of the situation here when you make your plans. I also was conscious of your nature: you want to hear the most pleasant news, but afterwards you find fault, if anything does not turn out in accordance with your expectations; as a result of this, I thought it safer to tell you the truth. (Thuc. 7.14.4)

Not only is the critic's voice now blended with that of the subject of his work, but through this echo Dionysius calls our attention to the fact that Nicias' hard words in fact reprise the themes of 1.22.4 – pleasure on one side, truth ('clear knowledge') and usefulness on the other;[21] just as Dionysius here alludes to Thucydides 7.14.4 and through that passage to 1.22.4, so in 7.14.1 the Thucydidean Nicias had 'alluded to', and thus confirmed the truth of, the historian's words at 1.22.4. Dionysius and Thucydides can indeed speak with one voice.

In 1.22.4 Thucydides expresses the hope that a particular section of his audience will 'judge' (κρίνειν) his work helpful. Dionysius does not use the verb at *Thuc.* 25.2 (above pp. 37–8), but it is obviously implicit in his renewed appeal to his audience. Here again we are taken back to the prologue of the work: in *Thuc.* 2.4 Dionysius notes that the work's addressee and τῶν ἄλλων φιλολόγων ἕκαστος, 'all other men of learning', will judge whether his words are 'true and appropriate to himself'. If the

---

[20] Aujac 1991, 125 suggests ἡδίω μὲν <ἂν> εἶχόν σοι, presumably in part to bring this even more closely in line with the Thucydidean model.
[21] Cf. also Weaire 2005, 255–6 and De Jonge 2017, who, however, associate the final sentence of the work only with Thuc. 1.22.4.

critic's job is to pass κρίσις about classical texts (award prizes in the various categories of style, in fact, cf., e.g., *Isoc.* 11.1–5), then the critic too will be judged. As is well known, the language of judging, of accusation and defence, is everywhere scattered throughout Dionysius' critical works; nit-picking criticism can be συκοφαντεῖν (*Thuc.* 2.2), and one's opponents – as, most famously, Callimachus' were – are, unlike Dionysius himself (*Thuc.* 2.3, 34.5), driven by envy and malice (4.1). The critic is, quite literally, on trial for his life,[22] and – as was normal in trials of the classical period – it is the defendant's life which must be laid bare by his defence. So it is that Dionysius tells us that he has only once before 'in his whole life' brought an accusation against anyone (κατηγορῶ τινος, *Thuc.* 2.3), and that was 'on behalf of πολιτικὴ φιλοσοφία', in other words in defence of everything 'we' hold dear, and he did this to ward off unjust attacks against her.[23] If Dionysius cannot, unlike Socrates in Plato's *Apology*, legitimately claim that he has never had anything to do with 'courtrooms' before, he can at least disclaim any experience of malicious or carping criticism (in both senses) (*Thuc.* 2.3), and also call 'witnesses' (*Thuc.* 3.3) to the fact that what he has been doing, and will do in the current treatise also, is entirely within the best traditions of classical practice. The witnesses he calls are Aristotle and Plato: their disinterested concern with truth, one which naturally leads them to be in part critical of their predecessors, is the same as Dionysius' (*Thuc.* 3.3–4). If we are tempted here to observe that elsewhere Dionysius has very harsh words for Plato's 'envious' attacks on his predecessors and, particularly, on Homer, we should recall the overriding importance to Dionysius, as to Isocrates, of the ideas of τὸ πρέπον and καιρός, of choosing the appropriate arguments to fit the rhetorical circumstances: these ideas apply as much to works of criticism as they do to the great works of the past on which criticism is practised. Dionysius is on trial and his arguments are indeed appropriate to the situation.

The forensic world of classical Athens, no less than the political and rhetorical arenas of contemporary Rome, is thus a crucial part of the living context in which the Augustan critic – both judge and judged – plies his trade; it is indeed central to the classicizing ideals which Dionysius promulgates that the Athenian and Roman situations form a continuum embodying similar ethical and rhetorical values. This context, however,

---

[22] Cf. Pavano 1958, 14.
[23] It is normally thought that this refers to a lost treatise against the Epicureans, cf., e.g., Bonner 1939, 11–12 and above p. 2.

has no room for the faint-hearted. If some of Dionysius' opponents – not, of course, Quintus Aelius Tubero and the rest of 'the jury' to whom Dionysius addresses himself (*Thuc.* 2.1) – will criticize his τόλμα (2.2), Dionysius' only concern, as it has been throughout his career, is the truth:

> τούτους οὖν ἐπὶ πάντων ἐγὼ τῶν ἐμαυτοῦ θεωρημάτων κανόνας ὑποτιθέμενος οὔτε πρότερον ὤκνησα τὰ δοκοῦντά μοι φέρειν ἐς μέσον οὔτε νῦν ἀποτρέψομαι.
>
> I have adopted these principles in all my investigations and I have never in the past shrunk from placing my views in the public domain and I will not hold back now. (*Thuc.* 35.1)[24]

Dionysius will not be silenced from placing his views ἐς μέσον, 'into the public arena', just as (elsewhere) he will speak freely, μετὰ παρρησίας (*Dem.* 23.1), thus enjoying the same freedom as a citizen of classical Athens.[25] There is something Periclean about his (alleged) fearless consistency (cf. Thuc. 2.61.2), or perhaps rather something Demosthenic. The formulation οὐκ ἀποτρέψομαι is found only here in Dionysius, but turns up three times in a single speech of Demosthenes and twice in the 'prologues' transmitted with the Demosthenic corpus, which Dionysius might well have accepted as genuine.[26] Demosthenes was not just, for Dionysius, the greatest classical orator and rhetorician,[27] but he was also a famous figure who said what needed to be said, even when it was deeply unpopular.

The same is not true for Dionysius' opponents, who play to the masses (*Thuc.* 4.1, cf. 2.3) with, as far as Dionysius' somewhat elliptical phrasing allows us to judge, the spiteful (ἐπίφθονον) charge that Dionysius is neither the historian Thucydides was nor the orator that Lysias, Demosthenes and the others were:

> There is one further matter in which I must offer a defence: it is a charge motivated by envy (ἐπίφθονον ... κατηγόρημα) and one which wins the approval of the many, but is easily rebutted as unsound.[28] If my powers (ἡ δύναμις) fall short of those of Thucydides and the other historians, I have not also lost the right to examine them. Those who do not have the same artistic skills as Apelles and Zeuxis and

---

[24] The text at the beginning of the passage is uncertain, but the sense is clear.
[25] Discussed by Wiater 2011a, 319–20.
[26] Cf. Dem. 24.2.1, 104.3, 200.2, Dem. (?) *Exord.* 23.1, 32.3; the last passage, 'I shall not turn away from saying what I think', is particularly close to Dionysius.
[27] See Yunis in this volume, p. 84.
[28] The translation in Aujac 1991, 48 suggests that she understands Dionysius to be saying that he is being charged with jealousy, not that the charge is motivated by spite; that does not seem to me the natural way to read the text. Pavano 1958 and Usher 1974 adopt the view that I have followed here.

Protogenes and the other famous painters are not prohibited from passing judgement on them, and the same is true for craftsmen who fall short of Pheidias and Polycleitus and Myron. I pass over the fact that the layman (ὁ ἰδιώτης) is no less competent a critic of many things than the expert (ὁ τεχνίτης), the things indeed which are apprehended by irrational perception (δι' αἰσθήσεως ἀλόγου) and by the emotions, and that every art aims at such criteria and takes its beginning from them. (*Thuc.* 4.1–3)

At issue is the relation between being a critic and being a practitioner of the art of which you are a critic, a subject famously discussed by T.S. Eliot in his 1923 essay on 'The Function of Criticism', not (incidentally) the only point of contact between that essay and the works of Dionysius: when Eliot observes that 'comparison and analysis ... are the chief tools of the critic', any reader of the *Letter to Pompeius* can almost hear Dionysius nodding in vigorous agreement.

Dionysius' answer to the charge falls at first glance into two related parts. One does not need to be a Rembrandt or a Vermeer to be an art critic, so why should you need to be a Thucydides to write critically about historiography? At one level this might seem in fact a rather silly charge to throw at Dionysius, however it is to be understood; Aristophanes' *Frogs* had indeed dramatized the idea that Aeschylus and Euripides were 'experts' (τεχνῖται) in the criticism of tragedy, but the critical tradition had long been in the hands of those with little claim to be themselves makers of creative art. In Dionysius' case, however, the charge might have pricked a nerve. We have already seen how Dionysius has suggested that what he is doing is an activity parallel to that of the classical writers, that he is in fact in part ventriloquising Thucydides, but it would not have been hard simply to point out that that is not really so. Moreover, Dionysius, like his addressee, was himself a writer of history. Whatever the chronological relationship between his rhetorical works and the final form of the *Roman Antiquities*, the first part of which was apparently published in 8/7 BC (cf. *Ant. Rom.* 1.7.2), it would (again) not have been difficult, particularly for Thucydides' many fans (of whom more anon), to point out that Dionysius' δύναμις as a historian fell very well short of the historian he chose to criticize.

The second part of Dionysius' defence against the charge, a defence introduced with the *praeteritio* of a past master, is that the layman (ἰδιώτης) is as good a judge as the expert (τεχνίτης) when it comes to works of art which are to be apprehended by 'irrational perception' (αἴσθησις ἄλογος) and the emotions, and that these are in fact the target of 'every art'. The text here is problematic, but the distinction between two kinds of critic, the layman and the expert, is a fundamental part of Dionysius' criticism throughout the rhetorical works;[29] both are able to judge literature by the 'irrational criterion', the criterion of which one cannot give an 'account' (cf., e.g., *Dem.* 24.11), though the αἴσθησις of the expert may have been honed and trained through long habituation – Longinus famously describes ἡ τῶν λόγων κρίσις as the 'final product (ἐπιγέννημα) of much experience' (*Subl.* 6.1) – and it is the expert who will be able to add a technical, critical λόγος on top of the αἴσθησις.[30] One of Dionysius' clearest and best known statements of principle occurs in the *Lysias*:

> Teachers of music advise those who wish accurately to listen to musical harmonies, so that they should not miss even the smallest difference in the scale, to train their hearing and to seek no more accurate criterion than this. I too would urge those who read Lysias and wish to understand the charm (χάρις) of his writing to do the same:[31] over a long period of time and with long practice and the use of irrational feeling they must train their irrational perception. (*Lys.* 11.3–4)

The analogy which Dionysius, very typically, uses is music, but we might be tempted rather to think of wine-tasting, another act of connoisseurship practised among consenting adults, and one which depends upon an 'irrational' talent honed by long years of both practice and 'theory'; Cicero in fact uses such an analogy of rhetorical style (*Brut.* 287–8). Why, however, does Dionysius introduce this matter of the αἴσθησις ἄλογος at *On Thucydides* 4.3? In his commentary on the *On Thucydides*, Giuseppe Pavano suggests that Dionysius' critics had been demanding *ingenium* from the critic as well as *ars*, and Dionysius' appeal to the universal αἴσθησις ἄλογος is one answer to that challenge.[32] Dionysius would of course normally regard himself as a τεχνίτης, so there is a kind of *a fortiori* argument: 'if an ἰδιώτης can judge such matters, then how much more right has a τεχνίτης such as myself'. Coming, however, immediately after a roll call of the greatest painters and sculptors of the Greek past, it is very hard not to feel that τεχνίτης also evokes the sense 'artist', and this shift, effected through a semantic glide in an important word, is not in fact untypical of Dionysius' criticism. The conventional dichotomy between

---

[29] Cf., e.g., Damon 1991, 45–9.
[30] On the αἴσθησις ἄλογος, cf., e.g., Schenkeveld 1975, 1988; Porter 2006; Viidebaum and Yunis in this volume, pp. 100, 116–20.
[31] On Lysias' χάρις, cf. Viidebaum in this volume.   [32] Pavano 1958, 16–17.

'layman' and 'expert', so familiar to Dionysius' audience, and Dionysius' favourite theme of 'irrational perception' are here reinforced, and in fact shown to be correct, by the manifest example – so manifest it requires no discussion – of art criticism. I shall return presently to Dionysius' reliance on appeals to what everyone knows.

I have been talking freely about Dionysius' 'opponents', and it is well known that if ancient critics (like some modern scholars) did not have opponents, they tended to invent them; the agonistic context of criticism, just one more part of the 'trial' in which Dionysius is involved, was fundamental from the earliest period – we might think of competing sophists or competing sophistic interpretations (cf. Plato, *Protagoras*) or the rhapsode Ion's pride in his superiority to other interpreters of Homer (Plato, *Ion* 530c9-d3).[33] Callimachus, for example, begins his most famous and influential poem with a 'Reply' to his own malicious and envious (as he would have us believe) critics, and ancient scholars at least thought they could identify these 'Telchines'.[34] Some at least of Dionysius' targets, if not his opponents, recur later in the treatise when, in the context of Thucydides' speeches, he turns his attention to Thucydides' fan club, 'those who admire him beyond what is reasonable/moderate (τὸ μέτριον), as though he differed in no way from those who are divinely inspired' (*Thuc.* 34.3). That Thucydides did have such a fan club of admirers and imitators in Rome we know from other sources (cf. Cic. *Orat.* 30–2) – Dionysius' addressee Tubero appears to have been among them – and this should not surprise:[35] the style of the speeches is so idiosyncratic that the claim to appreciate them and then to be able to imitate them would have been an irresistible way for some to establish intellectual and cultural credentials which set them apart from others; it is easy enough to think of modern parallels for such fashionable trends in the worlds of music, art and scholarship. It is, as always, τὸ μέτριον, the happy 'nothing in excess' middle way, which for Dionysius is to be imitated, for πολιτικοὶ λόγοι have, after all, a practical aim and a real audience. Those parts of Thucydides which are to be imitated (*Thuc.* 27.3) are those where ordinary people will find nothing outlandishly difficult and hard-to-follow to put them off, and the educated specialist will not be able to exercise his μῶμος, 'fault-finding', on anything which is common, trite and unpolished. Dionysius, like Demosthenes in rather more serious times, will not allow his audience to sleepwalk to disaster. The fans, however, like infatuated

---

[33] Cf. Hunter 2012, 91.   [34] Cf. the 'Florentine scholium', Callim. fr. 1b Harder.
[35] Cf., e.g., Weaire 2005; Canfora 2006; De Jonge 2008, 214–15; De Jonge 2011; De Jonge 2017.

lovers, will hear nothing at all against anything their darling ever wrote, in fact he is the epitome of all beauty and all the virtues; like lovers, they are slaves to the beloved (*Thuc.* 34.5), their critical judgement in a stupour (*Thuc.* 34.6), whereas Dionysius and his ilk are incorruptible:

> Those who preserve an attitude which is uncorrupted (ἀδέκαστος) and employ correct standards in the examination of literature, whether they have the gift of some natural power of judgement or have built up strong criteria of judgement through instruction, neither praise everything equally nor find fault with everything, but they offer appropriate acknowledgement to what is successful, and withhold praise from passages in which mistakes are made. (*Thuc.* 34.7)

Dionysius is here quite close to Plutarch who compares an unwillingness to find any fault with the figures of Homeric poetry, which amounts (again) to an 'enslavement of the judgement', to those who imitate Plato's stoop or Aristotle's lisp (*Mor.* 26b); for Plutarch, too, it is rather a matter always of judging what is appropriate, πρέπον, for this is what the critic does, and when something falls short the critic (or student) must not hesitate to say so. The critic is not a worshipper at a shrine, even if σέβας, religious awe, is due to the great figures of the past (cf. *Pomp.* 1.1); Homer for one had long since been regarded as divine (θεῖος) and accorded cult. Where Plutarch is concerned with the moral behaviour and utterances of the characters of classical literature, Dionysius is concerned with style (as a reflection of ethical προαίρεσις – the manner of your life and the manner of your writing are not to be separated (cf. *Orat. Vett.* 4.2), and here he will distribute both praise and blame as indeed appropriate (*Thuc.* 1.1, 34.7) and without fear or favour. Here in fact is another way in which Thucydides failed to live up to Dionysian principles: Thucydides went through Athens' mistakes and defeats in great detail, but 'when things went according to plan, he either did not mention them at all or did so as though under compulsion' (*Pomp.* 3.15).

The critic, then, has clear and strong principles of criticism, κριτήρια: we are most certainly not in a postmodern free-for-all in which subjective diversity is to be celebrated (cf. *Thuc.* 34.6). Authority derives not just from the use of appropriate κριτήρια, but also from the (real or alleged) tradition in which the critic is working. Dionysius is always anxious to stress that his critical views and practice fall within familiar parameters and have authoritative models (cf. above on *Thuc.* 3.3–5). One aspect of this is his frequent recourse to what we call rhetorical questions of the 'Who would not agree...?' or 'Who is so ignorant as not to realise...?' kind with which his work is littered;[36] the rightness of the critic's views is a matter of shared human sensibility – 'it is impossible to hold another view', he says on one occasion (*Dem.* 13.2) – a sensibility shared not just by like-minded εἰδότες ('connoisseurs'):

> There is no one who does not agree, on the basis of his own experience and what he has heard, that Lysias is the most persuasive of all orators. (*Lys.* 10.2).

We need critics not to startle us with their brilliance, people – as Dionysius puts it elsewhere – 'who judge matters with an eye to their own reputations rather than to the truth' (*Dem.* 23.6),[37] and, as Dionysius' successors, modern scholars must count themselves fortunate that no such literary critics exist on either side of the Atlantic today. What we need is, unsurprisingly, what Dionysius has on offer: a critic who will set forth the emotions he feels when reading the great figures of the past, emotions which, he assures us, are 'common to everyone and not unique to him' (*Dem.* 21.4), a critic, in other words, who is able to articulate a set of shared values and responses. T.S. Eliot (again), at least, would recognize the discourse. Dionysius, moreover, has no wish to appear 'to make novel and paradoxical claims', παράδοξα καινοτομεῖν πράγματα (*Thuc.* 2.2): the text and construction are unfortunately uncertain, but this phrase has a strongly negative flavour in Greek, much more so than the 'lone pioneer breaking new and unexpected ground' of the standard English translation.[38] If, on the other hand, κοιναὶ δόξαι, 'common opinions' (*Thuc.* 2.2), are wrong, they need to be corrected, and this – after all – has happened throughout history. When Dionysius comes in the *Letter to Pompeius* to defend the criticism (κατηγορία) of Plato to be found in his treatise on Demosthenes, he assures his addressee that he has done nothing 'new or paradoxical or contrary to universal belief' (*Pomp.* 1.2). Dionysius is able to produce a roll call of names to show that he was 'neither alone nor the first' (*Pomp.* 1.15) to criticize (in a negative sense) Plato; the list is a very heterogeneous one, but the key point is that these figures are alleged (with greater and lesser degrees of truth) to have been engaged in the business 'not of making fun [of Plato] out of spite or quarrelsomeness but of

---

[36] Cf., e.g., Wiater 2011a, 285–6. Such a rhetoric was already commonplace with the *logographoi* of the classical period, according to Arist. *Rh.* 3.1408a33–6, and was successful because 'the listener agrees out of shame not to know what everyone else knows'; Aristotle is sometimes thought to have Isocrates, in particular, in mind, but this is certainly not a necessary inference.
[37] Cf. Wiater 2011a, 339. Aujac mistakenly translates δόξας here as 'l'opinion'.
[38] Usher 1974, 465.

searching for the truth'.³⁹ That Plato is 'a great man of nearly divine nature' (*Pomp.* 2.2) should not, then, protect his style from the relentless pursuit of critical truth, and it never has.⁴⁰

Dionysius' self-defence in the *Letter to Pompeius* sheds considerable light on one conception of the critic's task. He first distinguishes what he claims to have done from the business of ἔπαινος, 'praise', in which it is virtues, ἀρεταί, rather than τὰ ἀτυχήματα, 'failures', which should take precedence (*Pomp.* 1.3); this is the generic principle, the καθεστηκότες νόμοι, which govern what he almost immediately afterwards calls 'encomium' (*Pomp.* 1.4). This was not, so we are told, what Dionysius was doing: he in fact was trying to establish relative claims among great figures by the comparative method. Rather than considering (again) just how disingenuous this defence may be, let us rather concentrate on the language of criticism. Of particular importance to Dionysius will have been (as always) Isocrates (note, in particular, the 'generic' concerns – the difference between defence and encomium – with which Isocrates' *Helen* opens), but from the very earliest days critical practice had been indissolubly linked to praise and blame; this may be traced back to the emergence of criticism from the internal self-reflection of poetry itself – some poets, most notably Homer himself, were engaged in the business of celebration (κοσμεῖν), whereas for others the task was blame (ψόγος), and critical practice followed suit. 'Praise and blame' are another way in which the public language of oratory and rhetoric provides the context for what the Dionysian critic does: the figures of the past are held up to a 'public' examination, and the natural mode of such examination, if indeed its crucial importance is to be acknowledged, is encomium or attack.⁴¹

As, however, Aristotle knew very well, the two practices of praise and blame attract people of different moral characters and are revelatory of the difference. Hence Dionysius is always at pains, whether he is discussing the figures of the past or his own critical practice, to examine the διάθεσις, 'attitude', with which views are expressed. Thus, for example, Plato's manifold virtues are spoiled by the spirit of τὸ φιλότιμον, 'competitiveness, desire for praise', which was engrained in his nature (*Pomp.* 1.12), a spirit most on show in his envy of Homer; Longinus, however, shows us how

---

³⁹ Both Usher 1974 and Aujac 1991 understand κωμῳδοῦντες to refer to what Plato's critics actually did do, but this seems to ignore the careful balance of the sentence, and Dionysius does not want any suggestion here that he too is involved in κωμῳδεῖν; it is unclear how Fornaro 1997, 115–16 construes the sentence.
⁴⁰ I am not convinced by Fornaro 1997, 156 that we should see irony in this description of Plato.
⁴¹ For some relevant passages on 'praise' and 'blame' in oratory and rhetoric, cf. Lausberg 1960, 55.

precisely the opposite, positive 'spin' could be put on this same eristic relationship – one can wish to compete for glory with the great figures of the past, and it was very much to Plato's credit that he did so (*Subl.* 13.4). As for Dionysius himself, it is (again) 'truth' which is his constant watchword (*Pomp.* 1.6), and it is a pity that it was not Plato's (*Pomp.* 1.14). Truth is, however, not simple, and Dionysius' flexible conception of it deserves a moment's notice.

In chapter 45 of the *On Thucydides* Dionysius criticizes the historian for giving Pericles such a defiant speech in book 2 when the Athenians turned against him, a speech which could only have made the Athenians angrier, rather than a pleading speech of apology:

> It would be amazing, if Pericles, the greatest orator of the time, did not know what anyone of average intelligence knew, namely that those who unsparingly praise their own virtues are always burdensome to the audience, but especially in trials before a law-court or assembly; here the risk they face is not loss of honour but punishment (μὴ περὶ τιμῶν...ἀλλὰ περὶ τιμωριῶν). In such circumstances, they are not only burdensome to others, but the cause of misfortune to themselves, as they attract popular malice (φθόνος). Where the judges and the prosecutors are the same, one needs endless tears and appeals for pity to achieve the good will of your hearers. (*Thuc.* 45.3)

Aspasia perhaps saw Pericles in floods of tears, but the Athenian assembly never did. Dionysius finishes his analysis of this particular Thucydidean misjudgement as follows:

> As I said at the beginning, the historian is expressing his own opinion about Pericles' virtue and he has said these things inappropriately (παρὰ τόπον). Certainly, he should have expressed whatever view he wanted about the man, but he should have given him humble words and ones capable of assuaging anger when he was on trial; this would have been appropriate (πρέπον) for a historian who wished to imitate the truth. (*Thuc.* 45.6)

In her edition Aujac suggests that there is an allusion here to Thucydides' own famously problematic account of his procedure with regard to speeches:[42]

> καὶ ὅσα μὲν λόγῳ εἶπον ἕκαστοι ἢ μέλλοντες πολεμήσειν ἢ ἐν αὐτῷ ἤδη ὄντες, χαλεπὸν τὴν ἀκρίβειαν αὐτὴν τῶν λεχθέντων διαμνημονεῦσαι ἦν ἐμοί τε ὧν αὐτὸς ἤκουσα καὶ τοῖς ἄλλοθέν ποθεν ἐμοὶ ἀπαγγέλλουσιν· ὡς δ' ἂν ἐδόκουν ἐμοὶ ἕκαστοι περὶ τῶν αἰεὶ παρόντων τὰ δέοντα μάλιστ' εἰπεῖν,

---

[42] Aujac 1991, III n. 1.

ἐχομένῳ ὅτι ἐγγύτατα τῆς ξυμπάσης γνώμης τῶν ἀληθῶς λεχθέντων, οὕτως εἴρηται.

> As to what was said by all parties, either in the run-up to the war or when they were actually engaged in it, it has been difficult to recall the exact wording of what was said, both for me with regard to speeches I myself heard and those who have supplied me with reports from elsewhere. Therefore, I have recorded what seemed to me it was most appropriate for anyone to say in the situation prevailing at any time, while remaining as close as possible to the general import of what was in truth said. (Thuc. 1.22.1)[43]

Two related points of interest arise, whether or not we accept that Dionysius is indeed alluding to this passage of Thucydides. One is whether Dionysius understood (or chose to interpret) Thucydides' τὰ δέοντα, 'what the case demanded', itself of course an expression redolent of rhetorical theorizing, as τὰ πρέποντα, 'what was appropriate', for Dionysus the most potent determinant of what was to be said. Whether or not we believe that there is a fundamental contradiction at the heart of Thucydides' programme for his speeches,[44] we can nevertheless see how the Thucydidean expression differs from the Dionysian πρέπον, but it is also clear how one could take them as essentially synonymous, and how Dionysius might well have done so.[45] Secondly, Dionysius might be saying that an orator such as Pericles will certainly have followed the rules of rhetoric as known to Dionysius,[46] and so this is the kind of speech which Thucydides should have given him. This may be another example of what Stanley Bonner called Dionysius' 'singular lack of mental elasticity',[47] but it is also much more interesting than that. What is clear is that 'imitation' is Dionysius' business, not Thucydides' (the historian, alas, was not one of Dionysius' pupils), and 'truth' may not be the Thucydidean 'what was truly said', that is, a matter of historical record, but rather the 'truth' imposed by a way of looking at the world, a way governed by rules determining how to behave and speak in particular situations, a rhetorical 'truth' in other words about τὸ πρέπον, just as appeals to 'life' in literary critical situations ('O Menander and life. . .') are not pleas for documentary realism.[48] There is of course a connection between the

---

[43] My translation of this tormented passage has, of course, a very limited purpose.
[44] Helpful summary of the arguments and some of the bibliography in Hornblower 1987, 45–66, adding Schütrumpf 2011.
[45] Dionysius' discussion of 2.60.5 immediately before (*Thuc.* 45.1–2) is not, I think, decisive against this view.
[46] Cf. Pavano 1958 ad loc.   [47] Bonner 1939, 72.
[48] Cf. further Halliwell 2002, 292–5; Hunter 2014, 373–9.

two forms of 'truth', and a more intimate one than our own preconceptions might allow us to accept: a rhetorical view of what the world is like is indeed just that – a view of what the world is like – and is not necessarily consciously partial or selective. We may compare, while acknowledging the important differences, the links which Dionysius creates in the opening of the *Roman Antiquities* between historical 'truth', 'the origin of φρόνησις and σοφία' (*Ant. Rom.* 1.1.2), and the choice of grand, uplifting themes which will benefit readers (1.1.2, 3.6).[49] In a rhetorically informed world, whether that issues in rhetorical criticism or historiography, truth is never neutral, it must always serve proper and important ends.

When Dionysius says that 'someone whose aim is truth and who wants to be an imitator of nature (τὴν ἀλήθειαν...τις ἐπιτηδεύων καὶ φύσεως μιμητὴς γίνεσθαι βουλόμενος) would not go wrong if he followed the model of Lysias' composition, for one which is truer (ἀληθεστέραν) than this cannot be found' (*Lys.* 8.7), it is again not a view of what a defendant 'really said' which is at issue. Dionysius is of course under no illusion that the truth of Lysias' style is a reproduction of 'the way people spoke'; perhaps to us, paradoxically, it is in fact rather 'truer' than that.[50] For Dionysius, Lysias is ποιητὴς κράτιστος λόγων who has discovered his own kind of ἁρμονία in prose, which is as different as one may be from ordinary conversation (*Lys.* 3.8); Lysias is however also a ποιητής who avoids any suspicion of the ποιητικόν (*Lys.* 14.1).[51]

My comparison to the rich ancient tradition about how comedy, and above all Menander, 'imitated life' is not chosen at random. As one looks through ancient discussions of Menander, it is hard not to be reminded of Dionysius' Lysias and of his *On Lysias*. The surviving epitome of Dionysius' praise of Menander in *On Imitation* praises the purity and clarity of comic diction in general and of Menander's mastery of τὸ πραγματικόν in particular (Menander T87 K-A). We may perhaps fill this out a little from Quintilian's discussion, as the general closeness of Quintilian to Dionysius in these famous chapters is a commonplace: for Quintilian, Menander *omnem uitae imaginem expressit*, 'represented a total image of life' (*Inst.* 10.1.69), and his plays were thus a particularly important model for the budding orator, both because of their rhetorical *copia et eloquendi facultas* and because of the way in which the speeches were suited to a very wide range of characters. The three leitmotifs of ancient criticism

---

[49] Cf. Oakley in this volume, pp. 130, 138–9.
[50] On Dionysius' presentation of Lysias, cf. esp. Viidebaum in this volume.
[51] Cf. De Jonge 2008, 253–6.

of Menander are in fact the purity of his language, his portrayal of character and his *charites*, and this group of virtues makes it hard indeed not to think of Dionysius' *Lysias*; the Menander of the extant epitome of Plutarch's *Comparison of Aristophanes and Menander*, for example, is very close to Dionysius' Lysias.[52]

However unusual much of Dionysius' extant criticism may seem to us, therefore, he can be seen, at least in part, to be operating with ethical and rhetorical categories and distinctions which were fundamental to ancient criticism of all kinds. It is indeed perhaps the fusion of traditional categories with a distinctive brand of classicizing aestheticism which is the most striking aspect of Dionysius' criticism. Dionysius was heir to more than one critical stream, and the debates which are on show in his treatises offer a remarkable view of a particular moment and a particular place – Augustan Rome – in the history both of criticism and of the idea of the critic.

---

[52] On this work, cf. Hunter 2009, 78–89. On χάρις, Viidebaum in this volume.

CHAPTER 2

Experiencing the Past: Language, Time and Historical Consciousness in Dionysian Criticism

Nicolas Wiater

Introduction

Konrad Heldmann is probably pronouncing a widely held view when he states that '[i]t is well known that the Greek Atticists appealed to the "good old times"'.[1] The purpose of this chapter is to argue that Dionysius' image of the past and the role it plays in his classicist criticism is more complicated than that. My argument is organized in three sections.

The first section argues that an 'idealized' image of the past, while certainly present in Dionysius' writings, coexists with a much more 'realistic', 'historicizing' image of fifth- and fourth-century Athens and its inhabitants. Dionysius is well aware that the contemporaries of the authors whose texts he regards as representative of 'the classical' – a concept in which aesthetics, politics and morals are inextricably intertwined – were far from conforming to this ideal. Dionysius therefore separates the classical texts and the ideas which they, quite literally, embody from their fifth- and fourth-century background: Dionysius' primary focus is the past as it is encoded and, hence, experienceable, in the classical texts, the 'past-as-text' or, as I suggest to call it, as a 'structure of feelings', rather than the historical people who wrote, performed and listened to them. The classical texts take the place of their authors. This abstraction of the classical ideal from its cultural, historical and political context dissociates being classical from the exclusive identity of fifth- and fourth-century Athenians. Thus, the 'classical' becomes transferable, as it were, to Augustan Rome, where it can finally realize its full potential to create a classical present and future.

While the first section focuses on the relationship between the classical texts and their historical context, the second section explores the relationship between the classical past-as-text and the classicist reader. How is the classical past created and experienced as a 'structure of feelings' through the

[1] Heldmann 1982, 105, with further references; cf. also 143.

classicist's daily contact with the texts? Dionysius, I will argue, construes the relationship with the past as a continuous quest for an intimacy with the classical (past-as-)text that can never be achieved: every act of reading/performing the classical texts opens up a gap between the intensity of the classicist's experience of the text and the imagined intensity of the experience of the same texts by an ideal classical audience, thus prompting the classicist to try even harder to further reduce this gap. The immediate 'identification between past and present, self and other', as Porter put it,[2] is not the driving force behind classicism as a cultural practice; rather it is a continuous, but never fulfilled attempt to close the gap between past and present in and through the reading process. The same mechanism informs Dionysius' view of the Augustan present as a permanent transformative state, a time oriented towards an ever-receding horizon of the promise of a classical future which has almost, but not quite yet, been reached.

The identification of the classical past with the texts and their effect, aesthetic as well as moral, on the reader (the past as a 'structure of feelings') also enables Dionysius to connect more immediately with the past by interfering with the classical texts. The final section of this chapter argues that such an immediate, 'invasive-constructive'[3] interaction with the past, is enacted through one of the key practices of classicist criticism which has so far been discussed primarily from the point of view of its didactic function, the so-called *metathesis*, the re-writing of passages of the classical texts. *Metathesis* allows Dionysius to engage with the past by manipulating the texts which embody it and thus to create the very classical ideal which he and his readers strive to reach.[4]

1. 'Historical Past' and 'Experienced Past': The Past as Text and a 'Structure of Feelings'

The foundation of any form of classicism is the desire to re-establish in the present the standards of a remote past which for whatever reason are perceived as having been neglected, corrupted or forgotten in the intervening period.[5] Classicism thus seems to entail a one-sidedly positive, even idealized vision of that remote, 'classical' past (the 'good old times');[6] this, we might presume, leaves little room, perhaps even discourages more historically minded, scrutinizing approaches, since these imply the risk of

---

[2] Porter 2006a, 45, cited below, p. 69. [3] I explain this term below, p. 77.
[4] On *metathesis*, see also De Jonge 2005; Yunis and De Jonge in this volume, pp. 90–1 and 257–8.
[5] See Gelzer 1979, now itself a classic. [6] Cf. the quotation from Heldmann above, p. 56.

producing a more balanced and, hence, less appealing image of the 'classical' period.

Such an 'idealizing' image of the classical Athenians certainly exists in Dionysian classicism. It is well illustrated by passages such as Dionysius' criticism of the Melian Dialogue (Thuc. 5.84–116) in his essay *On Thucydides* (37–41). The Melian Dialogue is one of a series of examples from Thucydides' work designed to illustrate Thucydides' success or failure as an author, both in terms of the contents of his work and its style (*Thuc.* 25.1).[7] For Dionysius, the Melian Dialogue is particularly significant because he regards it as invented in its entirety by Thucydides since the latter was not present at the event (*Thuc.* 41.3): the Dialogue is all Thucydides and therefore representative of the characteristics and tendencies of his work in general. Moreover, Thucydides' admirers regarded the Dialogue as one of the strongest parts of the *History*; Dionysius' criticism of this part of Thucydides' work in particular will therefore be an especially effective refutation of their views (*Thuc.* 37.1).[8]

Dionysius' focus in his discussion of the Dialogue is on its contents: contrary to the view of Thucydides' admirers, Dionysius holds, the Melian Dialogue is aesthetically unsatisfactory because it presents a deliberately negative image of Thucydides' Athenian contemporaries. The ruthless imperialism endorsed by Thucydides' Athenians, Dionysius says, makes them resemble 'barbarian kings' (*Thuc.* 39.1), while Thucydides should have portrayed his contemporaries as 'leaders of the city with the best laws in the world', who 'during the Persian War chose to leave their land and their city rather than submit to any base imposition' and 'had civilised the life of all mankind' (*Thuc.* 41.6). Adopting the image of Athenian civic identity familiar from Isocrates' speeches and the Funeral Oration,[9] Dionysius has here all but reduced the 'classical Athenians' to abstract, moral and political categories designed immediately to appeal to the classicist reader and to prompt his intuitive, emotional involvement and identification with them.

Yet, Dionysius' attitude to the classical past is somewhat more complex than passages such as *Thuc.* 41.6 might lead us to believe. In fact, this 'idealizing' view of the classical past coexists with a 'historicizing', more realistic one. This 'historicizing' mode is found, for example, in Dionysius'

---

[7] The passage is cited by Hunter in this volume, pp. 37–8.
[8] For a detailed discussion of Dionysius' criticism of the Melian Dialogue, see Wiater 2011a, 154–65. On Thucydides' fans in Rome, see De Jonge 2011; De Jonge 2017; Hunter in this volume, pp. 48–9.
[9] On the influence of Isocrates on Dionysius' thought, see Hidber 1996, 44–51; Wiater 2011a, 65–77; see also Hunter in this volume, p. 41.

discussion of the chronology of Demosthenes' and Aristotle's works in the *First Letter to Ammaeus* (11.1–4), where Dionysius is arguing against an anonymous Peripatetic who had claimed that Demosthenes had learned his wonderful rhetorical technique from Aristotle's theoretical works on rhetoric; Dionysius sets out to disprove that claim by relating Demosthenes' and Aristotle's works to political-historical events, thus showing that Demosthenes was already a famous and successful orator when Aristotle published his rhetorical treatises.[10] In order to do so, he presents his readers with several quotations from the works of the Atthidographers (Athenian local historians), in this case Philochorus, to bolster his chronology of Aristotle's and Demosthenes' works. Dionysius' attitude to the classical past here is fundamentally historicizing, inasmuch as he seeks to localize individual works within a carefully researched and chronologically precise framework of political and cultural events.

There is thus a remarkable 'doubleness of attitude'[11] towards the classical past in Dionysius' critical writings: Dionysius is clearly capable of regarding the fifth- and fourth-century Athenians, including the authors whose works he admires, as historical people who lived in a specific cultural, historical and social environment, and from his knowledge of local Athenian histories he must have been aware that Thucydides' portrayal of his contemporary Athenians was much more likely to be true than the alternative, idealizing construction of 'Athenian-ness' proposed by many of the classical texts. This awareness does not, however, prompt him to question the relevance of this idealizing image of classical Athenian-ness; on the contrary, he even seeks to superimpose it upon Thucydides' more realistic portrayal of his contemporaries. Instead, he keeps these different views of the classical past separate by confining their use to specific contexts: he applies the 'historicizing' mode when discussing chronological or philological matters such as the authenticity of certain speeches, the development of stylistic characteristics or, as in the *First Letter to Ammaeus*, the chronology of different works; the 'idealizing' mode, by contrast, seems to dominate his evaluation of the contents of these works.

This is all the more remarkable as the same classical authors on whose authority Dionysius' positive image of being a classical Athenian is based, often chastise their own audience for falling short of this ideal. Isocrates in particular was by no means blind to the flaws of his contemporaries. In fact,

---

[10] On *Amm.* 1 see Wiater 2011a, 29–52, 303–10 (with further literature).
[11] I am borrowing this term from MacFarlane 2007, 29 (who uses it with reference to Romantic attitudes to 'originality'); for the term 'doubleness' in relation to Dionysius, see also Connolly in this volume, pp. 269–70.

Isocrates creates the idealizing image of Athenian identity to which Dionysius subscribes with reference to the ancestors (πρόγονοι), not his contemporary audience. It is they whom he portrays as representatives of the set of moral and political values (most prominently δικαιοσύνη, σωφροσύνη, εὐσέβεια, ἐλευθερία, ὁμόνοια) that form the basis of Athenian political and moral superiority,[12] whereas he often chastises his actual audience for failing to live up to the standard of Athenian civic identity set by the ancestors.

That Dionysius was well aware of Isocrates' negative portrayal of his Athenian contemporaries, which was, after all, not so very different of Thucydides' representation of the Athenians in the Melian Dialogue, is evident from passages such as the following one from *On Isocrates*, which reveals an interesting tension between Dionysius' idealizing evaluation of the passage – he cites the passage as a demonstration of the remarkable aesthetic quality (the 'strength', ἰσχύς) of Isocrates' style in his *On the Peace* (41–2) – and the passage's contents, Isocrates' harsh criticism of his audience:[13]

> He has [...] composed a most beautiful encomium (ἐγκώμιον κάλλιστον) of justice and has outlined his criticism of the existing state of affairs (τὰ καθεστηκότα πράγματα μεμψάμενος). He follows this with a comparison between the Athenians of his day and their ancestors: '[...] Suppose that a stranger from some other country were to come to Athens, having had no time to become tainted with our depravity, but coming suddenly face-to-face with what goes on here, would he not think that we were mad and beside ourselves when we pride ourselves on the deeds of our ancestors and think fit to praise our city by recounting the deeds of their time, and yet behave in no way like them, but in the very opposite way?' (*Isoc.* 17.1)[14]

The tension between Dionysius' positive assessment of the passage as a 'beautiful praise' (ἐγκώμιον κάλλιστον) of justice (δικαιοσύνη), one of the key values of the ideal Athenian citizen (see above), and its contents, Isocrates' rebuke of his Athenian contemporaries as undermining this very ideal (τὰ καθεστηκότα πράγματα μεμψάμενος), reflects the coexistence of the two contrasting modes of viewing the classical past, the 'historicizing' and the 'idealizing', in Dionysius' classicism, which, in turn, seem to

---

[12] For Isocrates, see Too 1995, esp. 58–60; on the role of the ancestors in ancient oratory, Jost 1936, esp. 138–9 on Isocrates.
[13] Dionysius cites (and rewrites) the same passage from Isocrates in *Dem.* 17–20: see Yunis in this volume, pp. 90–1.
[14] Translations in this chapter are adapted from Usher 1974–1985 and Cary 1937–1950.

mirror the opposition between the πρόγονοι and the real audience which is so forcefully established by Isocrates.

Surprisingly, however, and in stark contrast to his criticism of the Melian Dialogue, Dionysius does not even comment on Isocrates' negative portrayal of his Athenian audience; on the contrary, the contrast only seems to intensify the positive qualities of the passage, in which ethics and aesthetics are closely interrelated: the attitude of the ancestors, the 'beauty' of the ideal past envisaged by Isocrates and Dionysius alike (ἐγκώμιον κάλλιστον), is independent of the actual historical circumstances of Isocrates' speech, the documentary value, so to speak, of Isocrates' criticism. What counts for Dionysius is that Isocrates himself represents and seeks to implement δικαιοσύνη in and through his speech by employing the full array of his oratorical skills to praise it.[15]

This might also help explain why Dionysius accepts the indirect negative image of the historical Athenians in Isocrates' speeches, but is positively outraged at Thucydides' portrayal of the Athenians in the Melian Dialogue. I have argued elsewhere that the source of Dionysius' outrage was the failure of Thucydides' image of the Athenians to conform to the standard of the 'ideal' Athenians put forward in Isocrates' speeches; Thucydides, put differently, should have used his work to present an idealized, rather than a 'realistic' image of his Athenian contemporaries.[16]

The above discussion of the passage from Isocrates' *On the Peace* suggests a different, more complex explanation. The passage shows that a critical, even negative image of the fifth- and fourth-century Athenians as such is clearly not a problem for Dionysius. This view receives further support from several passages in Dionysius' historical work, the *Roman Antiquities*, where Dionysius himself adopts a similarly critical stance. At *Ant. Rom.* 1.3. 1–2, for example, he dismisses the empires of Athens and Sparta as inferior not only to that of Rome, but even to the barbarian empires of the Assyrians, Medes, Persians and Macedonians.[17] Even more striking is his polemical criticism of Athenian and Spartan politics, which is remarkably similar to his own criticism of Thucydides' portrayal of his Athenian contemporaries in the Melian Dialogue:

> The Athenians in the case of the Samians, their own colonists, and the Lacedaemonians in the case of the Messenians, who were the same as their brothers, when these gave them some offence, dissolved the ties of kinship (τὴν συγγένειαν), and after subjugating their cities, treated them with such

---

[15] On the close interrelation of language and civic identity in Isocrates, see Too 1995.
[16] See Wiater 2011a, 157–65, esp. 164.   [17] On this passage cf. Martin 1993; Wiater 2018a.

cruelty (ὠμῶς) and beastliness (θηριωδῶς) as to equal even the most savage of barbarians (τοῖς ἀγριωτάτοις τῶν βαρβάρων) in their mistreatment of people of kindred stock (τῆς εἰς τὰ ὁμόφυλα παρανομίας). One could name countless aberrations (ἡμαρτημένα) of this sort made by these cities, but I pass over them since it grieves me to mention even these instances.[18] (*Ant. Rom.* 14.6.3)

If the negative image of the historical Athenians as such is not the issue in Dionysius' criticism of the Melian Dialogue, what is? A possible answer lies in the role and attitude of the speaker in Isocrates' speech and Thucydides' Dialogue. There is a noticeable difference in the passage from Isocrates between the way in which, according to Isocrates, his historical audience behave and the way in which they should behave; Isocrates' speech is beautiful despite its unpleasant contents because the negative image of the Athenians constitutes the basis, as it were, on which Isocrates develops his view of the ethical standards which the Athenians *should* follow and which is represented by Isocrates' very speech. In the passage from *On the Peace*, there is a gap between the historical Athenians and the idealized image of the Athenians which is advertised by Isocrates and adopted by Dionysius; the gap makes this idealized image shine forth even more strongly.

There is no such gap between ideal and 'real' in the Melian Dialogue. Here, Thucydides has an official representative of the Athenian people adopt and, hence, advertise the exact same kind of attitude towards power which Dionysius himself so explicitly criticizes in the passage from the *Roman Antiquities* cited above. There is no moral-ethical yardstick against which the reader could evaluate the Athenian's ideas, and, therefore, the passage has no positive ethical impact such as results from the awareness of the gap separating ideal and real in the Isocrates passage. As Dionysius says (*Thuc.* 41.8), 'when the leaders of a state, entrusted by her with great power and appointed to represent her on missions to other states, seem to express certain views, those views are assumed by all to be those of the state which sent them out'. It is this 'totality' of the condemnable attitude represented by the Athenian spokesman and the lack of an alternative perspective which is so firmly anchored in Isocrates' speech in the contrast between the Athenians of the present, on the one hand, and the (idealized) Athenians of the past

---

[18] I discuss this passage in the larger context of Dionysius' image of Athens and its relationship with his image of the Romans in Wiater 2018a.

and Isocrates himself, on the other, which makes the Melian Dialogue an ethical as well as an aesthetic failure.[19]

The discussion so far has shown that Dionysius' classicism does not entail an uncritically, one-sidedly positive image of the fifth- and fourth-century Athenians. Dionysius is well aware that the 'classical' moral, political and aesthetic values, the 'classical Athenian character' which constitutes the basis of his 'classicist ideology', is an idealized concept developed under and in response to the specific historical, cultural and social circumstances of fifth- and fourth-century Athens; he is also aware that the people who lived at the time were anything but representatives of this 'classical' ideal. Dionysius, to put it differently, is fully aware that the 'classical ideal' which he endorses and which he seeks to impart to his readers, is and always has been a culturally and historically contingent construction that was at odds with the reality already at the time of its creation. Dionysius does not suppress passages that prominently display this divergence between ideal and real, nor does he attempt to mitigate or gloss over Isocrates' criticism of the Athenians. On the contrary, it seems to be this very gap between the 'ideal' Athenians envisaged by Isocrates and his Athenian contemporaries that increases the importance and exemplary value of this classical ideal; the classical ideal to a considerable extent owes its very status as an ideal and, hence, as a desirable goal, to the existence of this gap and Dionysius' and his readers' awareness of it.

It is the correlative, and, perhaps, most important consequence of this awareness of the gap between historical Athenians and the ideal Athenian that this ideal can now be abstracted from the historical, cultural and social circumstances of its creation. After all, the political, moral and ethical values which Isocrates wants his audience to adopt have always and consciously been an anachronism (Isocrates introduces them as the values of the πρόγονοι!) inasmuch as already in the fifth and fourth centuries their intended effect was to inspire the desire to return to a better past. As I will argue now, the process of abstracting the classical ideal from its original context and transferring it to the present, where it is to serve essentially the same purpose as in the past, just more successfully, is a crucial element of Dionysius' classicist criticism.

An important step in this process of abstracting 'the classical' from its fifth- and fourth-century Athenian background is the shift away from the

---

[19] *Thuc.* 41.7: 'In the Melian Dialogue the wisest of the Greeks adduce the most disgraceful arguments, and invest them with the most disagreeable language'. *Thuc.* 39.6 (on Thuc. 5.95): 'A base sentiment, awkwardly expressed'. Cf. Fox 2001, 83 on the 'overlap between the moral and the aesthetic'.

actual, historical Athenians as potential representatives of the classical ideal to the classical texts and their distinctive combination of ethics and aesthetics as its, quite literal, 'embodiment'. This shift is observable already in Dionysius' discussion of the passage from Isocrates' *On the Peace* (above), which, as pointed out, focuses on the moral and aesthetic properties of the text as a manifestation of the ancestral virtues while neglecting Isocrates' negative image of his Athenian contemporaries: it is the potential moral, political and aesthetic effect of Isocrates' speech that is important, not its actual effect on Isocrates' audience. But the same shift towards the classical texts as the embodiment of the classical Athenian character, rather than the historical Athenians themselves, also informs Dionysius' programmatic definition of 'selective μίμησις',[20] as he presents it in his 'classicist manifesto',[21] the preface to his collection of essays *On the Ancient Orators*:

> Who are the most important of the ancient orators and historians? What manner of life and style of writing (προαιρέσεις τοῦ τε βίου καὶ τοῦ λόγου) did they adopt? Which characteristics of each of them should we appropriate and which should we avoid? (*Orat. Vett.* 4.2)

The preceding discussion suggests that Dionysius is not referring to 'style of life' and 'style of writing' as two separate categories.[22] On the contrary, the author's 'style of writing' is itself both an expression of, and way of implementing, his 'style of life', just like Isocrates' 'most beautiful encomium of justice' delivered to his depraved contemporaries is informed by and a manifestation of Isocrates' 'classical' morals and way of life. In the same way, Dionysius speaks of the 'beauty of Isocrates' subjects' (τῶν ὑποθέσεων τὸ κάλλος) with specific reference to the ethical contents of his speeches and their importance for their addressees' successfully playing a leading role in political life – in the past as well as the present.[23]

This explains the discrepancy noticed by scholars between Dionysius' stress on the 'manner of life' of the classical authors and the surprisingly little attention he does pay to their lives:[24] it is not through his biographical sketches that Dionysius intends to illustrate the classical authors' characters and moral and political attitudes. Like the quotations from historical works in the *First Letter to Ammaeus* mentioned above, the primary function of

---

[20] See Hidber 1996, 56–75; Hunter 2009, 107–27; Wiater 2011a, 77–92; cf. De Jonge's 2008 index s.v. 'imitation'.

[21] See the title of Hidber 1996: *Das klassizistische Manifest des Dionys von Halikarnass*.

[22] Cf. *Ant. Rom.* 1.1.3: 'it is a just and a general opinion that a man's words are the images of his mind'. Cf. Fox 2001, 83; Fox 2011, 99.

[23] *Isoc.* 4.2–4, cited below, n. 29.   [24] Hidber 1996, 72–3.

such biographical elements is to locate the works of these authors within a larger political, social and chronological context, rather than to (re)construct their 'manner of life'. The latter Dionysius expects to access through the aesthetics of these authors' texts, understood as an immediate, and immediately experienceable, expression of their identity, their characters and moral and political values. Isocrates, Lysias and Demosthenes matter most to him not as historical persons, as human beings who lived their lives according to certain moral or political standards, but as ciphers for a complex of aesthetics and political and moral values which is represented by their texts and which he and his readers can experience and connect with through studying and reading/performing these texts.[25] Adapting a concept developed by Raymond Williams, I suggest to call this emotional-aesthetic construction of the past and the people who represented it, the past as a 'structure of feelings'.[26]

This abstraction of the classical ideal from the concrete historical circumstances in which it was created, I would suggest, is directly linked to the peculiar perception of the relationship between past and present that underlies Dionysius', and, indeed, any form of classicism (see above): classicism operates on the premise that the remote past is somehow closer to the present than the period immediately preceding it. Idealizing this historical period itself and, hence, the historical fifth- and fourth-century Athenians as representatives of the classical ideal would link the classical ideal to the specific historical period in which it emerged and, thus, reveal any attempt to share and even continue this ideal as preposterous: the classical values and way of life would have become obsolete once the specific historical period in which they existed had ended; moreover, if the classical way of life was an exclusive attribute of the historical Athenian citizens – associated, as it was in Isocrates and others, with the specific moral and political tradition of the Athenian πρόγονοι – Dionysius and his addressees would have been excluded from it even if they had lived in fifth- and fourth-century Athens. Like Dionysius, most of them, as far as we know, were not from Athens, and some were not Greeks at all.[27] By the rules of classical Athenian democracy, which prescribed that both parents had to be Athenian citizens for their children to be Athenian citizens as

---

[25] On this process see the following section.
[26] First used in his *A Preface to Film* (Williams and Orrom 1954), the concept remains important in Williams' writings; see, e.g., Williams 1977, 128–35; Williams 2005, 26–31. I am using the term here without any Marxist connotations.
[27] On Dionysius' 'literary circle', see De Jonge 2008, 32–4; Wiater 2011a, 22–9.

well,[28] neither Dionysius nor the majority of his addressees would have been likely to be acknowledged as real Athenians in the historical past.

Dissociating the historical past from the experience of the past as a 'structure of feelings' thus dissociates 'being classical' from being born to Athenian parents and living in Athens in the fifth and fourth centuries BC. Consequently, Dionysius not only privileges Isocrates' text, and its message of the beauty of justice, over the actual attitude and character of Isocrates' classical audience, but also stresses the general, transtemporal value and effect of his writings (*Isoc.* 4.2–4).[29] By abstracting the didactic power of Isocrates' speeches from their original time, place and addressees, Dionysius underlines that it is the speeches themselves and their moral aesthetics that are the carriers of 'being classical' and can, therefore, be transferred to, and their message implemented in, Augustan Rome. The texts thus take the place of their authors and become, quite literally, embodiments of the classical ideal:[30]

> Generally speaking, two different forms of μίμησις can be found with regard to ancient models: one is natural (φυσικός), and is acquired by intensive learning and common nurture (ἐκ πολλῆς κατηχήσεως καὶ συντροφίας); the other is related to it, but is acquired by following the precepts of handbooks (τῶν τῆς τέχνης παραγγελμάτων). About the first, what more is there to say? And about the second, what is there to be said except that a certain natural charm and freshness (αὐτοφυής τις [...] χάρις καὶ ὥρα) emanates from all the original models (τοῖς ἀρχετύποις), whereas in the artificial copies (τοῖς δ' ἀπὸ τούτων κατεσκευασμένοις), even if they attain the height of imitative skill, there is present nevertheless a certain element of contrivance (τὸ ἐπιτετηδευμένον) and unnaturalness (οὐκ ἐκ φύσεως ὑπάρχον) also? (*Din.* 7.5)

The key terms 'natural' and 'intensive learning and common nurture' are particularly significant in the present context: in Dionysius' classicist ideology, the direct, 'physical' contact with the real, historical people, with Isocrates, Demosthenes and Lysias, which was the prerogative of the historical Athenians of the fifth and fourth centuries, is no longer

---

[28] See Ober 1989, 6; 97–8 (citizenship and exclusivity); 261–2 ('pure bloodline' and autochthony).

[29] 'The influence of these [Isocrates' writings] would make anyone who applied himself to his works not only good orators, but men of sterling character [τὰ ἤθη σπουδαίους], of positive service to their families, to their state and to Greece at large. I therefore affirm that the man who intends to acquire ability in the whole field of politics [τῆς πολιτικῆς δυνάμεως], not merely a part of that science, should make Isocrates his constant companion'; cf. Gabba 1991, 33–4; Fox 1996, 73; Wiater 2011a, 70–1.

[30] Cf. Wiater 2011a, 77–92, esp. 89–91. I agree with Halliwell 2002, 13–14, that the term *mimesis* is too complex to be translated adequately; the reductive rendering 'imitation' is especially to be avoided; I tentatively suggest 'appropriation'. Cf. further Halliwell 2011, 208 n. 2.

necessary to become classical. Instead, the classicists develop an equally close bond with their works, a 'common nurture', constituted by the intensive and long-term study of these texts from early childhood. It is from this process of 'growing up' with the texts as though they were childhood friends, from entering into some sort of community with them as though they were real people, that 'naturalness' results, in other words, that one becomes a 'natural' classical Greek.[31]

Thus, it is the texts and their moral-political-cum-aesthetic quality that become the focus of being classical, not the historical people who wrote and performed them in specific historical circumstances and in front of a specific historical audience. To the extent that this approach weakens the prestige of Athens as a physical, historical and geographical location in Dionysius' classicist worldview,[32] it strengthens that of Augustan Rome: in Dionysius and his contemporaries in Augustan Rome, Isocrates' speeches will finally find the appreciative audience they deserve; here, Dionysius and his fellow classicists can become the 'classical Greeks' they desire to be, in a new, modern environment that is free of the temporal, cultural and social obstacles that separate them from fifth- and fourth-century Athens. Rather than being the 'new Athens', Augustan Rome has substituted it, just as the classical texts have substituted their authors.[33]

The paradoxical coexistence of the 'historicizing' and the 'idealizing' view of the past in Dionysius' literary criticism thus turns out to be an essential element of his classicist thought: by creating awareness of the difference between the 'classical ideal' that is represented by the classical texts and the historical audience of these texts, who often fell noticeably short of this ideal, Dionysius creates a gap between the historical fifth- and fourth-century Athenians and 'classical Athens' as a mental-emotional construct. The classical ideal was created in specific historical, cultural and social circumstances, but these very circumstances did not allow 'the classical' to realize its full potential. The historical Athenians did not become the Athenians they could have been had they heeded the advice of Isocrates and others like him: they did not become 'classical'. It is this gap that Dionysius and his fellow classicists fill and that gives meaning to their endeavor to 'be classical' themselves: the distance between the historical Athenian audience and Dionysius and the 'practitioners of πολιτικοὶ

---

[31] On the 'natural' in Dionysius' rhetorical works, see also Yunis in this volume, pp. 90–1.
[32] On the marginalized role of Athens in late Hellenistic and early Imperial Greek literature, see Schmitz and Wiater 2011b, 35–41.
[33] See further below, pp. 68–72.

λόγοι'[34] creates a consciousness of the fact that the potential of the classical texts, the 'classical ideal' that they encode, did not come to fruition three hundred years earlier. While the foundations for the classical style of life-and-speaking were laid in fifth- and fourth-century Athens, it is only in Dionysius' time that this classical ideal is finally implemented systematically and successfully by Dionysius and his community.[35]

2. The Otherness of the Past as the Core of Classicist Self-Fashioning

In the previous section I argued that for Dionysius the classical past is not the specific period of fifth- and fourth-century Athens, but a mental-emotional construct, a 'structure of feelings' encoded in the classical texts which was created in fifth- and fourth-century Athens, but was not implemented at that time. The 'classical past' exists for Dionysius only as the complex of aesthetic, political and moral ideas represented by the texts, not as a historical period that once existed, was lost and now needs to be re-established. In this section, I will explore how this classical past is created and interacted with in the daily practice of classicist reading and how this process of reading thus becomes a way of enacting a specific relationship among past, present and future.

Dionysius' description of his experience of Demosthenes' texts illustrates how the past as a 'structure of feeling' is evoked and experienced in the classicists' daily practice as well as the nature of classicist reading as a practice charged with a strong temporal dimension:[36]

> When I pick up one of Demosthenes's speeches, I am possessed (ἐνθουσιῶ): I am subdued and overpowered (ὑπαγόμεθα καὶ κρατούμεθα), feeling one emotion after another – disbelief, anguish, terror, contempt, hatred, pity, goodwill, anger, envy – every emotion in turn that can sway the human mind (κρατεῖν [...] ἀνθρωπίνης γνώμης). [...] And I have often wondered what on earth those men who actually heard him make these speeches could have felt. For if we, who are so far removed in time and unaffected by the events (ἡμεῖς οἱ τοσοῦτον ἀπηρτημένοι τοῖς χρόνοις καὶ οὐθὲν πρὸς τὰ πράγματα πεπονθότες), are so subdued and overpowered (ὑπαγόμεθα καὶ κρατούμεθα) that we follow wherever the speech leads us, how must the Athenians and the rest of the Greeks have been excited at the time by the

---

[34] As I have argued elsewhere (Wiater 2011a, 48), this term refers to 'Dionysius' ideal readers, i.e., those readers who are defined, and define themselves, by adopting Dionysius' conception of classical rhetoric (πολιτικοὶ λόγοι) and by subscribing to his critical methods'.
[35] Here I differ fundamentally from Fox 2011, 98.
[36] On this passage, see also Yunis in this volume, p. 101.

orator addressing them on live and personal issues (ἐπὶ τῶν ἀληθινῶν τε καὶ ἰδίων ἀγώνων) [...]. (*Dem.* 22.2–5)

The difference which Dionysius establishes between Demosthenes as performer of his own works and his contemporary audience as their recipients, and Dionysius' reading/performance-cum-reception of Demosthenes' speeches recalls the difference between specific historical people who wrote, performed and experienced the classical texts and the texts themselves becoming the sole medium in which this experience is encoded and can be (re-)created and felt by the classicist critic in the present.[37] The classicist reader thus overcomes the separation of speaker and audience that was characteristic of the speeches' performance in their original setting and unites both roles in himself: his own performance of Demosthenes' text creates the conditions that allow the text to work its 'magic' (terms and phrases such as ἐνθουσιῶ, δεῦρο κἀκεῖσε ἄγομαι, and ὑπερφυές conceptualize this act of reading/performing/listening as a state of rapture under divine influence),[38] casting the classicist reader in what could be called a 'liminal role' between active reading and passive receiving, between being in control of the performance and being controlled ('seized') by it, and, thus, between past and present (note in particular δεῦρο κἀκεῖσε ἄγομαι which translates the critic's relationship with the past text into a violent movement of the critic's body in the present).

Dionysius' description of his experience of Demosthenes' texts seems to confirm Jim Porter's statement that

> [c]lassicism in any age involves its practitioners in more than an intellectual or visualized approximation to the past, because it involves them in a multiply layered experience of that past. [...] Classicism entails that individuals take on a *hexis* or a *habitus* and that they make it their own: one no longer merely inhabits the past like a tourist; one comes to be inhabited by it. The identification between past and present, self and other, is immediate, or at least it is imagined and felt (or pretended) to be so.[39]

Both the results of the previous section and the passage cited above confirm that Porter is right to stress the 'experiential' character of the classicist critic's relationship with the past, what I have suggested to call the past as

---

[37] See previous section.
[38] Cf. Kirchner 2005; De Jonge 2008, 332–40; Wiater 2011a, 263–76. Longinus conceptualizes the experience of the sublime in similar terms; see De Jonge 2012b, 286.
[39] Porter 2006a, 45. On the classical *habitus* or *hexis*, Porter 2006b, 308–10; Wiater 2011a, 236, 252–4, 257–63.

a 'structure of feelings' that is accessible and experienceable through the text. But the preceding discussion has also suggested that this same immediate, 'experiential' relationship with the past presupposes an awareness of the difference between past and present, between the historical Athenians in the fifth and fourth centuries and the construct of the 'classical Athenian'. Dionysius' description of his experience of Demosthenes' text, I argue, shows that the same awareness of a gap separating past and present also underlies classicism at the 'micro-level', the continuous contact with the classical texts and, through them, the classical past, through the intensive reading/performing of the classical texts.

The most important aspect of the above passage from this point of view is the relationship between Dionysius as reader/performer/audience of Demosthenes' speeches and his construction of a classical, fourth-century audience as recipients of the same texts. Dionysius conceptualizes the intensity and quality of his own experience by measuring it against the imagined intensity and quality of the experience of a contemporary audience. Here, Dionysius' image of the historical Athenians listening to Demosthenes' speech is remarkably more positive than Isocrates' characterization of his Athenian contemporaries discussed in the previous section. This difference is explained by the fact that in the above passage, Dionysius constructs Demosthenes' historical audience as a more intensely and immediately involved version of himself. In so doing, Dionysius deliberately creates a standard of 'authenticity of reception' that is impossible to reach. Moreover, it is the very intensity of Dionysius' experience of Demosthenes' speeches that creates the awareness of the gap between himself and the 'original' audience: 'If we, who are so far removed in time and unaffected by the events, are so subdued and overpowered that we follow wherever the speech leads us, how must the Athenians and the rest of the Greeks have been excited at the time by the orator [. . .]' (*Dem.* 22. 3–5, cited above). The very moment at which the contact with the past is at its most intense, at which the classicist reader's body is, quite literally, 'seized' by the past, is also the moment that creates the awareness of the difference between the emotional experience of Dionysius and that of Demosthenes' live audience. The only way the past can emerge as 'present' is as being-lost.[40]

This difference between Dionysius' and the imagined classical audience's reception of the classical texts legitimizes Dionysius' critical method

---

[40] I borrow this expression from Zizek 1997, 15.

on which his intense experience of these texts is based and the quality of which he advertises in his essays:[41] the only way to achieve an even more intense and 'authentic' experience of the classical texts would be actually to become one of these Athenians whom Demosthenes addressed on 'live and personal issues'. Since such a return to the past is impossible and – as I argued in the previous section – not even desirable, the kind of experience of the classical texts provided by Dionysius is the best available; barring becoming a fourth-century Athenian, there is no alternative.

The very possibility of such a 'near-authentic' experience presupposes, even requires, the awareness of a difference remaining between Dionysius' and his fellow classicists' reception of the text, and that of Demosthenes' contemporary audience: an essential part of the reception process as Dionysius describes it here is the relentless striving after a goal that is impossible to reach. It is this continuous attempt to get as close to 'the original' as possible that endows the classicist reading process with meaning.[42] Classicist reading, to return to Porter's statement, seems to be less about an 'immediate identification' with the past, an effacement, as it were, of the difference between 'self and other'. It rather presupposes the awareness of this difference, however small it might be, which is re-established every time the classicist performs/experiences the classical texts.

This constant re-opening of the gap between classical past and present is thus not only an essential condition of the ongoing productivity of classicism as a cultural practice, but it also firmly locates this practice in the present as the place and time where the classical ideal is being (re-)enacted. What drives classicism is, therefore, not, as is often assumed, the desire to return to the past:[43] as I have argued in the preceding section, there are no 'good old times' for Dionysius; the classical past is great because it has provided exemplary ideas and concepts necessary to create a better present and future, but it did not itself conform to these exemplary ideas and concepts. On the contrary, the full social and cultural force of these ideas and concepts still remains to be realized. The driving force behind classicism is the engagement with the classical past as a process, the continuous attempt to experience and implement the classical ideal, the classical past as

---

[41] Cf. Wiater 2011a, 232–3, 235–63.
[42] In contrast to my discussion of *Dem.* 22.2–5 in Wiater 2011a, 231–3, which too one-sidedly focused on this difference as a problem for Dionysius and his attempts to resolve it, I would argue now that the awareness of the difference between Dionysius and the 'classical audience' is a productive and even necessary part of the reception process; this difference is, moreover, created by Dionysius himself: there was, after all, no need for him to make that imagined difference an integral part of his conception of the experience of the classical texts.
[43] *Pace*, e.g., Gabba 1991, 23.

a 'structure of feelings', in one's own time in order to make the present (including the critic himself) 'classical'. His concern is not the re-creation of fifth- and fourth-century Athens, the re-definition of Rome, as it has often been put, as a 'new Athens'[44], but making Augustan Rome classical. Such a project can make sense in only one way: if the awareness of the difference between fifth- and fourth-century Athens and first-century Rome, and between being a Greek in Augustan Rome and being a fifth- or fourth-century Athenian, is upheld – being a classicist makes sense only if one can strive to be(come) classical without stopping being oneself.[45]

Instead of a practice turned towards the past, it seems more appropriate to describe classicism as a practice situated at the intersection of past and future, the present playing a 'liminal role' between past and future, just as the reading process casts the classicist critic in a 'liminal role' between past and present.[46] The present thus becomes a transformative state, the catalyst which enables the transition from the corrupted, Asianist past to the better, classical future, as Dionysius formulates it in the preface to *On the Ancient Orators*:[47]

> We ought to acknowledge a great debt of gratitude to the age in which we live (τῷ καθ' ἡμᾶς χρόνῳ), my most accomplished Ammaeus, for an improvement (κάλλιον ἀσκημένων ἢ πρότερον) in certain fields of serious study, and especially for the considerable progress towards the better (ἐπίδοσιν [...] ἐπὶ τὰ κρείττω) in the practice of πολιτικοὶ λόγοι [...] I think that the cause and origin of this great revolution has been the conquest of the world by Rome [...]. This state of affairs has led to the composition of many worthwhile works of history by contemporary writers (τοῖς νῦν), and the publication of many elegant political tracts and many by no means negligible philosophical treatises; and a host of fine works, the products of well-directed industry, have proceeded (προεληλύθασι) from the pens of both Greeks and Romans, and will probably (κατὰ τὸ εἰκός) continue to do so (προελεύσονται). And since this great revolution has taken place in so short a time, I should not be surprised (οὐκ ἂν θαυμάσαιμι) if that craze for a silly style of oratory fails to survive another single generation (μηκέτι χωρήσει προσωτέρω μιᾶς γενεᾶς); for what has been

---

[44] See Hidber 1996, 75–81; more recently, Wiater 2011a, 56; De Jonge, rev. Wiater 2011a, *BMCR* 2012.06.41 (http://bmcr.brynmawr.edu/2012/2012-06-41.html).

[45] The importance of the future in Dionysian classicism is stressed by Fox 2011, although his primary focus is on the *Antiquities*; Heldmann 1982, 143, calls the role of the future in Dionysius 'programmatic'. Cf. the discussion below.

[46] See above, p. 69.

[47] On the role of time in *Orat. Vett.*, see Fox 2011a, 100–2. I have discussed the relationship between past and present in this passage in Wiater 2011a, 60–5, but failed adequately to take into account the importance of the future.

reduced from omnipotence to insignificance can soon (ἐξ ὀλίγου) easily (ῥᾴδιον) be wiped out altogether. (*Orat. Vett.* 1.1, 3.1–3)

The present which Dionysius pictures here is that of a continuous state of 'almost' (note the comparatives): in 'the age in which we live' there has been an 'improvement in certain fields of serious study', and the practice of πολιτικοὶ λόγοι has made 'progress' 'towards the better'; the production of fine works will 'probably continue', and Dionysius 'should not be surprised if' Asianist oratory were not to survive another single generation, as it 'can soon easily be wiped out altogether'.

The function of Dionysius' image of a better future is remarkably similar to the function of his image of the 'original classical recipient' in his description of his experience of Demosthenes' texts (above): Dionysius creates a horizon of the future which provides the ultimate goal of his critical and aesthetic criticism without ever being attainable. The only certainty about his (likely) prediction that Asianism will (probably) not survive another single generation is that it postpones the (foreseeable) victory of classicism into a future that neither Dionysius nor his readers will live to see. The temporal framework in which classicism operates is the limbo between the past and the ever-renewed promise of a better future, just as its daily practice derives its meaningfulness from the continuous attempt to achieve a standard of authenticity of the experience of the classical texts and a kind of intimacy with the ideas they represent that is designed to be unattainable.

How Dionysius envisaged the pursuit of the classical ideal to inform the daily life and activities of his readers in Augustan Rome is more difficult to assess because he never makes any explicit comments to that effect. Some suggestions are, however, possible, and shall bring this section to a close. Dionysius clearly assumed that the sort of knowledge (stylistic, political and moral) that his 'classical education' provided was to play an essential part in his readers' political and social lives. This we can gather from *Orat. Vett.* 1.4, where he explicitly links rhetorical practice to the exertion of political power.[48] As Thomas Hidber aptly put it in his commentary on the passage:

> Only a training worthy of a freeborn man engenders the ability to take responsibility in the community. In the present case, rather concrete

---

[48] Asianist rhetoric, he says there, 'made itself the key to civic honours and high office, a power which ought to have been reserved for the philosophic art' (τὰς τιμὰς καὶ τὰς προστασίας τῶν πόλεων, ἃς ἔδει τὴν φιλόσοφον ἔχειν, εἰς ἑαυτὴν ἀνηρτήσατο).

interests are at stake, namely filling positions in the administrations of towns, provinces, and the Roman empire [...].⁴⁹

The same connection between 'classical' rhetorical training and successful adult life is implied in the preface to his essay *On Composition*, a present to Metilius Rufus on his 'first birthday since reaching man's estate' (πρώτην ἡμέραν ἄγοντι γενέθλιον, *Comp.* 1.1),⁵⁰ and, as I have argued elsewhere, in the parallel Dionysius establishes between the rhetorical-moral education offered by his writings and the learning process which turned orators such as Demosthenes into exemplary rhetoricians *and* statesmen.⁵¹ Such pretensions were perhaps not quite as far-fetched as they might seem, given that some of Dionysius' readers did, in fact, belong to Rome's social and political elite,⁵² and Dionysius could reasonably expect that his education would also influence their behavior outside the 'classroom'. The kind of education which Dionysius offered to the members of his 'literary circle' was, after all, not so different from the Greek education which had been highly sought after by members of the Roman elite for generations: that Greek (rhetorical) education and Roman oratory and statesmanship went hand-in-hand had long been commonplace at Dionysius' time.⁵³

In concrete terms, Dionysius' education would, presumably, become part of the general 'habitus' of his readers and manifest itself in their

---

⁴⁹ Hidber 1996, 105: '[n]ur eine Ausbildung, wie sie eines freien Mannes würdig ist und wie sie allein die φιλόσοφος ῥητορική vermittelt, befähigt zur Übernahme von Verantwortung im Gemeinwesen. Konkret geht es hier um relativ handfeste Interessen, nämlich um die Besetzung von Ämtern in den Verwaltungen der Städte, Provinzen und des Reiches [...]'. Cf. further *Orat. Vett.* 1.7, 3.1.

⁵⁰ Cf. Wiater 2011a, 275–6; De Jonge in this volume, pp. 243, 247.   ⁵¹ Wiater 2011a, 257–63.

⁵² This is certain in the case of Q. Aelius Tubero, the historian and jurisconsult who lost against Cicero in the trial of Q. Ligarius in 46 BC, both of whose sons were *consules* in 11 and 4 BC, respectively; see Bowersock 1965, 129; Bowersock 1979, 68–71. Q. Aelius Tubero was also one of the sources of the *Roman Antiquities*: see Oakley in this volume, p. 154. See also Hunter in this volume, p. 37. The aforementioned Rufus Metilius might be identical with the proconsul of Achaea and legate to Galatia under Augustus; see Bowersock 1965, 132 with n. 2; Bowersock 1979, 70; De Jonge in this volume, p. 247.

⁵³ Already Polybius could capitalize on the idea of the formative influence of Greek knowledge and education on Roman politics and statesmanship when describing his relationship with the young Scipio Aemilianus (31.23–5); other examples include Cicero, whose education is too well known to need repeating here. The formative influence of rhetorical education underlies Cicero's characterization of the *Stoici oratores* Quintus Aelius Tubero (*Brut.* 116–17; *tribunus plebis* in 130 BC and adversary of the Gracchi, who unsuccessfully attempted to become *praetor* in 123 BC; cf. Jahn and Kroll 1964 *ad loc.*) and Spurius Mummius (Jahn and Kroll 1964, 94); Marcus Claudius Marcellus, Augustus' nephew, was taught by the 'Academic' Nestor of Tarsus (Strabo 14.5.14, 674C, 7–8 Radt); Lucius Aelius Tubero is known to have been a fellow student of Aenesidemus at the Academy, probably under Philo (Glucker 1978, 122–3). Augustus himself belonged to the school of Apollodorus of Pergamum (Suet. *Aug.* 89; Quint. *Inst.* 3.1.17–18), while the future Roman emperor Tiberius was taught by Theodorus of Gadara (Suet. *Tib.* 57; Sen. *Suas.* 3.7). The Greek philosophers who advised Roman statesmen and rulers also belong here; see Rawson 1989, esp. 237–46.

judgment on the quality of literature in general and speeches in particular – certainly at 'social events' such as the presentations of *declamationes* at which speakers as well as hearers (re-)asserted and furthered their social status through the conspicuous display of their rhetorical skills, knowledge of rhetorical technique and taste in matters of aesthetics and style;[54] but the judgment they expressed on political speeches at assemblies or even Senate meetings, as well as their own speeches given at these occasions, would also have reflected the training in aesthetics, style, and political and moral ideas which they had received from Dionysius.

As far as practical examples of such 'classical' speeches by Dionysius' recipients are concerned, the speakers and speeches in the *Roman Antiquities* are likely to have been intended by Dionysius as models of his readers', especially his Roman readers', own political practice.[55] Many of Dionysius' early Roman politicians both in the regal and the Republican period, including, for example, Romulus (*Ant. Rom.* 2. 3–26), Tullus Hostilius (*Ant. Rom.* 3.11) and the 'founder' of the Roman Republic Marcus Iunius Brutus (*Ant. Rom.* 4.74), successfully resolve the political and social problems of their times by drawing on their knowledge of the customs and institutions of the classical Greek past and creatively adapting these 'paradigms' (παραδείγματα, e.g., *Ant. Rom.* 3.11.4) to the requirements of the Roman present.[56] Along with these explicit references to the classical 'paradigms', the speakers continuously make reference to, explore the implications of and, above all, employ equally freely and strategically in the interest of their cause the same moral and political values that Dionysius regards as the core of the classical ideal (δικαιοσύνη, σωφροσύνη, εὐσέβεια, ἐλευθερία, ὁμόνοια).[57] Finally, many of these references themselves as well as the language and style of the speeches more generally often allude to specific passages from the classical authors: the 'constitutional debate' at 4.72–5, for example, evokes the similar debate in Herodotus

---

[54] The best way to get a sense of these presentations as 'social events' is reading Seneca the Elder's *Declamationes* and *Suasoriae*.

[55] Dionysius expects his Roman readers to follow the example of the early Romans as he portrays them in his narrative (*Ant. Rom.* 1.6.4). On the speeches in the *Roman Antiquities*, see Pelling, Fox, Schultze, Oakley and Hogg in this volume and Wiater 2018b, index s.v. 'Reden'.

[56] See, e.g., Richard 1993; Fromentin 2006; Wiater 2018a. On Romulus' speech (*Ant. Rom.* 2.3–26), see Fox in this volume, pp. 194–5. On Brutus' speech (*Ant. Rom.* 4.72), see Pelling in this volume, pp. 211–12.

[57] On these 'classical values', see above, p. 60. Of these terms and concepts, 'freedom' (ἐλευθερία) is the most prominent one in the *Roman Antiquities*, see, e.g., 3.23.8; 4.11.2, 23.2, 78.1; 5.64.2, 65.4; for εὐσέβεια, see, e.g., 3.17.2, 6, 28.6; 8.2.2, 32.2; δικαιοσύνη: 4.11.2; 5.66.2, 3; σωφροσύνη: 2.3.4; 3.36.4; 4.65.3; 5.66.2, 4; 6.96.2; ὁμόνοια: 4.26.1; 5.1.2; 6.43.3.

3.80–2,[58] the discussion of δικαιοσύνη in the speech of Appius Claudius Sabinus at 5.66–8 repeatedly evokes Plato's *Republic* (esp. 5.66.3, 67.4), and Tullus Hostilius (above) aligns himself with Thucydides' Funeral Oration both through his ideas and the phrasing in which he presents them;[59] and here, too, Dionysius' speakers use the classical phrases and expressions flexibly and freely, even mixing them with terms and phrases that do not occur in the classical authors at all,[60] thus continuously adopting and adapting the classical material to the requirements of its new, 'modern' context.

It is easy to see how such speeches could serve as models for the speeches of Dionysius' own readers, because they allowed them to combine their allegiance to the classical ideal with the political and moral heritage of the Roman *maiores*: speakers who followed the example of the speeches in the *Antiquities* were able to evoke the speeches of Romulus, Brutus and Appius Claudius in conjunction with the works of Herodotus, Demosthenes and Thucydides. From that point of view, then, many of Dionysius' Roman speakers might offer us a glimpse of how he envisaged the role of his own readers in Roman society and politics.

3. Re-Fashioning the Past: The Other Side of Metathesis

The previous section focused on the importance of the 'classical past' as an emotional-moral concept (a 'structure of feelings') embodied in the classical texts which provides classicists with the goal continuously to strive for in their endeavor to create a 'classical' present and future. While, as I argued there, the ultimate 'authentic' experience of the classical past-as-text remains impossible to achieve, the identification of past and text also allows the critic directly to interact with and even re-fashion that past as a 'structure of feelings' by interfering with the texts that represent and constitute it. This more active relationship with the classical past-as-text will be the topic of this final section. In particular I will focus on *metathesis*, the importance and function of which as a critical tool has been explored in

---

[58] Fromentin 2006 Waiter 2018a, 213–27. See also Pelling in this volume, pp. 214–15 on Hdt. 3.82 as a model in the *Ant. Rom.*

[59] Cf. *Ant. Rom.* 3.11.4: κοινὴν ἀναδείξαντες τὴν πόλιν, with Thuc. 2.39.1: τήν τε γὰρ πόλιν κοινὴν παρέχομεν; Richard 1993, 129; Fox 1996, 86. Other examples of Thucydidean influence (on the level of both style and content) include, for example, Dionysius' description of the siege of Fidenae, cf. esp. *Ant. Rom.* 5.41.3 (note in particular the rare χῶσις and the use of μετὰ τὸν πρῶτον ὕπνον) with Thuc. 2.76.4 and 7.43.2 (see the notes on the passage in Waiter 2018b), and his narrative of the trial of Coriolanus (*Ant. Rom.* 7.66), which evokes the *stasis* in Corcyra (Thuc. 3.82; Hogg 2008, 128–32). Cf. further Ek 1942; Fox 1996, 83–92; Usher 1982.

[60] On this latter point, see Usher 1982, 825–8.

exemplary and comprehensive fashion by Casper de Jonge.[61] In what follows I suggest to discuss this practice from a different angle: *metathesis*, I will argue, allows Dionysius to literally rewrite the past as a 'structure of feelings' and thus to exert immediate influence on the way in which it is experienced in the present.

The idea that 'the classical' is not a preexisting, well-defined concept, but is fashioned, as it were, out of the critical material by the skilled literary critic, underlies Dionysius' concept of 'selective μίμησις',[62] which lies at the heart of his classicist criticism and which he defines, as we have seen above, as follows:

> Who are the most important of the ancient orators and historians? [...] Which characteristics of each of them should we appropriate and which should we avoid? (*Orat. Vett.* 4.2)

As this passage shows, Dionysius takes neither the identity and number of the 'ancient authors and historians' for granted nor the characteristics which are to be 'appropriated' or, indeed, 'avoided'. The 'canon' on which Dionysius' criticism is based and, hence, the 'classical ideal' which he sets out to explain, has yet to be 'created' or, rather, constructed, through the critical analysis of the ancient texts. Only then can the texts of both past and present be measured against it and, if necessary, be modified accordingly. I suggest to call this an 'invasive-constructive' reading, as the process of constructing 'the classical' is coupled with an invasive critical assessment of the classical texts which results in discarding or altering anything the critic deems unworthy of (his conception of) 'the classical'.[63] 'The classical' is imposed on the material, not found in it.

The idea that Dionysius actively intervenes in the textual material in order to construct the 'classical' can fruitfully be brought into dialogue with the results especially of the first section of this chapter. I argued there that Dionysius privileges an anachronistic, idealizing concept of the past as a 'structure of feelings' based on and encoded in the classical texts, over a more 'historicizing' approach which treats the classical texts as documents to gain insight into the cultural, historical and social circumstances in which they were created, even though he is fully aware that this emotional concept of the past is and always has been an idealization. This privileging of the textual-idealizing over the historicizing image of the past is

---

[61] De Jonge 2005; De Jonge 2008, esp. 56–7 and his ch. 7 'Rewriting the Classics. Dionysius and the Method of Metathesis'. This section is a welcome opportunity to make up for the lack of any systematic treatment of this important aspect of Dionysius' criticism in my previous work.
[62] See above n. 20.   [63] Cf. Gelzer 1975, 166–7.

particularly evident in passages such as the following from *On Isaeus*, where the boundaries between the text and its extratextual reality are blurred. Contrasting the *ethopoiia* in Lysias' and Isaeus' speeches, Dionysius says:

> Who would not recognise Lysias' client as a sort of perfect specimen of the young, ordinary citizen minding his own business, differing in no way whatsoever from reality (ἀρχέτυπόν τινα [...] τῆς ἀληθείας); whereas the other speaker is a sort of copy (ἀπόγραφόν τινα), a manifest fiction of the rhetorician's art (οὐ λανθάνοντα ὅτι πέπλασται ῥητορικῇ τέχνῃ). The former's words and thoughts are obviously natural (τὸ αὐτοφυές; lit. 'naturally grown'), the latter's, artificially created (τὸ κατασκευές). (*Is.* 11.1)

While the real Athenian whom Lysias is portraying in his speech should be the 'archetype' of the speaker in the text, that is, the original pattern from which the text derives (the ἀπόγραφον),[64] it is the speaker created by Lysias who for Dionysius is the 'archetype' of reality, 'differing in no way whatsoever from' it. Due to Lysias' extraordinary technical skills, his text has rendered the extratextual reality that originally lay behind it obsolete.[65] This inversion is illustrated effectively through the contrast with Isaeus' text: unlike Lysias, Isaeus has not reached a level of technical perfection on which the skills efface themselves, and τέχνη and φύσις become virtually indistinguishable (τὸ αὐτοφυές).[66] Instead, his speaker is 'a sort of copy' and 'a manifest fiction of the rhetorician's art', thus emphasizing the gap between extratextual reality and text rather than effacing it.

Strictly speaking, both Lysias' and Isaeus' texts should equally be classified as 'copies' (ἀπόγραφα) of reality (ἀλήθεια) produced by 'the rhetorician's art'. Instead, Dionysius presents us here with a conception of τέχνη which in its most advanced form has the power to substitute the world outside the text with the world of the text, that is, with an aesthetic creation:[67] 'reality' and 'nature' have become literary-aesthetic concepts,[68] and the real Athenian who commissioned Lysias' speech for his appearance in trial has been replaced by the *ethos* of the Athenian, the 'natural Athenian' created by Lysias' rhetorical art.[69] The 'natural

---

[64] Cf. *Is.* 20.4: Lysias is superior to other orators as the original is superior to the copy (ὥσπερ ἀρχέτυπον ἀπογράφων ὑπερέχειν).
[65] Cf. Halliwell 2002, 294–5.
[66] On τέχνη and φύσις in Dionysius' thought, see De Jonge 2008, 251–328, esp. 253–73.
[67] Cf. Halliwell 2002, 295.
[68] Cf. De Jonge 2008, 256–73 on Dionysius' criteria for a 'natural' style or expression.
[69] The idea that art should surpass, and is therefore preferable to, reality is implied already in Arist. *Poet.* 1461b9–13; cf. Sharrock 1991, 38–9. It is then clearly expressed in Ovid's story of Pygmalion (*Met.* 10.247–9), on which see Elsner 2007, 122–3. The above observations should be read in conjunction with *Lys.* 8.5–7.

aesthetics' of Lysias' speeches thus make the past immediately and 'naturally' experienceable – within, of course, the limits of classicist experience of the past-as-text as discussed in the previous section.[70]

On Isaeus 11.1, in which the 'reality' and 'nature' of the past are conceptualized as products of art, demonstrates well how in Dionysius' thought the texts have substituted the historical past, thus resulting in the 'classical past-as-text' which is experienced through the act of performing/ reading these texts (the classical past as a 'structure of feelings'). The classicist practice of *metathesis*, I shall argue now, capitalizes on this identification of past and text. Due to the textual nature of the past, the emotional effect and, hence, the direct experience of that past is subject to control and manipulation by such critics as Dionysius. As De Jonge has shown, *metathesis* is directly related to 'selective' *mimesis* in that the manipulation of the classical texts is a powerful didactic instrument to teach Dionysius' readers how to write 'classical' texts themselves.[71] While this is undeniably the main purpose of *metathesis*, I want to suggest here that there is an additional dimension to this practice. *Metathesis* is also an important way of connecting, even interacting with, the past through interacting with the texts that embody it: by interfering with the textual structure of the original texts, the 'invasive-constructive' critic fashions the past as a 'structure of feelings' as well as the image of 'the classical Athenian' that results from reading the classical texts:

> ἥκιστα γὰρ ἰδιώτης ἂν οὕτως· 'οὐχ ἡγούμην δεῖν κατοκνῆσαι' οὐδέ γε τὸ 'δι' ὑμῶν πειρᾶσθαι τυγχάνειν τῶν δικαίων', ἀλλ' ἐκείνως πως μᾶλλον· 'τοσούτων γέ μοι συμπιπτόντων δυσκόλων ἐφ' ὑμᾶς ἠνάγκασμαι καταφυγεῖν, ἵνα τῶν δικαίων τύχω δι' ὑμῶν'.

> An ordinary speaker would be most unlikely to have said 'I have not thought it necessary to shrink', or indeed '[...] from trying to obtain justice from your hands', but would rather have expressed himself in the following way: 'Since so many difficulties are besetting me, I have been forced to seek your help in order to secure justice through you'. (*Is.* 11.4)

The preceding considerations suggest that there is more to passages such as this one than the mere attempt to make a stylistic point. We have here one of those cases criticized by Dionysius shortly before this passage (*Is.* 11.1, discussed above) in which Isaeus has not succeeded in creating an adequate

---

[70] This accords well with De Jonge's (2008, 58–9) observation that Dionysius uses the terms ὑποκείμενον and πρᾶγμα interchangeably for 'the thought (τὴν ὑποκειμένην διάνοιαν) or the referent (person or object) in reality'.
[71] Cf. De Jonge 2008, 367 n. 3, 369, 374, 390.

'reality effect' because his text does not conjure up the image of the 'ordinary Athenian citizen' (ἰδιώτης) expected and desired by the classicist critic.⁷² *Metathesis* allows Dionysius to correct this failure and create the kind of 'real' (ἀληθής) ordinary classical Athenian with which he and his readers desire to connect; by interfering with the text, and literally substituting the author's words with his own, he is directly interfering with the aesthetic reality of the past in order to achieve the desired experience of that past.⁷³

On Composition provides a good illustration of the extent to which *metathesis* is bound up with the emotional experience of the text and, going hand-in-hand with this, the reader's emotional relationship with the past. Here, Dionysius contrasts Herodotus 1.6 with two *metatheses*, one in the style of Thucydides and another in the style of Hegesias:

> μετατίθημι τῆς λέξεως ταύτης τὴν ἁρμονίαν, καὶ γενήσεταί μοι οὐκέτι ὑπαγωγικὸν τὸ πλάσμα οὐδ' ἱστορικόν, ἀλλ' ὀρθὸν μᾶλλον καὶ ἐναγώνιον· 'Κροῖσος ἦν υἱὸς μὲν Ἀλυάττου, γένος δὲ Λυδός, τύραννος δὲ τῶν ἐντὸς Ἅλυος ποταμοῦ ἐθνῶν· ὃς ἀπὸ μεσημβρίας ῥέων μεταξὺ Σύρων καὶ Παφλαγόνων εἰς τὸν Εὔξεινον καλούμενον πόντον ἐκδίδωσι πρὸς βορέαν ἄνεμον'. οὗτος ὁ χαρακτὴρ οὐ πολὺ ἀπέχειν ἂν δόξειεν τῶν Θουκυδίδου τούτων· "Ἐπίδαμνός ἐστι πόλις ἐν δεξιᾷ εἰσπλέοντι τὸν Ἰόνιον κόλπον· προσοικοῦσι δ' αὐτὴν Ταυλάντιοι βάρβαροι, Ἰλλυρικὸν ἔθνος'. πάλιν δὲ ἀλλάξας τὴν αὐτὴν λέξιν ἑτέραν αὐτῇ μορφὴν ἀποδώσω τὸν τρόπον τοῦτον. 'Ἀλυάττου μὲν υἱὸς ἦν Κροῖσος, γένος δὲ Λυδός, τῶν δ' ἐντὸς Ἅλυος ποταμοῦ τύραννος ἐθνῶν· ὃς ἀπὸ μεσημβρίας ῥέων Σύρων τε καὶ Παφλαγόνων μεταξὺ πρὸς βορέαν ἐξίησιν ἄνεμον ἐς τὸν καλούμενον πόντον Εὔξεινον'. Ἡγησιακὸν τὸ σχῆμα τοῦτο τῆς συνθέσεως, μικρόκομψον, ἀγεννές, μαλθακόν [...].

I alter the arrangement of the words in this passage [Hdt. 1.6], and I shall find that the manner of writing is no longer leisurely and historical, but direct rather, and forensic: 'Croesus was the son of Alyattes, and by birth a Lydian. He was king, on this side of the Halys, over nations; which river

---

⁷² See above, pp. 66, 78–9.
⁷³ The passage from *On Isaeus* belongs to the first (and most common) of the three types of *metatheses* identified by De Jonge 2008, 374, that is, *metatheses* that aim to bring out and correct stylistic defects in the original (De Jonge 2008, 375–9). My argument, however, works for all three; the difference is one of degree rather than kind: type-one *metatheses* such as the one discussed above completely change the aesthetic experience of the past by changing a particular passage of text; *metatheses* of the second type, which illustrate the virtues of the original texts by juxtaposing them with alternative, less effective expressions (De Jonge 2008, 379–84), contribute, through that contrast, to creating and maintaining a specific image of the classical past-as-text and the kind of experience that is expected from it, thus serving as a guideline for Dionysius' and his readers' assessment of the quality and 'realism' of the experience of the classical past afforded by specific texts. For an example of the third type of *metathesis* (*Comp.* 4.8–11), see below.

from the south flowing between Syria and Paphlagonia runs into the sea which is called the Euxine and issues towards the north'. This style would not seem to differ greatly from that of Thucydides in the words [Thuc. 1.24.1]: 'Epidamnus is a city on the right as you sail into the Ionian gulf; its immediate neighbours are barbarians, the Taulantii, an Illyrian race'. I shall alter the same passage once more and give a new form to it as follows. 'Alyattes' son was Croesus, by birth a Lydian, king over all nations was he, on this side of the river Halys; which river from the south flowing between Syria and Paphlagonia discharges itself to the north, into the Euxine-called sea'. This precious, degenerate, effeminate way of arranging words resembles that of Hegesias. (*Comp.* 4.8–11)

The comparison with the Hegesian rendering is particularly interesting: while Thucydides and Herodotus are both firmly located in the classical past, Hegesias is regarded by Dionysius as the 'archetype of Asiatic perversity'[74] with whom the classical style and morals broke down, and the Greek world was swamped with Asianism.[75]

Dionysius' rewriting of the Herodotus passage in the style of Hegesias is a *Gedankenexperiment* which allows him directly to confront the classical text with its Asianist Other. It is thus a striking illustration of how changes of style affect the entire nature of the classical texts and the experience of the past they represent.[76] Whereas the Thucydidean *metathesis* merely shifts the register of the passage from the 'leisurely and historical' to the 'direct and forensic' (*Comp.* 4.9),[77] the Hegesian *metathesis* completely changes the aesthetic experience of the passage: Herodotus' classical text has become 'finicky' (μικρόκομψον), 'degenerate' (ἀγεννές) and 'effeminate' (μαλθακόν) (*Comp.* 4.11). Along with the stylistic aesthetics, the entire moral content of Herodotus' passage has been perverted.

The contrast between Herodotus' classical passage and its Hegesian Other highlights once more the ideological dimension of classicist reading, that the past and its moral values are encoded in, and thus experienceable through, the classical texts. Dionysius' Hegesian experiment thus demonstrates *ex negativo* the historical dimension of *metathesis* and its implications for the classicist's relationship with the past. While correcting Isaeus' Athenian ἰδιώτης according to the classical standard enables the classicist reader to connect with the past, the Hegesian *metathesis* of Herodotus' text renders any such connection with the past impossible because it changes

---

[74] De Jonge 2008, 386.
[75] See *Orat. Vett.* 1.3–7, with Hidber's 1996 commentary; Wiater 2011a, 60–5, 93–100, 110–16.
[76] See *Comp.* 4.5.
[77] On the 'forensic' (ἐναγώνιος), see now Ooms and De Jonge 2013. The term is also used in the *Roman Antiquities*: see Fromentin 1993 and Oakley in this volume, p. 139.

the moral-aesthetic character of the past-as-text itself. In addition to their didactic function, *metatheses* thus (re)present a constant process of the critic's direct interaction with the aesthetic experience of the past, a process of working on the past which is constitutive of creating and maintaining the desired immediate connection with the past through the engagement with the text.

These observations also shed some interesting light on a phenomenon observed by De Jonge, that it is 'characteristic of his [Dionysius'] application of the rewriting method [...] that he explicitly involves the reader in his analysis'.[78] The process of re-writing the classical texts as a process of 'working on the past' is an aesthetic experience of the past shared by all classicists, while distinguishing them from all the others who lack the necessary refined literary taste and literary-critical training to perform this operation.

It is important to note, as De Jonge has pointed out, that 'Dionysius supposes that his readers are used to the technique of rewriting texts, and he is even confident that they can employ the method of *metathesis* themselves'.[79] The active involvement with the text and the 'structure of feelings' which they encode is thus integrated into the daily practice of the classicist critic. The continuous quest to identify the parts of the works that do not conform to the classical standard and to transform them into proper classical texts is part of the ongoing fight against Asianism and the crucial mission of establishing the classical standard in the present in order to create a 'classical future'.[80] The classicist critic is not only working on shaping the present according to the classical ideal, but he also is at the same time creating the precondition of this transformation by working on and, thus, ensuring the classical quality of the past itself.

---

[78] De Jonge 2008, 375.   [79] De Jonge 2008, 383.   [80] See above, pp. 72–3.

CHAPTER 3

Dionysius' Demosthenes and Augustan Atticism

Harvey Yunis

Dionysius' Rhetorical Project

In his literary essays and epistles, Dionysius of Halicarnassus ranges, selectively but widely, over the corpus of Greek prose-writers and poets as it existed in his day, examining how particular authors use language for expressive and aesthetic purposes. Out of this large group he focuses on the prose-writers of the classical period, especially the prose-writers of classical Athens. Regardless of the genre and occasion of their writings, these writers – orators, historians, philosophers – are rhetorical in the sense that they manipulate form for effect, or, to put the matter in a more Dionysian fashion, their writing styles are the result of self-conscious choices, which puts them in the realm of art. Dionysius compares the writers with one another, offers judgments about what constitutes good and bad kinds of style, and presents evidence to support his judgments. Occasionally he comments on the writers' choice of subject matter and considers questions of authenticity and chronology.[1]

Throughout, Dionysius' purpose is to offer his reader lessons on 'imitation' (μίμησις), that is, on the discriminating use of classical models of style so as to enable students to make their own compositions as effective as possible in regard to their own purposes. For Dionysius imitation is the ruling concept of rhetorical study and practice; it ties the study of the exemplary past to the creation of the new. What is imitated in this process are not the words or thoughts of earlier writers, but the beautiful, stimulating, expressive, and flowing patterns of diction, rhythm, sound, and thought that past masters were able to capture and embed in their discourses by means of the style they created and utilized. These lessons are available nowhere else apart from past models, certainly nowhere else with

---

[1] For an overview of Dionysius' literary essays and discussion of their chronology, see Bonner 1939; Grube 1965, 207–30; De Jonge 2008, 1–48. Translations of Dionysius in this chapter come from the Loeb edition of Usher 1974–85 with slight modifications for clarity.

such profusion and power. Yet because concepts and perceptions of beauty can be shared over the generations, imitation also requires a moral seriousness that is common to both the historical models and present-day practitioners. Further, imitation is an enduring process that reflects ever new appropriations: the historical models that are studied and imitated by current practitioners were themselves engaged in studying and imitating the models that were available to them.[2]

Dionysius' work on style and imitation helped to establish and fortify the trend of Atticizing literary style that began in the first century BCE and dominated over the next several centuries. One further element in Dionysius' stylistic work affected this trend even more. Dionysius singles out Demosthenes among his classical peers as the one writer most worthy of imitation; he describes in detail aspects of Demosthenes' style that rhetorical students need to learn to employ in their own compositions; and he develops a systematic approach to style that attempts to explain Demosthenes' supreme mastery. Thus, Dionysius was an early and influential proponent of Demosthenes as the primary historical model for rhetorical instruction, a position that Demosthenes maintained for as long as classical rhetoric endured as a compelling presence in education, literature, and politics, that is, until the end of antiquity.[3]

This chapter will examine the terms and method of criticism in the literary essays in order to discover the basis for and the value of Dionysius' judgments on Demosthenes and the other writers with whom Demosthenes is compared and contrasted. Dionysius' critical apparatus then becomes the basis for appreciating 'the beauty and pleasure' (τὸ καλὸν καὶ ἡ ἡδονή) of Demosthenes' best writing, which makes him preeminent among classical models. Finally, Dionysius shows that Demosthenes' aesthetic achievement, which helped to assure his speeches' success in their original setting, was simultaneously a pursuit of timeless literary

---

[2] Dionysius' treatise *On Imitation* in three books survives only in fragments (including an extended quotation by Dionysius himself) and an epitome. For the text, see Aujac 1992, 26–40, 87–99 (= *Pomp.* 3.2–6.11); for commentary on the epitome, see Battisti 1997. See Hidber 1996, 56–75; Wiater 2011a, 77–92 on Dionysius' theory and practice of imitation as these can be gleaned from the remains of *On Imitation* as well as the extant works. Hunter 2009 explores the antecedents to and later appropriations of Dionysius' theory of imitation. Flashar 1979b discusses the concept of imitation as used in classicizing agendas in the Hellenistic and Roman periods. Russell 1979 discusses the wider phenomenon of imitation in Greek and Roman literature of the Hellenistic period. On new appropriations: Demosthenes, Dionysius' chief model for imitation, himself imitated and selected the best features of all (previous) writers (*Din.* 6.4).

[3] In the sixth century CE in the Western Empire and the thirteenth century CE in the Eastern Empire. On Demosthenes' domination in the rhetorical world of late antiquity, see Drerup 1923, Pernot 2006.

fame. Thus, Dionysius views the Athenian politician as a model worthy of emulation in the new age being ushered in under Augustus. Demosthenes perfected the arts of composition and *thereby* made himself a standard of political, moral, and aesthetic unity.

We begin with a brief review of the context and premises of Dionysius' rhetorical approach in order to make clear in what way his method suits his purposes as a rhetorical critic working in Augustan Rome.

Dionysius' Augustan Atticism

Dionysius' brief preface *On the Ancient Orators*, which functions as both a manifesto of his views on Atticism and an introduction to his essays on the Attic orators, connects the Roman context to his own work.[4] In the essay, Dionysius appropriates an earlier debate among rhetorical experts in Rome that was framed as a dispute between Atticists and so-called Asianists in regard to proper style in rhetorical discourse. In this dispute, which preceded Dionysius by at least a generation, the terminology and stylistic tendencies of Greek rhetoric were mapped onto equivalent practices among Latin-speaking authors. Roman Atticists of Cicero's generation, who promoted the plain style and pure Attic diction of Lysias and Hyperides as the sole standard of Atticism, relegated Cicero to the Asianist camp because of the emotion, force, and fullness (*copia*) of his public orations, qualities which Cicero's Atticist opponents rejected and associated with the rhetoric of the Greek cities of Asia Minor. Cicero was clearly not going to cede the Atticist label to his opponents, and he responds in two ways. In the treatises *Brutus* and *Orator* (46 BCE), he rejects Lysias and Hyperides as the sole measure of Attic style, while pointing out the variety of styles employed by the different Attic orators, not least the forceful, emotional style of Demosthenes that he claims as his own chief model; and relying on Demosthenes' reputation as the heroic defender of Greek freedom, he injects considerations of political substance into his account of Atticism, which were intended to advance his own standing as the Roman Demosthenes and leading statesman of his day.[5]

Greek rhetoric of the Hellenistic period has largely been lost to the historical record, which limits our ability to understand the nuances of this dispute. Beyond the names of rhetoricians from Hellenistic Asian cities and

---

[4] Hidber 1996 is a commentary on and general study of the essay.
[5] See Cic. *Brut.* 284–91, 316, 325–26; *Orat.* 23–32, 230–31. On Roman Atticism, Cicero's response, and other antecedents of Dionysian Atticism, see Robling–Adamietz 1992; Wisse 1995; Hidber 1996, 30–37. On Cicero's effort to portray himself as the Roman Demosthenes, see Bishop 2015.

a few fragments attributed to them, we possess a significant corpus of rhetorically stylized royal correspondence and decrees preserved on stone, which provides a basis for assessing the stylistic developments of the Hellenistic period. But there is no evidence of an actual 'Asianist' school or movement of rhetoric in Rome that looked to the Greek Asian cities for inspiration. The stylistic tendencies which Cicero's Atticist opponents criticized and labeled as 'Asian,' mostly having to do with non-Attic diction, excessive embellishment, unconventional word order, and intrusively obvious and repetitive prose rhythms, seem rather to characterize Hellenistic Greek rhetoric generally. Further, in the terminology of Roman elites, 'Asian' was a term with connotations of decadence, flamboyance, and excessive wealth, while the term 'Attic' connoted the austerity, restraint, and nobility associated with classical Athens. In common with Cicero and other Atticists of his day, Dionysius makes use of Asianist terminology to advance his rhetorical agenda by attaching it to larger cultural norms.[6]

Although the common ground on this issue between Cicero and Dionysius is considerable, it is limited in ways that reflect the different contexts in which they operated. Dionysius shares with Cicero several points that pertain strictly to rhetorical theory (discussed below): the broad redefinition of Atticism to include the full spectrum of Attic orators as well as other Athenian prose-writers; the tripartite scheme for classifying rhetorical styles that was itself a common Hellenistic inheritance; and the choice of Demosthenes as the best Attic orator and the one most worthy of imitation.[7] But unlike Cicero, the Greek rhetorical teacher had no role in Roman politics and thus no stake in reviving Demosthenes for political

---

[6] On the ethnic connotations, see Quint. *Inst.* 12.10.17. On the sources and qualities of Greek rhetoric of the Hellenistic period, especially from the Greek cities of Asia Minor, see Norden 1909, vol. 1, 131–49; Wooten 1975; Kremmydas–Tempest 2013. For the evidence from inscriptions, see Chaniotis 2016. For the inscribed royal correspondence, see Welles 1934; for an updated list of sources, see Bencivenni 2014. Hegesias of Magnesia (third cent. BCE), credited as the first great exemplar of the bombastic Asian style (Cic. *Brut.* 286–87; Strabo 14.1.41; Longinus, *Subl.* 3.2), is disparaged by Dionysius at *Comp.* 4.11, 18.22–29. Caecilius of Caleacte, like Dionysius a Greek rhetorician in Augustan Rome and known to him (Dion. Hal. *Pomp.* 3.20), wrote (at least) two works in defense of Atticism against Asianism: *Against the Phrygians* and *How Attic Style Differs from Asiatic*; see Caecilius T 1 (= *Suda* K 1165 Κεκίλιος) in Woerther 2015, 1 with commentary 45–6. For 'Phrygians' as representatives of Asianism, cf. Dion. Hal. *Orat. Vett.* 1.7. Caecilius likely joined Dionysius in choosing Demosthenes as the best model for imitation; see Innes 2002, 276–84, and the four book titles that concern Demosthenes listed in Caecilius T 1.

[7] Direct influence of Cicero on Dionysius is entirely possible but not indicated by specific evidence. Yet, Dionysius' contacts with contemporary Roman intellectuals are well attested, so he was likely familiar with rhetorical theories circulating in Rome; see De Jonge 2008, 25–34 and the introduction to this volume, p. 8.

reasons of his own. Dionysius embraces Atticism and champions Demosthenes for aesthetic reasons, though there is a pointedly political side to the whole project of *On the Ancient Orators*. By divine grace or merely a fortuitous moment in history (*Orat. Vett.* 2.2), Dionysius was able to attach his rhetorical program to the great political movement of his day, namely, the new Augustan regime and in particular the regime's attempt to revive traditional values in politics, morality, and public aesthetics. Indeed, as Augustus was transforming Rome into a new, stable imperial capital, the question of style – in public buildings and private houses, in law, morality, and domestic life, in prose and poetry, in Rome and the cities of the empire – was deemed crucial for determining the future course of the city and empire. At that moment, style was more than just style: it was also a statement of attachment to the regime's favored political and ethical values that were meant to promote a renewal of Rome's pristine virtues.[8]

The manner in which Dionysius attaches his rhetorical program to the Augustan regime is itself a feat of rhetorical skill. First, he turns the contemporary quarrel of Atticism vs. Asianism into an epochal narrative of original glory (classical Athens), descent into depravity and chaos (Hellenistic Asianism following Alexander's death), and glory recovered (Augustan Atticism) (*Orat. Vett.* 1–2). The quarrel, in fact, now belongs to the past: Asianism and its kindred debased values have been vanquished from the empire by the good government and honorable values of the new regime (*Orat. Vett.* 3). Second, the role of the Augustan regime in securing the defeat of Asianism and the restoration of Attic values affords Dionysius the opportunity of expressing gratitude, which he does in a fulsome, grandiloquent style that in good Attic diction and despite its brevity suggests imperial panegyric of the high Roman Empire (*Orat. Vett.* 3.1).[9] The defeated party, an easy target, receives lavish abuse: beyond disparaging epithets – 'shameless,' 'histrionic,' 'illiberal' (1.3), 'vulgar,' 'disgusting' (1.4), 'brainless' (2.2) – Dionysius presents a vivid image of Asianism as a whore who has displaced and terrorized the chaste and lawful wife, namely,

---

[8] See Galinsky 1996 on the manifestations in art, literature, architecture, etc. of what he terms Augustus' cultural evolution. On rhetoric as part of the Augustan cultural program, see Lamp 2013. Suetonius records that Augustus himself criticized M. Antonius by asking whether he preferred the style of 'Asiatic orators' (*Aug.* 86.3). On the political allegiances and motives underlying Dionysius' account of Atticism and Asianism, see Spawforth 2012, 20–26. For a political reading of the essay that stresses the philo-Roman oligarchies of the eastern Greek cities, see Galinsky 1996, 340–42; Wiater 2011a, 95–100.

[9] On imperial panegyric, see Russell 1998; Pernot 2015, 24–26, 31–34. Dionysius aims his praise at Rome, foregoing mention of Augustus personally, but it is unequivocally clear that the new Augustan regime is the object of his gratitude.

Atticism, who is also called the 'Attic Muse' (1.5).[10] Finally, thanks to the new regime, Dionysius' essays on the Attic orators will find their proper audience and make a timely contribution. The essays will provide further impetus to the 'revolution' (μεταβολή, *Orat. Vett.* 3.1) of aesthetic and moral values which the regime has already initiated (*Orat. Vett.* 4.1), specifically, by offering a guide to the qualities of the Attic models that should be imitated and those which should be avoided (4.2). This kind of inquiry is new, at least insofar as Dionysius can determine (4.3).

The preface thus serves as a dramatic introduction to the literary essays, offering Dionysius' reader motivation to study them for both the aesthetic lessons in rhetorical imitation, available nowhere else, and the contribution which such lessons make towards aiding the Augustan regime in restoring world order. The large burden which Dionysius thereby imposes on himself is matched by the grandiloquent style of the essay. In other circumstances grandiloquence might give rise to the suspicion of irony or mere flattery. Here the suspicion can be dismissed, not only because of the evident seriousness of the literary essays, but also because of Dionysius' monumental history of early Rome, the *Roman Antiquities*. The scale and detail of the latter work, which in Atticizing style portrays early Rome in the mold of a virtuous archaic Greek *polis*, indicates the degree to which Dionysius was invested in Augustan Rome as the proper home for the revival of Attic rhetoric.[11]

Style in Postclassical Rhetorical Criticism

In exercising his critical faculties and issuing literary judgments, Dionysius is concerned with style. But what is style? And why is style the particular object of Dionysius' scrutiny? Dionysius' understanding of style is dependent on the premises of rhetorical criticism which he, along with his contemporaries, inherited from the same classical tradition that furnished the literary and rhetorical figures who function as models for Dionysius and his students to study, imitate, and emulate.

Style in the sense under consideration constitutes one pole of the comprehensive dichotomy of style (λέξις) and subject matter (πρᾶγμα), or form and content, that goes back at least to Plato and that, beginning

---

[10] On Dionysius' Asian whore and Attic Muse, see De Jonge 2014a, 393–98.
[11] On the Augustan perspective in the *Roman Antiquities*, see Gabba 1991, 23–59; Wiater 2011a, 165–225. On the Roman πόλις in Dionysius' history of Rome, see Fox in this volume, pp. 180–200.

with Aristotle, became standard in the classical rhetorical tradition.[12] Dionysius mentions the form-content distinction on several occasions, for instance at the beginning of the essay *On Composition*:

> In virtually all kinds of discourse two things require study: the ideas (τὰ νοήματα) and the words (τὰ ὀνόματα). We may regard the first of these as concerned chiefly with subject matter (ὁ πραγματικὸς τόπος), and the latter with expression (ὁ λεκτικὸς τόπος). (*Comp.* 1.5)[13]

Subject matter constitutes what the writer or speaker intends to convey, and it includes arguments and evidence used by the writer or speaker to support his case. Style constitutes how the writer or speaker conveys the subject matter, that is, the language chosen by the writer or speaker to put his case into words. Several aspects of Dionysius' method of criticism follow from this version of the form-content distinction.

First, for Dionysius style amounts to the entire linguistic edifice erected by the writer to put his case into words. In and of itself the text constitutes the style, which is both the result of the author's artistic choices and the source of the effects which the text produces on the reader. As such, the text furnishes Dionysius, or any student of rhetorical criticism, with the material to assess the author's art. The elements of this linguistic edifice include the following: the choice of words and the order in which they are put; figures of speech, metaphor, and simile; the length and structure of clauses and sentences; and the patterns of sound, rhythm, parallelism, antithesis, and variation that result from the choice and order of words. Every choice in regard to these items tends to produce a different effect on the reader or listener, and such effects can be evaluated as better or worse in relation to the writer's attempt to convey his subject matter to the intended audience. On this basis Dionysius can compare and contrast the various prose-writers and poets even though they wrote about different subjects in different genres at different times and addressed different audiences. Choosing

---

[12] Cf. Pl. *Resp.* 394c-d; *Ion* 530c; *Phdr.* 228d for formulations of the form-content distinction. Cf. Arist. *Rh.* 3.1.2, 1403b14-18 for his formulation of the form-content distinction, which is built into the structure of the *Rhetoric* as a whole, the first two books being devoted to subject matter, and the third book to style. On the theories of style that were developed in ancient Greek criticism, see De Jonge 2014b. On the (extensive) terminology of Greek and Latin stylistic theory, see Quadlbauer 1958, Chiron–Lévy 2010. By focusing on style and omitting content (for the most part), Dionysius is implicitly staking a claim about what is important in rhetoric. Compare the treatise *On the Sublime* (8.1), which makes great thoughts the primary element and strong emotion the second element in creating the effect of the sublime, style being relegated to tertiary status.

[13] Dionysius repeats the form-content distinction several times in the literary essays, often using different words but making essentially the same point; see De Jonge 2008, 53–59 for passages and discussion.

particular forms of linguistic expression with a view to affecting the reader in a particular way while conveying the relevant subject matter is a task shared by all the writers to whom Dionysius directs his attention.

Second, the form-content distinction makes feasible the foundational rhetorical principle that one message can be cast in different forms, each of which may affect the audience differently. Hence the reason for focusing on style as a crucial field of rhetorical artistry: without regard for the subject matter at issue and the particular message which the author wants to convey, the author faces a huge range of choices in order to present his message in particular words and thus to ensure that his audience receives his message in the most favorable way (*Comp.* 4.12). The inherent mutability of rhetorical form underlies Dionysius' practice of 'rewriting' (μετάθεσις), in which he displays a passage verbatim from an exemplary author and then rewrites it by using different words, by changing the order of the original words, by lengthening or shortening the clauses, or by changing the grammatical status of the clauses, all the while leaving the underlying meaning untouched.[14]

Dionysius' exercises in rewriting take different forms. He may rewrite a single clause of one of his exemplars by adding or deleting one or two words or by changing even a single letter; in these cases he is concerned to show how such small changes affect rhythm and euphony.[15] In other cases he rewrites extensively and presents what amounts to a stylistic commentary that refers to both the original and the rewritten versions. For example, in *On Demosthenes* 17–20 Dionysius first transcribes Isocrates 8 (*On the Peace*) 41–50, which constitutes the original passage that will be rewritten.[16] He then discusses the virtues and vices that are typical of Isocrates' style in the original passage. Finally, he rewrites large chunks of the original passage in a simpler, shorter, less hypotactic style, while simultaneously pointing out the flaws in the original passage. As a basis for rewriting or critiquing ornate or otherwise highly stylized passages of Thucydides, Isaeus, Isocrates, and Plato, Dionysius frequently invokes the concept of 'natural style' (τὸ φυσικόν), which includes both word choice and word order and aims chiefly at clarity.[17] Though natural style reflects the patterns and diction of everyday, non-technical language, it is nonetheless artificial, as is evident chiefly in Lysias, whose clear style is said to imitate nature (*Is.* 16.1). By

---

[14] On Dionysius' practice of rewriting, see De Jonge 2005.
[15] Single clause: *Comp.* 25.20, 23; single letter: *Comp.* 6.9.
[16] Dionysius also cites part of this passage in *Isoc.* 17: see Wiater in this volume, p. 60.
[17] Examples of Dionysius' concept of natural style: *Lys.* 2–4, 10.1; *Isoc.* 2; *Dem.* 9.10, 20.9; *Thuc.* 49; *Is.* 15.3. On the concept, see De Jonge 2008, 253–73.

rewriting, Dionysius turns the abstract principles of stylistic doctrine into concrete illustrations of actual stylistic choices and their impact on the audience. The didactic value is evident; one can easily imagine the usefulness of such exercises in rhetorical schools.[18]

Third, though style and subject matter are mutually autonomous, they are not unrelated. What chiefly affects the relation of style and subject matter is propriety (τὸ πρέπον), that is, the sense that some kinds of subject matter are more appropriately presented in one kind of style rather than another (*Comp.* 3.17, 20.1–22; *Dem.* 18.7).[19] Propriety is an elusive quality, and Dionysius avoids defining it. When propriety is maintained, it may pass unnoticed and for that reason allow the writer to retain the reader's attention without interruption. When propriety is breached, the resulting shock disrupts the reader's attentiveness and disables, so to speak, the writer's attempt to manipulate the reader through stylistic means (*Comp.* 20.1–2). Beyond examples that illustrate propriety, Dionysius advances an intuitive understanding in which propriety is related to proportion and aptness, notions that belong to common human experience and are applicable to the manner in which language is related to the world that the language refers to (*Dem.* 13.2, 44–45; *Lys.* 13.3; *Thuc.* 34.4, 50–51). For instance, the smooth, clear, plain style (as Dionysius describes it) of Lysias' judicial speeches is better suited – in the sense of better matching the subject matter according to audience expectations – to the mundane disputes related in those speeches than would be, for example, a grandiose, highly wrought style such as that of Gorgias (*Lys.* 3.1–7, 9). Similarly, Thucydides' style is better suited to the big themes of war, diplomacy, and social turmoil that constitute his subject matter (*Thuc.* 49.2–3). So much is straightforward. Dionysius' sense of propriety becomes unreliable when the obvious constraints of subject matter on style no longer apply, or where authors are willing to breach commonly held conceptions of propriety for the sake of particular effects. For instance, in regard to Socrates' first speech on *eros* in the *Phaedrus*, Dionysius famously mistakes Plato's ironic, humorous imitation of grandiose style for sincere but bombastic effect (*Dem.* 7.3–7).[20]

---

[18] On rewriting and the practice of *paraphrasis* in the rhetorical schools, see De Jonge 2005, 474–75.
[19] Propriety has two other functions in Dionysius: first, in regard to the relationship between style and audience, in which a simple, straightforward style is suited to an audience of ordinary citizens, while a sophisticated style is appropriate for an audience of well-educated citizens (*Dem.* 15); second, in regard to the judicious use of melody, rhythm, and variety in the act of composition (*Comp.* 11.1, 6; *Dem.* 47.4). A breach of propriety in any of these senses is liable to alienate the reader or listener.
[20] Likewise, Dionysius mistakes Thucydides' purpose when criticizing his style in the Melian Dialogue (*Thuc.* 40–41) and Pericles' last speech (*Thuc.* 45).

Fourth, style in the sense under discussion is analyzed by Dionysius into two more specific formal elements, which warrant study separately: diction, which is the author's choice of words (λέξις in the narrow sense, ἑρμηνεία, ἐκλογὴ τῶν ὀνομάτων); and composition (σύνθεσις, ἁρμονία), which is the order in which the author places his chosen words and thereby forms meaningful semantic units such as phrases, clauses, and sentences.[21] Composition not only affects the reader's or listener's ability to comprehend what is being said, but it also creates subsidiary effects, such as the rhythmical and melodic aspects of language, the fluidity and ease of pronouncing a text, and the rapidity and pacing of the reader's or listener's understanding of the author's meaning. For this reason, Dionysius examines diction and composition separately in the essay *On Demosthenes*, devoting the first half of the essay to diction (1–33), the second half to composition (34–58), the latter being the exclusive subject of the essay *On Composition* in regard to a range of authors.

Beyond the premises that support the coherence of Dionysius' critical method, one further aspect of Dionysius' critical milieu also requires preliminary mention. In the case of speeches delivered before live audiences, vocal delivery and physical gestures can affect audience reception as much as, or even more than, the manner of linguistic expression achieved through word choice and word order. Hence, it was standard in classical rhetorical criticism to include the speaker's delivery and gestures, in addition to the style of linguistic expression, as belonging to the overall means by which the speaker conveys his substantive message and affects his audience.[22] Now, Dionysius is well aware that Demosthenes' speeches were originally composed for delivery to live audiences and were thus delivered (*Dem.* 53.1–4), and he allows himself to imagine that Demosthenes must have been a master of delivery (*Dem.* 22.4–7). Contending that 'the style itself prescribes to the sensitive reader the kind of delivery that will be required' (*Dem.* 53.6), Dionysius uses examples from Demosthenes 9 (*Third Philippic*) to illustrate the type of delivery that is prescribed by the text (*Dem.* 54). But in fact Dionysius is concerned with Demosthenes and the other classical prose-writers as authors of written texts. Thus, even though Dionysius has much to say about the musical quality of artistic prose, especially in the hands of Demosthenes, and even

---

[21] Dionysius makes further distinctions in regard to linguistic usage and parts of speech; cf. *Thuc.* 22; De Jonge 2008, 91–165. But the basic distinction between diction and composition provides the organizing principle for his discussions of style. On composition, see De Jonge in this volume, pp. 242–66.
[22] On delivery and gestures in Greek rhetoric, see Edwards 2013a; in Roman rhetoric, see Hall 2007.

though Dionysius and his students must have enunciated the speeches of Demosthenes and the other Attic orators in declamatory fashion (*Dem.* 53.5), for Dionysius this quality is created purely by the author's compositional art and exerts its influence primarily in the act of reading. Of course, it was in written form that Dionysius and contemporaries knew and studied the fifth- and fourth-century texts.

Dionysius' Tripartite Stylistic Scheme

In the essay *On Demosthenes* Dionysius uses a three-fold scheme to classify and analyze the compositional styles of the writers he discusses: the grand, austere, or difficult style that, for him, is typified by Thucydides; the smooth, plain, or simple style that is typified by Lysias; and the middle or mixed style that is in principle the best kind of style. Dionysius views Plato and Isocrates as exponents of the mixed style, but he champions Demosthenes as both the master of the mixed style and the best prose stylist of all.

Dionysius' three-fold scheme seems to have been a staple of Hellenistic rhetorical theory, though we have no certain knowledge of its origins. It is invoked in the anonymous *Rhetorica ad Herennium* (4.11–16), which stems from the early first century BCE and is clearly based on Hellenistic material; it is used by Cicero in his dialogue *Orator* (65–99); and Quintilian discusses it as a common way of classifying the various styles that one encounters in the inherited literary canon (*Inst.* 12.10.58–65).[23] Yet the three-fold scheme has been characterized as lacking subtlety, and criticized for being too simplistic or reductive, for, as with the colors of a painter's palette, the varieties of style are surely greater than three. For instance, writing about two centuries after Dionysius, Hermogenes of Tarsus developed a far more elaborate system of classifying styles. He posited seven basic types of style which are themselves complicated by various sub-types so as to yield twenty different kinds of style. Hermogenes' system has therefore been cited as a more sophisticated stylistic theory than that of Dionysius, that is, one that is better capable of explaining the literary phenomena which constitute the subject matter of this kind of theory in the first place.[24]

Yet to prefer Hermogenes' stylistic theory to that of Dionysius just because it offers a greater number of classificatory headings misses the mark. Clearly, one could enlarge and enhance Hermogenes' scheme too,

---

[23] On the historical development of the doctrine of three kinds of style, see Hendrickson 1905.
[24] Hermogenes, *On Types of Style* (= Wooten 1987). See Wooten 1989 for the critique of Dionysius.

just by creating more such headings based on finer distinctions and finding appropriate examples. But such a procedure would amount to a mere exercise in theorizing. More to the point is to examine how Dionysius uses the stylistic theory at his disposal, and what he contributes to our understanding of the subject-matter – namely, the choice and ordering of words in artistic prose – which the theory aims to elucidate.

To begin with, Dionysius himself anticipates the objection based on the small, limited number of basic types of style. Acknowledging that 'as in personal appearance, so in literary composition, an individual character is associated with each of us,' he mentions the analogy of the painter's palette while rejecting its relevance to the study of literary style and composition (*Comp.* 21.1–2). Dionysius argues that none of his three basic styles exist in a pure form in any author, and any real example of literary style contains elements of the three basic styles to one degree or another, just as the four basic elements of the natural world (earth, air, water, fire) exist only in compounded forms in the real world (*Dem.* 37.2). Thus, all styles can be analyzed in the tripartite scheme by assessing the degree to which each of the basic styles is present in any particular case. For instance, according to Dionysius, Demosthenes, the middle style master, uses the grand style and seems Thucydidean in the *Third Philippic*, which, like Thucydides' history, concerns war (*Dem.* 9). Yet Demosthenes uses the plain style and seems Lysianic in the speech *Against Conon*, which, like Lysias' forensic speeches, is a private judicial matter (*Dem.* 12–13). These comparisons suggest that the subject matter of the discourse influences the author's stylistic choices, which raises the question of stylistic propriety. But a prior point must be considered: far from detracting from its usefulness, the simplicity and structure of Dionysius' tripartite stylistic actually enhances its usefulness.

First, by ultimately assigning every author to one basic style in spite of the evident admixture of other styles – as Thucydides, Lysias, Demosthenes each represent a single basic style in spite of inevitable variation in their writing – one ends up describing the predominant feature of each author, which is informative in itself and also contributes to the creation of a literary history. When Dionysius chooses particular passages to illustrate each author's dominant style – for example, the Corcyra passage and Pericles' speeches from Thucydides (*Thuc.* 28–33, 42–47), Lysias' speech *Against Diogeiton* (*Lys.* 21–27, preserved only here), the central passage of Demosthenes' speech *On the Crown* which culminates in the oath by the fighters of Marathon (*Dem.* 31), passages in which each author is, so to speak, most himself – Dionysius thereby creates an identity for each author within a history of literary style that encompasses the entire inherited canon of Greek authors, both prose-writers and poets. For while Dionysius is mainly concerned with prose-writers, in the treatise *On Composition* he places the major poets of the Greek tradition alongside the prose-writers within a common three-fold compositional scheme in order to illustrate how they too put words together (*Comp.* 21–24). In this respect Dionysius anticipates Quintilian (*Inst.* 12.10.64–65).

Second, by using the three-fold scheme to characterize all instances of literary style, instances which admittedly are not pure examples of any one of the three basic styles, Dionysius cultivates the reader's judgment in discerning and evaluating stylistic differences, which is a crucial part of stylistic imitation, especially when the artistic tendencies are subtle ones. When Dionysius offers his own judgments, he usually brings forward supporting evidence, which makes the judgments instructive and provides the material for further discussion. For instance, he often specifies the qualities in the quoted passage that he is emphasizing or introducing as innovative.[25] Sometimes he includes a brief comment along with another illustrative passage.[26] Sometimes he omits any explanation of his own, preferring to let the reader see for himself the qualities that led Dionysius to quote the passage; for instance, *On Demosthenes* 19.1 offers a typical comment following the quotation of a long passage of Isocrates: 'Any reader can judge for himself whether my argument is sound and Isocrates is inferior in these qualities by examining the passage which I have just quoted.'[27] Further, although Dionysius' literary history is not undertaken without due regard for external evidence regarding dates, events, and influences of one writer on another, as in his argument in the *First Letter to Ammaeus* that Demosthenes' preserved speeches preceded Aristotle's composition of the *Rhetoric*, style is a subject that has a timeless character outside the rhythms of political history. Hence his willingness to compare any writer in any genre from Homer to the end of the classical period with any other. It is fair to say that Dionysius is inventing a history of his subject – the history

---

[25] E.g., quotation of Socrates' first speech on *eros* in the *Phaedrus* is accompanied by discussion of its stylistic problems (*Dem.* 7.1–6); quotation of Dem. 9 (*Third Philippic*) is accompanied by discussion of its Thucydidean qualities (*Dem.* 9); quotation of Isocrates 17 (*Trapeziticus*) is followed first by a general statement about Isocrates' style in this passage, on which Dionysius expects universal agreement, and then by detailed discussion of the artificial qualities of the passage (*Isoc.* 19–20).

[26] E.g., quotation of Socrates' palinode in the *Phaedrus* is followed by a quotation of Pindar, *Paean* 9 and just the comment: 'In this [i.e., the Pindar passage], as in the Plato passage, is not the imagery inappropriate?' (*Dem.* 7.7).

[27] Similarly, Dionysius' practice of rewriting passages is often meant to speak for itself: e.g., *Comp.* 7.5–6, 8.3–4. On this aspect of Dionysius' rewriting, cf. Damon 1991, 52; De Jonge 2005, 473–5.

of literary style – at the same time as he explains what that history consists in.

Yet a further advantage of Dionysius' tripartite stylistic scheme lies in the nature of its structure, that is, not in the mere fact of three basic styles, but more particularly in the constellation of three concepts that are related to each other in a way that mimics the Aristotelian pattern of a virtuous mean situated midway between two opposed, vicious extremes. This point does not concern the question of the extent to which Dionysius' tripartite scheme is descended from Aristotle, Theophrastus, or later Peripatetics. It is clear, in any case, that Aristotle's thinking on diction contains the idea of two extremes around a virtuous mean: excellent diction must not only be clear, but also 'neither banal nor above what the subject deserves, but appropriate (πρέπουσαν)' (*Rh.* 3.2.1, 1404b1-4), where propriety occupies the place of the virtuous mean. Aristotle's thinking on prose rhythm likewise involves a mean with two opposed extremes (*Rh.* 3.8.1-3, 1408b21-32). Since the historical development of Greek stylistic doctrine led from Aristotle and Theophrastus to Dionysius (and beyond), it is unsurprising that Dionysius makes profitable use of the idea of a mean in his own teaching.[28] Yet there is a different point to make regarding the incisiveness and flexibility of Dionysius' tripartite Aristotelian pattern as a vehicle for theorizing about literary phenomena generally.

As in Aristotle, so in Dionysius the opposition of the two extremes and the middle position of the third praiseworthy concept help to define all three elements more clearly, indeed more dynamically, than is possible for a merely descriptive array of stylistic concepts such as that used by Hermogenes. For instance, in the only preserved work devoted solely to literary style that likely precedes Dionysius, the treatise *On Style* attributed to Demetrius which probably stems from the second century BCE, the author deploys a four-fold scheme of literary styles: plain (ἰσχνός), grand (μεγαλοπρεπής), polished (γλαφυρός), and forceful (δεινός).[29] Despite its historical interest and the occasional insight, Demetrius' treatise tends to be merely descriptive and does not provide the sort of systematic, open-ended, normative analysis that is available in Dionysius. By virtue of the

---

[28] Dionysius cites Theophrastus for the classification of Thrasymachus as an early exponent of the middle style (*Dem.* 3.1). Cf. *Comp.* 16.15; *Isoc.* 3.1; *Lys.* 14.1–5 for other instances where Dionysius cites Theophrastus on style. For the mean in the stylistic doctrines of Aristotle and Theophrastus and their influence on Dionysius, see Bonner 1938. On Theophrastus' theory of style and his adoption of the mean in stylistic discourse, see Innes 1985. For Aristotelian influence on Dionysius, see also Fox and Viidebaum in this volume, pp. 108, 193.

[29] Demetr. *Eloc.* 36. On Demetrius' doctrine and terminology of style, see Chiron 2010.

tripartite, Aristotelian scheme, every author whom Dionysius discusses, prose-writer or poet, is put into a meaningful, immediately perceptible relation with every other author whom Dionysius has considered and classified. Both similarities and differences among all these writers are made evident. Thucydides, Lysias, and Demosthenes thus form a sort of baseline for understanding style; and all other writers, in prose and verse, are put into relation with those three and with each other by virtue of their allotted places in the tripartite scheme. It is a convenient and useful way to classify, and thus to understand, the entire canon, at least with respect to style.[30]

It is a notable feature of Dionysius' stylistic theory that while he is constantly holding three stylistic concepts in balance and in play at once, he is also constantly varying the names of his three concepts and pointing to different qualities that each concept contains. This point holds true both for the general stylistic issues raised in the various treatises devoted to individual writers, that is, on matters related to diction, and for the more specific question of composition or word order in the treatise devoted to that subject. In both cases, while Dionysius uses a variety of terms for both stylistic extremes, we always know what he is talking about because they function as mutually defining opposites. Thus, early in the extant portion of the treatise devoted to Demosthenes (the opening of the treatise being lost), Dionysius defines the grand and plain styles by a series of contrasts between them (*Dem.* 1–3): the grand style is far from normal speech, the plain style resembles ordinary speech; Lysias, the plain stylist, stands to Thucydides, the grand stylist, as the lowest note on a musical scale stands to the highest; the grand style startles, the plain style soothes; the one induces strain, the other relaxes, etc. The styles of Thrasymachus, Isocrates, and Plato are then introduced as different ways of seeking a middle ground between the two extremes (*Dem.* 3–7). When Dionysius is finally about to introduce Demosthenes, he first compiles a list of the opposite qualities of the two extreme styles (*Dem.* 8): grand–simple, elaborate–plain, strange–familiar, ceremonial–practical, serious–light-hearted, intense–relaxed, sweet–bitter, sober–emotional. Demosthenes' overall style, which is the middle way, is then described as a mixture of this series of opposite qualities (*Dem.* 8.4).

---

[30] *Comp.* 22–24 sets out lists of prose-writers and poets who are categorized in the tripartite scheme of austere, smooth, and middle or mixed forms of composition. One prose-writer and one poet are chosen to exemplify each category: Pindar and Thucydides exemplify austere; Sappho and Isocrates exemplify smooth; Homer and Demosthenes exemplify mixed.

Though Dionysius often uses the term 'middle' (μέσος) for his third, ideal form of style, his most interesting and effective idea for rhetorical style is his use of the concept of mixture for the middle style. In addition to the term 'mixed' (μικτός, *Dem.* 8.4), as just illustrated in regard to Demosthenes, he also uses the term 'well-blended' (εὔκρατος, *Comp.* 24.1).[31] Now, the idea of mixing does not belong to Aristotle's tripartite classification of virtues and vices. Demetrius broaches the idea of mixing styles (*Eloc.* 36), but does not elaborate the idea. Dionysius uses the idea to explain how a praiseworthy middle style is constituted. When in the treatise *On Composition* Dionysius introduces his preferable, middle type of composition, which is the 'well-blended' type that contains judiciously chosen elements of the austere and smooth extremes, he cites the Aristotelian framework to account not for the particular qualities of this style of composition or for the idea of a mixture, but merely to explain that it occupies the middle position in an Aristotelian framework and that, for that reason too, in addition to its inherent qualities, it must be deemed to be the best (*Comp.* 24.1–2).

Although Aristotle does not employ the idea of a mixture of the two vicious extremes in his moral vocabulary of virtues and vices, and although he does not speak of mixing styles in the *Rhetoric*, it is nevertheless in Dionysius' idea of mixing styles that he creates a conceptual link with Aristotle's substantive stylistic doctrine based on the idea of propriety (πρέπον). In the *Rhetoric* Aristotle makes two claims about propriety: first, excellent style must be 'neither banal nor above what the subject deserves, but appropriate' (3.2.1, 1404b3-4); second, 'style will have propriety...if it is proportionate to the subject matter of the discourse' (3.7.1, 1408a10-11). The latter point is followed by examples that demonstrate the kinds of style that are appropriate to the expression of certain emotions, states of mind, or subject matter. For Dionysius the middle style, at least in the hands of Demosthenes, is well-blended, and therefore praiseworthy, precisely because it brings in the other styles when they are appropriate and to the extent that they are appropriate. For instance, Demosthenes' style largely resembles that of Thucydides, but it differs from it by limiting the use of obscure or striking language and injecting clarity, which is a concession to the practical requirements of competitive public oratory, a concession that Thucydides never had to make (*Dem.* 10).

---

[31] On Dionysius' concept of mixture for the middle style, see Martinho 2010.

Beauty, Pleasure, Music

Towards the end of the treatise *On Demosthenes*, Dionysius introduces a concept that stands alongside and in addition to the tripartite scheme of grand, plain, and middle. 'Virtually every work, whether it is created by nature or mothered by the arts, has two objectives, beauty and pleasure' (τὸ καλὸν καὶ ἡ ἡδονή, *Dem.* 47.2).[32] By including works of nature alongside works of art, Dionysius maintains the teleological view of nature that belongs to the philosophical tradition of Plato, Aristotle, and the Stoics, and uses it to advance his view of the proper goal of art. In the *Phaedrus* Plato introduced the notion of organic composition to explain the purpose and coherence of a work of art by reference to the same qualities in works of nature. Organic composition in a work of rhetorical art means, among other things, that the parts of the discourse are 'appropriate to each other and the whole' (*Phdr.* 264c), which adds yet another criterion for propriety beyond the original ones that pertain to the subject matter and the audience. Dionysius' comments on the beautiful and pleasurable musical qualities of Demosthenes' prose rely on the idea that the parts of his composition are appropriate to each other and the whole.

With regard to beauty and pleasure in the essay *On Demosthenes*, Dionysius attributes to Demosthenes two insights: that beauty and pleasure must both be present in order for each to be complete; and that beauty is the goal of the severe type of composition and pleasure that of the smooth type (*Dem.* 47.2–3). Then, as if acting on these insights, Demosthenes is said to have discovered that beauty and pleasure both have the same elements: melody (μέλος), rhythm (ῥυθμός), variation (μεταβολή), and propriety (τὸ πρέπον) (*Dem.* 47.4; *Comp.* 11.1–2). Demosthenes achieves propriety, once again, by mixing the extreme styles in such a way as to produce the most beautiful and pleasing combinations of musical and rhythmical sounds. Although, following Aristotle's line of thought, Dionysius claims that Demosthenes observes propriety in relation to his subject matter (*Dem.* 44–46, 48.4–5), in fact Dionysius says little about how the subject matter affects propriety. He focuses instead on how Demosthenes uses the musical elements of prose, melody, and rhythm to create a sense of propriety (*Dem.* 48). When Dionysius speaks at greater length about propriety in the treatise *On Composition*, his main example comes from Homer, the Sisyphus passage from *Odyssey* 11.593–96 (*Comp.*

---

[32] Cf. *Comp.* 10; *Dem.* 36.3 for similar claims. On beauty and pleasure in the essay *On Composition* in particular, see Donadi 1986.

20). The underlying idea is that the appropriate use of these musical elements is created in relation to the subject matter, to the character of the speaker, and to the emotions being invoked in the audience.

In attempting to explain how the combinations of syllables and individual letters composed by Demosthenes produce their beautiful and pleasing musical and rhythmical effects, Dionysius focuses mostly on features that are a matter of mere perception, that is, hearing in particular; these features are classified as appealing to 'the irrational capacity of the mind' (τὸ ἄλογον τῆς διανοίας κριτήριον) (*Thuc.* 27.1), or to 'irrational perception' (ἄλογος αἴσθησις, *Lys.* 11.8).[33] Indeed, Dionysius also mentions musical and rhythmical features that are analyzable by 'the mind's rational capacity' (τὸ λογικόν [τῆς διανοίας κριτήριον]) (*Thuc.* 27.1), and on this basis he attempts to analyze the rhythms of Demosthenes' prose into the meters or quasi-meters of poetry (*Comp.* 25.16–28). But the attempt is dense and unproductive, and ultimately plays an insignificant role in regard to beauty and pleasure.[34] Rather, Dionysius argues at length that Demosthenes composed with a view to the effect on the 'ear' (ἀκοή), and that the ear has its own natural sense of beauty and pleasure (*Dem.* 22; *Comp.* 10.2, 11.6–14, 23.20–23; *Lys.* 11). These claims are supported by detailed discussions of passages, ranging from just a few words to several pages, in which the sounds and rhythms produced by the author's combinations of syllables and letters are evaluated for their smoothness, flow, and musical qualities (*Comp.* 22–24). To do no more than refer to the ear to explain such effects may seem inadequate, as if one were merely giving a name to what still requires explanation. In this case, however, it is more informative to refer to well-known natural capacities that have been demonstrated empirically by expert writers such as Demosthenes than to attempt to explain in the abstract how such capacities can be manipulated systematically by quasi-metrical combinations of syllables and letters.[35]

---

[33] On 'unreasoning perception' in Dionysius, see also Hunter and Viidebaum in this volume, pp. 46–8, 117–20.

[34] See Damon 1991, 53–55; De Jonge 2008, 340–47 on the problems in Dionysius' attempt at a rational analysis of musical and rhythmical effects as conducted in *On Composition* 11.15–23, 17–18, 25. The rational capacity is sometimes referred to in the literature as the 'technical' capacity, that is, in accord with the (rational) principles of the art (τέχνη). On these terms and Dionysius' discussions of aesthetic effect and perception generally, see Damon 1991. On the background connection between rhetoric and music, see Wysłucha 2012.

[35] Dionysius likely had two main sources for his account of irrational perception of aesthetic effects: Cicero, *Orator* 149–203, which discusses rhythmical and musical euphony in oratory and refers to the ear as the evaluative faculty; and the so-called 'critics' (κριτικοί), who, as evidenced in Philodemus, *On Poems*, espoused the view that 'sound is the sole criterion for excellence in verse' (Janko 2000, 121). On the Hellenistic euphonist 'critics,' see Porter 1995. On their connection with

Dionysius' account of Demosthenes' beautiful and pleasing musical and rhythmical effects is compelling because it reveals a Demosthenes who is quite different from, and in fact somewhat opposed to, the Demosthenes of the treatise *On the Sublime*. That treatise, in effect, praises Demosthenes for his moments of brilliance, his intermittent but transcendent strokes of originality and insight expressed in unusual language. Now, Dionysius is not unaware of the sublime aspect of Demosthenes: Dionysius claims to be transported when reading Demosthenes, and he compares the experience of reading Demosthenes to the ecstasy of Corybantic rites (*Dem.* 22.2–3).[36] The treatise *On the Sublime* offers similar ways of describing Demosthenes' sublime moments (1.4, 12.4–5, 38.5). But what Dionysius actually gives us in his account of Demosthenes' art is rather a Demosthenes who is persistently intriguing and pleasing, who creates discourse in which beauty and pleasure are less intense than the sublime, but still available throughout and constantly changing in large and small ways.[37]

Political Discourse and Literary Fame

Dionysius insists that, like painter, sculptor, or poet, Demosthenes was concerned with the smallest level of detail, from sentence to word to syllable to the sounds of individual letters (*Dem.* 51.7).[38] Demosthenes' attention to minute detail seems as undeniable as it is difficult to elucidate. Recall just one of the examples that Dionysius presents in this regard (*Comp.* 6.8–9), the deictic *iota* in the opening sentence of the speech *On the Crown* – εἰς τουτονὶ τὸν ἀγῶνα, 'in this trial *here*' – where the sound and rhythm are far more pleasing, and convey a more august sense of the opening of a serious enterprise, than would be the case without the *iota*.[39] In the *Phaedrus* Socrates had decried prose-writers such as Lysias and Isocrates who waste time in the laborious pursuit of artistic combinations of words, even while they give no thought to what they are saying (278d): '[such a prose-writer] has nothing more valuable than the things he composed (συνέθηκεν) or wrote while turning them upside down (ἄνω κάτω στρέφων) over time, pasting them together and taking them apart.'

Dionysius, see De Jonge 2008, 193–204; Viidebaum and De Jonge in this volume, pp. 114–15 and pp. 246–7.
[36] The passage is cited by Wiater in this volume, pp. 68–9.
[37] See De Jonge 2012b on connections between the sublime (ὕψος) in Dionysius and Longinus.
[38] See Viidebaum in this volume.
[39] De Jonge 2008, 379–80 explains the *iota* here with reference to euphony in conjunction with surrounding consonants.

Dionysius alludes to this passage precisely in order to reject the claim that attention to minute detail is incompatible with the talent and purpose of a great political orator: anyone who 'is surprised that so great a man [i.e., Demosthenes] should be such a victim of misfortune that whenever he writes speeches he turns his words upside down (ἄνω καὶ κάτω στρέφειν)...trying to introduce into the language of political oratory melody, rhythm, and meter, the ingredients of music and poetry, which are entirely foreign media,' is mistaken (*Dem.* 51.2–3). Along with Demosthenes and Isocrates, Plato himself is characterized by Dionysius as a serious writer who composed 'in an exquisitely chiselled and turned style' (*Dem.* 51.4).[40]

Dionysius makes one additional point that complicates his basic tripartite scheme even more, and it too enhances his account of Demosthenes as practicing both political oratory and literary art at the same time. In several passages Dionysius attributes to Demosthenes two distinct goals in his rhetorical compositions, both of which help to explain certain features of Demosthenes' style (*Dem.* 10, 15, 32, 51). First, Demosthenes' speeches stem from actual political and legal contests in democratic Athens; that is, he was seeking to persuade his audience of ordinary Athenians to accept his plea and to reject that of his opponent in a contest to be decided on the spot. This goal accounts for the adversarial quality of the orator's speeches, which lends urgency and liveliness to his style and for which Dionysius uses the term ἐναγώνιος, meaning in a literal sense 'competitive,' 'adversarial,' and in a metaphorical sense 'engaging.'[41] For Dionysius the engaging aspect of Demosthenes' writing distinguishes him from Thucydides (*Dem.* 10), on the one hand, whose severe and difficult style, with its grammatical complexities and strange word order, would alienate an audience of average citizens, and, on the other hand, from Isocrates (*Dem.* 20) and Plato (*Dem.* 30.3, 32), who, though they employ the middle style like Demosthenes, do so with a feebleness or laxity that prevents them from engaging their readers' emotions. Dionysius is here recognizing a crucial connection between style and occasion: Thucydides, Isocrates, and Plato composed, of course, not for actual rhetorical contests with audiences acting as judges, as Demosthenes clearly did, but merely for readers who,

---

[40] Dionysius defends the combination of verbal artistry and serious content at *Dem.* 52; *Comp.* 25.29–44. See Hunter 2012, 151–84 on Dionysius' views on the styles of the *Phaedrus*.
[41] This usage occurs at *Dem.* 10.3, 18.4, 20.3, 21.4, 58.3, etc. On the meaning of the term as used by Dionysius and other literary critics, see Ooms and De Jonge 2013. The term and its stylistic implications go back to Aristotle's 'agonistic style' (λέξις ἀγωνιστική, *Rh.* 3.12). See also Oakley in this volume, p. 139.

whatever else they may take away from their reading, were not forced to decide between opposing speakers addressing them in person and in the moment. Modern scholars have remarked on the differences in content that arise between speakers addressing actual democratic audiences and writers, like Plato and Isocrates, who address readers outside of an actual political context. These differences are due to the expectations of mass democratic audiences that made it difficult, if not impossible, for speakers addressing such an audience to flout the pieties of Athenian democratic ideology.[42] Dionysius points out stylistic differences that arise from the same differences in the original contexts.

Yet if Thucydides, Isocrates, and Plato naturally aspire to the literary fame for which their written, non-agonistic genres of literature – history and philosophy – are best suited, Dionysius does not allow Demosthenes to fall short of these rivals in the pursuit of enduring literary fame. Thus the second goal that Dionysius attributes to Demosthenes. Enlarging on the differences between Demosthenes and Thucydides, Dionysius formulates Demosthenes' dual pursuit of immediate agonistic victory and permanent literary fame thus:

> But [Demosthenes'] aim is to satisfy the special needs of his case, and he makes his style conform to this practical requirement, not solely to that of permanent literary value, which the historian had in mind. Accordingly he never abandons clarity, which is the first requisite of actual competitive rhetoric (τοῖς ἐναγωνίοις λόγοις); while in addition he earns a reputation for eloquence (τό τε δεινὸς εἶναι δοκεῖν), which is clearly his primary object. (*Dem.* 10.3)

Just what Dionysius means by attributing to Demosthenes the desire for 'a reputation for eloquence' may not be clear at first. After all, Demosthenes was forced to defend himself against attacks by Aeschines in which the latter represented him as a sophistic rhetorician bent on deceiving his Athenian audiences.[43] That is clearly not the sort of reputation for eloquence that Demosthenes pursued, even though the word 'eloquent' (δεινός) in Dionysius' formulation may seem to suggest it. Dionysius himself deals with Aeschines' attacks on Demosthenes' style as part of his response to standing objections to Demosthenes' artistry (*Dem.* 35.3–8, 55). Rather, it is in the subtlety and finesse of Demosthenes' musical and

---

[42] The kernel of the argument is expressed at Pl. *Ap.* 31e-32a, where Socrates decries the impossibility of addressing the Athenian δῆμος frankly. See Yunis 1996, 125–32, 153–61, 238; Ober 1998, 206–13; Saxonhouse 2006, 146–78.
[43] Aeschin. *In Ctes.* 16, 137, 168, 174 (δεινὸς λέγειν), 200, 202, 207, 215 (δεινὸς δημιουργὸς λόγων).

rhythmical effects that Dionysius finds evidence of Demosthenes' pursuit of literary fame (*Dem.* 51.3, 52; *Comp.* 25.1–10). In Dionysius' view, such artistry would indeed affect Demosthenes' original audiences of average citizens; after all, they affect the ear naturally. But being ill-equipped by background or training to appreciate fine art, those audiences could hardly be expected to understand that such effects do belong to the business of the practical, busy orator-politician (*Comp.* 25.5–6). Yet such fine artistic effects would be noticed by the few elite, discerning members of Demosthenes' original audiences, as well as by the students of literature of succeeding generations, like Dionysius himself, who study texts as works of art. So Dionysius praises Demosthenes not only for mixing styles, but for mixing the goals of immediate agonistic victory and enduring literary fame (*Dem.* 15.6–7). In Dionysius' view, he did that in a way and to an extent that was equaled by no other classical writer.

Dionysius' Augustan Atticism Again

Dionysius' critical approach was clearly instrumental in moving Demosthenes and Atticism to the center of education in formal discourse from the Augustan age onwards. Before and after him Dionysius had colleagues in this enterprise (Cicero, Caecilius, Longinus, Quintilian, Hermogenes, Aristides, etc.). But one can point to aspects of this task that can be ascribed to Dionysius in particular. There is, of course, the sheer detail, scope, and relentless focus of his rhetorical doctrines; these have been discussed. Beyond that, however, there is a romantic element that provides motivation for the educational enterprise as a whole. In the essay *On the Ancient Orators* Dionysius produced a compelling picture of a well-ordered society in which high moral, political, and aesthetic values are interdependent and find expression in mutually supporting venues, genres, and media (*Orat. Vett.* 3).[44] In this image of a model society, the aesthetic is on a par with the political, and both are essential components of the communal striving which the Augustan regime was attempting to renew. Dionysius' portrayal of Demosthenes – the exemplary diction, composition, musical qualities, and outstanding fame – enables Dionysius to cash in, so to speak, on the promise of the type of society that is implied in the introductory essay. By demonstrating Demosthenes' unique and surprising artistic depth and breadth, Dionysius transformed him into palpable proof

---

[44] Cited by Wiater in this volume, pp. 72–3.

that the promise of the Augustan age was not fantasy. The figure of the historical Demosthenes, as Dionysius portrays him, becomes the model not only of wonderful, effective writing, but also of what the citizens of the Augustan empire, both Greeks and Romans, can achieve. It was perhaps an appropriate idea for the moment.

CHAPTER 4

Dionysius and Lysias' Charm

Laura Viidebaum

Introduction

On Lysias is the first instalment of, and in many ways an introductory work to, Dionysius of Halicarnassus' project of providing critical discussions of ancient orators he considers worthwhile for study and imitation.[1] It is perhaps not coincidental that Lysias, a metic living and writing in imperial Athens of the fifth and fourth centuries BC, is selected to launch the critical work of Dionysius, a Greek critic and historian writing in Augustan (imperial) Rome.[2] Indeed, Dionysius might have felt more proximity to this author than to any other Attic orator: both Lysias and Dionysius were involved in their contemporary intellectual life and were writing as subjects of an imperial power, but they were not really able to take an active part in its politics. Dionysius was not, however, the first critic to take an interest in Lysias, who was a prominent figure in literary criticism well before Dionysius (e.g., in the Atticist movement). Hence, the question of Lysias' role in Dionysius' writing also involves trying to come to terms with Lysias' overall importance at that specific time and place, Augustan Rome. Indeed, there seems to be something about Lysias that makes him a very attractive author for literary critical enterprises, and, as this chapter will hope to show, this 'something' is best understood through Dionysius' concept of 'charm' or χάρις.

It is relatively secure that Dionysius' essay on Lysias was his first contribution to the bigger project *On the Ancient Orators*. The essay, the longest of his three essays on the ancient generation of orators (Lysias, Isocrates, Isaeus), is roughly divided into two sections, the first dedicated to Dionysius' assessment of Lysias' speeches by reference to specific

---

[1] I would like to thank Richard Hunter for reading and commenting on innumerable drafts of this chapter over the past years. I would also like to thank Casper de Jonge and the anonymous referees for their helpful comments on an earlier draft. All remaining errors are, of course, mine.
[2] On Dionysius as a 'migrant thinker', see Connolly in this volume.

characteristics of Lysias' style, the second part analysing examples from Lysias' speeches to sustain claims made in the first part. According to Dionysius, Lysias 'wrote many well-arranged speeches to the law-courts and the council and the assembly, as well as panegyrics, erotic discourses and letters' (*Lys.* 1.5). Dionysius continues: 'he overshadowed the fame of those orators who came before him and those who blossomed in his own time, leaving not many opportunities to improve for those to come in all these forms of writing, by Zeus not even in the most trivial' (οὔτε γ' ἐν ταῖς φαυλοτάταις, *Lys.* 1.5). Lysias was, then, a writer accomplished in many genres, and yet Dionysius consistently emphasises Lysias' excellence in court speeches and the most trivial matters. Indeed, for the rest of the essay Dionysius leaves aside, without further comment, his letters, his amatory discourses and the other works which 'he wrote for amusement' (μετὰ παιδιᾶς ἔγραψεν), and focuses only on 'the serious speeches which he wrote for the law-courts and for the assembly' (οἱ σπουδῇ γραφόμενοι δικανικοὶ λόγοι καὶ συμβουλευτικοί, 3.7). He shows an awareness of Lysias' diverse literary production, but in this essay Dionysius decisively moves towards associating Lysias' talents primarily with the private speech genre – a genre that is less obviously politically charged in the context of fourth-century BC Athens as well as Augustan Rome.[3] Or perhaps not least relevant for the intended aims of Dionysius' critical essays – i.e., to cultivate rhetorical knowledge among young ambitious Romans[4] – was the fact that judicial oratory was often regarded as a legitimate and efficient way for young men to start their career and attract attention through eloquence.[5] In other words, to be able to discuss how to excel in the private speech genre might have made Dionysius' overall project more topical under Augustus and, as such, appealing for potential pupils.

With regard to Dionysius' critical method, his essay on Lysias shows him to be of an eclectic persuasion. Indeed, not only does he follow the (Peripatetic) theory of the virtues of style (more below), but throughout this essay Dionysius appears to make use of many different rhetorical theories and systems: he makes productive use of Theophrastus (*Lys.* 6.1, 14.1), of Isocrates or, perhaps more appropriately, the Isocrateans (*Lys.* 16.5), and of older rhetorical handbooks (*Lys.* 24.1–4). In so doing, Dionysius is not particularly concerned to stick to one specific system of

---

[3] Kennedy 1972, 303–4. As a way to gain and exercise political power, Cicero in *De or.* 2.333 clearly prefers deliberative oratory to judicial or epideictic. Fantham 1997 offers a good overview of the changes in public oratory from Republican to Augustan Rome.
[4] On Dionysius' audience, see Schultze 1982; Luraghi 2003; the introduction to this volume, pp. 31–3.
[5] E.g., Fantham 1997, 120–2; Rutledge 2007, 111.

virtues and to describe Lysias according to the terminology of a particular school. Instead, as he tells us at *Lys.* 10.3, he could name many more virtues of style, leaving it essentially open from where he is drawing his terminology and system. He was willing to mix, in other words, different theories and practices provided that they helped to better explain the work under discussion.[6]

The importance of the theory of the virtues (ἀρεταί) for Dionysius' discussion of different elements of style intimates the strong influence of Peripatetic criticism on Dionysius' thought and terminology.[7] In the *Letter to Pompeius*, which is probably very close (in time of composition) to his *On Demosthenes* and *On Thucydides*, Dionysius mentions the distinction between two different kinds of virtues (*Pomp.* 3.16–21), the essential virtues and the ancillary virtues. The main difference between the different virtues is that the 'essential' virtues have to be present in every speech, 'to make clear and manifest what one wishes to say, but they do nothing more'; the ancillary virtues have more influence and 'they show the δύναμις of the orator and they lend him his glory and fame'.[8]

Even though Dionysius does not mention the two-fold division of the virtues of style into essential and ancillary explicitly in his *On Lysias*, Bonner is surely right that the list Dionysius produces in this essay is in some important way indebted to that theory and connected to passages from his other works cited above.[9] The one significant difference between the virtues of style in *On Lysias* and those in his *Letter to Pompeius* is that compared to the latter the former essay displays a very clear distinction and an almost definition-like treatment of the virtues. Every virtue is mentioned in lucid and clear terminology, and the terms are often followed by brief explanations. Dionysius lists the following virtues of style: purity (καθαρότης), ordinary expression (κύρια καὶ κοινὰ ὀνόματα), lucidity (σαφήνεια), brevity (βραχύτης), compactness (στρογγυλότης), vividness (ἐνάργεια), characterisation (ἠθοποιία), propriety (τὸ πρέπον), persuasive (πιθανή) / convincing (πειστική) / natural (πολὺ τὸ φυσικόν) style, and charm (χάρις). This critical terminology is used throughout Dionysius' rhetorical works, and his efforts to create a clear-cut critical vocabulary and

---

[6] Cf. De Jonge 2008, 34–41. See Porter 2016, 221–2 on the apparent contradictions in, and flexibility of, Dionysius' method.
[7] Bonner 1939, 15–24 discusses the development of the theory about the virtues of style in Dionysius' work. See also Schenkeveld 1964, 72–6; Innes 1985. Dionysius mentions this system explicitly in his later essay *Thucydides* (22.2–3). For Peripatetic influence on Dionysius' rhetorical works, see also De Jonge 2008, 34–5; Yunis and De Jonge in this volume, p. 96 and pp. 248–9. For Peripatetic influence on the *Roman Antiquities*, see Fox in this volume, p. 193.
[8] Schenkeveld 1964, 74.   [9] Bonner 1939, 45.

method to analyse Lysias (and, by extension, all subsequent orators) have had a profound impact on subsequent rhetorical criticism of this author.

Of all the Lysianic virtues, Dionysius mentions Lysias' pure Attic language first (καθαρός ἐστι τὴν ἑρμηνείαν πάνυ, *Lys.* 2.1). In the context of the Atticist-Asianist controversy, putting this quality in such a prominent position, and ahead of the Peripatetic/Aristotelian 'lucidity' (σαφήνεια), is certainly a significant (political) move.[10] Dionysius explicitly says that purity is 'the first and most important element in speeches' (πρῶτόν τε καὶ κυριώτατον ἐν λόγοις), and of all other writers the only one closest to Lysias in this stylistic virtue was Isocrates.[11] A similar Atticist background seems to lurk behind his second virtue, which Dionysius describes as Lysias' skill to express ideas in 'standard, ordinary, moderate language' (ἡ διὰ τῶν κυρίων τε καὶ κοινῶν καὶ ἐν μέσῳ κειμένων ὀνομάτων ἐκφέρουσα τὰ νοούμενα ἑρμηνεία, *Lys.* 3.1). Here, Dionysius does not use a critical term for the quality (e.g., ἁπλότης or ἀφέλεια, cf. *Dem.* 2.1) and is thus pushed to spell out what this virtue really entails: the use of ordinary language makes Lysias' style accessible and dignified without recourse to poetical devices (ποιητικῆς οὐχ ἁπτόμενος κατασκευῆς). Yet, Dionysius warns us, Lysianic simplicity is deceptive, and the common words and language that he uses conceal a highly artistic prose. It is not simply everyday speech that Lysias reproduced in his speeches,[12] but a highly sophisticated art of simplicity. In fact, proof of the artistic labour behind the effect of a 'simple and common expression' is that of all the followers of Lysias it was Isocrates, this time the young Isocrates, famous for his elaborate style, who came closest to imitating Lysias' artistic and deceptive simplicity. After some remarks about lucidity and brevity, Dionysius moves on to sketch out the ancillary virtues, with the intention of highlighting Lysias' superiority in these elements over all other orators. Lysias excels in vividness (ἐνάργεια),[13] especially in observing 'human nature'

---

[10] On Atticism and classicism, see Gelzer 1979; Gabba 1982; Hidber 1996; Porter 2006; De Jonge 2008, 9–20; De Jonge 2014a; Kim 2014. See also Yunis in this volume, pp. 85–8.

[11] Hunter in this this volume, pp. 54–5, points out that the ancient criticism of Menander is very close to Dionysius' presentation of Lysias, featuring purity of language, character portrayal, and χάρις.

[12] At first, it might seem that Dionysius contradicts what he has said above in *Lys.* 4.5. Upon closer inspection, however, it becomes clear that he is showing us here the way in which a style that uses common words (κοινὰ ὀνόματα κτλ.) differs from everyday speech (λόγος ἰδιώτου).

[13] Aristotle writes in his *Rhetoric* about ἐνέργεια (rather than ἐνάργεια), but the context is similar: Aristotle aims to elucidate what it means to bring something 'before the eyes' (πρὸ ὀμμάτων) and defines this characteristic in the following way: λέγω δὴ πρὸ ὀμμάτων ταῦτα ποιεῖν ὅσα ἐνεργοῦντα σημαίνει (1411b25-6). He uses ἐνάργεια in the *Poetics* (17 1455a22-6). A good discussion of their difference in Aristotle is Eden 1986, 71–5. For ἐνάργεια in Dionysius' *Roman Antiquities*, see Oakley in this volume, p. 140.

(φύσιν ἀνθρώπων, *Lys.* 7.3), and characterisation (ἠθοποιία),[14] where he is again depicted as an excellent conveyor of truthfulness (ἀλήθεια) and the best example for anyone intending to become an imitator of nature (φύσεως μιμητής, *Lys.* 8.7). The emphasis on Lysias' proximity to natural language and truthfulness is striking and indeed suggestive of the way in which Lysias' prose works: it is enchanting through its very simplicity, which suggests both linguistic and moral trustworthiness.

In order to emphasise Lysias' character appropriations, Dionysius links Lysias' skill at characterisation with the virtue of a simple and common style. That Dionysius aims to establish a link between the two virtues becomes clear when he writes that 'the impression (χαρακτήρ) of this harmonious [composition] seems to be somehow un-laboured (ἀποίητος) and inartificial (ἀτεχνίτευτος)' (*Lys.* 8.5), concluding, however, that 'it is more carefully composed than any work of art' (8.6), that 'this artlessness is itself the product of art' (πεποίηται γὰρ αὐτῷ τοῦτο τὸ ἀποίητον), and that 'it is in the very appearance of not having been composed with masterly skill that the cleverness lies' (καὶ ἐν αὐτῷ τῷ μὴ δοκεῖν δεινῶς κατεσκευάσθαι τὸ δεινὸν ἔχει). This compares well with what he claimed a few passages before under the topic of 'common language/simplicity', namely that despite his apparent simplicity Lysias 'is the most accomplished literary artist' (ἔστι ποιητὴς κράτιστος λόγων, *Lys.* 3.8).[15] It is probably significant that of all the 'ancillary' virtues of Lysias, charm (χάρις) is the one that receives fullest treatment and attention by Dionysius. He must have felt that this element characterises Lysias' style particularly aptly and thus warrant a more elaborated discussion in the treatise. Indeed, the heightened pace with which Dionysius rushes through some of the last virtues of style in his discussion of the terminology seems to build up a sense of culmination when he finally comes to Lysias' χάρις, which counts surely as the most enigmatic of Lysias' virtues. To conclude his otherwise mechanical list of virtues with a long discussion of literary/Lysianic charm is perhaps the

---

[14] For the sake of convenience, I will translate ἠθοποιία here as 'characterisation', even though a good case could be made for a translation that would emphasise the moral qualities and normative connotations inherent in Dionysius' use of this notion. There is some controversy concerning Dionysius' concept of characterisation: is it referring to 'literary types' or 'individual characterisation'? The former position is defended by Bruns 1896, followed by Büchler 1936 and most recently Weissenberger 2003, 75. The advocates of 'individual characterisation' in Lysias include most famously Usher 1965. I hope to address the topic of characterisation and its use in Dionysius elsewhere.

[15] Dionysius' emphasis on this deceptive quality of Lysias' style, his δεινότης, strongly resembles Phaedrus' judgement of Lysias in Plato's *Phaedrus* (227c5, 228a2).

most striking aspect of the essay,[16] especially as Dionysius seems to use this notion as a way to explore the limits of criticism and artistic creation more generally.

Χάρις before Dionysius

To assess the significance of χάρις in Dionysius' discussion of Lysias and of a successful literary style more generally, let us take a brief look at the importance of this concept for poetics and literary criticism before Dionysius. Despite several studies tackling various different connotations of χάρις, there has not been much discussion of the presence and importance of χάρις in the domain of literary criticism and rhetoric.[17] The ancient Greek poetical tradition and rhetoric/literary criticism share a common interest in, and concern with, education and, perhaps even more importantly, with persuasion.[18] While it is a commonplace to regard rhetoric as profoundly engaged with persuasion, it is also in Pindar and Bacchylides, that is to say in the poetic tradition, that we find assurances that persuasion is as crucial to poetry as it is to rhetorical and oratorical practices. Indeed, Pindar's *Olympian* 1, for example, not only expresses an anxiety about poetry's persuasiveness, but it also demonstrates a connection between χάρις (or Χάρις/Χάριτες in most cases) and persuasion: 'Χάρις, who fashions all gentle things for men, by bestowing honour makes even what is unbelievable (ἄπιστον) often believed (πιστόν | ἔμμεναι τὸ πολλάκις)' (Pind. *Ol.* 1.30–2).[19]

Even though both poets predominantly invoke the goddesses (rather than use the noun χάρις or adjective χαρίεις),[20] this usage is metonymically associated with the concept and impact of χάρις found (and discussed) in earlier poetry. This reading of the persuasive qualities of χάρις, which emphasise its ability to dazzle our senses and, if necessary, deceive our judgement, brings us to the old and well-known Hesiodic story of Pandora

---

[16] For Usher 1974, 18–19 this gives the entire essay a 'Janus-like quality, looking inwards to the earlier systems of the ancient rhetoricians, of Theophrastus and Hermagoras, and outwards to the later intuitive criticism of Dionysius in the *De Compositione Verborum*, and of the author of the treatise *On the Sublime*'.
[17] Most of these studies focus on poetic, social, political or erotic usages (e.g., MacLachlan 1993, Latacz 1966, Hunter 2007), but there is also plenty of work done on its religious use (e.g., Harrison 2003, Moussy 1966). See now, however, Porter 2016, esp. 226–9 on χάρις in Dionysius.
[18] See for example Pl. *Phdr.* 234e5, where Socrates refers to Lysias (mockingly?) as a poet (ποιητής).
[19] See also Bacchyl. *Epin.* 9.1–2: Δόξαν, ὦ χρυσαλάκατοι Χάρι[τ]ες, | πεισίμβροτον δοίητ'[...], 'Grant the renown that persuades men, O Graces [...]'.
[20] Cf. Gerber 1982, 64–5.

(*Works and Days* 59–82), whose irresistible attraction is the work of Aphrodite and the 'grace (χάρις) and painful desire and limb-devouring cares' that she shed 'around her head' (65–6). In these contexts, χάρις is used by the poets (from Hesiod to Bacchylides) to denote the desired impact of a work of art on its audience. Understandably, however, these sources do not embark on any more detailed discussion about what exactly χάρις is and how it functions.

Another discipline where χάρις plays an important role is art criticism, where χάρις seems first to have become an important critical term around the beginning of the Hellenistic period.[21] In his analysis of χάρις in art (criticism), Pollitt argues that the notion contains two (mutually dependent) sets of meanings: the 'objective' χάρις describes 'the outward grace or beauty of a thing', and the 'subjective' χάρις approximates 'grace' or 'favour' 'which one receives from another or which one bestows on another'. Pollitt suggests that Latin authors may have attempted, at least to some extent, to differentiate the two meanings by translating the 'objective' χάρις with *venus* or *venustas*, which is exclusively used to refer to external and/or visible grace, and the 'subjective' χάρις with *gratia* or *ingenium*.[22] It is worth noting, moreover, that the Latin *venustas* seems to have become an important term in art criticism by the time of Vitruvius, an older contemporary of Dionysius, who advocates this notion as a cornerstone of the science of architecture and relates *venustas* to the impression of exterior beauty, which resides in the justly calculated internal symmetry (*De arch*. 1.3.2).[23] Vitruvius' complex blending of the external and internal aspects of *venustas* also intimates that in art criticism the concept is not very clear-cut and is perhaps best understood instead as oscillating between these two categories, encompassing references to external beauty as much as to internal ingenuity. More importantly, as suggested in Vitruvius' emphasis on *venustas*, this notion plays a significant role in Augustan aesthetics and the politics of architecture. *Venustas* is closely associated with Venus, and as Indra McEwen points out, this goddess became particularly relevant within the Roman power struggles of the first century BC.[24] The fact that *venustas* occupied such a prominent position in Roman politics and aesthetics provides an interesting background from which to assess Dionysius' decision to highlight χάρις as the most impressive aesthetic category of Lysias' style. If nothing else, with this

---

[21] Pollitt 1974, 301, referring back to Schlikker 1940.   [22] Pollitt 1974, 298–9, 380.
[23] On Vitruvius and *venustas*, see McEwen 2003, 198–212. On Dionysius and Vitruvius, De Jonge 2008, 33–4, 191.
[24] McEwen 2003, 203–10; Beard, North, and Price 1998, vol. 1, 144–5.

choice of terminology Dionysius positions himself amidst contemporary Roman aesthetic ideals and their underlying political implications.

In the context of art criticism, most examples seem to point towards an understanding of χάρις as somehow opposed to the laborious, profound, and serious, in the wake of Apelles, who was one of the most renowned Greek painters famous for the outstanding grace (*venustas*) of his art.[25] This resonates also among Dionysius' writings and in the literary and art criticism of the time more broadly.[26] Without assuming that art criticism had a direct impact on Dionysius' essays, our evidence of an increased discussion of this notion in various areas of cultural production suggests that by the first century BC χάρις had become an important critical term to be used in the context of Roman aesthetics.[27] The connection to art criticism appears relevant to Dionysius' use of art and artists in his rhetorical essays more generally. It is noteworthy that Dionysius refers to artists several times in his works, and there might be three possible explanations for the function of these comparisons and analogies in his work.[28] First, the artists that Dionysius is referring to all represent the classical world (just like Lysias and Isocrates), and therefore help evoke the classicising ideal that he wants us to 'imitate'. Second, appealing to contemporary art criticism implies its acceptance and high regard as a form of intellectual activity, so that being acquainted with the most famous artists and having the relevant vocabulary to discuss them was part of elite παιδεία.[29] It might be, then, that Dionysius, whose works on Attic orators introduce his ideas about rhetorical teaching/training, is drawing on the (perhaps more widely spread and accepted) terminology of art critics to legitimise his concepts and interpretations, reassuring his reader that he is merely applying to literary criticism ideas that have become current and accepted in other, but more relevant, arts.[30] Third, it seems that Dionysius has a tendency to import analogies from art when he is dealing with concepts that cannot be defined with precision, and where other art

---

[25] Plin. *HN* 35.79–97; Pollitt 1965, 158–63.
[26] Dionysius makes reference to Apelles twice in his writings (*Din.* 7.7; *Thuc.* 4.2), but he never compares Lysias to Apelles.
[27] This suggestion is in line with De Jonge 2012, where the emergence of yet another important concept, that of the sublime (ὕψος), is traced back to the Augustan period and linked to Greek classicism.
[28] On analogies between writing and visual arts in Dionysius (and Horace), see also De Jonge in this volume, pp. 250–1.
[29] Tanner 2006, 250–76 is helpful here. For more on Vitruvius' self-positioning in the Roman cultural climate, see Nichols 2009; Wallace-Hadrill 2008, 144–210.
[30] Benediktson 2000, 111 similarly suggests that Dionysius uses analogies to the visual arts 'to defend his approach'.

forms might potentially be useful for comprehending his insights.³¹ Underlying this is an idea that literary criticism is (or should be) very similar to other art forms, thus making such analogies and comparisons between disciplines legitimate.³² Also, as will be suggested below, Dionysius seems to hold that one crucial aspect that literary/rhetorical criticism shares with music and visual arts is its dependence on sense perception.³³

In this context it is important to mention Philodemus, whose critical work is an important source for a group of literary critics – the *kritikoi* – who argued for the importance of sense perception in literary production.³⁴ Dionysius' dependence on and use of these critics is ambivalent, and their ideas can be found in unequal measure throughout his works. Due to the interest of the *kritikoi* in sounds and euphony, it is to be expected that Dionysius is relying on their ideas most prominently in his work *On Composition* and far less in his critical essays on ancient orators.³⁵ Nevertheless, there are interesting connections with the latter treatises, and, for instance, I count altogether at least three relevant usages of χάρις in the fragments of Philodemus' *On Poems* 1 that refer to 'radical euphonists' and approximate to Dionysius' treatment of χάρις in his critical essays.

These three uses occur in fragments where Philodemus is debating the views of Pausimachus.³⁶ Papyrus column 83 in book one of Philodemus' *On Poems* brings us straight to the centre of the euphonists' position: Philodemus argues here that according to Pausimachus good verse depends only on sound, and that it is from there, i.e., the sounds, that our irrational delight comes (24–6: τὴν [μὲ]ν χά- / ριν τὴν ἄλογον π[αρ]ὰ τοῖς / αὐτοῖς ἀνατιθείς [. . .]). This seems supported also by column 89 where Philodemus communicates a further aspect of Pausimachus' views, according to which there is an important distinction to be made between the immediacy of hearing, to which Pausimachus claims we can easily assign our delight (14–16: [μό]- / νῳ δ' ἀποδιδόναι τ[οὐ]- / τωι τὴν χάριν), and a more complicated process of explanation, which will most probably incorporate some form of logos or rationalised action. Even though

---

³¹ These concepts include καιρός, τὸ μέτριον, and – as will be discussed in more detail below – χάρις (cf. Dion. Hal. *Lys.* 11).
³² Cf. Benediktson 2000, 108.
³³ Porter 2011 seems to corroborate this view with his emphasis on the ambivalent materiality of Hellenistic (and post-Hellenistic) aesthetics.
³⁴ On Philodemus and the *kritikoi*, see also the introduction and De Jonge in this volume, pp. 22–3, 246–7.
³⁵ For a brief overview of Dionysius' engagement with the *kritikoi* in *Comp.*, see De Jonge 2008, 37–41.
³⁶ The source text for the following quotations is Janko 2000. On Pausimachus' theory of composition, see also De Jonge in this volume, pp. 261–2.

χάρις is not here accompanied by the adjective ἄλογος, the context makes it clear that it is precisely the irrational sensory experience of χάρις that is contrasted with the logos-involved explanation.[37] The third occurrence of χάρις is in papyrus column 100, which seems to support the same point. In this passage, Pausimachus compares two people, one speaking Greek and another a foreign language (βαρβαριζόντων ἑτεροεθνῶν), and argues that one is listened to with pleasure (ἡδέως), the other not. This is because, according to Pausimachus, it is the sound (in the Greek language) that produces 'what is particular with regard to our pleasure' (οὕτω τοίνυν καὶ ἐπὶ τῶν ἑλληνιζόντων ὁ μὲν ἦχος ἀποτελεῖ τὸ ἴδιον κατὰ τὴν χάριν).[38] Even though the rationale behind this latter claim is not entirely clear,[39] Pausimachus appears to associate the concept of χάρις clearly with our perception of sounds that appeals to the irrational part of our body and, at the same time, constitutes the primary function or very essence of poetry. Poems *qua* poems should be assessed, according to him, on the basis of sound, and successful poems/sounds induce χάρις. The similarities and differences between the *kritikoi* and Dionysius on the notion of χάρις will be highlighted below after a closer look at Dionysius' exposition of the term. For the time being, however, the fact that both the *kritikoi* and Dionysius dedicate considerable energy to elucidating the concept of χάρις indicates that it probably played a pivotal role in the debates about the art, literature, language, and philosophy of perception that circled around in the second and first centuries BC.

Dionysius and Lysias' χάρις

To return to Dionysius' essay *On Lysias* and his discussion of χάρις, we find the description of χάρις extending over several chapters of the work, the longest section dedicated to a single virtue of style. Dionysius claims that Lysias' χάρις is his 'finest and most important quality, and the one above all which enables us to establish his peculiar character' (*Lys.* 10.3). Even though nobody else excelled him in χάρις, those who imitated it appeared superior to others because of this quality alone (10.4). It is 'some sort of charm that blossoms forth in all his words' (ἡ [τις] πᾶσιν ἐπανθοῦσα τοῖς

---

[37] See below for a discussion on Dionysus' ἄλογος αἴσθησις.
[38] Gomperz restored 'pleasure' (χάριν) from *PHerc.* 994 col. 6, 9–11.
[39] It seems to be vulnerable to the claim that the Greek-speaker produces pleasure in the (Greek-speaking) listener, precisely because the latter can understand what is being said. This would, however, contradict the positions of the euphonist critics who downplay the importance of meaning over that of sound.

ὀνόμασι <χάρις>) and it is 'something bigger than all words and more wonderful' (πρᾶγμα παντὸς κρεῖττον λόγου καὶ θαυμασιώτερον, 10.5). Yet, it is also a challenging term, as Dionysius concedes when he says that it 'is very easy to see and it is to everyone, layman and expert alike, manifest, but it is most difficult to express in words, and not simple even for those with exceptional descriptive powers' (καὶ οὐδὲ τοῖς κράτιστα εἰπεῖν δυναμένοις εὔπορον, 10.6). Dionysius connects χάρις and the impossibility to determine in exact terms what it is with other difficult, but very productive literary critical terms, such as 'timeliness' (καιρός, 11.2) and 'the mean' (τὸ μέτριον). In all these cases, 'it is with senses and not with reason that we comprehend' (αἰσθήσει γὰρ τούτων ἕκαστον καταλαμβάνεται καὶ οὐ λόγῳ, 11.3).

We see here the similarities between Dionysius and the views of the *kritikoi* outlined above, but also their distance from each other. Pausimachus had argued that χάρις appeals to the irrational in us and constitutes the core of any poetic aspiration. Dionysius also claims that χάρις is an irrational sensation and one that proves for him the most essential quality of Lysias. There is, clearly, some common ground between these two positions, and Dionysius' dependence on some of the ideas of the *kritikoi* has been discussed and demonstrated particularly in relation to his *On Composition*.[40] There are, however, substantial differences between the *kritikoi* and Dionysius' thought. Firstly, and quite obviously, in this essay Dionysius makes no attempt to actually understand χάρις as comprising sounds, and, if anything, he is clearly struggling to provide his readers with a clear definition of the concept.[41] To be sure, Dionysius emphasises the centrality of sense perception, but he is not clear which senses he has in mind (his examples range widely from music to painting and sculpture), or how the experience of this phenomenon could be broken down into smaller pieces (in a way similar to the *kritikoi*). Hence, Dionysius is reluctant to participate in the debate of whether it is sound or sense that should have primacy in oratorical compositions. Secondly, instead of focusing on one particular constituent of χάρις (as the *kritikoi* do in prioritising the aural perception of sounds), Dionysius concentrates almost exclusively on a specific author whom he considers to be the best learning-source for χάρις – Lysias.

---

[40] The most recent and thorough treatment of this topic is De Jonge 2008; see also De Jonge in this volume, pp. 261–2.
[41] In *Comp.*, however, where Dionysius also mentions χάρις, the concept is associated with ἡδονή (11.2), which *is* explained in terms of sounds and syllables (14–19).

Since definitions and words do not bring us closer to this term, Dionysius turns to another art where senses are heavily involved – music. Borrowing from music teachers, who advise their pupils simply to cultivate their ear, which is the most accurate criterion of music (*Lys.* 11.3), Dionysius recommends his students who wish to learn the nature of Lysias' χάρις 'to train the unreasoning perception over a long time with consistent study and unreasoning experience' (χρόνῳ πολλῷ καὶ μακρᾷ τριβῇ καὶ ἀλόγῳ πάθει τὴν ἄλογον συνασκεῖν αἴσθησιν, 11.4). In other words, the first step towards a full appreciation of Lysias' mastery is to simply listen to and read numerous speeches by Lysias without making any attempt to critically discuss or otherwise engage with the work. This constant exposure to Lysianic style will form one's senses in a way that will eventually lead to a general understanding of his particular style and make sure that any non-Lysianic feature will immediately stand out.

How exactly this 'unreasoning perception' (ἄλογος αἴσθησις)[42] is related to Lysianic χάρις, however, is not entirely clear. Could Dionysius' method that he recommends for understanding Lysias' χάρις be meaningfully used to determine the qualities and idiosyncrasies of any author, and not just those of Lysias? Indeed, a passage from his essay *On Demosthenes* reveals that this seems to be the case. Dionysius discusses the melodious composition of Demosthenes and recommends to those wishing to exactly understand Demosthenes' composition (σύνθεσις) to judge the most important and significant individual elements of the composition, the first being melody (ἐμμέλεια), the best means of judging which is the 'instinctive feeling' (ἄλογος αἴσθησις). Dionysius adds, however, that this requires much practice (τριβὴ πολλή) and prolonged instruction.[43] Even though in this passage Dionysius connects the 'instinctive feeling' more precisely with melody in style, thus giving his reader a little more specific information about ἄλογος αἴσθησις than in his essay on Lysias, its continued association with the aural aspects of style clearly suggests that Dionysius' thinking has not dramatically changed between writing *Lysias* and *Demosthenes*. Dionysius still considers the 'ear' a crucial organ for the evaluation of literary value and artistic success. And it is significant that this method, if that is the right way to call it, is associated with the universal impression of an author and his works, so that Dionysius associates Lysias' χάρις not so much with a particular virtue of style, but

---

[42] See also Yunis and Hunter in this volume, pp. 47–8, 100.
[43] Dion. Hal. *Dem.* 50.3. On Dionysius' treatment of Demosthenes, see Yunis in this volume, with further bibliography.

rather with the overall effect of his work. We get, thus, a little bit closer to understanding what kind of work the notion χάρις is actually doing for Dionysius, for we have been able to narrow down the dimensions of where to look for the Lysianic χάρις – it is the overall and broader effect of the work that Dionysius' notion of χάρις is concerned with.[44]

Perhaps we can get closer to the notion of χάρις by looking at the role of ἄλογος αἴσθησις in Dionysius' criticism. His treatment of the concept has received a thorough analysis by Cynthia Damon, who has demonstrated how Dionysius' own critical activity reflects his position on the importance of ἄλογος αἴσθησις as a cornerstone in literary criticism.[45] Damon's article was a direct response to Schenkeveld's negative assessment of Dionysius' critical capacity, where he argued that Dionysius had conflicting views regarding the two notions ἄλογος αἴσθησις and τὸ λογικὸν κριτήριον.[46] Schenkeveld rightly pointed out, however, that ἄλογος αἴσθησις is a notion that Dionysius attributes both to the layman and the critic alike.[47] In other words, Lysias' charm that is conveyed to any reader or listener through the 'instinctive feeling' is perceived similarly by everyone regardless of their previous experience or expertise in criticism. In trying to understand how this concept works in Dionysius' writings, Damon argues that he deals with the notion of ἄλογος αἴσθησις in two stages: when analysing a passage, he first sketches out a general impression that is accessible to both the layman and the critic, and then goes in greater depth and highlights elements that are more relevant to the critic.[48] This confirms the previous assessment about the semantic field of χάρις as a notion that captures the broad effect of the work rather than a specific aspect of it. It is important that Dionysius associates this effect with both the expert and the layman alike. From the critics' perspective, however, the pedagogical method based on ἄλογος αἴσθησις, as referred to in *On Lysias*, is open to further challenges. Most of all, it seems to presuppose that we have a canon of Lysias' works (or of any author for that matter) that is representative of his whole literary activity, which could then be used for this kind of learning. However, Dionysius does not address this question and instead goes on to claim that charm is such a fundamental feature to understanding Lysias' style that it also becomes a very useful tool for assessing the authorship of speeches that have come down under his name.

---

[44] This overall effect of χάρις could possibly be compared to what Aristotle and Theophrastus seem to have called τὸ ἡδύ. See Innes 1985, 256.
[45] Damon 1991.   [46] Schenkeveld 1975.   [47] Schenkeveld 1975, 95, 103.   [48] Damon 1991, 49.

There is circularity in this argument: being trained with Lysias' speeches will enable the critic to identify those which have distinctly non-Lysianic elements, which will lead to simply confirming over and over again the existing canon. Would Dionysius have realised the circularity of this argument and regarded this as a problem? His essay indicates that he was all too aware of questions regarding authenticity and had spent time thinking about the methods for establishing or overruling authorship claims. At the same time, Dionysius does not question the validity and authorship of the canon that he himself has established and regarded as authentic. In other words, despite emphasising the problem of authorship, Dionysius ignores it when he sets up his methodology about how to approach Lysias, falling back on his confidence in the established corpus of Lysias' speeches. The situation is even more striking when we notice that none of Lysias' speeches that Dionysius mentions and quotes in his critical essays has been preserved elsewhere, and that he does not in turn make any references to speeches that have come down to us as part of the Lysianic corpus.[49] It seems, then, that as much as Dionysius trusted his Lysianic canon to be stable and the speeches he quotes in the essay to be widely known, there might have been more fluctuation and uncertainty about Lysias' speeches than appears on the surface. This casts a shadow over Dionysius' tacit assumption of a 'stable' canon and his unwillingness to engage with this topic at greater length.

Another sign of this uncertainty is perhaps discernible in Dionysius' eagerness to withhold judgements based solely on the (cultivated) 'instinctive feeling' (ἄλογος αἴσθησις) about the author and instead to make use of alternative information when deciding about the authenticity of a text. For example, while arguing that it is Lysias' charm that will eventually decide whether the speech is genuine or not, Dionysius also makes use of chronological data and other information available to him before making up his mind. Speeches involving Iphicrates, an Athenian general, provide some insight into Dionysius' critical thinking (*Lys.* 12.2–9): the first speech concerning the statue of Iphicrates seemed suspicious to Dionysius on chronological grounds, while the second concerning a defence for impeachment did not display the Lysianic charm. A closer investigation revealed to Dionysius that they were written by the same hand, but that

---

[49] Of the three speeches quoted at length in the second half of the essay, the first three sections of speech 32 (*Against Diogeiton*) are also attested in Syrianus' commentary on Hermog. *Id.* (88. 15–89.15), sections of speech 33 (*Olympiakos*) are preserved in Diod. Sic. (14.109), [Plut.] *X orat.* (836d), and Theon's *Progymnasmata* (63), and for speech 34 (*On Preserving the Ancestral Constitution*) Dionysius appears to be our only source.

this hand could not have been, for chronological and stylistic reasons, Lysias'. Despite his confidence about the importance of χάρις as a defining element of Lysias' speeches, Dionysius himself admits the need for more clear-cut evidence before confidently arguing for or against Lysias' authorship.

A review of Dionysius' critical writings more generally and the way χάρις is used there helps somewhat to narrow down the range of meanings associated with the term. It is especially productive to look at comparisons with other orators. Lysias is opposed to Isocrates, for example, in that Lysias is described as being more skilled (σοφώτερος) in small subjects (ἐν τοῖς μικροῖς), Isocrates as more impressive (περιττότερος) in grand subjects (ἐν τοῖς μεγάλοις) (*Isoc.* 3.7). In this section, Lysias' 'lightness' and 'charm' is explicitly contrasted to Isocrates' grand and dignified rhetorical art (*Isoc.* 3.6). Also, Lysias' style of composition is simpler, Isocrates' more elaborate, so that 'the former [is] more convincing in creating the appearance of truth (τῆς ἀληθείας εἰκαστής), the latter the more powerful master of technique (τῆς κατασκευῆς ἀθλητής)' (*Isoc.* 11.5). Dionysius highlights, once again, Lysias' skill at creating illusions or resemblances to truth, without necessarily presenting truth. When comparing Lysias with Isaeus, he resorts to the language of the visual arts: Lysias, by his simplicity and charm (κατὰ τὴν ἁπλότητα καὶ τὴν χάριν), resembles 'older paintings which are worked in simple colours without any subtle blending of tints but clear in their outline, and thereby possessing great charm (πολὺ τὸ χαρίεν ἐν ταύταις ἔχουσαι)' (*Is.* 4.1); Isaeus, on the other hand, is a representative of 'later paintings that are less well-drawn but contain greater detail and a subtle interplay of light and shade, being effective because of the many nuances of colour which they contain' (*Is.* 4.2). Lysias' style is thus straightforward and uncompromising, but perhaps not altogether as serious as this description would suggest.

The rhetorician Demetrius had already linked Lysias with χάρις: in his *On Style* they were both associated with wit and humour. Paragraphs 128–89 of Demetrius' *On Style* tackle the elegant (γλαφυρός) style,[50] which he describes as 'a speech with charm and a graceful lightness'

---

[50] I follow the conventional practice of referring to the author of *On Style* as Demetrius. Regarding the date of the work, I tend to support the growing consensus among recent scholarship (e.g., Chiron 1993, Innes 1999, Schenkeveld 2000) that the work belongs to a relatively early period (second/first century BC). This would make Demetrius a contemporary of the art critics mentioned above and thus further support the view that this concept had a relatively wide circulation already around the second and first centuries BC.

(χαριεντισμὸς καὶ ἱλαρὸς λόγος, *Eloc.* 128).⁵¹ He then goes on to divide χάρις into two larger categories: the poetic χάρις, which is more imposing and dignified (μείζονες καὶ σεμνότεραι), and a more ordinary χάρις, which is closer to comedy and resembling jests (σκῶμμα). Demetrius invokes Lysias as an example for the latter kind and quotes some of his passages to illustrate the comic χάρις. This seems to corroborate the view that Lysias' style gives an impression of 'everyday' language, a 'natural', non-rhetorical and non-artistic style that charms and deceives us by its very appeal to truthfulness and simplicity.

A passage from *On Demosthenes* (54.8), despite its fragmentary form, might suggest that witticism was also one of the meanings that Dionysius had in mind. Dionysius there equates charm (χάρις) with wit (εὐτραπελία) and says that Demosthenes' style lacks wit, which most people call charm (ἡ Δημοσθένους λέξις λείπεται εὐτραπελίας, ἣν οἱ πολλοὶ καλοῦσι χάριν). This passage is corrupt, and in his reconstruction Usher suggests that Dionysius intended to evoke here a comparison with Lysias.⁵² Be that as it may, what matters for the present purpose is that εὐτραπελία is used as a synonym for χάρις and that this juxtaposition helps to narrow down the broad spectrum of possible meanings used for χάρις. It is thus somehow associated with the small, the commonplace, and the witty.

Lysias' Charm in Rome

Details about how exactly these associations work and why Dionysius decided not to specify the notion are left unclear. In fact, perhaps the obscurity and impenetrability of χάρις served a purpose for Dionysius. In the particular social and educational context of Augustan Rome, it might have helped Dionysius to reassert the authority of (Greek) rhetorical teaching and teachers, who will have sat down with their authors and trained their senses to recognise different stylistic features characteristic of different authors. Rather than simply a craft that can be learned through 'rulebooks', rhetoric and style – or at least their most accomplished and successful elements – are conceived of as arts that require well-trained

---

⁵¹ Grube 1961, 31 is very critical of Demetrius' treatment of the elegant style and claims that he goes too far in incorporating laughter and jokes into this category. With regard to terminology, Grube notices that Demetrius' overall confusion of this style is reflected in the way he strikingly abandons γλαφυρός and adopts χάρις instead to discuss the core features of this style.

⁵² Usher 1974 prints the text without Reiske's addition of <οὐ> before λείπεται, which completely changes the interpretation of the passage. Other editors are more cautious and Aujac 1988, for example, adopts Reiske's addition. It is true that Dionysius does not hint anywhere else in his critical essays that Demosthenes did not have enough charm.

teachers and experience. And these associations of χάρις just mentioned – the small, the commonplace, and wit – might have held particular appeal for young Romans and Dionysius' potential students: here was an entertaining Greek author who would not put off students (and Romans more generally?) with his philosophical gravity,[53] and who at the same time has much to teach about 'playful intellectualism'. Next to the political potential of χάρις (as a Greek equivalent to the Latin *venustas*) as an aesthetic category in Augustan Rome, Dionysius' emphasis on Lysias' charm shows how a Greek writer could be successfully used to capture the new trends in contemporary Roman (Augustan) rhetoric.

Dionysius was generally alert to the topic of appropriate audience and styles, and his concern for the 'uneducated' reader is also strongly present in his discussions of ἄλογος αἴσθησις and the 'instinctive feeling' that affects the critic and the non-critic alike. His criticisms of Thucydides (e.g., *Thuc.* 24) and Isocrates (e.g., *Isoc.* 3), for example, condemn their obscurity (Thucydides) and overly ornate style (Isocrates). This preference for simplicity and clarity that emerges from Dionysius' discussion of Attic prose also reflects Roman literary tastes and rhetorical education, and – if true – could be regarded as a confirmation of the above sentiment about the potential attractiveness of an author like Lysias for a Roman audience. After all, Lysias had been the primary model of stylistic purity in the circles of Roman *Attici*, the opponents of Cicero, just a few decades before Dionysius' arrival in Rome.[54]

However, this conclusion might appear problematic when we look at what Dionysius explicitly tells us about his intellectual environment and his potential readership. In his preface to *On the Ancient Orators*, Dionysius claims that the changed appreciation of rhetoric is indebted to 'the conquest of the world by Rome' (ἡ πάντων κρατοῦσα Ῥώμη), and he continues by arguing that 'her leaders are chosen on merit, and administer the state according to the highest principles. They are thoroughly educated (εὐπαίδευτοι πάνυ) and in the highest degree discerning, so that under their ordering influence the sensible section of the population (τὸ φρόνιμον τῆς πόλεως μέρος) has increased its power and the foolish have been compelled to behave rationally' (*Orat.*

---

[53] It seems that the introductions of Cicero's work may be particularly relevant as reflecting the responses of his contemporary Romans to Greek culture and literature. See Baraz 2012 for a more detailed discussion.
[54] Cicero defends himself against C. Licinius Calvus and the other *Attici* in *Brutus* and *Orator* (46 BC). See *Brut.* 67 on Lysias as the champion of the *Attici*. On Roman Atticism, see Wisse 1995; De Jonge 2008, 12–13; Yunis in the current volume, pp. 85–8.

Vett. 3.1).⁵⁵ In other words, Dionysius claims that the level of education among the populace has arisen in Rome and we can expect this to have a direct effect on Dionysius' evaluation of his students and readers. And indeed, he makes several gestures towards his imagined readership that support his high regard for their cultural education. In his essay *On Lysias*, for example, Dionysius characterises his audience as 'those knowing' or 'connoisseurs' (εἰδότες, 10.1) and later on as 'well-educated and moderate minds' (ψυχαὶ εὐπαίδευτοι καὶ μέτριαι, 20.2), thus suggesting that he has high expectations for the intellectual capacity of his imagined readership.⁵⁶

Yet perhaps these apparently conflicting views of Dionysius' intended audience are not necessarily mutually exclusive. Rome has already demonstrated her dislike for the ornate and excessive ('Asianic') style that emerged in the Hellenistic period (*Orat. Vett.* 3), emphasising τὸ ὄφελος and τὸ φρόνιμον in both rhetoric and style. Dionysius, building on this intellectual climate that prefers the simple over the complex, and the useful over the pleasurable, will thus find a favourable audience when commencing his critical essays with the Greek orator that most fulfils these conditions – Lysias. By proposing Lysias as the first role model for style, Dionysius is at the same time fashioning his audience as 'learned' men who already know that it is simplicity and effectiveness, the very virtues he ascribes to Lysias, that are to be valued highly in oratorical performance. In other words, Dionysius attracts the Roman readership to the Greek models by appealing to the virtues to which Romans are already committed and flattering them for having duly recognised these virtues thanks to their wide learning.⁵⁷ Furthermore, if it is indeed true that Rome was suspicious of Greek intellectuals and philosophers, and did not have high regard for their abstract argumentation and emphasis on theory,⁵⁸ this might also cast

---

⁵⁵ Cf. De Jonge and Yunis in this volume, pp. 87–8 and 264.
⁵⁶ More parallels are collected in Hidber 1996, 120. Wiater 2011a, 270–8 emphasises Dionysius' strictly elitist approach to his readership and demonstrates its connections with his classicism. It is surely true, as Wiater maintains, that Dionysius' writings were addressed to the Roman elite, but we might not want to dismiss the possibility that the Roman elite was not as eagerly invested in classicism as Dionysius' rhetoric invites us to believe. Emphatically labelling one's audience as 'knowledgeable' and 'well-educated' might also have been a rhetorical strategy used by Dionysius to flatter his readers and create an appealing image that they might find difficult to reject.
⁵⁷ Cf. Suet. *Aug.* 86. See De Jonge in this volume, p. 264.
⁵⁸ Cicero has made this intellectual climate plain in his attempts to counter these accusations. He discussed this topic in depth in his lost *Hortensius*, but we see his continued engagement with this environment, for example, in his *Tusculan disputations* (2.1). For thorough discussion of this passage, see Gildenhard 2007, 156–66. Cf. also Griffin 1989, 18–22, for a good analysis of Roman suspicions about philosophy in public life; Baraz 2012, 13–43.

Dionysius' discussion of the ἄλογος αἴσθησις in a new light: when Dionysius argues that the most important quality of Lysias' style is his charm (χάρις), which according to him depends on ἄλογος αἴσθησις and cannot be understood through logical/abstract reasoning, he might in fact have put his finger on the Roman virtue of style *par excellence*. Even more than the emotion and powerfulness of a Demosthenes, this experience-based and sense-dependent charm that does not lend itself to theoretical discussion is what might have spoken most closely to the Roman oratorical practice.[59] Hence, with his notion of 'charm' Dionysius appears to have given the Romans a useful critical tool with which to justify their high regard of Lysias and the kind of rhetoric that is associated with it.[60]

---

[59] Cf. Gabba 1982, 48.
[60] Wisse 1995 suggests that the Atticist movement originated among the Romans, a view which potentially strengthens my argument.

PART 2

Dionysius and Augustan Historiography

CHAPTER 5

The Expansive Scale of the Roman Antiquities

S. P. Oakley

Introduction

The great expansiveness and detail of the eleven extant books of Dionysius' *Roman Antiquities*, caused in part by the inclusion of a very large number of speeches, is perhaps their best-known feature.[1] In this chapter Dionysius' own remarks on the writing of history, in both his theoretical treatises and the *Roman Antiquities*, will be examined in order to show how they do much to explain this expansiveness, and two episodes that may serve as a general illustration of his techniques will be analysed. Some suggestions will be made as to where in the Roman annalistic tradition Dionysius found the material that allowed him to write at such length, and the chapter will end with discussion of a battle scene that exhibits characteristic Dionysian or Roman annalistic expansion. Throughout, comparison of the *Roman Antiquities* with Livy's *Ab urbe condita*, the only other extended narrative of early Rome that survives, will be used to illustrate Dionysius' techniques.

The length of the work

Dionysius' history is vastly more expansive than Livy's, especially at its beginning: Livy takes one book to cover the regal period, Dionysius takes four or, to put it another way, Dionysius' account occupies 540 pages of Carl Jacoby's standard Teubner text, whereas Livy's occupies 75 pages of Robert Ogilvie's standard Oxford Classical Text, which has about 20% more words on a page.[2] Livy ends his book 2, after 153 pages of Ogilvie's text, at the end of

---

[1] The length of some of Dionysius' programmatic pronouncements on the writing of history means that readers of scholarship on him are usually offered summary, paraphrase, or a translation, but rarely his actual Greek. I am grateful to editors and publishers for allowing here a confrontation with Dionysius' actual words and to Dr C. C. de Jonge, Dr Y. Gershon, and Professor R. L. Hunter for improving an earlier version of this chapter.

[2] On p. 11 of each text I found that Jacoby had 186 words, Ogilvie 227.

468 BC; Dionysius has reached the end of 468 BC at *Ant. Rom.* 9.58.8, after 1,109 pages of Jacoby's text. Dionysius reaches the end of 449 BC, the year in which the decemvirate was overthrown and Ap. Claudius the decemvir was prosecuted at *Ant. Rom.* 11.50.2, after 1305 pages of Jacoby's text, Livy at 3.64.11, after 232 pages of Ogilvie's text. Since the rest of book 11 of the *Roman Antiquities* suffers from excerpting, and books 12–20 of the work survive only as excerpts or in epitome, it is difficult thereafter to conduct so precise a comparison, but, if only books 12–20 had survived, we should probably marvel less at their expansiveness, since the scale of Livy's narrative eventually surpasses that of Dionysius. Livy has reached 293 BC by the time that his text breaks off at the end of book 10, a point that Dionysius seems to have reached in book 17 or 18. And Dionysius reaches the eve of the First Punic War in 264 BC only two (or three) books and part of a book later. Livy takes a full five books (11–15) to get from 293 to 264 BC.

As these figures show, the two writers devoted particular attention to different epochs of earlier Roman history. Livy treated the regal and early Republican period briefly and with a sustained note of detached irony. His narrative becomes a little more expansive from book 3 onwards and much more expansive from book 6, after Rome recovers from its sack by the Gauls.[3] Dionysius seems to have been somewhat less interested in this later period of the conquest of Italy and much more interested in the regal period and early Republic. Two episodes in particular caught his attention: the decemvirate, which he describes in book 11, and, above all, the account of the First Secession of the Plebs and its aftermath which leads into the Coriolanus story, that is, the years 494–488 BC.[4] In Livy these seven years occupy 2.28.1–40.14, just over sixteen pages (pp. 108–24) of Ogilvie's text. In Dionysius they run from *Ant. Rom.* 6.34.1 to 8.63.4, that is, 315 pages of Jacoby's text. In other words, Dionysius' narrative is over fifteen times as long as Livy's.

Dionysius' Own Pronouncements on a Suitable Scale for the Writing of History[5]

Though many modern readers have found the length of the *Roman Antiquities* excessive, Dionysius himself thought hard about the sense of

---

[3] On the relative expansiveness of Livy in books 6–10, see, e.g., Oakley 1997–2005, vol. 1, 112.
[4] The fullest analysis of the Coriolanus episode is Noè 1979. For the decemvirate, see Hogg in this volume, p. 223.
[5] My comments in this section concentrate on analysis of material in Dionysius' theoretical treatises that is germane to my theme of expansiveness and detail; I have not attempted a full account of

proportion needed in a work of history. *On Thucydides* 13–17 gives an insight into his thinking on how much fullness was required in any episode. The section begins thus:[6]

> Ὅτι δὲ καὶ περὶ τὰς ἐξεργασίας τῶν κεφαλαίων ἧττον ἐπιμελής ἐστιν, ἢ πλείονας τοῦ δέοντος λόγους ἀποδιδοὺς τοῖς ἐλάττονων δεομένοις ἢ ῥᾳθυμότερον ἐπιτρέχων τὰ δεόμενα πλείονος ἐξεργασίας, πολλοῖς τεκμηρίοις βεβαιῶσαι δυνάμενος, ὀλίγοις χρήσομαι.
>
> Although able to confirm with many instances that in the elaboration of his subjects he was less than careful, either allowing more words than was necessary for matters that deserved fewer or lazily dashing over those that needed more elaboration, I shall use a small number. (*Thuc.* 13.1)

Dionysius begins his critique (*Thuc.* 13.2) with naval battles, finding fault with Thucydides for devoting less space at 1.100.1 to the famous victory of Cimon at Eurymedon than to the smaller and less significant battles of 429 BC recounted at 2.83–4. Then he turns to infantry battles, and notes (*Thuc.* 13.3–14.2) that Thucydides narrated the campaign at Pylos and Sphacteria in book 4 ἀκριβῶς καὶ δυνατῶς, πλείους ἢ τριακοσίους στίχους αὐτὸς ἀποδεδωκὼς ταῖς μάχαις 'with detail and power, allowing more than three hundred lines for these battles', even though in his own summary of the action he showed that the numbers involved were insignificant. Yet a little later Thucydides (4.54.2) narrates the campaign of Nicias at Cythera, in which greater forces were involved, ἐπιτροχάδην ('hastily') and the Athenian capture of Aeginetans in Thyrea equally briefly. Next (*Thuc.* 14.3–15.2) Dionysius discusses embassies, and criticises Thuc. 2.59.1–2, in which Thucydides states very briefly that the Athenians had sent an unsuccessful embassy to Sparta to sue for peace, for lacking both the names of the ambassadors and the speeches which offered the arguments of the Athenians and the Spartans, as though the episode were trivial. Yet when describing the embassy sent by Sparta to Athens to request the recovery of the men captured at Pylos, Thucydides records the speech of the Spartan envoy and the reasons (τὰς αἰτίας) for an agreement not having been reached. In Dionysius' view (*Thuc.* 15.1–2), if it was necessary to describe the later embassy fully (ἀκριβῶς), the earlier one should have been given the same treatment, and vice versa. He turns next to Thucydides' account of the capture of cities, some of which he found supremely compelling, others cursory and lacking in

---

Dionysius' views on how history should be written. On Dionysius' criticism of Thucydides, De Jonge 2017 provides a good recent introduction, with further bibliography.

[6] Translations are my own.

emotional power.[7] Comparing books 1 and 8 (*Thuc.* 16.1–4), he finds the absence of speeches from book 8, in which the events described were so momentous, and their abundance in book 1, in which the events were less weighty, worrying. Discussing the Mytilenean affair, he finds troubling Thucydides' omission of speeches from the first meeting at Athens but his inclusion of them for the second.[8] Dionysius then (*Thuc.* 18.1–7) finds fault in Thucydides' giving his only funeral oration to Pericles and not placing it in a year of more significant Athenian military action. The section closes with criticism of material in Thucydides' proem that Dionysius considered superfluous (*Thuc.* 19.1–21.1).

The weaknesses in Dionysius' judgements on Thucydides have often been pointed out (most obviously, in the section which we have analysed he takes no account of the requirements of *uariatio*),[9] but the attitudes summarised above do much to explain the full coverage found in the *Roman Antiquities*.

Programmatic Comment in the *Roman Antiquities*

In the main body of the *Roman Antiquities*, there are four important passages in which Dionysius comments on his own historical techniques. The first is his prologue (1.1–8), which contains the most extensive comments in the *Roman Antiquities* on the writing of history; what Dionysius says here may be taken to apply to the work as a whole. The other three (*Ant. Rom.* 5.56.1, 7.66.1–5, 11.1.1–6) defend and explain Dionysius' practice in episodes that he admitted that he had written expansively, but they too contain remarks that have a general application.[10]

Dionysius' argument in his preface may be paraphrased as follows. Historians should choose a subject which is 'outstanding' (μεγαλοπρεπεῖς) and important and has 'utility' (*Ant. Rom.* 1.1.2 ὠφέλειαν) for readers. There is no more 'outstanding' and 'useful' subject (1.2.1 μεγαλοπρεπῆ ... ὠφέλιμον) than Dionysius', since Rome's empire is the largest and most enduring ever known (1.2–3).[11] Her early history is a fitting subject because it has never

---

[7] The narratives of the captures of Plataea (Thuc. 3.52–68), Mytilene (Thuc. 3.27–50), and Melos (Thuc. 5.84–116) are singled out for praise, Thuc. 1.114.3, 2.27.1, and 5.32.1 for adverse criticism.
[8] See Thuc. 3.36–49.   [9] Many of Dionysius' arguments are evaluated in Pritchett 1975.
[10] Much of the material that I discuss here is discussed also by Verdin 1974, whose analysis concentrates on *Ant. Rom.* 11.1.1–6, and more generally by Noè 1979, 36–9 and Gabba 1991, 73–85. On the preface see also Schultze 2000, esp. 6–12; Hogg 2008, 13–67; on *Ant. Rom.* 11.1–6 see Halbfas 1910, 56–7; Hogg 2008, 163–5; Hogg in this volume, p. 226. For the rhetorical treatises as evidence for Dionysius' own practice, see also Sacks 1983, 74–6.
[11] Similar remarks may be found at *Ant. Rom.* 5.75.1.

The Expansive Scale of the Roman Antiquities

received satisfactory treatment, and hence Greeks are ignorant of the character of those who established Rome as a power (1.4–5). Dionysius will demonstrate in his first book that the Romans are Greeks (1.5.1); then from his second onwards he will write 'about the deeds which they performed immediately after the foundation and about their modes of life, from which their descendants arrived at so great an empire', 'leaving out so far as I am able nothing that is worthy of record (τῶν ἀξίων ἱστορίας)' (1.5.2). For 'no full and precise (ἀκριβής) history of these matters has been published in Greek but only summary (κεφαλαιώδεις) epitomes that are altogether short' (1.5.4). In arguing for the truth of this proposition, he states (1.6.1) that Hieronymus of Cardia, Timaeus, Antigonus, Polybius, and Silenus and others each recorded only a few matters which they had not 'fully and precisely' (ἀκριβῶς) researched. Fabius and Cincius Alimentus, Romans who wrote in Greek, did write fully and precisely (ἀκριβῶς) about their own times, but each 'ran through' (ἐπέδραμεν) events after the foundation only 'summarily' (κεφαλαιωδῶς) (1.6.2). From Dionysius' writing up 'fully and precisely' (1.6.3 ἀκριβῶς) a subject that has been neglected by earlier writers, those early Romans who deserve honour will be immortalised; current and future Romans will be inspired to emulate them; and Dionysius will repay his debt to Rome. Next, he explains his qualifications for the task, stating that he has been in Italy a long time, has learnt to read Latin, and has read a large number of Latin writers (1.7.1–4).[12] Finally, he outlines the scope of the work: it will range from myths about the earliest settlers in Italy down to the beginning of the First Punic War (1.8.1–2). What follows may be quoted in full:

> ἀφηγοῦμαι δὲ τούς τε ὀθνείους πολέμους τῆς πόλεως ἅπαντας, ὅσους ἐν ἐκείνοις τοῖς χρόνοις ἐπολέμησε, καὶ τὰς ἐμφυλίους στάσεις ὁπόσας ἐστασίασεν, ἐξ οἵων αἰτιῶν ἐγένοντο καὶ δι' οἵων τρόπων τε καὶ λόγων κατελύθησαν· πολιτειῶν τε ἰδέας διέξειμι πάσας ὅσαις ἐχρήσατο βασιλευομένη τε καὶ μετὰ τὴν κατάλυσιν τῶν μονάρχων, καὶ τίς ἦν αὐτῶν ἑκάστης ὁ κόσμος· ἔθη τε τὰ κράτιστα καὶ νόμους τοὺς ἐπιφανεστάτους διηγοῦμαι καὶ συλλήβδην ὅλον ἀποδείκνυμι τὸν ἀρχαῖον βίον τῆς πόλεως. (3) σχῆμα δὲ ἀποδίδωμι τῇ πραγματείᾳ οὔθ' ὁποῖον οἱ τοὺς πολέμους <μόνους> ἀναγράψαντες ἀποδεδώκασι ταῖς ἱστορίαις οὔθ' ὁποῖον οἱ τὰς πολιτείας αὐτὰς ἐφ' ἑαυτῶν διηγησάμενοι οὔτε ταῖς χρονικαῖς παραπλήσιον, ἃς ἐξέδωκαν οἱ τὰς Ἀτθίδας πραγματευσάμενοι· μονοειδεῖς γὰρ ἐκεῖναί τε καὶ ταχὺ προσιστάμεναι τοῖς ἀκούουσιν· ἀλλ' ἐξ ἁπάσης ἰδέας μικτὸν ἐναγωνίου τε καὶ θεωρητικῆς,[13] ἵνα καὶ τοῖς περὶ τοὺς

---

[12] On Dionysius' transcending of the Roman tradition of local history, see Marincola 1997, 245–6. For brief comment on this passage from another point of view, see below, p. 153.

[13] Since three classes of reader follow ἵνα καί, a third adjective is very likely to have been lost here: Stephanus, followed by Jacoby, supplemented to θεωρητικῆς καὶ ἡδείας, Cary 1937–50, 1.26 to

πολιτικοὺς διατρίβουσι λόγους καὶ τοῖς περὶ τὴν φιλόσοφον ἐσπουδακόσι θεωρίαν καὶ εἴ τισιν ἀοχλήτου δεήσει διαγωγῆς ἐν ἱστορικοῖς ἀναγνώσμασιν, ἀποχρώντως ἔχουσα φαίνηται.

I recount all the foreign wars that the city fought in those times and all the internal political conflicts when there was strife, showing from what causes they arose and through what methods and words they were resolved. I shall expound all the forms of constitution that the city used, both when ruled by kings and after the dismissal of those who ruled alone, and what were the arrangements of each of these. I expound the most important practices and the most striking laws and, in short, I put on display the whole life of old in the city. (3) I give a form to my enterprise not like that given by those who give a record of wars in their histories nor like those who expound constitutions on their own nor like the lists of dates which those who have worked on *Atthides* have published: these works are monotonous and swiftly become annoying to those who hear them. Its form is a mixture of every kind, both that found in political debate and theoretical, in order that it may appear satisfactory to those who are employed in political discussion and to those who are busy with philosophical theorizing and to any who want untroubled entertainment in their reading. (*Ant. Rom.* 1.8.2–3)

The next passage is attached to his narrative of 500 BC:

Ἄλλος μὲν οὖν ἄν τις ἀποχρῆν ὑπέλαβεν αὐτὸ τὸ κεφάλαιον εἰπεῖν, ὅτι συλλαβὼν τοὺς μετασχόντας τῶν ἀπορρήτων βουλευμάτων ἀπέκτεινεν, ὡς ὀλίγης τοῖς πράγμασι δηλώσεως δέον· ἐγὼ δὲ καὶ <u>τὸν τρόπον</u> τῆς συλλήψεως τῶν ἀνδρῶν ἱστορίας ἄξιον εἶναι νομίσας ἔκρινα μὴ παρελθεῖν, ἐνθυμούμενος ὅτι τοῖς ἀναγινώσκουσι τὰς ἱστορίας οὐχ ἱκανόν ἐστιν εἰς ὠφέλειαν τὸ τέλος αὐτὸ τῶν πραχθέντων ἀκοῦσαι, ἀπαιτεῖ δ' ἕκαστος καὶ τὰς <u>αἰτίας</u> ἱστορῆσαι τῶν γινομένων καὶ <u>τοὺς τρόπους</u> τῶν πράξεων καὶ <u>τὰς διανοίας τῶν πραξάντων</u> καὶ <u>τὰ παρὰ τοῦ δαιμονίου συγκυρήσαντα</u>, καὶ μηδενὸς ἀνήκοος γενέσθαι τῶν πεφυκότων τοῖς πράγμασι παρακολουθεῖν· τοῖς δὲ πολιτικοῖς καὶ πάνυ ἀναγκαίαν ὑπάρχουσαν ὁρῶν τὴν τούτων μάθησιν, ἵνα παραδείγμασιν ἔχοιεν πρὸς τὰ συμβαίνοντα χρῆσθαι.

Perhaps someone would have supposed that it suffices just to give a summary [of these events], namely that after rounding up those who had taken part in this clandestine conspiracy he executed them, as if there was little need of explanation for these facts. However, thinking the manner in which the men were gathered together to be worthy of history, I decided not to pass it over, reckoning that for those who read historical works it does not suffice for their edification if they learn just about the outcome of what happened but rather that each yearns to know the reasons behind events, the manner in which things were done, the motives of those of those who did

---

θεωρητικῆς καὶ διηγηματικῆς. Fromentin 1993, 183 argues that Dionysius' combination of oratorical and philosophical prose makes history 'le genre littéraire par excellence'.

them, and what events were caused by divine intervention – indeed to hear about all of the matters that arose as a consequence of these actions. And for those involved in politics I realize that knowledge of these matters is absolutely necessary in order that they may have prior examples to apply as circumstances arise (*Ant. Rom.* 5.56.1).

The other two passages are attached to the two episodes that have already been singled out: the First Secession of the Plebs and the tale of Coriolanus in its aftermath, and the fall of the decemvirate. That for the earlier story occurs after Coriolanus' conviction:

Ἡ μὲν δὴ πρώτη Ῥωμαίοις ἐμπεσοῦσα μετὰ τὴν ἐκβολὴν τῶν βασιλέων στάσις ἔσχε τοιαύτας αἰτίας καὶ εἰς τοῦτο κατέσκηψε τὸ τέλος· ἐμήκυνα δὲ τὸν ὑπὲρ αὐτῶν λόγον τοῦ μή τινα θαυμάσαι, πῶς ὑπέμειναν οἱ πατρίκιοι τηλικαύτης ἐξουσίας ποιῆσαι τὸν δῆμον κύριον, οὔτε σφαγῆς τῶν ἀρίστων ἀνδρῶν γενομένης οὔτε φυγῆς, οἷον ἐν ἄλλαις πολλαῖς ἐγένετο πόλεσι. ποθεῖ γὰρ ἕκαστος ἐπὶ τοῖς παραδόξοις ἀκούσμασι <u>τὴν αἰτίαν</u> μαθεῖν καὶ τὸ πιστὸν ἐν ταύτῃ τίθεται μόνῃ. (2) ἐλογιζόμην οὖν, ὅτι μοι πολλοῦ καὶ τοῦ παντὸς δεήσει πιστὸς εἶναι ὁ λόγος, εἰ τοσοῦτον ἔφην μόνον, ὅτι παρῆκαν οἱ πατρίκιοι τοῖς δημοτικοῖς τὴν ἑαυτῶν δυναστείαν, καὶ ἐξὸν αὐτοῖς ἐν ἀριστοκρατίᾳ πολιτεύεσθαι τὸν δῆμον ἐποίησαν τῶν μεγίστων κύριον, δι' ἃς δὲ συνεχωρήθη ταῦτ' <u>αἰτίας</u> παρέλιπον· διὰ τοῦτ' ἐπεξῆλθον ἁπάσας. (3) καὶ ἐπειδὴ οὐχ ὅπλοις ἀλλήλους βιασάμενοι καὶ προσαναγκάσαντες, ἀλλὰ λόγοις πείσαντες μεθήρμοσαν, παντὸς μάλιστ' ἀναγκαῖον ἡγησάμην εἶναι τοὺς λόγους αὐτῶν διεξελθεῖν, οἷς τότ' οἱ δυναστεύσαντες ἐν ἑκατέροις ἐχρήσαντο. θαυμάσαιμι δ' ἄν, εἴ τινες τὰς ἐν τοῖς πολέμοις πράξεις ἀκριβῶς οἴονται δεῖν ἀναγράφειν, καὶ περὶ μίαν ἔστιν ὅτε μάχην πολλοὺς ἀναλίσκουσι λόγους, τόπων τε φύσεις καὶ ὁπλισμῶν ἰδιότητας καὶ τάξεων τρόπους καὶ στρατηγῶν παρακλήσεις καὶ τἆλλα διεξιόντες ὅσα τῆς νίκης αἴτια τοῖς ἑτέροις ἐγένετο· πολιτικὰς δὲ κινήσεις καὶ στάσεις ἀναγράφοντες οὐκ οἴονται δεῖν ἀπαγγέλλειν τοὺς λόγους, δι' ὧν αἱ παράδοξοι καὶ θαυμασταὶ πράξεις ἐπετελέσθησαν. (4) εἰ γάρ τι καὶ ἄλλο τῆς Ῥωμαίων πόλεως μέγα ἐγκώμιόν ἐστι καὶ ζηλοῦσθαι ὑπὸ πάντων ἀνθρώπων ἄξιον κἀκεῖνο ἐγένετο κατ' ἐμὴν δόξαν τὸ ἔργον, μᾶλλον δ' ὑπὲρ ἅπαντα πολλὰ καὶ θαυμαστὰ ὄντα λαμπρότατον, τὸ μήτε τοὺς δημοτικοὺς καταφρονήσαντας τῶν πατρικίων ἐπιχειρῆσαι αὐτοῖς, καὶ πολὺν ἐργασαμένους τῶν κρατίστων φόνον ἅπαντα τἀκείνων παραλαβεῖν, μήτε τοὺς ἐν τοῖς ἀξιώμασιν ἢ διὰ σφῶν αὐτῶν ἢ ξενικαῖς ἐπικουρίαις χρησαμένους διαφθεῖραι τὸ δημοτικὸν ἅπαν καὶ τὸ λοιπὸν οἰκεῖν ἀδεῶς τὴν πόλιν· (5) ἀλλ' ὥσπερ ἀδελφοὺς ἀδελφοῖς ἢ παῖδας γονεῦσιν ἐν οἰκίᾳ σώφρονι περὶ τῶν ἴσων <καὶ> δικαίων διαλεγομένους πειθοῖ καὶ λόγῳ διαλύεσθαι τὰ νείκη, ἀνήκεστον δ' ἢ ἀνόσιον ἔργον μηθὲν ὑπομεῖναι δρᾶσαι κατ' ἀλλήλων· οἷα Κερκυραῖοί τε κατὰ τὴν στάσιν εἰργάσαντο καὶ Ἀργεῖοι καὶ Μιλήσιοι καὶ Σικελία πᾶσα καὶ συχναὶ ἄλλαι πόλεις. ἐγὼ μὲν οὖν διὰ ταῦτα προειλόμην ἀκριβεστέραν μᾶλλον ἢ βραχυτέραν ποιήσασθαι τὴν διήγησιν· κρινέτω δ' ἕκαστος ὡς βούλεται.

The first civil strife that enveloped the Romans after the expulsion of the kings had such causes and proceeded to this end. I have extended my account of these matters lest anyone should wonder how the patricians could bear to make the populace master of such a power when there had been neither the slaughter nor the exile of aristocrats that took place in many cities. For everyone who hears remarkable things yearns to learn their cause and in this alone places his trust. (2) Therefore, since I considered that my account would entirely lack any credibility if I said merely so much (namely that the patricians handed over their own power to the populace and that, although they could have continued to run the state as an aristocracy, they made the people master of the most important matters) and left on one side the reasons through which this settlement was agreed, I have accordingly gone through all these reasons. (3) Moreover, since the two sides did not subdue and constrain each other with arms but rather made changes after persuading each other with speeches, I considered it to be especially necessary to expound the words used by those who wielded power on each side. I should regard it as remarkable if some thought it necessary to describe the affairs of war in detail (ἀκριβῶς) and to spend many words on one (say) battle, going through the appearance of the terrain and the specific character of the armaments and the nature of the tactics and the exhortations of the generals and other such things but, when describing political upheavals and conflicts, they do not think it necessary to spread abroad the words through which the extraordinary and noteworthy events [in them] were brought to pass. (4) For if anything else about the Roman state is greatly to be praised and worthy of emulation by all mankind, it is, in my opinion, this achievement, which even beyond all the many remarkable achievements of Rome is resplendent, namely that the members of the popular party, though despising the patricians, did not lay hands on them nor seized all their possessions carrying out a massive slaughter of the most powerful; and those in positions of power did not destroy all the popular party either by means of their own resources or using foreign aid and then govern the city in the future without fear. (5) Rather, discussing what was fair and just like brothers with brothers or children with parents, they ended their disputes by persuasive argument and they did not bring themselves to carry out any incurable or evil deed against each other – the kind of things that the Corcyraeans carried out in their civil dispute and the Argives, Milesians, all Sicily, and many other city-states. For these reasons I have preferred to write an exposition that is more detailed than brief. Let each offer the verdict that he thinks fit. (*Ant. Rom.* 7.66.1–5).

The final passage is the opening of book 11, where Dionysius offers a long account of his rationale for describing the crisis of the decemvirate. Coming exactly halfway through the work, this passage comes with all the programmatic force of a second preface:[14]

Ἐπὶ δὲ τῆς ὀγδοηκοστῆς καὶ τρίτης Ὀλυμπιάδος, ἣν ἐνίκα <στάδιον> Κρίσων Ἱμεραῖος, ἄρχοντος Ἀθήνησι Φιλίσκου καταλύουσι Ῥωμαῖοι τὴν τῶν δέκα ἀρχὴν ἔτη τρία τῶν κοινῶν ἐπιμεληθεῖσαν. ὃν δὲ τρόπον ἐπεχείρησαν ἐρριζωμένην ἤδη τὴν δυναστείαν ἐξελεῖν, καὶ τίνων ἀνδρῶν ἡγησαμένων τῆς ἐλευθερίας, καὶ διὰ ποίας αἰτίας καὶ προφάσεις, ἐξ ἀρχῆς ἀναλαβὼν πειράσομαι διελθεῖν ἀναγκαίας ὑπολαμβάνων εἶναι καὶ καλὰς τὰς τοιαύτας μαθήσεις ἅπασι μὲν ὡς εἰπεῖν ἀνθρώποις, μάλιστα δ' ὅσοι περὶ τὴν φιλόσοφον θεωρίαν καὶ περὶ τὰς πολιτικὰς διατρίβουσι πράξεις. (2) τοῖς τε γὰρ πολλοῖς οὐκ ἀπαρκεῖ τοῦτο μόνον ἐκ τῆς ἱστορίας παραλαβεῖν, ὅτι τὸν Περσικὸν πόλεμον – ἵν' ἐπὶ τούτου ποιήσωμαι τὸν λόγον – ἐνίκησαν Ἀθηναῖοί τε καὶ Λακεδαιμόνιοι δυσὶ ναυμαχίαις καὶ πεζομαχίᾳ μιᾷ καταγωνισάμενοι τὸν βάρβαρον τριακοσίας ἄγοντα μυριάδας αὐτοὶ σὺν τοῖς συμμάχοις οὐ πλείους ὄντες ἕνδεκα μυριάδων, ἀλλὰ καὶ τοὺς τόπους, ἐν οἷς αἱ πράξεις ἐγένοντο, βούλονται παρὰ τῆς ἱστορίας μαθεῖν, καὶ τὰς αἰτίας ἀκοῦσαι, δι' ἃς τὰ θαυμαστὰ καὶ παράδοξα ἔργα ἐπετέλεσαν, καὶ τίνες ἦσαν οἱ τῶν στρατοπέδων ἡγεμόνες τῶν τε βαρβαρικῶν καὶ τῶν Ἑλληνικῶν ἱστορῆσαι, καὶ μηδενὸς ὡς εἰπεῖν ἀνήκοοι γενέσθαι τῶν συντελεσθέντων περὶ τοὺς ἀγῶνας. (3) ἥδεται γὰρ ἡ διάνοια παντὸς ἀνθρώπου χειραγωγουμένη διὰ τῶν λόγων ἐπὶ τὰ ἔργα καὶ μὴ μόνον ἀκούουσα τῶν λεγομένων, ἀλλὰ καὶ τὰ πραττόμενα ὁρῶσα. οὐδέ γ' ὅταν πολιτικὰς ἀκούσωσι πράξεις, ἀρκοῦνται τὸ κεφάλαιον αὐτὸ καὶ τὸ πέρας τῶν πραγμάτων μαθόντες, ὅτι συνεχώρησαν Ἀθηναῖοι Λακεδαιμονίοις τείχη τε καθελεῖν τῆς πόλεως αὐτῶν καὶ ναῦς διατεμεῖν καὶ φρουρὰν εἰς τὴν ἀκρόπολιν εἰσαγαγεῖν καὶ ἀντὶ τῆς πατρίου δημοκρατίας ὀλιγαρχίαν τῶν κοινῶν ἀποδεῖξαι κυρίαν οὐδὲ πρὸς αὐτοὺς ἀγῶνα ἀράμενοι, ἀλλ' εὐθὺς ἀξιοῦσι καὶ τίνες ἦσαν αἱ κατασχοῦσαι τὴν πόλιν ἀνάγκαι, δι' ἃς ταῦτα τὰ δεινὰ καὶ σχέτλια ὑπέμεινε, καὶ τίνες οἱ πείσαντες αὐτοὺς λόγοι καὶ ὑπὸ τίνων ῥηθέντες ἀνδρῶν καὶ πάντα, ὅσα παρακολουθεῖ τοῖς πράγμασι, διδαχθῆναι. (4) τοῖς δὲ πολιτικοῖς ἀνδράσιν, ἐν οἷς ἔγωγε τίθεμαι καὶ τοὺς φιλοσόφους, ὅσοι μὴ λόγων, ἀλλ' ἔργων καλῶν ἄσκησιν ἡγοῦνται τὴν φιλοσοφίαν, τὸ μὲν ἥδεσθαι τῇ παντελεῖ θεωρίᾳ τῶν παρακολουθούντων τοῖς πράγμασι κοινὸν ὥσπερ καὶ τοῖς ἄλλοις ἀνθρώποις ὑπάρχει· χωρὶς δὲ τῆς ἡδονῆς περιγίνεται τὸ περὶ τοὺς ἀναγκαίους καιροὺς μεγάλα τὰς πόλεις ἐκ τῆς τοιαύτης ἐμπειρίας ὠφελεῖν, καὶ ἄγειν αὐτὰς ἑκούσας ἐπὶ τὰ συμφέροντα διὰ τοῦ λόγου. (5) ῥᾷστα γὰρ οἱ ἄνθρωποι τά τε ὠφελοῦντα καὶ βλάπτοντα καταμανθάνουσιν, ὅταν ἐπὶ παραδειγμάτων ταῦτα πολλῶν ὁρῶσι, καὶ τοῖς ἐπὶ ταῦτα παρακαλοῦσιν αὐτοὺς φρόνησιν μαρτυροῦσι καὶ πολλὴν

---

[14] On this passage, see also Hogg in this volume.

σοφίαν. διὰ ταύτας δή μοι τὰς αἰτίας ἔδοξεν ἅπαντα ἀκριβῶς διελθεῖν τὰ γενόμενα περὶ τὴν κατάλυσιν τῆς ὀλιγαρχίας, ὅσα δὴ καὶ λόγου τυχεῖν ἄξια ἡγοῦμαι.

In the eighty-third Olympiad, in which Criso of Himera was victorious on the race-course and Philiscus was archon in Athens, the Romans abolished the decemvirate, which for three years had been entrusted with the government of their affairs. Taking up the tale from the beginning, I shall attempt to expound both how they attempted to remove a powerful clique that had put down roots, and the arguments and pretexts that they used. I regard knowledge of matters such as these to be necessary and edifying for all (if I may say so) men, but particularly those who concern themselves with philosophical contemplation and the practical conduct of a state's affairs. (2) For it is inadequate for many men to take just this from a history that in the Persian War (if I may take this as an example) the Athenians and the Spartans were victorious in two sea-battles and one infantry-battle, fighting against a foreign foe at the head of three million men when they themselves with their allies numbered no more than 110,000. Rather, they wish also to learn from a history the places in which the events happened, and to hear the reasons for which these remarkable and unexpected deeds were accomplished, and to ask who were the leaders of foreign and Greek forces and to be ignorant of none whatsoever of the events accomplished in these struggles. (3) For every person's mind delights in being led through words to deeds, and not only in hearing what was said but in visualizing what happened. Nor, when they learn about politics, is it enough for them to hear a summary version or the outcome of events, for instance that the Athenians agreed with the Spartans, without making a struggle against them, to take down the walls of their own city and to cut through their ships and to let a garrison into their citadel and to accept an oligarchy at the head of their affairs rather than their ancestral democracy; rather, they think it proper to be instructed as to what were the exigencies holding the city in their grip on account of which it submitted to these terrible and baneful conditions, what were the arguments that persuaded them and by what men they were spoken, and everything that has a bearing on these events. (4) For men concerned with government (amongst whom I include even philosophers, at least those who regard philosophy to be the practice not of fine words but of fine deeds) share with other men the taking of pleasure from an all-embracing contemplation of the circumstances that accompanied action. However, in addition to this pleasure, they have an advantage: this training allows them in difficult times greatly to assist their states and to lead them willingly by argument to a suitable course of action. (5) Men learn most easily what profits and harms them when they see these things depicted in many examples and they bear witness to the intelligence and great wisdom of those who summon them to these examples. For these reasons I decided to expound in detail (ἀκριβῶς) everything that happened at the time of the abolition of the decemvirate, at least what I regarded as worthy of record. (*Ant. Rom.* 11.1.1–5)

Dionysius' main concern in the prologue is to defend the importance and worthiness of early Roman history as a subject and to show that he is qualified to write about it. Implicit throughout is the notion that an important subject needs to be explained clearly and that such an explanation needs fullness; hence his contrasting his own work with those that are summary (*Ant. Rom.* 1.5.4, 6.2). In the three later passages Dionysius reveals that he is perfectly aware that the narratives to which they are attached are long (*Ant. Rom.* 5.56.1; 7.66.1, 3, 5; 11.1.5), and he provides justification for this length. His fundamental argument is very similar to that found in the prologue: events which are extraordinary and noteworthy (*Ant. Rom.* 7.66.1, 3–4; 11.1.2),[15] and hence deserving of a place in a work of history (5.56.1),[16] should be treated in appropriate detail.[17]

In the passage quoted above in full from the prologue, Dionysius states that he intends to record the entire (ὅλον, 1.8.2) life of the city, dealing with both war and politics, in contrast to writers who deal with only one or the other. This comprehensiveness in both spheres is emphasised in 1.8.2–3 by the adjectives ἅπαντας, πάσας, and ἁπάσης.[18] The contrast between warfare and politics returns in the last two passages, in which elaborate accounts of warfare are set against elaborate accounts of political events (7.66.3, 11.1.2–3), and in our fourth passage Dionysius says that he finds it surprising that some historians did not think that political events should be recorded in this way. Dionysius nowhere reveals any dislike of military narrative, of which there was much in the *Roman Antiquities*, but politics were particularly important for his own work, since the development of the Roman Republican constitution, of which he so much approved, is perhaps its dominant theme and more important

---

[15] For the importance of including what was θαυμαστόν and παράδοξον, see *Pomp.* 6.4. In the *Ant. Rom.* Dionysius is in fact relatively restrained in his reporting of the marvellous, coupling these words or their cognates to describe events or people at *Ant. Rom.* 3.13.3, 21.1, 22.10, 47.4; 4.2.3; 5.8.6; 6.13.4. On 3.22.10 see Oakley 2010, 119.

[16] For the idea of an event's being not ἱστορίας ἄξιον, cf. *Ant. Rom.* 6.1.1, 10.53.8, 11.62.4, where the expression seems to mean little more than 'nothing of note'; it is used in a stronger sense at 6.83.2. See further Oakley 1997–2005, vol. 2, 138–9.

[17] The comprehensiveness of the expected detail is brought out by the use of the adjective ἀνήκοος at *Ant. Rom.* 5.56.1 and 11.1.2.

[18] That Dionysius' notion of a comprehensive history derives from Theopompus (thus Gabba 1991, 73–9) may be right, but it should be remembered that (1) we know very little about Theopompus, and (2) the view that Dionysius especially admired him rests largely on *Pomp.* 6.1–11.

than the many wars that he describes. He certainly devotes more space to politics than, for example, Herodotus, Thucydides, or Polybius.[19] In our third passage he states at 7.66.4–5 that the most remarkable aspect of Roman politics is the manner in which the Romans settled their differences by discussion rather than by killing their opponents (as in so many instances of στάσις in Greek cities).

Thucydides' penetrating discussion of the causes of the Peloponnesian War set a standard for later historians, who felt obliged to explain why things happened as they did.[20] Causes are mentioned in the prologue at *Ant. Rom.* 1.8.2 (αἰτιῶν),[21] and in the other passages we are told that detail is needed is to give the αἰτίαι for events (5.56.1, 7.66.1–2, 11.1.1), especially those that are extraordinary and surprising, so that they appear credible (7.66.1–2). The detail should explain how events happened as they did: note the use of τρόπος at 1.8.2, 5.56.1, and 11.1.1.[22] This point is brought out further in three bald summaries of events that show just how uninformative such summary narratives of this kind are: at *Ant. Rom.* 7.66.2, of the establishment of the tribunate of the plebs; at 11.1.2, of the Persian war against Xerxes;[23] and at 11.1.3, of the settlement imposed by Sparta on Athens at the end of the Peloponnesian War. The theme had been hinted at already in 1.8.3, where Dionysius had referred to the tediousness of chronographies.[24]

Like so many other ancient historians, Dionysius emphasises the didactic role of his work.[25] The ὠφέλεια ('utility' or 'profitability') of his subject

---

[19] Compare the remarks of Delcourt 2005, 65.
[20] At *Pomp.* 6.7 Dionysius praises Theopompus for his skill in revealing αἰτίαι.
[21] The context is quoted fully above.
[22] The word should not be dismissed as never more than the equivalent of such generally colourless terms as Latin *quo modo* or English 'how'. We shall see how the use of the word in the programmatic passage at *Ant. Rom.* 5.56.1 is picked up throughout Dionysius' narrative of 500 BC. It appears in another programmatic context at *Ant. Rom.* 3.18.1, in the context of the triple combat of the Horatii and Curiatii. Other passages in which Dionysius uses it of events that he has described at some length include *Ant. Rom.* 2.7.1, 34.1; 3.65.1; 4.12.3, 63.3 (a good example); 5.75.1; 6.92.6; 8.17.6; 9.35.1. At 10.47.3 Siccius Dentatus is said to have described the τρόπος of a battle: that one of Dionysius' characters should share an interest with the narrator is unsurprising.
[23] Hogg 2008, 163–4 shows that *Ant. Rom.* 11.1.2 δυσὶ ναυμαχίαις καὶ πεζομαχίᾳ μιᾷ recalls Thuc. 1.23.1 δυοῖν ναυμαχίαιν καὶ πεζομαχίαιν (on these same events). See also Hogg in this volume, p. 227. The effect of this is to place Roman history on the same level as that of Greek history and for Dionysius to challenge Thucydides (I am less certain than Hogg that Dionysius does not wish to disparage Thucydides).
[24] In these passages Dionysius' thought may be compared with the traditional contrast of bald annalistic narrative with fully fledged *historia*. See, e.g., Asellio F1 and 2 Cornell (and Peter) = Gell. 5.18.7–9; Cic. *Fam.* 5.12.5, *De or.* 2.51–4.
[25] On didacticism in historiography, reflection on which goes back to Thuc. 1.22.4, there is a vast bibliography. For a basic gathering of material, see, e.g., Scheller 1911, 73–8; Avenarius 1956, 22–6;

is emphasised from the outset (*Ant. Rom.* 1.1.2 ὠφέλειαν, 1.2.1 ὠφέλιμον), and this word or its cognates recur in two of the later passages (5.56.1, 11.1.4).²⁶ Dionysius' work, he says, will be especially useful for those engaged in politics, whether in the practice of it or in theorising about it. Such men are mentioned at the end of the preface (8.3) and then in two of the later passages: at 5.56.1 and 11.1.5 he refers to the provision of παραδείγματα ('examples') for them;²⁷ at 11.1.1 and 4 (passages particularly germane to our theme) to their need for a fully detailed account of the overthrow of the decemvirate.²⁸

In the prologue Dionysius promises to recount the words that were used in the resolution of political conflict (*Ant. Rom.* 1.8.2), and ἐναγωνίου ('found in political debate') at 1.8.3 prepares us for the numerous symbouleutic speeches in the *Ant. Rom.*²⁹ The importance of speech becomes particularly clear at 7.66.4–5, where Dionysius points out that an extraordinary aspect of Roman history is the resolution of political conflict by speech rather than violence, and at 11.1.4, where he suggests that lessons learnt from the discussions of the Romans of old may be put to use by the politicians of his own day.³⁰

At the end of the prologue Dionysius states (1.8.3) that a subsidiary reason for the inclusion of both war and politics is to prevent the annoyance that comes from the monotonous (μονοειδεῖς) format of less comprehensive works.³¹ This hint at the pleasure that can be given by reading works of history is developed more fully in the final passage,³² where he notes the pleasure that can be given by a lengthy narrative (*Ant. Rom.* 11.1.3

Fornara 1983, 104–20. For Dionysius, see, e.g., Verdin 1974, 299–300; Schultze 1986, 137–8; Gabba 1991, 78–85.

²⁶ At *Pomp.* 6.4 Theopompus is praised for this quality. See further Verdin 1974, 296–7.
²⁷ On παραδείγματα see also Dionysius' remarks at *Ant. Rom.* 5.75.1. The use of παραδείγματα made by his characters in speeches is discussed by Schultze 2012, 126–37.
²⁸ See also *Ant. Rom.* 5.75.1; *Pomp.* 6.5; and (for discussion) Verdin 1974, 297–8; Wiater 2011, 204 n. 525.
²⁹ For the interpretation of this adjective, see Sacks 1986, 389–90; Ooms and De Jonge 2013; Yunis in this volume, p. 102.
³⁰ See also Verdin 1974, 300.
³¹ Dionysius is alert elsewhere to the importance of variety; see, e.g., *Pomp.* 3.11–12 (where Herodotus' practice is contrasted with Thucydides', to the latter's disadvantage); *Pomp.* 6.3–4 (where the πολύμορφον ['many-faceted'; the opposite of μονοειδές] quality of Theopompus' history is praised). However, he was well aware that digressions could be seen as indulgent: he defends his own practice (*Ant. Rom.* 7.70.1) and criticises some of those in Theopompus (*Pomp.* 6.11). See Schultze 1986, 137 with further bibliography.
³² It would be more than a hint if at *Ant. Rom.* 1.8.3 Stephanus' supplement θεωρητικῆς <καὶ ἡδείας> is right; but though attractive it is not necessary. For other conjectures see above, p. 131 n.13.

ἥδεται, 4 ἥδεσθαι, ἡδονῆς). Therefore, the desire to give pleasure becomes yet another stimulus to an expansive style of writing.[33]

In the second half of the final passage, the language of sight is pervasive (*Ant. Rom.* 11.1.3 ὁρῶσα, 4 θεωρίᾳ, 5 ὁρῶσι), and Dionysius seems to be implying that a detailed narrative encourages vividness, what the ancients called ἐνάργεια.[34] In the *Letter to Pompeius* he uses similar language in describing one of the virtues of Theopompus:

> τὸ καθ' ἑκάστην πρᾶξιν μὴ μόνον τὰ φανερὰ τοῖς πολλοῖς ὁρᾶν καὶ λέγειν, ἀλλ' ἐξετάζειν καὶ τὰς ἀφανεῖς αἰτίας τῶν πράξεων καὶ τῶν πραξάντων αὐτὰς καὶ τὰ πάθη τῆς ψυχῆς, ἃ μὴ ῥᾴδια τοῖς πολλοῖς εἰδέναι, καὶ πάντα ἐκκαλύπτειν τὰ μυστήρια τῆς τε δοκούσης ἀρετῆς καὶ τῆς ἀγνοουμένης κακίας.

The ability not only to visualize and describe with regard to each event what is clear to everyone but also to scrutinize obscure explanations of both events and the actions of those who brought them to pass and the passions of the soul, which are not generally easy to grasp, and to unveil all the secrets of apparent virtue and unrecognized vice. (*Pomp.* 6.7)

Since Dionysius himself does not give much weight to this idea in his second preface, and since he never uses ἐνάργεια in the *Roman Antiquities* (and uses the cognate ἐναργής only twice in unremarkable contexts),[35] discussion need only be brief,[36] but it is obvious that expansive use of details can make a narrative more vivid, and this was recognised by other ancient theorists.[37]

---

[33] How far a work of historiography should give pleasure as well as be useful had been made a subject for debate perhaps for the first time at Thuc. 1.22.4, where Thucydides admits that the absence of τὸ μυθῶδες ('the romantic') from his reporting may make it ἀτερπέστερον ('less pleasurable'). In the following sentence he uses the word ὠφέλιμα ('useful') of his work. Many ancient historians touch on the topic, and Lucian devotes par. 9–13 of *Hist. conscr.* to it. Among modern discussions see, e.g., Avenarius 1956, 26–9; Fornara 1983, 120–34; Schultze 1986, 136–7; Wiater 2011, 162–4. Discussion of the roles of utility and pleasure in historiography was part of a wider discussion of their roles in ancient literature as a whole; among many texts see, most famously, Hor. *Ars P.* 333–4 *aut prodesse uolunt aut delectare poetae | aut simul et iucunda et idonea dicere uitae*, 'poets wish either to be useful or to give pleasure or at the same time to say things that are pleasing and helpful for living'. See also Hunter in this volume, pp. 40–1.

[34] This virtue of style is defined by Dionysius in *Lys.* 7.1. Cf. Viidebaum in this volume, p. 109.

[35] See *Ant. Rom.* 1.25.3, 2.60.5.

[36] On ἐνάργεια in the historians, see, e.g., Scheller 1911, 57–61; Avenarius 1956, 133–40; Verdin 1974, 303–4.

[37] See Demetr. *Eloc.* 209: γίνεται δ' ἡ ἐνάργεια πρῶτα μὲν ἐξ ἀκριβολογίας καὶ τοῦ παραλείπειν μηδὲν μηδ' ἐκτέμνειν, οἷον ὡς δ' ὅτ' ἀνὴρ ὀχετηγὸς καὶ πᾶσα αὕτη ἡ παραβολή· τὸ γὰρ ἐναργὲς ἔχει ἐκ τοῦ πάντα εἰρῆσθαι τὰ συμβαίνοντα, καὶ μὴ παραλελεῖφθαι μηδέν 'Vividness comes first from precision in the use of language and from cutting nothing out. For example, "As when a conduit-maker" [Hom. *Il.* 21.257] and all the following simile; it has a vivid quality from all the circumstances being described and nothing being left out.'

Ἀκρίβεια[38]

Ἀκρίβεια and its cognates occur regularly in the passages that have been discussed above (see *Thuc.* 13.3, 15.1; *Ant. Rom.* 1.5.4, 6.1, 2, 3; 7.66.3, 5; 11.1.5). Their implications of both fullness and precision are not easily matched by any one English word – hence my translation of ἀκριβῶς as 'fully and precisely'. Dionysius' understanding of the term will have been shaped by both his rhetorical and critical and his historical studies.

Like some other terms deployed in Greek literary criticism, ἀκρίβεια could be referred to either style or content, and Dionysius uses it of both in his discussion of the characteristics of Attic orators. By suggesting that an orator uses language 'precisely', he seems to imply not just that the orator wrote refined Attic but that he handled with precision the detail so important in forensic oratory.[39]

Thucydides' proclamation of his quest for ἀκρίβεια in a famous programmatic passage (1.22.1–2) ensured that it became a cardinal virtue for a Greek historian, about possession of which he had to boast, Xenophon alone being secure enough in his abilities not to proclaim allegiance to it.[40] Fantasia has detected two main strands in Greek historians' use of the concept. The first refers to the precision that comes from autopsy and personal involvement: Dionysius uses it regularly of precision and certainty in historical writing, both in the context of chronology (*Ant. Rom.* 1.74.4, 7.1.4)[41] and more generally (*Ant. Rom.* 1.29.2, where he admits that it can be difficult to achieve; see also 1.30.3, 31.4; 2.2.3, 48.2; 5.48.3; 10.57.5; 12.10.2).[42] The second refers to a narrative that is precise because it is

---

[38] Fantasia 2004, which includes extensive bibliography and citation of key ancient texts, supersedes previous synoptic treatments; Kurz 1970 discusses the development of the concept down to Aristotle; for the *Ant. Rom.* Schultze 1986, 126–7 is succinct and pertinent. Some of what they say is reworked in this paragraph. See also Geigenmueller 1908, 14–15 (for the rhetorical treatises); Verdin 1974, 301; also Hunter 2003, 216–19 = 2008, 1.437–40 on ἀκρίβεια's associations with the written word as opposed to orality (and also to grandeur).

[39] For full lists of Dionysius' use of the term in his critical works, see Geigenmueller 1908, 14–15; Aujac 1992, 190. Some examples: τὸ ἀκριβές and its cognates are coupled regularly with τὸ καθαρόν and its cognates: see *Dem.* 4.1 (of Lysias and Isocrates: see Viidebaum in this volume), 11.1 (of Lysias), 13.1 (of Lysias and Demosthenes), 18.1 (of Isocrates). In such passages τὸ καθαρόν seems to refer to purity in dialect and style, τὸ ἀκριβές to precision in argument. Dionysius couples it also with τὸ ἰσχνόν ('leanness') at *Dem.* 6.3–4 = *Pomp.* 2 (twice of Plato) and *Dem.* 11.1 (of Lysias and Demosthenes), as well as with τὸ σαφές ('clarity') at *Dem.* 13.1 (of Lysias) – for the association of these two terms, see also *Ant. Rom.* 1.30.3.

[40] Xenophon never uses ἀκρίβεια or its cognates in this sense.

[41] So first Thucydides (1.97.2, 5.20.1–3).

[42] That for Dionysius ἀκρίβεια could denote certainty is shown by some passages in speeches in which his characters use the term; note esp. *Ant. Rom.* 4.47.6 (contrasted with conjecture), 4.81.4 (as previous example), 10.10.1 (contrasted with rumours).

detailed.[43] This is the sense in which we have met the term in all but one of the passages cited at the head of this section,[44] and at *Ant. Rom.* 3.18.1 he refers to the term twice at the start of his very expansive version of the triple combat of the Horatii and the Curiatii and its aftermath.[45] Note also *Ant. Rom.* 1.23.1, where he tells us that there would be much to say about the Pelasgi, should he wish 'to write in detail' (τὴν ἀκρίβειαν γράφειν).[46]

That the same term could be used by Dionysius both alongside τὸ ἰσχνόν ('leanness') to denote Lysias' style and to describe expansively detailed historiography may seem surprising: the link is the precise handling of detail, required in oratory to make a case plain and in historiography to provide a properly elaborate narrative.

A Summary of Dionysius' Views on Fullness of Narrative

Dionysius' main contentions may be summarised as follows: (1) there should be a consistency of treatment (this appears more in *Thuc.* than in the programmatic passages of the *Ant. Rom.*); (2) episodes of consequence should be written up at a length that reflects this consequence; and (3) in episodes in which speeches played an important part, the arguments found in those speeches should be fully reported.

By and large, Dionysius does manage to put most of his precepts into practice in the *Roman Antiquities*. There is in general a consistency of treatment, in which most events, both political and military, are written up fully. This is not to say that he always wrote as fully as he might have done. In some passages he himself states that his account is summary, for example, on the laws of Romulus,[47] on Numa's religious

---

[43] From many passages cited by Fantasia 2004 for the latter notion, adumbrated in Thucydides (1.97.2, 6.54.1), see, e.g., Polyb. 2.40.4–5, 3.87.9, 9.20.4. An interesting passage from a late historian is Euseb. *Hist. eccl.* 2.5.6, where Eusebius says that in his *Embassy* Philo wrote ἀκριβῶς about the events in which he was involved, but that he proposes to omit much of the detail (Rufinus here translates ἀκριβῶς as *singillatim*, for which usage in an historian cf. Sall. *Iug.* 42.5). From outside historical narrative, see Aeschin. 2.118; Dio 50.18.2, 56.44.2 (neither referring to Dio's own narrative); Julian. *Ep.* 98.80; Porph. *Vit. Pyth.* 37.7. Further examples of this usage are cited by Kurz 1970, 158. Lucian *Hist. conscr.* 19–20 pokes fun at mindless ἀκρίβεια.

[44] *Ant. Rom.* 1.6.1 is the exception. This emphasis on fullness and detail is particularly clear in those passages in which the term is contrasted with κεφαλαιωδῶς ('summarily') or its cognates; see *Ant. Rom.* 1.5.4, 6.2; 11.1.3–5. At 5.56.1 the term τὸ κεφάλαιον is used of a summary narrative that is contrasted with a fuller one, but ἀκρίβεια is not mentioned.

[45] For the role of ἀκρίβεια in shaping his narrative of this tale, see Oakley 2010, 120–6.

[46] Perhaps also *Ant. Rom.* 2.61.3, where we are told that 'arguing' (ἀκριβολογεῖσθαι) about divine myths would need many words.

[47] *Ant. Rom.* 2.27.5 (including ἐπὶ κεφαλαίων); also 2.24.1.

institutions,[48] and on Larcius' handling of the first dictatorship.[49] On the Twelve Tables he states that it was proper neither entirely to pass them by (especially when they were so different from Greek legislation) nor to give too extended an account of them.[50] Such comments are perhaps intended to convey a sense of proportion and discrimination.[51] Episodes of consequence are written up at greater length than less important episodes. These include not only those already singled out (the establishment of the tribunate of the plebs and the tale of Coriolanus and the ending of the decemvirate), but also, e.g., the expulsion of the Tarquins in 510 BC (4.63.1–85.4) and the instituting of the dictatorship in 498 BC (5.59.1–77.6). He includes, as has already been observed, a large number of speeches, and, appropriately, these tend to cluster in the more important episodes. Especially in such episodes, readers are able not only to evaluate the arguments of individual speakers, but to see how they respond to earlier arguments and how they in turn generate further debate. Again, he sometimes remarks that he is giving only the gist of a speech,[52] and again such remarks may be intended to draw attention to his awareness of the need for proportion.

Perhaps more than any other passage, *Ant. Rom.* 1.8.2–3 from the end of the preface (quoted above) takes one to the heart of what the *Ant. Rom.* is about. Dionysius has created a vast tableau on which he has seized the chance to describe the development of what we should call an archaic πόλις.[53] We see the dangers that beset such a state from the outside. We see the development of its constitution from the inside, from monarchy to aristocracy to the mixed constitution that Dionysius and others so admired. We see at work the exemplars of the different political types that were to be found in archaic πόλεις: the benevolent king, the good tyrant, the bad tyrant, the die-hard oligarchs and aristocrats, the subversive democratic revolutionaries whose words cannot be trusted, and the type that Dionysius admired most, the moderate aristocrats. Such men argued their cases, and Dionysius' speeches let us hear them argue. The verisimilitude goes further: some of these speeches are very long and must almost have matched the length of interventions in real-life assemblies. In short, the *Roman Antiquities* is a fascinating study of political

---

[48] *Ant. Rom.* 2.63.1 (including again ἐπὶ κεφαλαίων); also 2.74.1.
[49] *Ant. Rom.* 5.75.1 (including the adverb συντόμως).   [50] *Ant. Rom.* 11.44.5.
[51] See also *Ant. Rom.* 2.64.5; and note the remarks of Schultze 1986, 137.
[52] See, e.g., *Ant. Rom.* 8.70.1, 10.55.1, 11.60.2.
[53] On the πόλις in the *Roman Antiquities*, see Fox in this volume.

thought in action: without the vast length, and without the succession of speeches, especially in these two episodes of crisis, we should never be taken so fully into the interior life of this πόλις.⁵⁴

Since to paraphrase and discuss some of these longer episodes would take an inordinate amount of space, I have chosen two shorter episodes to illustrate Dionysius' techniques: his account of the conspiracy to restore Tarquinius Superbus in 509 BC and his account of events in 500 BC.

The Conspiracy to Restore the Tarquins and the Retirement of Collatinus

The way in which speech and detail combine to explain an event is illustrated nicely by *Ant. Rom.* 5.1.1–13.5, which deal with events in the opening year of the Republic (509 BC), down to the voluntary retiring of Collatinus into exile and the execution of those who had conspired to restore Tarquinius Superbus.

After the expulsion of Tarquinius Superbus, Lucius Junius Brutus and Lucius Tarquinius Collatinus were made the first consuls (5.1.2). A vote in the assembly confirmed the exile of Tarquinius Superbus' family (5.1.2), and the people then swore an oath that they would never take back into the city either him or any of his descendants (5.1.3). Dionysius describes various political measures which had the effect of making the people well disposed to the newly governing aristocracy (5.1.3–2.3), but then states that a conspiracy arose to restore the Tarquins (5.2.3).

After his expulsion, Tarquin had moved to Tarquinii in Etruria, whence his family had come to Rome (5.3.1–2). There he gave an account of his misfortunes (a brief summary of his speech is given in *oratio obliqua*) and persuaded the Etruscans to send an embassy to Rome on his behalf, telling the ambassadors what to say (5.3.3). Speaking in the Roman senate, they said that Tarquin requested the opportunity to speak in the senate and afterwards, if the senators agreed, before the people. He would give an account of himself and would try to persuade them to take him back as king or as a private citizen. The ambassadors ended their speech by saying that it is just (τὸ δίκαιον) to give everyone the right to speak in his own defence; and that if the Romans did not wish to do this they should not antagonise the city that was appealing on his behalf (5.4.1–3). Brutus then said that any return was impossible because of laws and oaths passed by the

---

⁵⁴ That the details are largely imaginary raises other questions, some of which I touch on at the end of this paper.

Romans, but that if the ambassadors had any other moderate demands they should announce them (5.5.1). The ambassadors said that they were surprised by this denial of justice, but then made another request that they regarded as equally just: that Tarquin should be allowed back his property (5.5.2). When the ambassadors had withdrawn, the senate deliberated. Brutus advised that the possessions of Tarquin should be retained, as punishment for the wrongs that he had done to the people and because of 'expediency' (τὸ συμφέρον), lest Tarquin should use the money to prepare war against Rome. Collatinus said that they ought to return the money, lest they should seem to have expelled the Tarquins for the sake of their possessions and lest they should give them 'a just excuse for war' (πρόφασιν πολέμου δικαίαν); in his view it was unclear whether Tarquin would wage war with it, but very clear that he would use its being withheld as an excuse to fight. Torn between the expediency of Brutus' view and the greater justice of Collatinus', the assembly debated for several days, before deciding to return Tarquin's property. The envoys congratulated them on their putting justice before expediency (5.5.3–6.2). The ambassadors then stayed in the city on the pretext of arranging Tarquin's affairs, but really stirring up dissent: they gave letters from the Tarquins to some, took letters to the Tarquins from others, and arranged conspiratorial meetings. Among the conspirators were Titus and Tiberius the sons of Brutus, Marcus and Manius Vitellius, the children of his sister, and Lucius and Marcus Aquillius, the sons of Collatinus' sister; it was in the house of these last that the meetings were held (5.6.2–4).

The conspiracy was discovered because Vindicius, a slave from Caenina in the house of the Aquilii, became suspicious of the conferences of his masters and, listening through a door, learnt of their plan to bring back the Tarquins. He reported what he had discovered, not to the consuls (lest they should take no action because their relatives were involved) but to Publius Valerius, who went around the next day with retainers and arrested the conspirators. Signed and sealed letters were found in which the conspirators had mentioned who were the men on whom Tarquin could count (5.7.1–5).

Brutus as consul took possession of the letters that had been found and examined them in public. Recognising the seals of his sons, he ordered that their letters be read out, gave them the chance to speak in their defence, and, when they said nothing, ordered their execution. Listening neither to the crowd, who wished to grant the lives of the young men to their father, nor to the lamentations of his sons, he watched their execution with an unflinching gaze (5.8.1–6). Next, he turned his attention to the Aquillii.

When given the chance to speak in their defence, they threw themselves at the feet of the other consul, Collatinus. Brutus ordered them to be dragged away to death unless they wished to speak in their own defence, but Collatinus asked him to step aside and begged him to relent. He asked that their punishment be remitted first because of their youth and then as a gift to himself (the only one that he would request). When both requests were refused, he asked for a lesser punishment, saying that it was absurd for the Tarquins to be punished only with exile, their supporters with death (5.9.1–3). When he got nowhere, he said that since he had power equal to Brutus he would use it to take the children away. Brutus replied, 'While I am alive, Collatinus, you will not be able to set betrayers of their country free. In fact, in the not too distant future you too will pay a suitable penalty' (5.9.3).[55]

Brutus then called an assembly and made a speech. He described how the conspiracy had been discovered and said that Collatinus was preventing the punishment of his nephews, which action (if successful) would in turn prevent Brutus from punishing others. Noting that Collatinus had earlier argued that the Tarquins should be granted their goods, he suggested that his behaviour pointed to his violating his oath, to his being friendly towards the Tarquins, and to his positioning himself to receive favours from them if they returned; he therefore proposed that Collatinus be stripped of his magistracy and sent into exile (5.10.1–7). When Collatinus called him a betrayer of his friends, continued to plead on behalf of his nephews, and refused to allow a vote on himself, the crowd became increasingly angry (5.11.1–2). Then Spurius Lucretius, Collatinus' father-in-law, requested permission to speak. He urged Collatinus to resign his office and withdraw willingly to another city, since he could not easily continue as consul if the people were unwilling; and he urged Brutus not to humiliate his colleague by exiling him but to allow him simply to withdraw from Rome and to keep his possessions (5.11.2–3). Collatinus reluctantly agreed, and Brutus praised him, arranging for the city to make a gift to him, which he supplemented from his private funds. Brutus oversaw the election of Valerius as suffect consul and the execution of all the conspirators (5.12.1–13.1).

This narrative and its parallel in Livy (2.2.2–5.10) differ in several ways that reveal the characteristics of their authors.[56] But the greatest

---

[55] Οὐκ ἐμοῦ γ', ἔφη, ζῶντος, ὦ Κολλατῖνε, τοὺς προδότας τῆς πατρίδος ἰσχύσεις ἐξελέσθαι· ἀλλὰ καὶ σὺ δώσεις δίκας ἃς προσῆκεν οὐκ εἰς μακράν.

[56] For a comparison of the two from a Livian perspective, see Burck 1964, 52–3.

difference comes from Livy's separation of the tale of the retirement of Collatinus, which he reports as occasioned solely by his bearing the name Tarquinius, from that of the conspiracy of the youths. He therefore presents two discrete episodes.[57] Yet Dionysius' fullness allows his narrative to bring out how the semi-voluntary withdrawal of Collatinus is a direct consequence of earlier events. The decree of exile and the oath sworn by all the Romans reappear immediately as a reason for denying the Tarquins a return to Rome and then later when the conspirators are punished and Collatinus is suspected. The refusal to allow the Tarquins to return raises the question of their possessions, and Collatinus' arguing for a position that the narrative voice agrees to be just, namely that the possessions of the Tarquins should be returned to them, leads first of all to the envoys from the Tarquins' staying in the city to arrange their affairs and, later, to Collatinus' being suspected of sympathies towards them. Whilst in the city the envoys help to coordinate the conspiracy in which Collatinus' nephews are implicated and for which their house was a base. What follows demonstrates both the expediency of Brutus' advice that the possessions of the Tarquins should not be returned to them and Vindicius' good sense in not going to the consuls, since (we may conjecture) Collatinus might very well have wished to hide the complicity of his relatives. (Incidentally, Vindicius' approaching Valerius provides another unifying link, since Valerius will shortly be elected suffect consul.)

Much of the speech in these chapters is in *oratio obliqua*, some of it summary. In this form we find Tarquin's speech at Tarquinii about his fortune (5.2.2), the first speech of his envoys at Rome (5.4.1–3), the speeches of Brutus and Collatinus to the senate as they deliberate their response to the envoys (5.5.3–4), Collatinus' speech in his defence (5.11.1), Lucretius' advice to the consuls (5.11.2), and Brutus' speech of submission to Lucretius. But *oratio recta* is used for Brutus' firm rebuttal of the envoys' first speech (5.5.1), for the envoys' second speech (5.5.2–3), for the dialogue between Brutus and Collatinus (5.9.3), and for Brutus' speech to the assembly advocating the punishment of Collatinus (5.10.2–7). This direct speech serves to underline climactic moments and to keep Brutus prominent, as he had been at the end of book 4. All in all, Dionysius' use of

---

[57] It is likely enough that these two differing approaches to these events were found already in Livy's and Dionysius' sources, but possible that one of the two Augustan authors has innovated on the existing tradition.

speech serves its purpose of giving the reasons why people acted as they did.[58]

Dionysius' desire to give a proper explanation of events leads him often into repeating sections of narrative in speech, albeit summarised and slanted towards the point of view of the speaker.[59] *Ant. Rom.* 5.10.3–4, where Brutus explains about the conspiracy to the assembly that had convened, is a good example of this.[60]

Subtly to delineate the characters of the participants in his history was not a particular concern of Dionysius', but he brings out Brutus' decisiveness (in rejecting the first embassy and in executing his own children), his hatred of the tyrants (visible throughout), and his impetuosity (in proposing to strip Collatinus of his office in an undignified manner). The contrast between *Ant. Rom.* 5.10.7 (ὃς τὸ μὲν σῶμα παρ' ἡμῖν ἔχεις, τὴν δὲ ψυχὴν παρὰ τοῖς πολεμίοις, 'you who keep your body among us, but your heart among our enemies') and *Ant. Rom.* 5.11.2 (τὸ μὲν σῶμα παρὰ τοῖς ὑποδεξαμένοις ἔχειν, τὴν δὲ ψυχὴν παρὰ τοῖς προπέμπουσι, 'keep your body among those who welcome you in but your heart with those who send you on your way') is a nice touch, underlining Brutus' change of tone. Collatinus, by contrast, seems to be as prone to emotion (*Ant. Rom.* 5.11.1, 12.1) as he had been at the end of book 4, after his wife, Lucretia, had been raped and had then taken her own life (4.70.2).

Dionysius on 500 BC

Dionysius' narrative of events in 500 BC stretches from *Ant. Rom.* 5.52.1 to 5.57.4, twelve pages of Jacoby's text; he finds a great deal worthy of record, which well illustrates his interest in detail. The fact that he attached to this narrative the passage of programmatic comment quoted at pp. 132–3, in which he justifies his lengthy treatment and relates it to his aims in writing history, would on its own invite analysis. But a further provocation to investigate is provided by Livy, whose parallel narrative is extremely brief:

---

[58] The amount of speech in this episode is modest in comparison with some others, but the preceding episode, dealing with the expulsion of the Tarquins, had been packed with speeches, and Dionysius may have thought that some variety was in order.

[59] See Schultze 1986, 128.

[60] But his reference to Rome's being protected by θεῶν τινος εὐνοίᾳ ('the good will of one of the gods', *Ant. Rom.* 5.10.4) recalls not events of which he could have been aware but a comment by the historian himself (προνοίᾳ θεῶν 'by the providence of the gods', *Ant. Rom.* 5.7.1).

Consules Ser. Sulpicius M'. Tullius. Nihil dignum memoria actum.

Servius Sulpicius and Manius Tullius were consuls. Nothing was done that is worthy of record. (Livy 2.19.1)

We are now nine years into the Republic, but Tarquinius Superbus and his family are still trying to persuade other Latin states to reinstate them. Dionysius tells us (*Ant. Rom.* 5.52.1–6) that nearby Fidenae was in revolt from Rome, that a Roman army under one of the two consuls was attacking it, and that some tried to persuade the Latin assembly to support the recall of the Tarquins, but that the populace of the Latin states was in general against such action. Therefore, Tarquin and his great supporter Mamilius of Tusculum try a new method (*Ant. Rom.* 5.53.1–4): they would encourage civil dissension at Rome. Knowing that there was a problem of indebtedness there and that some creditors were behaving harshly, they sent to Rome both an embassy that would demand from the senate the restoration of the Tarquins and with it men who were to bribe some Romans to take part in a conspiracy against the ruling aristocracy; those bribed included not only the free poor but also slaves. The leaders of the conspiracy were to seize the commanding heights of the city, and the slaves were to kill their masters. The conspiracy was revealed by a θεία πρόνοια 'foreknowledge coming from the gods' (5.54.1): two brothers in the conspiracy called Publius and Marcus Tarquinius (the name shared with the last king of Rome seems to be a coincidence) had visions of a terrible punishment. When they consulted soothsayers, they were advised to reveal their plans to the consul. He kept them in his house, responded to the Latin embassy with an emphatic negative (Dionysius reports the speech in *oratio recta* at 5.54.5), arranged for the Latins to be escorted out of the city, told the senate about his new information, and was given by the senate the authority to take such action as he saw fit. He decided to arrest only the ringleaders, and then only by producing incontrovertible proof. To his thoughts on this matter, and Dionysius' approval of them, we shall return shortly (*Ant. Rom.* 5.54.1–55.3).

Then comes the programmatic passage at *Ant. Rom.* 5.56.1 quoted above, in which Dionysius explains why he narrates this tale at such length, mentioning *inter alia* that he thought it important for readers to know the τρόπος by which the conspirators were captured, the αἰτίαι for events, and the role played by divine intervention. The τρόπος is soon revealed: young senators are sent to take control of the fortified parts of the city; armed knights are placed in the forum; and the army is recalled from Fidenae. The informers were then told (5.57.1) to arrange for the chiefs of the conspiracy to assemble in the forum around midnight. When these conspirators had arrived, the armed men moved into place and the forum was surrounded so that no one could escape. Daybreak revealed that the other consul and his army were now back, encamped on the Campus Martius. The consuls summoned the people to an assembly, challenged the conspirators (none of whom denied the charge), and consulted the senate, which recommended the death penalty if the people sanctioned it, and the reward of citizenship for the Tarquinii. The people accepted the decree, and the conspirators were put to death; no reprisals were carried out against others involved in the conspiracy (5.57.1–58.4).

It becomes clear that programmatic comment and narrative are closely linked. We have seen already how the reference to τρόπος in the programme is immediately taken up by the narrative, and the reference to events occasioned by divine intervention looks back to the visions of the two Tarquinii. As for the αἰτίαι, these have been brought out at great length at the beginning of the narrative. Most interesting, however, is the passage (which has another τρόπος) in which Dionysius comments on the thinking of the consul Sulpicius:

> καὶ λαβὼν ἐξουσίαν παρ' αὐτῶν αὐτοκράτορα τοῦ διερευνήσασθαι τοὺς μετασχόντας τῶν ἀπορρήτων βουλευμάτων καὶ τοῦ κολάσαι τοὺς ἐξευρεθέντας, οὐ τὴν αὐθάδη καὶ τυραννικὴν ἦλθεν ὁδόν, ὡς ἕτερός ἄν τις ἐποίησεν εἰς τοσαύτην κατακλεισθεὶς ἀνάγκην· ἀλλ' ἐπὶ τὴν εὐλόγιστόν τε καὶ ἀσφαλῆ καὶ τῷ σχήματι τῆς καθεστώσης τότε πολιτείας ἀκόλουθον ἐτράπετο. (2) οὔτε γὰρ ἐκ τῶν οἰκιῶν συλλαμβανομένους ἄγεσθαι τοὺς πολίτας ἐπὶ τὸν θάνατον ἀποσπωμένους ἀπὸ γυναικῶν τε καὶ τέκνων καὶ πατέρων ἐβουλήθη, τόν τ' οἶκτον ἐνθυμούμενος, οἷος ἔσται τῶν προσηκόντων ἑκάστοις παρὰ τὸν ἀποσπασμὸν τῶν ἀναγκαιοτάτων καὶ δεδοικώς, μή τινες ἀπονοηθέντες ἐπὶ τὰ ὅπλα τὴν ὁρμὴν λάβωσι, καὶ δι' αἵματος ἐμφυλίου χωρήσῃ τὸ ἀναγκασθὲν παρανομεῖν· οὔτε δικαστήρια καθίζειν αὐτοῖς ᾤετο δεῖν, λογιζόμενος, ὅτι πάντες ἀρνήσονται καὶ οὐθὲν ἔσται βέβαιον τοῖς δικασταῖς τεκμήριον οὐδ' ἀναμφίλεκτον ἔξω τῆς μηνύσεως, ᾧ πιστεύσαντες θάνατον τῶν πολιτῶν καταψηφιοῦνται· (3) καινὸν δέ τινα <u>τρόπον</u> ἀπάτης ἐξεῦρε τῶν νεωτεριζόντων, δι' οὗ πρῶτον μὲν αὐτοὶ μηδενὸς ἀναγκάζοντες εἰς ἓν χωρίον ἥξουσιν οἱ τῶν ἀπορρήτων βουλευμάτων ἡγεμόνες, ἔπειτ' ἀναμφιλέκτοις ἁλώσονται τεκμηρίοις, ὥστε μηδ' ἀπολογίαν αὐτοῖς καταλείπεσθαι μηδεμίαν, πρὸς δὲ τούτοις οὐκ εἰς ἔρημον συναχθέντες τόπον οὐδ' ἐν ὀλίγοις μάρτυσιν ἐξελεγχθέντες, ἀλλ' ἐν ἀγορᾷ πάντων ὁρώντων γενόμενοι καταφανεῖς ἃ προσήκει πείσονται, ταραχή τ' οὐδεμία γενήσεται κατὰ τὴν πόλιν οὐδ' ἐπαναστάσεις ἑτέρων, οἷα συμβαίνειν φιλεῖ περὶ τὰς κολάσεις τῶν νεωτεριζόντων, καὶ ταῦτ' ἐν ἐπισφαλέσι καιροῖς.

And taking sole authority from them (*sc.* the senators) to track down those who were taking part in these clandestine plans and to punish those whose involvement had been discovered, he did not advance down a vicious and tyrannical route as another person might well have done when cramped by such an emergency; rather, he turned to a route that was rational and safe and consistent with the established constitution. (2) He did not want to gather citizens from their houses and lead them to death, tearing them away from their wives and children and fathers, because he realized what kind of lamentation there would be among the relatives of each when they were torn away from those close to them, and because he feared that some driven to panic should make a dash to arms and the resulting transgression to which they had been forced should issue in civil bloodshed. Nor did he think it appropriate to set up trials for them, calculating that all would deny the charge and that, apart from the information supplied by the informer, there would be no secure and indisputable proof for the judges on the basis of which they could vote for the death of citizens. (3) He devised a new method of deceiving the revolutionaries by means of which first the leaders of the conspiracy would assemble with no one else compelling them into one place, then they would be convicted by indisputable evidence with the result that no defence was left for them. In addition, they would not be assembled in a deserted place nor would their involvement be proved in front of a few witnesses. Rather, being visible to the eyes of all in the forum they would suffer a fitting punishment, and there would be no commotion in the city nor riots of others in sympathy, the kind of things which tend to happen when revolutionaries are punished, especially in perilous circumstances. (*Ant. Rom.* 5.55.1–3)

The moderation with which Dionysius makes Sulpicius behave chimes with the general political outlook of the *Roman Antiquities*, in which extreme voices are abhorred and the absence of violence is celebrated: the negative connotations of τυραννικήν and αὐθάδη, a word from a root that is found nearly a hundred times in the *Roman Antiquities*, need no illustration. The emphasis at the beginning of the passage on Sulpicius' acting in accordance with the constitution is picked up later in the story, when he consults the senate, and the senate proposes a decree to be passed by the people. As numerous references to such decrees in Dionysius attest,[61] this was what Dionysius regarded as constitutional procedure, and it was a procedure of which he much approved. In allowing the people to vote on a matter of capital punishment, the senate was respecting a popular right, the introduction of which Dionysius had described at *Ant. Rom.* 3.22.6. Particularly interesting is Dionysius' drawing attention to

---

[61] For discussion see Bux 1915; Cary 1937, xxv–xxviii.

Sulpicius' humanity in avoiding raids on houses and to (in Dionysius' view, at least) his good sense in avoiding trials for those involved in the conspiracy. This is picked up in the programmatic passage by his comment on the need to know the intentions of those involved in the action (τὰς διανοίας τῶν πραξάντων). In this passage more than anywhere in his account of the story, Dionysius points to lessons from which politicians may learn.

The striking contrast with Livy may be explained by the different aims of the two authors. Livy, writing a briefer narrative that is building up to the climactic Battle of Lake Regillus, perhaps not unreasonably judged this material unworthy of record. Livy's comment makes sense only if he did find in his sources something similar to what Dionysius relates; it therefore provides evidence for his abbreviation of his sources.[62] Dionysius' history needed a wealth of detail to make its impact, and therefore he seized upon the tale, and upon the lessons that could be learnt from it. He never mentions Livy in his work; but it would be strange if he had never read him, and it is possible that the programmatic passage that we have been discussing is a rebuke aimed at Livy.

Dionysius and His Sources[63]

A critical modern historian of early Rome has to face up to the likelihood that most of the details in our extant narratives were invented, certainly for the period before the 440s BC, for which the narrative of Dionysius is wholly extant. Just conceivably the Romans may have known the names of magistrates, they may have been able to assign them more or less to the correct year, they may have had records of the years in which legislation was passed and in which victories and triumphs occurred, but it passes belief that they knew the proximate causes of these wars or had detailed information about political strife. For no Roman wrote history before Fabius Pictor c. 200 BC, and there is no known mechanism by which such details could have been securely transmitted over a period of more than 250 years. It follows that most of the details in Livy, let alone the more expansive Dionysius, were invented.

Hitherto we have analysed the details of Dionysius' narrative without any discussion of whether he or his sources were responsible for their

---

[62] See below, pp. 153–4.
[63] In much of this section, I return to material discussed at much greater length both by others and in Oakley 1997–2005, vol. I, 21–108, where my own views are expounded. Since this is not the place for a full inquiry into the evidentiary basis of early Roman history, I am deliberately brief and dogmatic.

The Expansive Scale of the Roman Antiquities 153

creation and whether they were in any sense 'true'. This procedure is legitimate, since the impact and literary texture of the finished *Roman Antiquities* deserves analysis in its own right, and the effect of recounting any particular detail remains the same whether or not Dionysius was the first to record it. Besides, no one should yearn for a return to the days when extant ancient historians seemed sometimes to be valued as much for the extent to which they could be used in the reconstruction of lost writers as for what they themselves had achieved. Nevertheless, it would make a difference for our appreciation of Dionysius' achievement if we knew how much of this detail he had taken over from his sources. Dionysius himself was alert to the possible charge of invention, fearing that readers on finding material not recounted by Hieronymus or Timaeus or Polybius might suspect that he had made it up; hence his justification of his narrative by his pointing to the opportunity for gathering information given by his long stay in Rome and by his reading of Latin sources.[64] Without new discoveries of lost writers, the matter cannot be finally settled, but there is reason to believe Dionysius when he says that he did not invent large swathes of his narrative.

Livy's fame, the fact that he wrote 142 books (of which the surviving 35 occupy much space), and the loss of other histories of the Roman Republic tempt classical scholars into thinking that the scale of his account of early Roman history was normal or large – and that Dionysius' was therefore exceedingly abnormal. Certainly, Livy's first five books offered a more expansive account of early Roman history than that found in early annalists such as Fabius Pictor and Lucius Calpurnius Piso Frugi. Yet it would be a mistake to underestimate the length of some of Livy's Roman annalistic predecessors, especially Gnaeus Gellius, who wrote at the end of the second century.[65] The loss of Gnaeus Gellius is hugely frustrating. It seems very likely that much of the detail in later narratives of early Roman history appeared in some form or other in his history, perhaps often for the first time.[66] And this history seems to have been very long: F3 Cornell, dealing with the Rape of the Sabine Women, is cited from book 2 (Livy narrates it on p. 14 of Ogilvie's text); F5, from book 3, shows the same story continuing; F8 (= Macrob. *Sat.* 1.16.21), from book 15, deals with Roman history in 389 BC, and corresponds to something narrated by Livy in book 6, chapter 1. If F10 (= Charisius, *GLK* 1, 54) is reliable, then Gellius

---

[64] *Ant. Rom.* 1.7.1–4; σχεδιάζειν is the verb that he uses in 1.7.1 to describe this invention.
[65] On Gellius see most recently J. Briscoe, in Cornell 2013, vol. 1, 252–5, vol. 2. 362–83, vol. 3. 229–42.
[66] On Gellius' invention of detail, see Badian 1966, 11–12 ('the expansion of the past' is his memorable heading); Wiseman 1979, 20–3; Briscoe loc. cit., vol. 1, 254.

wrote at least 97 books. These books can hardly have extended as far as 100 BC, by which date he probably was dead. Livy reached 100 BC in only 69 books. Different annalistic writers will have invented different details, but Gellius must have invented a great deal. A powerful motive for the invention must have been the desire to write a history that offered more than just an annalistic record of who held what magistracy: Dionysius need not have been the first historian of Rome to have been interested in ἀκρίβεια. The length of the histories of Licinius Macer and Valerius Antias is harder to estimate, but both could have been more expansive than Livy's.[67]

How far did Gellius influence our extant narratives? Since Livy never mentions him, there is no reason to believe that he ever consulted him, but that does not mean that Gellius had no influence on the details of his history. Livy does tell us that he used Valerius Antias, Claudius Quadrigarius, Quintus Aelius Tubero, and Licinius Macer: all of these wrote late enough to use Gellius, and there is good evidence that the last did use him.[68] Dionysius is different: he tells us (*Ant. Rom.* 1.7.3) that Gellius was one of the authors whom he consulted, and he goes on to cite him, five times;[69] by comparison, he cites Valerius Antias once, Licinius Macer six times, and Quintus Aelius Tubero, his patron, just once.[70] We do not know much about how Dionysius used his sources. It is rash to assign large portions of his text to a particular individual source, as was occasionally attempted by the older *Quellenforscher*, since Dionysius was quite capable of blending and adapting his sources.[71] However, if a book of Gellius was roughly the size of a book of Livy, his history was able to provide Dionysius with much of the detail that he needed, and Dionysius' Gellian length makes it reasonable to suggest that he did so provide, probably both directly and through other sources' use of him.[72] This does not mean that Dionysius did not consult other sources (we know that he did), change details, improve details, and invent further details. He may even have invented whole scenes and episodes, especially those involving speeches. He used many sources and he exhibits a rhetorical polish that Gellius is hardly likely to have matched, but

---

[67] On Macer see Walt 1997; Oakley in Cornell 2013, vol. 1, 320–31, vol. 2, 672–97, vol. 3, 418–49; on Antias, Rich in Cornell 2013, vol. 1, 293–304, vol. 2, 548–99, vol. 3, 330–67, all with further bibliography and extensive discussion.
[68] For recent discussion see Walt 1997, 85–7; Oakley in Cornell 2013, vol. 1, 327 (with further references).
[69] *Ant. Rom.* 2.72.2, 76.5, 4.6.4, 6.11.2, 7.1.4.
[70] On Quintus Aelius Tubero, see Wiater in this volume, p. 74 n.52.
[71] For older source-criticism of Dionysius, see, e.g., Bocksch 1895; Klotz 1938.
[72] See Walt 1997, 85–7 and Oakley in Cornell 2013, 1 327.

perhaps in Dionysius' work we may catch (albeit dimly) some glimpses of what Gellius' narrative was like.

Detail in Battle Scenes

Although the massive scale of Dionysius' narrative is observed most readily in his extended portrayal of internal politics at Rome and in the speeches that he wrote to complement his narrative, it is apparent also in his narratives of Rome's external relations and battles, many of which are recounted with elaborate detail. In addition to the general consideration that Gnaeus Gellius and other annalists are likely to have influenced his narrative, there are three good reasons for thinking that Dionysius did not have to create all of his battle scenes *ex nihilo* and that a considerable portion of them was inherited: first, he occasionally states that some lengthy narratives were found already in his sources;[73] second, parallel narratives (usually that of Livy) sometimes contain the same details, thereby showing that they must go back beyond Dionysius; third, many of the same τόποι recur in the battle descriptions of Dionysius and Livy, suggesting that they were motifs that both they themselves and their predecessors used to add colour to their accounts of battles. Nevertheless, to assume that Dionysius deployed such τόποι in precisely the same way as his sources and that he was incapable of making original use of them would be to fall into the fallacy of assuming that innovation occurred only in writers lost to the modern scholar.[74]

A good example of a detailed battle-narrative is found in Dionysius' account of 487 BC. The question of the authenticity of the details in it is posed starkly by comparison with Livy, since this is another year for which there is an extreme contrast between the narratives of Dionysius and Livy:

> Consules T. Sicinius et C. Aquilius. Sicinio Volsci, Aquilio Hernici – nam ii quoque in armis erant – prouincia euenit. Eo anno Hernici deuicti: cum Volscis aequo Marte discessum est.
>
> The consuls were Titus Sicinius and Gaius Aquillius. The Volsci were assigned to Sicinius as his province, the Hernici (for they too were under arms) to Aquilius. The Hernici were defeated in that year; from battle with the Volsci the Romans departed on even terms. (Livy 2.40.14)

---

[73] See above all *Ant. Rom.* 9.18.5–22.6 on the defeat of the Fabii at the Cremera.
[74] Some of the schematism in Dionysius' battle scenes is brought out by Gaida 1934, the only extended study of the topic.

If any authentic notice of the events of 487 BC survived, it can hardly have recorded more than the names of the magistrates and the outcomes of the wars. Since this is precisely the form that Livy's narrative takes, he perhaps chose to follow a source or sources that offered no elaboration and no invention of plausible detail; and if all the lost annalistic writers had written as Livy writes, then we could be sure that Dionysius himself had invented the details that we have just discussed. However, in books 1–2 Livy often abbreviates ruthlessly from longer narratives and may very well have done so here; it is safer to presume that at least some of what Dionysius says was found in his sources.

Dionysius reports that in response to aggression from the Hernici (who had previously been allied to Rome), the Aequi, and the Volsci, tribes whose lands were close to those of Rome, the senate had sent an embassy to the Hernici asking them to make reparations and had ordered the consuls to carry out a levy of all Roman forces. We join the narrative just after the Hernici have said that they are happy to go to war.

> Ταῦτα ἡ βουλὴ μαθοῦσα ἐψηφίσατο νείμασθαι τὴν καταγραφεῖσαν ἐκ τῶν νεωτέρων στρατιὰν τριχῇ· τούτων δὲ τὴν μὲν μίαν ἄγοντα Γάϊον Ἀκύλλιον τὸν ὕπατον ὁμόσε τῇ Ἑρνίκων στρατιᾷ χωρεῖν· καὶ γὰρ ἐκεῖνοι ἤδη ἦσαν ἐν τοῖς ὅπλοις· τὴν δ' ἑτέραν Τίτον Σίκκιον ἐπὶ Οὐολούσκους ἄγειν, τὸν ἕτερον τῶν ὑπάτων, τὴν δὲ λοιπὴν τρίτην μερίδα παραλαβόντα Σπόριον Λάρκιον, ὃς ἦν ἀποδεδειγμένος ὑπὸ τῶν ὑπάτων ἔπαρχος τὴν ἔγγιστα τῆς πόλεως χώραν φυλάττειν· τοὺς δ' ὑπὲρ τὸν στρατιωτικὸν κατάλογον, ὅσοι δύναμιν εἶχον ἔτι βαστάζειν ὅπλα, ταχθέντας ὑπὸ σημαίαις τάς τ' ἄκρας φρουρεῖν τῆς πόλεως καὶ τὰ τείχη, μή τις αἰφνίδιος πολεμίων γένηται ἔφοδος ἐξεστρατευμένης τῆς νεότητος ἀθρόας· ἡγεῖσθαι δὲ τῆς δυνάμεως ταύτης Αὖλον Σεμπρώνιον Ἀτρατῖνον, ἄνδρα τῶν ὑπατικῶν. ἐγίνετο δὲ ταῦτ' οὐ διὰ μακροῦ.
>
> (65.1) Ἀκύλλιος μὲν οὖν ἅτερος τῶν ὑπάτων ἐν τῇ Πραινεστηνῶν χώρᾳ τὸν Ἑρνίκων στρατὸν ὑπομένοντα καταλαβὼν ἀντικατεστρατοπέδευσεν ὡς ἐδύνατο μάλιστ' ἀγχοτάτω σταδίους ἀπὸ τῆς Ῥώμης ἀποσχὼν ὀλίγῳ πλείους διακοσίων· τρίτῃ δ' ἀφ' ἧς κατεστρατοπέδευσεν ἡμέρᾳ, προελθόντων ἐκ τοῦ χάρακος τῶν Ἑρνίκων εἰς τὸ πεδίον ἐν τάξει καὶ τὰ σημεῖ' ἀράντων τῆς μάχης, ἀντεξῆγε καὶ αὐτὸς τὴν δύναμιν ἐν κόσμῳ τε καὶ κατὰ τέλη. (2) ἐπεὶ δ' ἀγχοῦ ἐγένοντο ἀλλήλων ἔθεον ἀλαλάξαντες ὁμόσε, πρῶτον μὲν οἱ ψιλοὶ σαυνίων τε βολαῖς καὶ τοξεύμασι καὶ λίθοις ἀπὸ σφενδόνης μαχόμενοι, καὶ πολλὰ τραύματα ἔδοσαν ἀλλήλοις· ἔπειτα ἱππεῖς ἱππεῦσι συρράττουσι κατ' ἴλας ἐλαύνοντες καὶ τὸ πεζὸν τῷ πεζῷ κατὰ σπείρας μαχόμενον. ἔνθα δὴ καλὸς ἀγὼν ἦν ἐκθύμως ἀμφοτέρων ἀγωνιζομένων, καὶ μέχρι πολλοῦ διέμενον οὐδέτεροι τοῖς ἑτέροις τοῦ χωρίου, ἐν ᾧ ἐτάχθησαν, εἴκοντες. ἔπειτα ἡ Ῥωμαίων ἤρξατο κάμνειν φάλαγξ, οἷα διὰ πολλοῦ τοῦ μεταξὺ χρόνου τότε πρῶτον ἠναγκασμένη

ὁμιλεῖν πολέμῳ. (3) τοῦτο συνιδὼν Ἀκύλλιος ἐκέλευσε τοὺς ἀκμῆτας ἔτι καὶ εἰς αὐτὸ τοῦτο φυλαττομένους ὑπὸ τὰ κάμνοντα τῆς φάλαγγος ὑπελθεῖν μέρη, τοὺς δὲ τραυματίας καὶ τοὺς ἀπειρηκότας ὀπίσω τῆς φάλαγγος ἀπιέναι. οἱ δ' Ἕρνικες ὡς ἔμαθον κινουμένους αὐτῶν τοὺς λόχους φυγῆς τ' ἄρχειν τοὺς Ῥωμαίους ὑπέλαβον, καὶ παρακελευσάμενοι ἀλλήλοις ἐμβάλλουσι πυκνοῖς τοῖς λόχοις εἰς τὰ κινούμενα τῶν πολεμίων μέρη, καὶ οἱ ἀκραιφνεῖς τῶν Ῥωμαίων ἐπιόντας αὐτοὺς δέχονται· καὶ ἦν αὖθις ἐξ ὑπαρχῆς ἀμφοτέρων ἐκθύμως ἀγωνιζομένων μάχη καρτερά· καὶ γὰρ καὶ οἱ τῶν Ἑρνίκων ἐξεπληροῦντο λόχοι τοῖς ἀκμῆσιν ὑποπεμπομένοις εἰς τὰ κάμνοντα ὑπὸ τῶν ἡγεμόνων. (4) ἐπειδὴ δὲ περὶ δείλην ὀψίαν ἦν ἤδη, παρακαλέσας τοὺς ἱππεῖς ὁ ὕπατος νυνὶ δὴ ἄνδρας ἀγαθοὺς γενέσθαι, ἐμβάλλει τοῖς πολεμίοις κατὰ τὸ δεξιὸν κέρας αὐτὸς ἡγούμενος τῆς ἴλης. οἱ δ' ὀλίγον τινὰ δεξάμενοι χρόνον αὐτοὺς ἐγκλίνουσι, καὶ γίνεται φόνος ἐνταῦθα πολύς. τὸ μὲν οὖν δεξιὸν τῶν Ἑρνίκων κέρας ἐπόνει τ' ἤδη καὶ ἐξέλειπε τὴν τάξιν, τὸ δ' εὐώνυμον ἔτι ἀντεῖχε καὶ περιῆν τοῦ Ῥωμαίων δεξιοῦ· μετ' ὀλίγον μέντοι καὶ τοῦτ' ἐνέδωκεν. (5) ὁ γὰρ Ἀκύλλιος τοὺς ἀρίστους τῶν νέων ἐπαγόμενος παρεβοήθει κἀκεῖ παραθαρρύνων τε καὶ ἐξ ὀνόματος ἀνακαλῶν τοὺς εἰωθότας ἐν ταῖς πρὶν ἀριστεύειν μάχαις, τά τε σημεῖα τῶν λόχων, ὅσοι μὴ ἐρρωμένως ἐδόκουν ἀμύνεσθαι, παρὰ τῶν σημειοφόρων ἁρπάζων εἰς μέσους ἐρρίπτει τοὺς πολεμίους, ἵνα τὸ δέος αὐτοὺς τῆς ἐννόμου τιμωρίας, εἰ μὴ ἀνασώσαιντο τὰς σημαίας, ἄνδρας ἀγαθοὺς εἶναι ἀναγκάσῃ· τῷ τε κάμνοντι αὐτὸς παρεβοήθει μέρει ἀεί, τέως ἐξέωσε τῆς στάσεως καὶ θάτερον κέρας. ψιλωθέντων δὲ τῶν ἄκρων οὐδὲ τὰ μέσα παρέμεινε. (6) φυγὴ δὴ τῶν Ἑρνίκων τὸ μετὰ τοῦτ' ἐγίνετο ἐπὶ τὸν χάρακα τεταραγμένη τε καὶ ἄκοσμος, καὶ οἱ Ῥωμαῖοι αὐτοῖς κτείνοντες ἠκολούθουν. τοσαύτη δ' ἄρα προθυμία παρὰ τὸν τότ' ἀγῶνα τῇ Ῥωμαίων στρατιᾷ ἐνέπεσεν, ὥστε καὶ τοῦ χάρακος τῶν πολεμίων πειρᾶσθαί τινας ἐπιβαίνειν ὡς ἐξ ἐφόδου χειρωσομένους· ὧν οὐκ ἀσφαλῆ τὴν προθυμίαν οὐδ' ἐν τῷ συμφέροντι γιγνομένην ὁρῶν ὁ ὕπατος, σημαίνειν κελεύσας τὸ ἀνακλητικὸν κατεβίβασε τοὺς ὁμόσε χωροῦντας ἄκοντας ἀπὸ τῶν ἐρυμάτων, δείσας, μὴ ἐξ ὑπερδεξιῶν βαλλόμενοι σὺν αἰσχύνῃ τε καὶ μετὰ μεγάλης βλάβης ἀναγκασθῶσιν ὑποχωρεῖν, ἔπειτα καὶ τὴν ἐκ τῆς προτέρας νίκης εὔκλειαν ἀφανίσωσι. τότε μὲν οὖν – ἤδη γὰρ ἦν περὶ δύσιν ἡλίου – χαίροντές τε καὶ παιανίζοντες οἱ Ῥωμαῖοι κατεστρατοπέδευσαν.

When the senate learned about these things it voted that the army which had been conscripted from the young men should be divided into three parts; that the consul Caius Aquillius should lead one part of these to confront at close quarters the army of the Hernicans, since these were already in arms; that the other consul Titus Siccius should lead another of these against the Volscians; that Spurius Larcius, who had been appointed as an additional magistrate by the consuls, should take command of the remaining third part and guard the land nearest the city; that, in addition to this levy of troops, those who still had power to carry arms should be divided into companies to guard the heights and walls of the city, lest there should be any unexpected attack of the enemy after the assembled youth had been marched out; and that Aulus Sempronius Atratinus, a consular, should take command of this force. These dispositions did not take long to be carried out.

(65.1) Aquillius, one of the two consuls, finding the army of the Hernicans waiting in the territory of the people of Palestrina, camped opposite them as close as he possibly could, being distant from Rome a little more than two hundred stades. On the second day after he had encamped, when the Hernici had come down from their camp to the plain arrayed for battle and had raised their battle-standards, the consul also led out his force in ranks and order. (2) When they came close to each other, they ran forwards raising the war-cry at the same time. First, the light-armed troops fought with the throwing of javelins, bows, and the hurling of stones from slings, and they inflicted many wounds on both sides. Next cavalry charging forwards in their troops clashed with cavalry, and infantry in their detachments with infantry. Then there was a splendid contest between the two sides fighting with great vigour, and for a long time they remained steady, with neither side ceding to the other any of the ground on which they had been drawn up; but then the battle-line of the Romans began to tire – unsurprisingly since then for the first time in a long while it had been compelled to take part in a war. (3) Seeing this, Aquillius ordered those of his troops who were fresh and had been kept in reserve for this purpose to come up alongside those parts of the battle-line that were struggling, and those who were wounded and exhausted to retreat behind the battle-line. When the Hernici realised that the Roman detachments were changing position, they imagined that they were beginning to flee and, encouraging one another, they thrust in closely packed formation into those parts of the enemy army that were changing position, and the fresh Romans resisted them. And all over again there was a mighty battle, with both sides fighting vigorously: for the ranks of the Hernicans were also filled with fresh men sent up by their commanders to those parts that were struggling. (4) And when it was drawing late in the afternoon, the consul encouraged his cavalry to show themselves brave men and, himself leading the troop, he made them charge the enemy on their right wing. Resisting for only a little time, the enemy began to give way, and there was a massive slaughter. Therefore the right flank of the Hernici was in difficulties and withdrew from the line of battle, but their left flank still resisted and had the advantage over the Roman right. But after a little time this too gave way: (5) Aquillius, gathering the best of the young men, had come to the Romans' assistance, raising their spirits, and calling by name on those who had been accustomed to display valour in previous battles; and, seizing from the standard-bearers the standards of those detachments that did not seem to be defending themselves bravely, he hurled them into the middle of the enemy so that fear of just punishment if they did not rescue the standards should force the men to

The Expansive Scale of the Roman Antiquities 159

be brave; and he himself helped the ailing wing all the time until he had dislodged the enemy's other wing from its position. Nor did the centre remain firm once the extremities of the line of battle were laid bare: (6) after this there was a confused and disordered flight of the Hernici to their camp, and the Romans followed, killing them. Such boldness took hold of the Roman army during this part of the contest that some men attacked the camp of the enemy in the hope of capturing it on the first assault; but the consul, seeing that this boldness was both dangerous and occurring at an inopportune time, ordered the signal for the retreat to be sounded and brought down from the fortifications those who were fighting at close quarters, even though they were unwilling. He feared that they would be bombarded by men in a higher position, would be compelled to retreat in shame and with great loss of life, and would lose the glory of their earlier victory. Therefore, since the time had reached sunset, in good cheer and singing songs of victory the Romans encamped. (*Ant. Rom.* 8.64.3–65.6)

This passage is replete with commonplace motifs, all of which may be paralleled from elsewhere in Dionysius or Livy: the division of the Roman forces,[75] with the older soldiers being left behind to defend the city;[76] the appointment of a city prefect;[77] the replacement of tired soldiers with those who were fresh;[78] the address by Aquillius to individual troops by name;[79] the reference to great slaughter;[80] the cavalry charge;[81] the contrasting fortunes of the two wings of the Roman army;[82] the hurling of the Roman standards into the enemy ranks;[83] the assault on the camp of the enemy.[84] Other details that suggest accuracy are the fairly precise reference to the spot in which Aquillius pitched camp and the delay in battle until the second day after pitching camp. Whether owed to authentic records or to the inventions of the historical tradition, the record of Rome's battles in

---

[75] Here, if the older men are counted, we have in effect a fourfold division of the Roman forces. *Ant. Rom.* 5.75.4 and 6.2.3 differ only in that the city prefect is stationed inside the city. For a threefold division of the Roman forces, with one part left to guard the city, see *Ant. Rom.* 9.69.2, 10.22.2, 11.23.1.
[76] For the older men so used, see *Ant. Rom.* 5.45.3, 75.4; 6.42.1; 9.5.3; Livy 5.10.4, 6.6.14, 10.21.4. Often Dionysius makes clear that these older troops were left with the city prefect, and, at 6.2.3, where he does not mention the character of the forces left with the prefect, it is reasonable to assume that he was thinking of the older men.
[77] See Oakley 1997–2005, vol. 2, 745–7.
[78] See Oakley 1997–2005, vol. 3, 419, where this passage might have been cited.
[79] See Oakley 1997–2005, vol. 2, 768–9.
[80] Φόνος πολύς is as common in Dionysius as *magna caedes* in Livy. Slightly different from what we have here is καὶ γίνεται μέγας ἀγὼν καὶ φόνος ἐξ ἀμφοτέρων πολύς *uel sim.*, which is found at *Ant. Rom.* 1.87.1, 9.20.4, 11.47.5 in formulaic descriptions of battles.
[81] See Oakley 1997–2005, vol. 1, 620.
[82] See Oakley 1997–2005, vol. 1, 462–3, where again this passage might have been cited.
[83] See Oakley 1997–2005, vol. 1, 466, where again this passage might have been cited.
[84] See Oakley 1997–2005, vol. 1, 622–3 (normally the attack of the victorious army is successful).

the fifth and fourth centuries can seem almost endless. Anyone who wished to offer military narrative with the detail that ἀκρίβεια demanded was faced with the problem of how to write these battles up at length. One answer was to make use of a series of stock τόποι which could be varied and used in different combinations, occasionally with a striking novel aspect thrown in. This has been Dionysius' technique here.[85]

Conclusion

Among ancient historians Dionysius is unique in having written literary critical treatises that include ample discussion of historiography, as well as a work of history with many original characteristics, of which its expansiveness is one of the most notable. In this essay this expansiveness of the *Roman Antiquities* has been illustrated by several comparisons with Livy, and an explanation for it has been sought in Dionysius' own views on the writing of history. It has also been suggested that the Roman annalistic tradition could have provided Dionysius with much of the raw material that he needed in order to write at such length.

---

[85] But we cannot know whether he was the first to use these τόποι in describing this battle.

CHAPTER 6

Ways of Killing Women: Dionysius on the Deaths of Horatia and Lucretia

Clemence Schultze

1. Introduction

The present paper examines what Dionysius of Halicarnassus makes of two stories of women who leave their homes, and die by violence.[1] Contexts and circumstances differ greatly, but both accounts come from the corpus of traditional material which Dionysius' annalistic predecessors handed down. They were accordingly impossible to ignore but required appropriate reworking so as to fit Dionysius' end of demonstrating the purposive yet stable development in Roman society and character. These two accounts require that the reader be guided towards an appropriate understanding of the respective protagonists' conduct. Close reading aims to show how Dionysius' narrative choices emphasise the more archaic elements of the first tale (that of Horatia, treated in section 2), aligning the personages and passions of the early regal period with those of epic and tragedy, and consciously marking the difference between the remote past and his own day. In the case of Lucretia (section 3), he shuns dramatic or picturesque variants in the interests of depicting the motivation of all the characters involved as beyond reproach, both personally and politically. This suits his objective of expounding and justifying Rome's most significant constitutional shift, from tyranny to Republic. Both stories, though treating events so distant from Dionysius' own time, have resonance for his Augustan Roman readership (section 4). One of these women is deemed wanton, the other one is paradigmatically chaste. The way in which the historian portrays their behaviour and fates is coloured by contemporary concerns for sexual morality and the policing of the

---

[1] Earlier versions of this chapter were presented at a seminar at Boston University in 2011 and at the Leiden conference 'Dionysius of Halicarnassus and Augustan Rome' in 2012. I thank participants at both for their observations, and I am especially grateful to Casper de Jonge for his valuable suggestions.

public–private divide. Section 5 considers how the principles for good historical writing, derived by Dionysius from the historians whom he regarded as models for imitation and adaptation, are manifested in these two narratives.

2. Horatia

The tale of Horatia (*Ant. Rom.* 3.21) is inset within the lengthy account of the Roman–Alban war during the reign of Tullus Hostilius, the third Roman king (*Ant. Rom.* 3.2–31). At stake is whether mother city Alba or her flourishing daughter colony Rome shall be supreme; the relationship between the two cities renders the situation reminiscent of a civil war. The ideological issue is over citizenship and constitution: are the guiding principles of the hegemonic power to be exclusivity and tradition, or openness and change?[2] The two kings agree to decide the dispute not by a pitched battle but by a contest of three champions – sets of brothers – from each side. Livy 1.24.1 problematises the entire story of the Horatii and Curiatii from the outset by claiming that opinions differ as to which family was the Alban one, which the Roman.[3] Dionysius, who often shows great concern to explain his criteria for selecting one variant account over another,[4] here does not even mention any divergence, but unquestioningly accepts the Horatii as Roman.

Dionysius' narrative (almost twice as long as Livy's)[5] places considerable emphasis upon tragic features of the story. He also stresses the role of providence and chance (conceived of as purposive rather than random).[6] 'Some divine providence', foreseeing the future conflict, had ensured that each city would have suitably doughty champions. The fact that these two sets of triplets were also cousins and hence bound to spill kindred blood and incur pollution is stressed repeatedly in the prolonged negotiations and speeches required for setting up the contest (*Ant. Rom.* 3.13–18).[7] This helps

---

[2] Richard 1993; Fox 1996, 82–92.   [3] Ogilvie 1965, 109, 450.   [4] Schultze 2000, section 7.3, 42–5.
[5] Livy 1.23–6 covers from pre-combat negotiations to Horatius' trial and the various expiations (and includes lengthy formulae ignored by Dionysius); this equates to *Ant. Rom.* 3.15–22 (respectively 9 and 17 Loeb pages). Livy's account of the entire Roman–Alban conflict (on which see Ogilvie 1965, 105–17), tinged with overtones of civil war (Batstone 2009, 33–5), differs considerably from Dionysius' amicable process of incorporation (Fox 1996, 82–92). At *Ant. Rom.* 3.18.1 Dionysius justifies his lengthy treatment as 'going through [matters] accurately (ἀκριβῶς, ἐπ' ἀκριβείας)': Schultze 1986, 126–7; Fantasia 2004. On Dionysius' attention to detail, see Oakley in the present volume, pp. 141–2.
[6] *Ant. Rom.* 3.13.3, 14.1–3; Oakley 2010, 121, 123; Wiseman 2002, 343–7; Whitmarsh 2016, 197–9.
[7] For ἄγος, see *Ant. Rom.* 3.15.2, 18.3, 22. For μίασμα and cognates, 3.15.3, 16.3, 21.5, 6.

to establish the situation as one embodying tragic elements which preclude any happy outcome. So does the appearance of the six combatants, who are described as 'dressed like men about to die' (ἔχοντας κόσμον οἷον ἄνθρωποι λαμβάνουσιν ἐπὶ θανάτῳ, *Ant. Rom.* 3.18.2) – the first occurrence in the story of clothing as a signifier. The young men mutually embrace, causing the spectators to reproach themselves for their own hardheartedness.

The course of the battle is recounted in a fashion drawing upon both epic combats from the *Iliad* and the celebrated description of the sea battle at Syracuse (Thuc. 7.71.1–4).[8] Sometimes the point of view is that of the spectating armies, sometimes that of the main Roman participant (*Ant. Rom.* 3.19–20). As sole survivor, the triumphant Horatius heads for the city, in order to be the first to bring the news of his victory to – not the king, but – his own father (*Ant. Rom.* 3.20.4).[9]

Dionysius has already pointed up the dramatic reversals represented in this story (πάθη θεατρικαῖς ἐοικότα περιπετείαις, *Ant. Rom.* 3.18.1). Now, at the outset of the next narrative stage, the authorial voice reiterates this notion: on the very same day, Horatius will fall from a 'wonderful and surprising distinction' to 'the thankless destiny of a sibling-slayer' (*Ant. Rom.* 3.21.1).[10] His sister (never named in Dionysius' narrative)[11] is foremost in dashing out of the city to meet him:

> ... [he was] disturbed at the first sight of her, that – leaving the household tasks she performed with her mother – she, a marriageable girl (παρθένος ἐπίγαμος), should have betaken herself into an unknown crowd. (*Ant. Rom.* 3.21.2)[12]

She outrages the proprieties by leaving the home where, as a virgin of marriageable age, she should be safely engaged in women's work. Horatius is at first inclined to view her disregard of decorum as merely 'some woman's thing she is suffering', as long as he believes it caused by concern for himself and grief for their two dead brothers (*Ant. Rom.* 3.21.2). But in fact she is 'mastered by love' (ἔρωτι κρατουμένη), with an 'unspoken passion' (πάθος ἀπόρρητον) for her slain fiancé and cousin:

---

[8] Walker 1993, 366–8; Oakley 2010, 122–6. Solodow 1979, 258 criticises Dionysius' tameness.
[9] Thomas 1984, 516–17 for fathers who willingly sacrifice sons for Rome.
[10] Herodotean: Pelling 2007, 255–6; Oakley 2010, 123–4.
[11] There seems no reason for him to suppress Horatia's name, but cf. Pericles in Thucydides 2.45.2. Heath 2005, 188–9, nn. 62–3, suggests that mythical women 'speak' through their spinning and weaving, citing Ferrari 2002, 11–86.
[12] The translations in this chapter are my own.

> Leaving the house – like the maenads (ὥσπερ αἱ μαινάδες) – she took herself towards the gates, without attending to her nurse who was calling her and running after her. (*Ant. Rom.* 3.21.3)

Only occasionally does Dionysius employ similes, so this association with Bacchic possession forcibly conveys the girl's frantic state.[13] It also reflects the description of Andromache leaving her house and the skilled textile work upon which she was engaged: 'she sped through the hall like a maenad (μαινάδι ἴση)' (Hom. *Il.* 22.460). To produce these high-prestige commodities is women's valued expertise; and it transpires that Horatia has already created such a piece for a special occasion. This is, significantly, the only particularised item among the spoils borne back by Horatius:

> ... a decorated robe (πέπλος ποικίλος) which she herself with her mother had woven and sent as a present to her fiancé for their future marriage, for it is the custom of the Latins to don decorated robes when they go for their brides. (*Ant. Rom.* 3.21.4)

Dionysius ingeniously contrives to remind the reader of the interior of the house, and how it had formerly fulfilled its proper role as the locus of skilled female domestic work, the place where women are protected. This association is, moreover, no mere nostalgia for the days of Andromache and Penelope, but speaks to the experience of Dionysius' contemporaries. Praise for good wool-working was more than epitaphic convention: the art was still practised in late Republican and Augustan times.[14] The troubled days of 52 BC had seen the house of interrex Marcus Lepidus invaded by Titus Annius Milo, and his wife's symbolic marriage bed and loom destroyed. These stood in the atrium, where this woman 'exemplary for her chastity...used to weave in accordance with ancient custom'.[15] Augustus' wife and female relatives were also tasked with spinning and weaving garments for the family, so as to reinforce an ideology of the traditional home.[16]

Horatia's unique piece of handiwork becomes the means of recognition (ἀναγνώρισις) and adds to the situation's pathos by signifying the marriage that will now not happen.[17] The mention of decorated attire for Latin

---

[13] 'Maenads' recalls the Bacchanalian episode of 186 BC: Livy 39.8–19, esp. 13–14, with Pailler 1988, 229–45, 523–32, 591–6; Henrichs 1978, 134–6; Takács 2000.

[14] Larsson Lovén 1998; Dixon 2001, 117–25.

[15] Asc., *Mil.* 43 C. See also 'Turia' of the so-called *Laudatio Turiae* (*CIL* 6.41062, lines 30–5) with Kierdorf 1980, 33–49; Hemelrijk 2004, 188.

[16] Suet. *Aug.* 64.2, 73.1, with Milnor 2005, 84–5; Langlands 2014, 121.

[17] On Aristotelian 'recognition' in the *Roman Antiquities*, see also Fox in the present volume, p. 193.

bridegrooms fulfils two ends: it ostensibly provides information for Dionysius' contemporaries, familiar with the plain or praetextate togas that constituted Roman formal dress; and it also marks a shared practice of betrothal gift-giving[18] which plays to Dionysius' constant theme that the Romans are, by descent and culture, truly Greek.

Elaborately wrought textiles, however, are also typically associated with funerary rituals, and it was the role of the women of the household to produce these too.[19] As noted above, Dionysius has termed the combatants 'men dressed for death'.[20] The betrothal robe that is now a blood-stained item of booty, as well as the verbal reminiscence of Andromache's distraught behaviour, goes some way to suggest that Horatia grieves with the same abandon as, and with (almost) the same right as, a wife. She expresses her grief as a tragic character might on stage, rending her own garment (χιτών), and beating her breast,[21] as she calls out her fiancé's name (*Ant. Rom.* 3.21.4). Significantly, the onlookers are struck with astonishment (κατάπληξις) rather than manifesting grief or sympathy, which suggests that Horatia has already passed the bounds of decorum.[22]

There follows an exchange of speeches. These are brief, and untypical of Dionysius' political debates in expressing confrontational attitudes that cannot be resolved by compromise or discussion. But here insults are traded, emotions run high, so that the tone resembles an ἀγών in a tragedy.[23] Private affections come up against civic values; no personal reconciliation between the siblings is possible, and so – in tragic fashion – a family is rent asunder. The sister picks up the notion of pollution and defilement already raised, addressing Horatius as 'most defiled of men (μιαρώτατε ἄνθρωπε)'. She reproaches him for being 'out of his wits with joy (ἐξέστηκας τῶν φρενῶν ὑπὸ τῆς ἡδονῆς)', and for 'having a beast's soul' (ἔχων ψυχὴν θηρίου)' (*Ant. Rom.* 3.21.5). He responds with a verbal attack, addressing her in turn as 'You defiled one!' (ὦ μιαρὰ σύ, *Ant. Rom.* 3.21.6). Disloyal to her country, and shameless in her conduct, she disgraces her family by this extravagant grief for the wrong victim, not manifested in the secrecy of darkness but 'before the eyes of all': her self-sought public

---

[18] A Greek bride presented the groom with a χλανίς for the prenuptial night (ἀπαύλια: Poll. 3.40): Redfield 1982, 194; Bundrick 2008, 321. For clothing as a gift, see Wagner-Hasel 2012; McNeil 2005.
[19] Closterman 2014, 171–4.
[20] Livy 1.26.2 with more probability but less pathos makes the recognition token a military cloak (*paludamentum*) woven by Horatia for her fiancé.
[21] Female mourning: Erker 2009, 135–49 (Rome); Garland 1985, 21–37; Rehm 1994, 11–29 (Greece).
[22] An instance of what Levene 1997, 132–3 terms 'analytic' emotion (rather than a shared 'audience-based' one).
[23] Rutherford 2012, 190–200.

appearance is not the least of her crimes. The climax of his reproaches puts her wrongdoing within the complex of family, living and dead: '... you false virgin, you brother-hater and disgrace to your ancestors!' (ὦ ψευδοπάρθενε καὶ μισάδελφε καὶ ἀναξία τῶν προγόνων).

As a ψευδοπάρθενος she is dishonoured, and she shames her parents (and, by implication, would disgrace also the family into whom she might marry); she 'hates' the dead brothers whom she does not mourn; and she is unworthy of her πρόγονοι. In short, the entire nexus of appropriate family relationships has been breached by her behaviour.[24] The Livian Horatius expresses a similar but more restricted notion: that brothers and country (*patria*) are forgotten by Horatia (Livy 1.26.4).

The culmination of Horatius' speech in Dionysius is to equate his sister with one whose body only lives, while her ψυχή is with the corpse whom she bewails, not with the father or brothers whom she disgraces. With this impassioned reproach, Horatius abandons moderation (τὸ μέτριον, *Ant. Rom.* 3.21.6) and kills her; their father accepts the deed because, like his son, he is a 'hater of vileness' (μισοπόνηρος, *Ant. Rom.* 3.21.6, 7). The father's stern (αὐθάδης) attitude is emphasised, and is carried to the length of refusing to allow the girl's body to be brought back into the house or be buried in the family tomb (*Ant. Rom.* 3.21.8).[25] He provides for the kindred a banquet (celebratory not funerary) in order to show that he rates his own disasters as less important than the common good of the country (*Ant. Rom.* 3.21.9). Meanwhile, Horatia's corpse is buried by passers-by as one that belongs to no family; and Dionysius specifically mentions the lack of a shroud (περιστολή).[26] This acts as a final reminder that Horatia has by her action of leaving the house deprived herself of home, kin and her role as maker.

In a striking fashion, Dionysius picks up Horatia's charge (at *Ant. Rom.* 3.21.5) of the beast-like nature of her brother and in the authorial voice applies it to Horatius senior, generalising further to include all Romans of that epoch:

> But so hating vileness and so stern were the manners and thoughts of the Romans then (οὕτω δὲ ἄρα μισοπόνηρα καὶ αὐθάδη τὰ τῶν τότε Ῥωμαίων ἤθη καὶ φρονήματα ἦν), and, if one compares them with the actions and lives of those now, so cruel and harsh and so little distant from the nature of

---

[24] On female and family honour, see Cohen 1991a; Bremmer 1997, 95–6; Langlands 2006, 31–2; McHardy 2008, 45–50.
[25] Gaughan 2010, 16.
[26] His description of the monuments (*Ant. Rom.* 3.22.7–10) omits Horatia's stone tomb (Livy 1.26.14).

wild beasts... (ὠμὰ καὶ σκληρὰ καὶ τῆς θηριώδους οὐ πολὺ ἀπέχοντα φύσεως). (*Ant. Rom.* 3.21.7)

The connotations of θηρίον and its cognates, when applied elsewhere in the *Roman Antiquities* to human beings, fall into four main groups: (a) ungoverned sexual relations; (b) fierce conduct in battle; (c) tyrannical behaviour or demeanour; and (d) uncivilised or un-Greek societal stages or actions.[27] So unfavourable are these associations that the authorial reiteration of this term deserves attention. Dionysius is ostensibly ascribing Horatius senior's action to the primitive state of society of the age of Rome's third king, but also (in view of the father's despotic ban on burying his daughter properly) suggesting that to take paternal power to this extreme has something tyrannical about it (if not actually barbarian: see *Ant. Rom.* 14.6.6, where fierce and brutal conduct towards kin renders Greeks unfit to be considered truly Greek).

So this terminology is notably at odds with the picture of the Romans collectively as humane – for φιλανθρωπία is a quality Dionysius regularly attributes to them.[28] But it fits the desired contrast here between the paternal harshness of an austere age, on the one hand (*Ant. Rom.* 3.21.8–10),[29] and, on the other, the gradual growth of political and judicial institutions towards greater responsibility, which is so marked a feature of Dionysius' conception of Rome's progress. The explicit comparison with present-day 'actions and lives' is at once complimentary to the prevailing social order, and also serves to place the story firmly in the distant past of epic and tragedy, a context where such things can happen.

Dionysius proceeds to deal briskly with King Tullus' dilemma: the choice between condoning a kin-murder which has already been approved by the victim's natural avenger, her father, versus condemning a popular hero and saviour of his country. His solution is to turn the matter over to the Roman people, who for the first time become judges in a capital case and acquit Horatius (*Ant. Rom.* 3.22.6). This development is rather casually handled by Dionysius, who gives very brief summaries (*Ant. Rom.* 3.22.4), sparing both the arguments as to the need for a trial and the actual trial speeches. The conflicted family situation is resolved by the negotiation of a new demarcation between the authority of the family and that of the state.[30] So by the omission of claim, counterclaim and trial speeches, as well

---

[27] (a) *Ant. Rom.* 2.24.4, 5. (b) 6.12.5, 32.3; 9.21.4; 14.10.1, 2. (c) 4.11.5; 5.15.1, 65.2; 6.20.2; 9.47.4; 12.2.8, 3.1; 14.12.1; 16.2.3. (d) 1.33.4; 6.79.3; 14.6.4, 6.
[28] *Ant. Rom.* 1.9.4, 89.1; 3.11.5. Φιλανθρωπία is a core value: Fox 1996, 55, 60, 62, 82, 89.
[29] Harris 1986, 82–6 lists known cases.   [30] Gaughan 2010, 12–22.

as of the archaic legal formulae prominent in Livy's version (Livy 1.26.5–8),³¹ Dionysius has left the sister and brother as the final two speakers, thereby emphasising the personal and emotional confrontation. Associated monuments are supposedly still visible in Rome:³² here he employs elements of aetiology and current practice so as to bring the issue into a contemporary frame of reference (*Ant. Rom.* 3.22.7–10). And his concluding words point up the resemblance to a tragedy, alluding to the περιπέτειαι, the reversals of fortune, which the story as a whole embodies (*Ant. Rom.* 3.22.10).³³

3. Lucretia

The story of Lucretia, Collatinus and Brutus and their involvement in the establishment of the Republic is a complex one, where variants and accretions have been combined and reworked over time. Wiseman has distinguished four main strands regarding 'Year One' of the Republic: the tales of Brutus, Lucretia, Publius Valerius and Marcus Horatius;³⁴ another player is Tarquinius Collatinus, Lucretia's husband, whose consular officeholding seems based on an Athenian model.³⁵ These stories were shaped into a complex and not fully coherent whole: awkward joins make for inconsistencies, so that some characters appear redundant, and the actions of others seem erratically motivated.³⁶ At latest by the time of Fabius Pictor, Collatinus had to be fitted into the family tree of the Tarquins (*Ant. Rom.* 4.64.3), leading to problems for chronographers and genealogists.³⁷ By the mid-second century, Brutus and Lucretia figured in stage dramas.³⁸ There may also have been Etruscan renderings of the story of Lucretia in which she figured as a (would-be) seductress; when father and/or husband arrived, her paramour escaped and she committed suicide. In such a version Etruscan Sextus Tarquinius is the hero (especially if the story had him resist Lucretia's overtures), while Romans – especially the unchaste Lucretia – are the villains. This, at any rate, is the interpretation offered of some urns from Volterra which probably date to the first century BC.³⁹

Rome, however, knew differently: Lucretia was exemplarily virtuous, and the familiar treatment by Livy has become the canonical one (Livy 1.57–60).⁴⁰ The young Tarquin princes, at the siege of Ardea, vie in

---

[31] Feldherr 1998, 123–44 on interplay between sacrifice and expiation in Livy.
[32] Andrén 1960; Wiater 2011a, 198–201.
[33] For another instance of περιπέτεια in the *Roman Antiquities*, see Fox in the present volume, pp. 191–2.
[34] Wiseman 2008c.   [35] Griffiths 2013.   [36] Wiseman 2008b.   [37] Gantz 1975; Schultze 1995.
[38] Wiseman 2008c, 313 with n. 15.   [39] Small 1976.   [40] Ogilvie 1965, 218–32.

praising the excellences of their wives. At Collatinus' suggestion, they test this by a surprise visit home and find their womenfolk partying – all except for Lucretia, Collatinus' wife, who is busy at home with her maidservants, spinning and weaving by lamplight. So she wins the palm for virtue – and she is beautiful too: hence Sextus Tarquinius' evil plot to seduce her.[41]

Dionysius' version of the story, however, omits almost all of this. There is no disputing or testing, no putting of the wives on display. Instead, the story begins when Sextus Tarquinius, doing military duties in Collatia, lodges as a matter of course at the house of his kinsman. His very presence there, and Lucretia's willing hospitality in the absence of Collatinus, implies trust on the part of both husband and wife:

> Collatinus chanced then to be at the camp, but his wife, a Roman woman, the daughter of Lucretius, a notable man, entertained him, as a kinsman of her husband, with great willingness and friendly cordiality. This woman, most beautiful of the women of Rome and most chaste (καλλίστην οὖσαν...καὶ σωφρονεστάτην), Sextus tried to corrupt, having for ages been prevented whenever he stayed with his kinsman, and now thinking that he had a suitable opportunity. Thus, after dinner, he went off to bed, waited a great part of the night, and when he thought everyone was asleep, he got up and came to the apartment where he knew Lucretia was sleeping, and without being noticed by her slaves, who were bedded down at the door of the apartment, he went in, sword in hand. (*Ant. Rom.* 4.64.4–5)

So Dionysius foregoes the delightful picture of Lucretia at work, which, for Livy, concretises her great glory as a wife. There is, as it were, no admittance to the atrium – not even through the end product of the work, as in the Horatia story. Instead, there is almost formulaic praise of her beauty and her σωφροσύνη. The contest over wives is not in Diodorus Siculus (10. 20–2), so Dionysius' annalistic source(s) may have lacked it too.[42] If, as Schubert argues,[43] Livy was the first to elaborate the contest over wives (derived from the Candaules and Gyges story in Herodotus 1.8–13) in the interests of making Collatinus a major participant in a story framed as a tragic triangle, Dionysius may have deliberately passed it over. That, of course, is to assume that Dionysius had read Livy – which is chronologically quite feasible[44] – but that he did not mention having done so.

It is clear, however, that whether or not the contest over wives was in his source(s), Dionysius found Herodotus' tale of Gyges, King Candaules of Lydia and his queen a distasteful one. He chooses it to demonstrate how

---

[41] Joshel 2002; Langlands 2006, 78–96.   [42] Schultze 2000, 21, 30–2.   [43] Schubert 1991, 85–9.
[44] See Oakley in the present volume, and the introduction.

ordinary words, well arranged, can create a narrative of great charm.[45] But he has nothing good to say about the story itself:

> The matter is not only lacking in dignity and unsuitable for fine narration, but it is also low, risqué, and closer to shamefulness than to fineness. But it is told very cleverly, and has become better to hear narrated than to see done. (*Comp.* 3.14)

Dionysius' distaste would tend to make him avoid the contest element. His Lucretia is depicted in a neutral and formal fashion. Her husband plays no part in putting her on view, nor in the rape scene is she viewed through Sextus' eyes. What is stressed there are his inducements to make her yield, couched in terms of power:[46] to reign now over Gabii, and in due course over the Romans and all the other nations subject to Tarquinius Superbus:

> 'For', he said, 'if you submit to gratify me, I shall make you my wife, and you will reign with me for now over the city my father has given me, then after his death, over the Romans, the Latins, the Tyrrhenians, and all the others whom he rules; for I know that I shall take over my father's kingdom, as is right, being his eldest son. Of the good things which belong to kings, all of which you will, with me, have power over – why need I teach you, since you well understand them. But if you try to resist, wishing to save your chastity (σώζειν βουλομένη τὸ σῶφρον), I will kill you and then slaughter one of your attendants, and place your bodies together, and will say that, having caught you behaving disgracefully (ἀσχημονοῦσαν) with the slave, I punished you to avenge the outrage (ὕβριν)[47] to my kinsman so that a shameful and blameworthy end will befall you, and there will be no tomb for your body, nor any of the other customary rituals (ὥστ' αἰσχρὰν καὶ ἐπονείδιστόν σου γενέσθαι τὴν τελευτὴν καὶ μηδὲ ταφῆς τὸ σῶμά σου τυχεῖν μηδ' ἄλλου τῶν νομίμων μηδενός)'. (*Ant. Rom.* 4.65.2–3)

It is not unusual for Dionysius to allow characters to put forward, in speeches, assertions or arguments belied by the 'facts' of the narrative. Here the claim that Sextus, as eldest son, will inherit the kingdom is clearly specious: no single Roman king yet has been the son of a ruling father. Moreover, he is revealing his inherited tyrannical tendencies by thus planning dynastic succession. So Lucretia is being offered the opportunity to be a Tanaquil or a Tullia, improper sharers in power. The duplicity of Sextus Tarquinius is apparent, as is the political aspect of the rape/marriage. Lucretia yields only under the intolerable threat of death with

---

[45] De Jonge 2008, 84–9. See also De Jonge in the present volume, pp. 257–60.
[46] Cf. Diod. Sic. 10.20.2.   [47] On adultery as ὕβρις, see Fisher 1992, 104–5.

dishonour plus the public disgrace of no burial (like Horatia). After the rape and Sextus' departure, Lucretia forthwith leaves Collatia for Rome.

She does so in a very different fashion from the maenad-like Horatia. Lucretia discreetly travels by carriage; she is clad in black, and has concealed a dagger in her clothing. Whereas Horatia's wild demeanour struck beholders with astonishment, Lucretia encounters sympathy but says not a word of her troubles; she is 'composed, thoughtful, with her eyes full of tears' (*Ant. Rom.* 4.66.1).[48] Lucretia breaks her silence only when she reaches her father's house at Rome.

Unlike Livy's Lucretia (Livy 1.58.5–6) with the mere four supporters whom she has summoned to Collatia, Dionysius' heroine shortly becomes the centre of a throng of onlookers. Some relatives just happen to be present when she arrives (*Ant. Rom.* 4.66.2). To these Lucretia makes her initial appeal (in the first direct speech Dionysius allows her), casting herself as a suppliant (ἱκέτις) before her father. She speaks of an outrage (ὕβρις) but reveals no details, requesting in another brief speech that he summon a larger gathering of φίλοι and more kinsmen with whom to take counsel (*Ant. Rom.* 4.66.3). This evokes the Roman notion of a *consilium* tendering advice and support.

These two speeches (the only direct ones that Dionysius attributes to Lucretia) carry the action forward to reach beyond the close family circle to a wider public, including Lucius Iunius Brutus and Publius Valerius Publicola. Dionysius then shifts to reported speech: 'She told them the whole matter, taking it from the beginning', followed by a generalised mention of her 'entreaties' and 'prayers' (*Ant. Rom.* 4.67.1). In none of these speeches is there any trace of the Livian Lucretia's determination never to be an instance of an unchaste woman who by surviving sets a bad example (Livy 1.58.10).[49] And there is no attempt (as in Livy 1.58.9) on the part of the onlookers to convince her of her innocence and right to live,[50] nor is there any apparent imputation or internalisation of shame. The emphasis, both in her own speech and in that of Brutus later, is on the terrible outrage she has suffered.

It is noteworthy that in both the rape episode itself and the subsequent reactions to it, shame is comparatively little mentioned. Of all the speakers depicted, Sextus Tarquinius puts by far the most stress on shame, threatening Lucretia with death with shame (θάνατον μετ' αἰσχύνης, *Ant. Rom.*

---

[48] While her demeanour fits the model of outraged *pudicitia* manifesting itself as *pudor* (Kaster 2005, 35–7), her words reveal none of the internalised shame that he analyses.
[49] Vandiver 1999, 215–6.
[50] Bauman 1993, 557–60 for 'blameless consent' (*inreprehensa voluntas*) under the *lex Julia*.

4.65.1). She will have a shameful and reproachable end (αἰσχρὰν καὶ ἐπονείδιστον...τελευτήν, 4.65.3). His tactic of accusing her of behaving dishonourably (ἀσχημονοῦσαν) with a slave (4.65.3) is effective, for she fears the dishonour (ἀσχημοσύνη) of this death (4.65.4). Sextus also says that in killing her he will claim to have avenged the *hubris* she has done to Collatinus (4.65.3). In her own words, Lucretia claims three times to have suffered ὕβρις (4.66.2 and twice in 4.66.3); she has undergone 'terrible things' (δεινά, 4.66.1, 2, 3, twice), and mentions 'shameful' ones (αἰσχρά) just once (4.66.3). Brutus stresses the ὕβρις that Lucretia endured (4.82.1, 2, 3). In regard to the sufferings of the Roman citizen body as a whole, he alludes to δεινά, χαλεπά and ὠμότης once each (4.71.3, 73.2); ὕβρις three times (4.71.4, 73.3, 78.1); and παρανομία four times (4.78.1, 2, 80.1, twice). The cumulative effect of this choice of words is to direct all the blame at the assailant, and, above all, to stress the ὕβρις and lawlessness that traditionally accompany tyranny.[51]

Lucretia herself is not accorded a suicide speech, but Dionysius reports her death thus:

> After that, embracing her father and making many entreaties both to him and to all present with him, and praying to the gods and other divinities to give her a speedy release from life, she drew the dagger that she had hidden under her robes,[52] and with a single stroke through her chest pierced her heart. (*Ant. Rom.* 4.67.1)

The female bystanders break out into lamentation, and those present vow to die for ἐλευθερία rather than to live under the ὕβρις of tyranny (*Ant. Rom.* 4.67.2).

This part of the narrative, starting from Lucretia's departure, constitutes a movement from the utterly private (the seclusion of her marital home in Collatia) via a transit stage where she remains mute, to a semi-public sphere where she gains a voice. The conclusion of this movement will eventually take Lucretia's body out into the fully public realm of the Forum of Rome, to be viewed by the city's whole population (*Ant. Rom.* 4.76.3).[53] Here she becomes, as it were, a passive interlocutor as Brutus, portrayed as the hero of the episode and architect of change, delivers a speech over her (see below). Meanwhile, Lucretia is ignored by Dionysius for two and a half chapters as he digresses into an explanatory flashback about Lucius Iunius

---

[51] Arist. *Pol.* 5.1310b40–1311b6, 1314b23–27, 1315a14–31. Cohen 1991b, 173–5; Fisher 1992, 27–30.

[52] The plural suggests *tunica* plus *stola*, denoting a modest woman: Scholz 1992; Sebesta 1998; Olson 2008, 27–36.

[53] Feldherr 1997, 148 on the similar – but less literal – movement in Livy 1.59.

Brutus (*Ant. Rom.* 4.67.3–69). This tends to check the emotion evoked by Lucretia's death, turning the narrative decisively away from her personal drama towards Rome's political future, just as Brutus will shortly bid the grieving family to do.

Only now does Tarquinius Collatinus make his appearance – when his wife is already dead (*Ant. Rom.* 4.70.2). His distraught demeanour is briefly but vividly presented: he embraces and calls upon Lucretia, and he is described as being 'out of his mind at this calamity' (ἔξω τοῦ φρονεῖν γεγονὼς ὑπὸ τοῦ κακοῦ).[54] Brutus sternly calls husband, father and household to order for excessive mourning, reminding them that vengeance comes first. This pointedly draws attention to Collatinus' behaviour: while natural and explicable on the personal level, it is wholly inadequate on the political level. The historian guides the reader's assessment of priorities by cutting short Collatinus' grief with a brief direct speech from Brutus, followed by a longer reported one. Here, then, is another phase of shifting from private to public, from mourning to action. The projected action is sealed by an oath of vengeance, led by Brutus and taken by all (*Ant. Rom.* 4.70.5–71.1).

Brutus then delivers three direct speeches. The first (*Ant. Rom.* 4.71) outlines a plan. Then an intermission, as it were, briefly reports the advocacy in turn of monarchy, senatorial rule and democracy (a miniversion of Herodotus' Persian debate of 3.80–2).[55] Brutus then directs a second substantial speech at the friends already present (*Ant. Rom.* 4. 73–5). He urges action, proposing various constitutional changes to be put before the δῆμος. It is a fine example of Dionysius' hyper-constitutionality: by the end its author uses expressions implying that Brutus is addressing a senate meeting (*Ant. Rom.* 4.75.4). A final lengthy harangue is spoken to the assembled people (*Ant. Rom.* 4.77–83).

Between Brutus' second and third speeches, the scene shifts to the Roman Forum, where Lucretia's body makes its final move into public view. The corpse is carried out in front of the senate house to be displayed in all its fresh horror: 'untreated for burial and stained with blood' (*Ant. Rom.* 4.76.3). Part of Brutus' final speech (*Ant. Rom.* 4.82.1–4) amounts to a funeral *laudatio* over Lucretia, using many of the tropes and forms characteristic of that genre.[56] Lucretia is set in a family context as a daughter and wife, and her resolute suicide is graphically related (*Ant.*

---

[54] Cf. *Ant. Rom.* 3.21.5, on Horatius, quoted above.
[55] Fromentin 2006. On this passage, see also Wiater in the present volume, pp. 75–6. Cf. also Pelling in the present volume, pp. 214–15 on the constitutional debate in *Ant. Rom.* 2.3.7–8.
[56] Kierdorf 1980, 112–16; Schultze 2011. Cf. Diod. Sic. 10.21 with Schubert 1991, 81 n. 4.

Rom. 4.82.1–2). The speaker then addresses her directly,[57] almost as if she lives again, entering into her state of mind, praising her manly staunchness and ascribing to her the motives which led to her action:

> 'O you remarkable woman, worthy of great praise for your noble disposition! You are gone, you are dead, being unable to endure the tyrant's outrage and despising all the pleasures of life in order not to suffer any such thing again. After this, Lucretia, when you, who happened to have a woman's nature, have shown the mental attitude of a noble man, shall we, who were born men, show ourselves worse than women in excellence? To you, because tyrannised one night your spotless honour was taken from you by force, sweeter and more blessed did death seem than life; and shall not the same thing apply to us, from whom Tarquinius, ruling as tyrant not for one day only but for twenty-five years, has taken all the pleasures of life in taking away our freedom?' (*Ant. Rom.* 4.82.3)

It is noteworthy how Dionysius makes Brutus report Lucretia's feelings and motivation far more forcefully than she was allowed to express them in the suicide scene: it is as if Lucretia, scarcely vocal herself, has been given voice by her champion. The power of the speech arouses strong and conflicting emotions in the audience: stirred by the call to freedom, but apprehensive of what that demands (*Ant. Rom.* 4.84.1). Its outcome is to spur the hearers to decisive action, and it is, accordingly, causational. This conforms precisely to the historian's rationale for the inclusion of speeches in history, expressed in methodological passages at *Ant. Rom.* 7.66.3 and 11.1.3–4. He considers them to rank with actions in a nexus of cause and effect: without speeches, no proper understanding of historical events can be obtained.[58] In this notable demonstration of ἐνάργεια,[59] Brutus' words extend and vividly embellish the narrative descriptions of the rape and the suicide, so that his supposed hearers and the reader can grasp the factors operative in creating significant political change.

4. The Augustan Context

'Before the institution of the *leges Iuliae*, the oversight of a woman's moral health was the responsibility of the male head of her household, either her father or her husband. . . .. For the first time under the adultery legislation,

---

[57] Paralleled in the *Laudatio Turiae* and Augustus' oration over Agrippa in 12 BC (Hemelrijk 2004, 186–7).
[58] Schultze 1986, 127; Marincola 2007, 126–7.
[59] Defined at *Lys.* 7.1. Marincola 2013, 83 observes that 'vividness *can* be a tool for raising the emotions but. . .it is also a tool for instruction and explanation by the historian'.

women were answerable to the state for their actions in the bedroom'.⁶⁰ The Julian laws *de maritandis ordinibus* and *de adulteriis coercendis* of 18 BC⁶¹ are of course not directly handled by Dionysius. Nevertheless, it is possible to relate some of the attitudes found in his work to these matters of contemporary concern.

In describing Romulus' legislation, Dionysius begins with measures relating to marriage and interaction with women, regarded as fundamental to the well-being of states. He dilates upon the inadequate institutions of lawgivers in other societies (Greek and barbarian) compared to the equitable forms devised by Romulus to promote stability both in marriages and in the state as a whole (*Ant. Rom.* 2.24–5). Equally approving is the description of the censor as overseer (ἐπίσκοπος) and guard (φύλαξ) of everything in the home – including the bedroom (*Ant. Rom.* 20.13.2). All this is fully in accordance with the Julian laws' aim of securing private family morality by legislative provisions.⁶² Romulus' system also inculcated respect and dutifulness on the part of children towards their parents (*Ant. Rom.* 2.26–7). This portion deals mostly with *patria potestas* with regard to adult sons, but there is a general message about the importance of well-regulated families which conduce to a well-regulated state.⁶³

Both these aspects – controlling women and exercising authority over sons – are in play in the Horatius–Horatia story. Firstly, there are verbal echoes. Dionysius' overall description of Romulus' legislation terms it 'austere, hating vileness and having much resemblance to heroic lifestyles' (*Ant. Rom.* 2.24.1). This recalls the judgement about the epoch of Horatius as 'stern and hating vileness' (*Ant. Rom.* 3.21.7, quoted above). Horatia has eluded paternal authority and put affection higher than honour. The shame that this entails is expressed in Horatius' offensive accusation that his sister is a 'false virgin', a ψευδοπάρθενος (quoted above), as if her autonomous act of leaving the house has actually destroyed her virginity. With it the family's honour is gone, and so this is tantamount to a self-chosen act of *stuprum*, deserving due penalty.⁶⁴ Punishment for this is meted out, in this instance, by a brother rather than a father, but the story as a whole endorses the exercise of *patria potestas*. The father disowns the daughter, forgives the son, stands by him at his trial, and claims the right to judge both his children (*Ant. Rom.* 3.22.4).

---

⁶⁰ Milnor 2005, 150. ⁶¹ Treggiari 1991, 60–80, 277–90; McGinn 1998, 70–104, 140–215.
⁶² Milnor 2005, 147–8. ⁶³ Thomas 1984; Gaughan 2012, 23–52. ⁶⁴ Fantham 1991.

The king agrees that both nature and law (φύσις and νόμος) give the father the right of avenging his daughter and (therefore) equally of letting his son off, if he so chooses (*Ant. Rom.* 3.22.5). This view resonates with recent and contemporary cases where paternal powers of *ius vitae necisque* were involved. Just within living memory was the case of A. Fulvius, the senator who executed his son for joining the Catilinarian conspiracy in 63 BC.[65] But in the time of Augustus, the *princeps* is found concerned in two cases where he exercised leniency. He rescued by his *auctoritas* an *eques* (Tricho) who had flogged his son to death and was being mobbed in the forum, and he recommended removal from the city for a senator's son (Tarius) whom his father was prosecuting for attempted *parricidium*.[66] These instances of the exercise of extreme paternal powers partly account for the fascination with which Dionysius describes this characteristically Roman institution.

In Dionysius' treatment of Lucretia, the insignificant role attributed to Collatinus requires explanation. Dionysius deprives him of all serious involvement, downplaying him in favour not only of Brutus, but even of his father-in-law, Spurius Lucretius. There is in fact good reason for writing Collatinus out of the story as far as feasible. It would be overly far-fetched to equate the competition of wives so graphically described by Livy with some kind of pimping on Collatinus' part, yet it is the case that *lenocinium* had become, under the *Lex Iulia de adulteriis coercendis*, an offence to which husbands were liable,[67] as they also were for providing a venue where adultery could take place.[68] Even if not criminally accountable, the man too complaisant, too careless or too weak to control his wife met with social opprobrium. Accordingly, Dionysius avoids the faintest hint that Collatinus might put his own wife on view, because even that would derogate from her modesty and chastity. That is why there is no contest as to the best wife and no display. This unfortunate husband must therefore be limited to weeping over his wife's body, but even in this he is so unrestrained as to incur Brutus' rebuke. This impugns his manliness and suggests he undervalues the political freedom to which Lucretia's suicide pointed the way. To Lucretia, as to 'Turia' of the *Laudatio Turiae*, is attributed true manly virtue. For such a significant turning point in the history of Rome, Dionysius requires flawless characters and motives above reproach.

---

[65] Sall. *Cat.* 39.5; Val. Max. 5.8.5; Dio 37.36.   [66] Sen. *Clem.* 15–16.1.
[67] McGinn 1998, 171–94. See also Cantarella 1991, 229–35; Edwards 1993, 37–62.
[68] McGinn 1998, 241–5.

5. The Historian's Principles

No longer is Dionysius' history routinely denigrated as hack work or mere flattery, unworthy of serious consideration.[69] Instead, it is recognised as a reimagining of early Rome aimed at creating a shift in understanding within Greco-Roman culture. His critical writings and their relationship to his historical opus have benefited over the past generation from many studies aiming at a more nuanced understanding of him as literary theorist and historiographer.[70] The present section briefly examines how Dionysius applies in the stories of Horatia and Lucretia the principles for historians which he articulates in his theoretical works and in the methodological passages of his history.

Foremost among the historian's duties is the choice of a good subject and fitting scope (*Letter to Pompeius* 3.2, 8–10; *On Thucydides* 6, 10, 12.1). That achieved, the individual events need to be selected and shaped. Herodotus receives praise for creating a harmonious whole over a huge time-span and area; this is combined with attractive variety between episodes (*Pomp.* 3.11, 13–14). Thucydides fails in this respect, and also with regard to appropriate length of treatment (*Pomp.* 3.12; *Thuc.* 9, 13.3, 14.3, 16.1). Xenophon is credited with good structure within the individual episodes (*Pomp.* 4.2). The relatively brief tale of Horatius and Horatia is framed as a personal narrative of tragic reversal, set within the larger account of a war. The latter situation is resolved through the negotiations and speeches which express the philanthropic principles that Dionysius holds to be characteristic of Rome, whereas the far more dramatic inset story highlights the individual cost. Change of pace and of focus provides variety. Lucretia's rape story functions as an initiating cause of action, and there follows a marked shift of attention from one protagonist to another, formed by the digression on Brutus. This takes the action from the private to the public sphere, where Brutus' three speeches place heavy emphasis upon the legitimacy of the lead-up process and on the traditionality of the new constitution itself. The lengthy working-out (ἐξεργασία) of these themes marks the extreme importance of a soundly based transition from one constitution to another, which it is important that the reader fully understands (cf. *Ant. Rom.* 7.66.2–5).

---

[69] See the introduction to the present volume, pp. 28–9.
[70] Wiseman 1979; Sacks 1983; Schultze 1986; Heath 1989; Gabba 1991; Fromentin 1993; Fox 1996; Hidber 1996; Marincola 1997; Luraghi 2003; Delcourt 2005; De Jonge 2008; Fox 2011; Wiater 2011a, 2011b; De Jonge 2017.

As regards the depiction (μίμησις) of emotion and of character, Dionysius awards Thucydides the palm for the former, Herodotus for the latter (*Pomp.* 3.18). Xenophon falls short here (*Pomp.* 4.4), while Theopompus' understanding of 'the emotions of the soul' is outstanding (*Pomp.* 6.7–8). Related to this aspect is that of providing speeches that convey sentiments appropriate both to speaker and situation (*Pomp.* 3.20; *Thuc.* 15.1–2, 17.2–18). In the account of Horatius, Dionysius uses a range of techniques to evoke the characters' feelings: depiction of action and appearance; description of thought processes; tokens – the bridegroom's robe – which evoke unfulfilled possibilities; and two speeches of notable brevity and forcefulness. His technique in the case of Lucretia is rather different. Both prior to and after her rape, opportunities for insightful analysis or the portrayal of emotional reactions are largely shunned; a demeanour that is subdued but not ashamed indicates controlled emotion. Greater emphasis is placed on speeches and their appropriateness to the speakers: Sextus Tarquinius' vigorous (yet specious) presentation of Lucretia's dilemma; her own restrained recounting of the ὕβρις she has undergone; and her posthumous 're-voicing' through Brutus' dynamic demonstration of her noble behaviour and suicide. Personal motivation and emotion is played down in favour of the wider political picture.

The historian's own disposition (διάθεσις) necessarily permeates every aspect of his work, in Dionysius' view. Every historian reveals himself as candid, fair, moral and well-judging, or the reverse: grudging, mean and carping (*Pomp.* 3.15, 4.2, 5.2, 6.6; *Thuc.* 8.2). These attitudes are manifested both in the overall treatment of large-scale events and in the presentation of individuals and small occurrences. Dionysius claims to be a right-thinking proponent of truth and justice (*Ant. Rom.* 1.6.5). In one of these accounts, he makes a rare authorial appearance, explicitly judging Roman behaviour of a remote epoch against that of his own day. But, as is his more usual practice, his διάθεσις emerges through respectful distancing from his characters and a concern for decency, virtue and moral behaviour.

6. Conclusion

In the story of Horatius, the sibling-slayer, Dionysius surely intended his Greek readers to recognise echoes of cultural practices known to them from literature. This small episode attributes to monarchical Rome features that simultaneously evoke myth, Homeric epic and Athenian tragedy. It is a brief glimpse of a somewhat more primitive society, one which bears out Dionysius' overall contention about the Greek nature of Rome from the earliest times. In Schmitz's neat phrase, here is an 'icon of Greekdom'.[71] Roman readers could no doubt see this too, and they would also identify continuities in the social system, such as *patria potestas*, that reinforced a reassuring self-image of traditions upheld and continuing.

The account of Lucretia's rape and the consequent momentous constitutional change offers the historian a different challenge. To emphasise the personal ordeal and the domestic drama would tend to direct the reader's attention and sympathy towards individual wrongs. Dionysius instead concentrates firmly on the abuse as a political act, demanding a more than merely familial revenge – an overthrow of the whole tyranny. To this end, Lucretia is reduced to an ideal of modest beauty, living more vividly after death in Brutus' later speech than in her own words; Collatinus is almost a cipher in order to throw all the blame upon Sextus Tarquinius. On the brink of significant political transformation, it is not the individual characters that matter but the collective character of Rome. Rome of those days is shown as a society where necessary change is achieved through argument-based consensus and with the assurance of stability: the implication is that this holds good for Rome of the Augustan age too.

---

[71] Schmitz 2011, 245.

CHAPTER 7

The Prehistory of the Roman polis in Dionysius

Matthew Fox

Introduction

This chapter discusses Dionysius' treatment of the first inhabitants of Italy, the pre-Romans who sustain his claims for the Hellenic ethnicity of the Romans, and who are the first historical characters in his history. How does he imagine these early inhabitants behaved? What was their society like? Rather than seeing what Dionysius tells us about them, I examine his techniques of representation, and consider what can be extrapolated from their details.[1] I will present passages from the start of the *Roman Antiquities* as a test case for a technique of close reading which observes the effects of large-scale ideas about history and political structures in verbal details. I explore how individual sentences can help clarify the relationship between Dionysius' picture of early society and his explicit (and better-studied) arguments about Rome. This focus on the small scale is aimed at providing new evidence for familiar questions about Dionysius' political orientation, as a Greek mediating a newly confident Augustan vision of Rome to a Greek audience across the Mediterranean.[2] The Hellenic origins of Rome's pre-founders and first inhabitants is the crux of Dionysius' framing of Rome's history so as to convince Greeks that Rome's hegemony made historical sense. It is also central to his polemic against Greek prejudice that Romans were barbarians. My reading will show that as he works with narrative to present what we should think of as an event-based representation of these theories, Dionysius does more than just reinforce a preconceived political agenda. Rather, his narrative, by playing with chronology and source-criticism, discloses the complexity of his political position. By taking that complexity into consideration, we can make significant progress in understanding how an idea that still excites ridicule –

---

[1] I thus aim to move the debate beyond the discussion of Gabba 1991, 98–124.
[2] There is a large literature on the nationality of Dionysius' audience. See, e.g., Schultze 1986; Luraghi 2003; Wiater 2014, 24–30; the introduction to the present volume.

that the Romans were Hellenes – could be regarded as credible, both to Dionysius and his readers.³ The idea seems absurd when it is presented as crude summary, but with careful work on his words, it gains in nuance, and emerges as Dionysius' adroit and self-aware response to a rich and chaotic set of traditions.

Recent studies provide a helpful foundation: Delcourt bringing a broad context to Dionysius' Hellenism; Wiater presenting *Roman Antiquities* in the light of Dionysius' theories of classicism.⁴ For the prehistoric narrative, Dionysius' relationship with Polybius is also important, since Dionysius' self-fashioning as a historian depends on refuting Polybius' insistence on the primacy of recent history, and on finding a productive way of handling prehistoric material.⁵ Dionysius expands Polybius' arguments about the inevitability of Rome's historical rise, showing that ethnic identity and political behaviour are causes, as much as constitutional and theoretical considerations. The political forces, as well as the place of origin, and the reasons for migration thus make the prehistorical Italians a useful resource for establishing ideas about ideal Helleno-Roman history, in terms both of what happened, and how best to write about it.

My approach takes its inspiration from White's idea of 'the historical field'.⁶ That term denotes the verbal processes by means of which the historian establishes the world to which readers can grant credence, and in White's analyses of the nineteenth-century canon, sentence-level analysis is a vital tool. Through such analysis, we learn about Dionysius' view of his role as a historian beyond what he tells us in his theoretical statements, enabling us to broaden his explicit political agenda into one that also includes a particular manner of engaging his readers, that being a political gesture in its own right. The advantage of examining the narrative texture is that it allows us to transcend the polarity of Roman/Greek, or Greek/Barbarian, around which Dionysius' *arguments* are articulated. Although once Rome is founded, Dionysius embarks enthusiastically on his task of representing Rome's leaders as fully formed in the model of their Greek relations, the prehistory is more cautious: exhorting

---

³ Ando 1999, 11 holds that Dionysius' remaking of Romans as Greeks 'persuaded nobody'.
⁴ Delcourt 2006, 130–53 describes the book 1 narrative as focussing on ideas, but neglects Dionysius' method of presentation; Wiater 2011a, *passim*, but esp. 165–98.
⁵ Dionysius includes Polybius in a list of stylistically unappealing historians at *Comp.* 4.15: cf. Pelling in the present volume, p. 203. On the polemic expressed by ending his history where Polybius starts, Gozzoli 1976; Wiater 2011a, 194–8; Pelling 2016; Pelling in the present volume, p. 204.
⁶ See White 1973, 5–7; 1978, 63–8.

readers to collaborate in the reconstruction of Roman ethnicity, and to accept that, given the nature of the evidence, his conclusions about Rome's origins are the most reasonable ones. In line with his views of historiography in his essays, his approach privileges an Herodotean interest in plurality and reader engagement, over a more authoritarian Thucydidean method.[7] Dionysius' discussion of Herodotus and Thucydides in the *Letter to Pompeius* 3 explains his preference for Herodotus in terms of formal decisions about narrative structure and style. It does not tackle head-on the topic of how to treat sources.[8] However, it will be evident that Dionysius takes a more Herodotean approach both to his source material and to his idea of the historian's authority, though in both areas, his presentation assumes a new and individual form.

Schwartz's discussion of Dionysius' failure to appreciate the distinctive nature of Roman political institutions, and his inaccurate use of Greek terminology, was based, in spite of his prejudices against Dionysius' rhetorical perspective, on a detailed examination of the text.[9] The terms of the debate have altered little in Ando's 1999 discussion, 'Was Rome a Polis?', in which he explores the difficulties Roman institutions presented to Greek historians.[10] My approach is different in that it starts not from political-theoretical categories designed to capture the 'real' historical nature of Rome's institutions, but from the texture of Dionysius' writing. As in my earlier studies, my aim is to try to understand why Dionysius describes Rome as he does, and from that to deduce something about the realities of living as a Greek intellectual in Augustan Rome.

The *polis* in Italy before Rome

From the outset, it is worth recalling how disordered the first book of *Roman Antiquities* is, how little concerned Dionysius is to provide a single coherent account, how eager to include variations in the sources. There are no less than five different waves of migration into Italy before he treats the

---

[7] For the contrast, Momigliano 1990; Foster and Lateiner 2012. For Dionysius' views on it, Wiater 2011a, 132–49. On the dialogic quality of Herodotus' persona, including his handling of sources, Dewald 1987, 2002; Baragwanath 2008, 55–9.
[8] Ek 1942, 5–47 is a meticulous examination of Dionysian echoes of Herodotean formulations for handling conflicting sources and events that require multiple explanations. Overall, Ek's dissertation provides excellent evidence for the Herodotean quality of Dionysius' writing.
[9] Schwartz 1903. On Schwartz's denigration of Dionysius, Gabba 1979, 1043–5; 1991, 5–9. Gabba 1994 rectifies my misunderstanding (Fox 1993, 31) of his interpretation of Schwartz's political context.
[10] Ando 1999. See too Hartog 1991: For Polybius, Champion 2004.

foundation of the city.¹¹ In narrating these, it is striking how much attention he bestows upon the process of historical research.¹² There are traces of an impulse to produce a linear historical narrative, but it is continually interrupted by the addition of variants and comparison of sources. Nevertheless, the *polis* is the fundamental element in Italian prehistory, even if the definition of that community remains vague. I examine some of the Italian examples, before turning to Rome.

At *Roman Antiquities* 1.16, the very start of his Italian prehistory, Dionysius states that the first people to inhabit 'these places' were Aborigines. Soon he has them sending out colonists from their cities (πόλεις) when lack of resources stresses the population, a story familiar in the Greek world.¹³ As well as πόλις, however, he also employs the term χωρίον (place), presumably to communicate either the variety of these communities, or the fact that not all were urban.¹⁴ However, the products of this colonizing expedition were unambiguously cities. This first wave, the displacement of Sicels by Aborigines, resulted in Antemnae, Tellenae, Ficulea, Tibur.¹⁵ This is the first case of a recurrent trope, of Dionysius connecting remains visible today with the most ancient prehistory. Although commonplace in much historiography, that is not a reason to overlook the effect it has within this particular account. Continuity with the present is a form of validation: the identification of prehistoric with modern cities provides an anchorage in verifiable material, and encourages readers to take seriously the historian's efforts.¹⁶

After the arrival of the Pelasgians from Greece, an alliance is formed that colonizes much of Italy, resulting in the displacement of both Sicels and Umbrians. Dionysius tells us that the two peoples, Pelasgian and Aboriginal, united in founding many cities. 'And the Pelasgians inhabited in common with the Aborigines many cities (πόλεις πολλάς), some of which were, before, inhabited by the Siceli and others they built themselves.'¹⁷

---

[11] See Gabba 1991, 107–11; Delcourt 2006, 201, 210. See also the introduction of the present volume, pp. 9–10.
[12] So, e.g., *Ant. Rom.* 1.13.4: an elaborate exhortation to readers to weigh up the evidence regarding the Aborigines (Oenotrians by descent); *Ant. Rom.* 1.22.2–5: several versions of the original location of the Sicels before they crossed over into Sicily. Scepticism even extends to central topics: 'there is much dispute about the date of the founders [of Rome] and their identity' (*Ant. Rom.* 1.72.1).
[13] *Ant. Rom.* 1.16.2.   [14] *Ant. Rom.* 1.16.4, 5.
[15] *Ant. Rom.* 1.16.5. Dionysius also draws attention to the still persistent traces of this struggle in the existence of a Sicel quarter in Tibur.
[16] On the limits of Dionysius' interest in such continuities, Pelling 2016.
[17] *Ant. Rom.* 1.20.5. Unless otherwise marked, I use Spelman's 1758 translation, with minimal modifications of spelling and punctuation, employing Cary's Loeb rewriting (1937–1950) where Spelman

Lest anxiety arise that these *poleis* are not so much cities, as city-states, Dionysius names them, and says that several were still inhabited in his own day. Striking is the inclusion of Croton (*Ant. Rom.* 1.20.4), at that point inhabited by the Umbrians, described as big and successful (εὐδαίμονα καὶ μεγάλην). Beyond the identity of the cities and the origin of their inhabitants, what dominates the writing is the manner in which Dionysius prevents readers from being drawn into a continuous narrative. Instead they are encouraged to reflect upon the continuity between prehistory and the present, and to remain aware of visible evidence for the long distant past. The description of the similarity of the religious rites of Falerii, one of the Pelasgian foundations, with those of Argos (*Ant. Rom.* 1.21), is a lengthier version of something that occurs regularly in a briefer form: the invitation to readers to compare the present with the distant past, and thus to reflect upon the historian's activities.

A revealing moment is the crisis over a divine demand for the Pelasgians to offer human sacrifices. Remember that the Pelasgians were in origin Greek, and after their sojourn in Italy many returned there: this was a response to a combination of natural catastrophes, and the difficult conditions placed on them by an oracle as a remedy to those same catastrophes (*Ant. Rom.* 1.23).[18] 'The first cause of the desolation of their cities seemed to be a drought, which laid waste the land' (1.23.2). They are settled in a number of cities, but the same fate affects them all. As one ethnic and social group, they carry the responsibility for their own failure to respond appropriately to the divine order. 'Using almost the same words' as Myrsilus the Lesbian,[19] Dionysius reports that the people consulted an oracle; he does not say which one, only that the respondent was 'the god'. Piecemeal, we learn more about the civic structures of these prehistoric communities. A second consultation of the oracle was prompted by one of the body designated as elders, τῶν γεραιτέρων τις. Continuing in *oratio obliqua*, Dionysius explains what the old man's reasoning was: they *had* made sufficient offerings in gratitude for their community's success, but had omitted to offer what was in fact dearest to the gods: human lives. Dionysius then sums up the response to this elder's

---

is infelicitous or obscure (Spelman-Cary). In a few cases, marked (Fox), I have retranslated to bring out an emphasis missing in either earlier version.

[18] Briquel 1993, 30–3 (summarizing arguments made more fully in Briquel 1984) points out that the Greek origin of the Pelasgians is central to the Hellenic genealogy of the Romans. It is this origin that distinguishes Rome from other cultures in Italy (notably the Etruscans – who are Briquel's theme in this work; cf. Briquel 1984, 629).

[19] I.e. Myrsilus of Methymna, *FGrH* 477.

interpretation of the oracle: '(...) some were of the opinion that he was in the right, others that there was treachery couched under his discourse' (*Ant. Rom.* 1.24.2).

The nature of this treachery (ἐπιβουλή) soon becomes clearer. The requirement for sacrifice produced conflict among the urban élite (οἱ προεστηκότες τῶν πόλεων). Disenchantment then descended the social hierarchy, as suspicion fell on those in power (ἔπειτα καὶ τὸ λοιπὸν πλῆθος δι' ὑποψίας τοὺς ἐν τέλει ἐλάμβανεν). In the following years, sacrificing of the youth continued; this reign of terror was being used by the magistrates to rid their cities of those they thought likely to ferment στάσις, as well as to eliminate enemies. The result was the terminal scattering of the Pelasgians, itself an explanation for the diversity of the historical traditions surrounding them.

What is the effect of these embryonic political structures, and what kind of historical reality do they evoke? Dionysius is striving to depict political processes that will prevent readers from reading this material as a myth that has been too heavily rationalized, while at the same time establishing a minimum level of plausibility. A distinct feeling for the primitive nature of this society does emerge: it is a πόλις structure, but not outlined with sufficient clarity to bring forth an anachronistic picture of a particular form of constitution. The failure to name the oracle is significant: it was either a god or a δαίμων that had given them the initial oracle: a striking contrast to the oracle obtained from Dodona, and quoted, from an account from a named historian, a few chapters earlier, when the Pelasgians begin their Italian exploits (*Ant. Rom.* 1.19). There is no formal assembly, and the choice of the word γεραίτεροι avoids using any term that suggests an assembly of elders; those in power are variously designated as οἱ ἐν τέλει, οἱ δυναστεύοντες.[20]

In these episodes Dionysius makes recurrent use of a dative participle construction, to evoke a hierarchy of historical agency, and thus a sense of causation and context.[21] Consider these three examples:

> As the Aborigines approached (ἐλθοῦσι δὴ τοῖς Ἀβοριγῖσι) with a great army, the Pelasgi, stretching out the symbols of supplication (...) (*Ant. Rom.* 1.20.1)

---

[20] This last term is used to describe those responsible for Rome's success in Dionysius' own time in *Oratt. Vett.* 3.1. See below, n. 24.
[21] Kühner-Gerth I 424–5, with similar usages in a range of historians from Herodotus onwards.

> Upon their consulting the oracle (μαντευομένοις δ' αὐτοῖς) what god, or genius they had offended to be thus afflicted, and, by what means they might hope for relief, the god answered that, having obtained what they desired, they had neglected to give what they had promised, but that the most valuable things were still due from them. (*Ant. Rom.* 1.23.4–5)
>
> While they were in this perplexity (ἀμηχανοῦσι δὲ αὐτοῖς), one of the elders, conjecturing the sense of it, told them they were very much mistaken, if they thought the gods complained of them without reason. (*Ant. Rom.* 1.24.1)

In each of these sentences, figures in the dative are made into a circumstance; they become the background against which a definable action occurs, to allow a distinct individual to take the initiative: a particularly bold old man; the god answering an oracle; the Pelasgians showing greater cultural cohesion than the Aborigines. But those who go into exile rather than submit to the caprice of their rulers also reveal something: these are people determined to transcend the barbarity of their own society, a barbarity denoted by the demand for human sacrifice. They would rather risk total dispossession (ἐφέστια, *Ant. Rom.* 1.24.3) than remain under the rule of a harsh god and his human agents. With such details, Dionysius produces a recognizable culture, without being explicit about political organization.

How Rome Became a *polis*

When we come to the emergence of Rome itself, Dionysius has several agendas. Most obtrusive, but also hardest to describe, is the unresolved juxtaposition of different accounts of the events that lead up to the foundation, and of the different strands in the narrative. They are all included: Italus, Saturn, the many stopping off points of Aeneas and Anchises; Heracles, Evander, Latinus; there is a substantial digression on the Greek origin of the Trojans (*Ant. Rom.* 1.61), an element sometimes overlooked, but which modifies too stark a polarity between Dionysius' and Vergil's views of Rome's origin.[22] There is a short version of Aeneas-to-Romulus, and then a longer one, again with variants. There is a further stab at the period in a discussion of the controversy over dating (*Ant. Rom.* 1.74.1). Throughout, Dionysius prevents readers from losing track of the multiplicity of versions, and from ignoring smaller scale

---

[22] Hill 1961; Gozzoli 1976, 155–6; Wiater 2011a, 213.

aetiologies in the quest for larger ones. Certainly, there are episodes where rationalizing techniques are in evidence, and others where variants are smoothed over. But there are also many where the variations in his sources are kept visible, and where the task of the historian becomes itself the object of attention. This task Dionysius is keen to share with his readers. The multiple tombs of Aeneas are a good example. They are described well before the main account of his death (at *Ant. Rom.* 1.64):

> But if it creates a difficulty, that the sepulcher of Aeneas is said to be, and is shown, in many places, it being impossible for the same person to be buried in more than one: let them consider that this difficulty is common to many, particularly to men of illustrious fortunes, and wandering lives (...) (*Ant. Rom.* 1.54.1)

This view of the attitude appropriate for interpreting the monuments and traditions supposes a more-or-less sceptical reader who just needs to examine the evidence to reach a reasonable conclusion. The many monuments to Aeneas demonstrate to some degree his presence. Dionysius does not, however, overstate the case, allowing for the most minimal interpretation of the evidence. At the very least, if there is a monument, Aeneas cannot have been unknown:

> What cause, then, can be assigned for the monuments erected to him in Italy, if he never reigned in these parts, resided there, or was entirely unknown to the inhabitants? (*Ant. Rom.* 1.54.3)

That is expressed as a deduction that any reader will need to draw. Dionysius here casts the interpretative responsibility firmly into the lap of the sceptics: they are invited to come up with their own *aetia* if they think Dionysius' account of the matter is incorrect. Slightly earlier, he is more direct – βούλομαι (I wish) the sentence emphatically begins:

> But I wish, concerning the arrival of Aeneas, not to give a cursory account, since some historians are ignorant about it, others give a different version. I shall draw on the most trusted of the Greek and Roman histories. This is what is said about him. (*Ant. Rom.* 1.45.4, translation Fox)

The reader should appreciate that Dionysius is doing his job properly by giving due weight to the complex traditions, both Greek and Roman, regarding Aeneas in Italy. It is not just the presentation of the evidence that is striking, but also the rhetoric used to involve the reader in weighing it up. Together with the great proliferation of accounts, this makes the pre-foundation story of Rome a demonstration of the complexity of the tradition, and of the problematic historical procedure necessary to give a responsible account. It is hard to imagine that Vergil is not a factor in these discussions about Aeneas. But Dionysius orientates his presentation not to provide a comment on Vergil, so much as to present the complex traditions which that master narrative had to tackle.

In this anarchic context, moments of clarity do emerge concerning Rome. The prehistoric account identifies the settlement of the Palatine hill as the original Arcadian basis of the city. It is a κώμη βραχεῖα, a small village:

> And the Arcadians, as Themis by inspiration kept advising them, chose a hill, not far from the Tiber, which is now near the middle of the city of Rome, and by this hill built a small village (κώμην βραχεῖαν) sufficient for the complement of the two ships in which they had come from Greece. Yet this village was ordained by fate to excel in the course of time all other cities, whether Greek or barbarian, not only in its size, but also in the majesty of its empire (κατά τε οἰκήσεως μέγεθος καὶ κατὰ δυναστείας ἀξίωσιν) and in every other form of prosperity (εὐτυχίαν), and to be celebrated (μνημονευθησομένην) above them all as long as mortality shall endure. They named the town Pallantium after their mother-city in Arcadia; now, however, the Romans call it Palatium, time having obscured the correct form, and this name has given occasion to many (πολλοῖς) to suggest absurd etymologies. (*Ant. Rom.* 1.31.3–4, translation Spelman-Cary)

Dionysius integrates the picture familiar from Roman sources – mostly Augustan, but a cliché a lot earlier – of the contrast between then and now. He inserts a synoptic vision of Rome, going from tiny village to the greatest metropolis ever known, in a remarkably structured sentence that fractures any sense of the self-contained nature of the historical narrative. The purpose of this moment is to move simultaneously back in time, to the original two-ships-worth of Arcadians, and forward, to the prediction of a distant future recollection of the whole history of Rome. That history is characterized in its totality as exceptional: the size of the settlement (οἰκήσεως μέγεθος) conjures up not the size of Rome's empire (the idea we might expect), but rather the dimensions of the inhabited city in Dionysius' own day (or in the future), the key idea of οἴκησις (settlement) being 'dwelling-place'.[23] The empire, and the administrative organization of the city, are alluded to in δυναστείας ἀξίωσις (translated above as 'majesty of empire').[24] As with the idea of οἴκησις (settlement), and the

---

[23] See LSJ s.v.
[24] Cf. οἱ δυναστεύοντες (those in power) in *Orat. Vett.* 3.1, where Dionysius credits Rome's current leaders for the beneficial turn against Asianic rhetoric.

following idea of generalized εὐτυχία (prosperity), Dionysius has in view the detached observer, someone who will conclude, making reasonable comparisons with other states, that Rome is in all respects the largest in history, the most magnificent. That is why, I think, he uses ἀξίωσις (majesty, or evaluation); this is a view from the outside, and if that outside is Hellenic in orientation, then the stress laid upon the first Arcadian settlers is particularly pointed. It was they who started the entire process, in their obedience to Themis, Evander's mother, but obviously also recalling the deity of Divine Right, who shares her name. Noteworthy too is the repeated use of the word χρόνος, and the strange juxtaposition of *personae*: the πολλοί at the end of the sentence are not so firmly located in time – they could be any kind of believer in incorrect etymologies. But as well as them, there is the nameless audience of Rome's colossal success, as well as those people implied in the participle μνημονευθησομένην (to be celebrated); people from the future will be engaged in this act of recollection. The historian's view is expressed as a consensus, built on observation in the present, of the past, and certain to remain the same in the future.

But before he comes to Rome in its own chronological place, the other urban forerunners are Lavinium and Alba Longa. Lavinium is on a hill near the sea:

> And, having received from the Aborigines some land for their habitation (χωρίον εἰς οἴκησιν), and everything else they desired, they built a town (πολίζονται) on a hill, not far from the sea, and called it Lavinium (Λαουΐνιον ὄνομα τῇ πόλει θέμενοι). (*Ant. Rom.* 1.45.1–2)

There is a low-key contrast between χωρίον (land) and whatever form of πόλις is implied in πολίζονται (they built a *polis*). Dionysius is hinting at a progression, as Alba Longa is clearly urban, involving the construction of a wall (1.45.2). Next, in a summary of events that are narrated in more detail later, the colonization and walling in of the Palatine constitutes the creation of the πόλις that is Rome:[25]

> They settle the places (οἰκίζουσι τοὺς τόπους), enclosing Pallantium with walls, so that then it first took on the form of a city (πόλεως σχῆμα). (*Ant. Rom.* 1.45.3, translation Fox)

In the fuller account of Aeneas a few chapters later, Lavinium is referred to first as a κτίσμα, a foundation (*Ant. Rom.* 1.59.3), and soon afterwards, as

---

[25] In the first full event in his history, the war in which Aborigines and Pelasgians unite to expel the Sicels from Latium (*Ant. Rom.* 1.9.1–2), the epochal change is from pre-urban to urban, denoted by the existence of walls. On walls as a definitive marker of a πόλις, Hansen and Nielsen 2004, 135–7.

a πόλις built as a memorial to Lavinia: not the daughter of Latinus (as in Vergil), but rather, of the Delian, Anius, who had sent his daughter as a priestess and prophet with Aeneas to Italy, where an illness killed her while the city was being constructed. In the next account, more closely resembling Vergil's, after Ascanius' death, the monarchic succession passes to Silvius, Ascanius' brother, instead of to Julus, his oldest son. That constitutional decision is produced by a vote of the δῆμος. Once again, Dionysius takes the opportunity for a proleptic vision, of the contribution of the Julii to Rome's entire history (*Ant. Rom.* 1.70.4). The combination of nascent political institutions and mention of the Julian house is purposeful: the pontifical status offered to Julus as compensation for Silvius' accession has popular support. So Dionysius can convey the idea of the piety of the δῆμος, both towards Julus, and towards Lavinia, and suggests, without obtrusive over-reconstruction, that none of this was accidental.

But when, soon afterwards, he finally comes to discuss the date of the foundation, scepticism takes the upper hand:

> As to the last settlement or founding of the city, or whatever we ought to call it, Timaeus of Sicily, following what principle I do not know, places it at the same time as the founding of Carthage, that is, in the thirty-eighth year before the first Olympiad; Lucius Cincius, a member of the senate, places it about the fourth year of the twelfth Olympiad, and Quintus Fabius in the first year of the eighth Olympiad. Porcius Cato does not give the time according to Greek reckoning, but being as careful as any writer in gathering the data of ancient history, he places its founding four hundred and thirty-two years after the Trojan war; and this time, being compared with the Chronicles of Eratosthenes, corresponds to the first year of the seventh Olympiad. That the canons of Eratosthenes are sound I have shown in another treatise, where I have also shown how the Roman chronology is to be synchronized with that of the Greeks. For I did not think it sufficient, like Polybius of Megalopolis, to say merely that I believe Rome was built in the second year of the seventh Olympiad, nor to let my belief rest without further examination upon the single tablet preserved by the high priests, the only one of its kind, but I determined to set forth the reasons that had appealed to me, so that all might examine them who so desired. In that treatise, therefore, the detailed exposition is given; but in the course of the present work also the most essential of the conclusions there reached will be mentioned. The matter stands thus: It is generally agreed that the invasion of the Gauls, during which the city of Rome was taken, happened during the archonship of Pyrgion at Athens, in the first year of the ninety-eighth Olympiad. (*Ant. Rom.* 1.74.1, translation Spelman-Cary)

The ἀπορία over datings extends even to the nature of the city itself; what should he call the foundation: is it an οἰκισμός or a κτίσις? Bear in mind that he is speaking here not of a prehistorical forerunner, but to the actual city of Rome that is still standing. It is a banal moment, but my aim is to make clear what the effect of such forms of expression is. Dionysius is engaging his readers with the inconsistencies of his sources, and the result is that moments of rationalized reconstruction remain just moments in an otherwise arduous presentation of the prehistorian's task.

These controversies yield to a more continuous narrative of the dynastic conflict in Alba Longa and the childhood of the twins. The demos-monarch situation which pertained in Ascanius' day has given way to something more structured. It is fear of upsetting a δῆμος blindly loyal to their king that prevents Numitor from objecting when Amulius enlists Ilia as a vestal (*Ant. Rom.* 1.76.4). But when Amulius summons Numitor to account for her pregnancy, it is before a συνέδριον, and Dionysius points out that the majority of council members (τὸ τῶν συνέδρων πλῆθος) is originally sympathetic to his defence of his daughter (1.78.2–4). However, responding to the same fear of the tyrant that had earlier motivated Numitor himself, the σύνεδροι follow Amulius' lead and condemn the fallen vestal to the traditional punishment.[26] The political structure seems to be that of a minimally democratic (or more strictly, oligarchic) tyranny, perhaps based on Hellenistic models.[27]

In general, there is a discernible move towards a more structured narrative, fewer methodological interruptions, and a greater sense of indulging in reconstruction. But Dionysius does not allow the difficulties of the source material to disappear for long. His writing pits a desire for accomplished historical vividness against the duties of a historian to instruct his readers. A hot moment for this comes just after Dionysius has indulged in the longest uninterrupted historical narrative so far, describing the adolescence of Romulus and Remus.[28] He has adopted an almost novelistic tone, narrating in a well-paced manner the capture of the twins' foster-father, Faustulus, caught sneaking into Alba Longa with the crib (σκάφη) in which the twins were exposed, intended as a recognition-token for Numitor. In a manner that reflects the theatrical cliché of the symbolic childhood object precipitating the dramatic περιπέτεια, Faustulus and his crib are

---

[26] On Numitor and Amulius, see also Pelling in the present volume, pp. 207–8.
[27] Livy also gives an Alban prototype of the Vestals, properly institutionalized at Rome by Numa: Livy, 1.20; cf. *Ant. Rom.* 2.66–9, Numa's practice here being 'not different from Romulus, the priesthoods originating in Alba'.
[28] *Ant. Rom.* 1.79–83.

captured, and the narrative races rather promptly to its conclusion: Numitor gathers a band of followers, and Amulius is defeated in a few lines.[29] The coda, however, is important:

> This is the account Fabius gives. But others, who hold that everything which has the appearance of a fable ought to be banished from history,[30] maintain that the exposition of the children, by the officers, contrary to their orders, is void of all probability (ἀπίθανον), and laugh at the tameness of the wolf, that suckled them, as an incident fraught with theatrical absurdity (ὡς δραματικῆς μεστὸν ἀτοπίας). Instead of which, they give this account of the matter: that Numitor (...). (*Ant. Rom.* 1.83.3–84.1)

Thus Fabius Pictor. Dionysius follows his account with a very different one, stressing the fanciful idealizing of Fabius' version, and inviting readers to identify with those who repudiate myth and theatrical absurdity. It is a remarkable disavowal of the entire preceding narrative, which although signalled at the start as following the majority of Latin accounts, reads very much as though it is endorsed by the author, who has taken some pains to make it lively and detailed.[31]

In the demythologized version, those who gave Laurentia the nickname Lupa are designated as 'those living around Pallantium' (οἱ περὶ τὸ Παλλάντιον διατρίβοντες), and to reinforce his claim of Greek identity for these inhabitants, Dionysius explains that *Loupa* (Λούπα) is a Greek word which has in more recent times been replaced by the more seemly ἑταίρα (*Ant. Rom.* 1.84.3–4). These people hanging round the Palatine are something like those inhabitants of the village that Dionysius had described earlier. The brief summary of the foundation that Dionysius gives at the start of *Roman Antiquities* book 2 sheds useful light. There, the twins are only mentioned after a more general statement that it was the Albans who instigated the move to urbanization, building a wall and ditch. The earlier community of farmers had settled there because of the abundant pasture, a nice counterpart to Vergil's evocation in *Aeneid* book 8, and here acting to provide a more credible vision of the community than in Fabius' version.[32]

---

[29] On peripety in the *Roman Antiquities*, see also Schultze in the present volume, p. 168.
[30] Ἕτεροι δὲ οὐδὲν τῶν μυθωδεστέρων ἀξιοῦντες ἱστορικῇ γραφῇ προσήκειν (...).
[31] Dionysius gives Fabius Pictor credit for the account, but also says that most other writers followed his lead: *Ant. Rom.* 1.79.4.
[32] 'The sixteenth generation after the Trojan war, the Albans built upon both these places, and surrounded them with a wall, and ditch: for, till then, there were only cottages of neatherds, and shepherds, and huts of other herdsmen; the land thereabouts yielding plenty of grass, not only for winter, but also for summer pasture, by reason of the rivers that refresh and water it' (*Ant. Rom.* 2.1.

Reconsidering the earlier, novelistic narrative, one feature of Dionysius' method stands out. Faustulus is betrayed by the crib (σκάφη) that he is carrying into the city. The story is structured as a formulaic rendering in historiographical guise of the tragic conventions described in Aristotle's *Poetics*, a tradition of analysis with which Dionysius was doubtless acquainted, even if not from that text.[33] The σκάφη is an example of the recognition token Aristotle associates with tragic ἀναγνώρισις (recognition), but once we are aware that Dionysius thinks this version is melodramatic, it works to betray the artifice of those same conventions. The use of this token exposes the theatrical nature of the incident, and reveals Dionysius' own narrative vividness as belonging to the realm of the stage, rather than the pages of history. The crib is a clue to the clichéd and theatrical quality of the tradition. As this is the first piece of extended narrative that Dionysius has provided, the disavowal of the dramatic trend in historiography should be given due weight.[34] The passage adds further layers of scepticism to the struggle to sift sources for reliable material that has already been so prominent. Here scepticism is dramatized, as Dionysius produces what is almost an *ekphrasis* of a different kind of historiography, attributed to what ought to be one of his best sources, Fabius Pictor. It is a form of theatrical storytelling that Dionysius will not endorse, however skilfully he can execute it. With this recognition token, Dionysius signals to his readers that such theatricality is another kind of problem in the sources, and that he, and they, need to continue to exercise caution in establishing the appropriate kind of written record. This episode demonstrates the limitations of applying a simple Herodotus/Thucydides dichotomy to Dionysius' problematization of his sources. By indulging in a theatrical form of narrative, and then explicitly deconstructing it, Dionysius is, perhaps, entering new territory.

To conclude, let us consider what happens when Rome is finally founded, and Dionysius begins his long account of the constitution of

---

1–2). See De Jonge in the present volume, pp. 265–6, on pastoral resonances between Dionysius and Vergil.

[33] Arist. *Poet.* 1454b-1455a. See De Jonge 2008, 107: 'Dionysius presumably did not know Aristotle's *Poetics*'. Ogilvie 1965, 53 reads the recognition scene in Livy's version as a nod to dramatic historiography; cf. Feldherr 1998, 166–9. For Peripatetic influence on Dionysius, see De Jonge 2008, 34–5, and index s.v. 'Peripatetic Tradition'; Wiater 2011a, 33–40, 51–2 on Dionysius' dislike of Peripatetic rhetorical criticism. For another recognition scene in the *Roman Antiquities*, see Schultze in the present volume, p. 164.

[34] Polybius' polemics against his predecessors is relevant here, the closest parallels perhaps being Phylarchus, in whom Polybius detects the fanciful (τερατεία, Polyb. 2.58–60), and Theopompus (Polyb. 8.9-11, accusing him among other things of ἀτοπία, absurdity, 8.9.5). Dionysius rehabilitates Theopompus at *Pomp.* 6, possibly thinking of Polybius: Fox 1996, 76–8.

Romulus. As a new city, Rome has no pre-existing political structures, so it is the mob (τὸ πλῆθος) that Romulus addresses on becoming king, Dionysius adding that only the influence of his maternal grandfather rendered him capable of mustering the people (*Ant. Rom.* 2.6.1–2). He is attempting to render plausible the idea of a displaced population under a young, inexperienced ruler. However, the reported speech that Romulus gives introduces a new kind of discourse into the historical field, one of moralizing on the value of the Romans. It is not the topics that are new: we find praise of the virtues of the Romans at the start and end of book 1; the end, in particular, is where Dionysius' patriotism unites praise of Roman virtues with pride in their Hellenic identity.[35] What is new is the transferral of this value system to the characters of history themselves. Until this point, they have remained the subjects of Dionysius' narrative observation. The distancing device is, in this case, the use of indirect speech.

Romulus' arguments are worth examining. Most pivotal is the sentence in which Romulus explicitly connects the morality of the individual to the nature of any political constitution:

> That those who employ themselves in the exercise of arms, and at the same time are masters of their passions, are the greatest ornaments to their country; and these are the men who provide both the commonwealth with impregnable walls, and themselves with a safe retreat. That the form of government supplies those who have prudently instituted it with men of bravery and justice, and who practise every other virtue; while, on the other hand, bad institutions render men cowardly and rapacious, and the slaves of foul desires. (*Ant. Rom.* 2.3.5)

In an echo of Themistocles, and perhaps Nicias, Romulus argues that it is not walls that safeguard a city; an interesting *topos* given the emphasis on walls in the definition of prehistoric πόλεις, and that the building of walls and houses is the only foundational act that precedes this speech (*Ant. Rom.* 2.3.1).[36] Romulus repudiates their significance: in external conflicts, it is the bravery of individuals and in internal struggles, the ὁμοφροσύνη (like-mindedness) of those participating that is the real bulwark of a city. Commonplace though this might sound, it is highly significant. It replaces an idea born in the context of the historiography of Athens with one central to the Romans' own conceptions of their own historical

---

[35] *Ant. Rom.* 1.89–90.
[36] Dionysius echoes the contrast between walls and the true identity of the city, rather than any one of the passages exploring this idea in either Herodotus (no reference in Ek 1942) or Thucydides: Hdt. 8.61 (Themistocles); Thuc. 1.94.4–5, 7.77.7 (Nicias). See Hornblower 2008, 720–1.

problems: the dialectic between external conflict and internal political tension. That dialectic is explored by Sallust, and it has been attributed to Posidonius, although the evidence is elusive.[37] Dionysius is giving an updated version of Polybius' emphasis on the constitution in explaining Rome's unique success, one that has its origins at the origins of the city, and furthermore takes account of the period of civil war through which Rome has just passed. The commitment to military exercise is complemented by the mastery of the appetites or passions; these fortify the city, as well as providing places of safety for individual lives. It is a precise articulation of a specific vision of virtue. This virtue is then directly linked to the form of constitution, the topic that dominates the remainder of Romulus' speech. The causal chain runs from constitution to individual character, rather than the reverse: good constitutions produce good men; poor arrangements produce men who are soft, greedy, slaves to their own desires.

Romulus' speech is followed by a general consultation of the public, and at this point, the nature of the Roman πολιτεία (constitution) as a monarchic regime based on popular goodwill receives its first exposition. Dionysius grants the people a direct speech (only the second in the work) characterizing them as obedient both to their own fathers and to their sense of tradition. Their first words are emblematic (*Ant. Rom.* 2.4.1): 'We do not at all desire a new form of government' (ἡμεῖς πολιτείας μὲν καινῆς οὐδὲν δεόμεθα). As the first words uttered by the new Romans, these are a striking challenge to Dionysius' persuasive powers, insisting that the identity of the Romans and their constitution were both well-established, even in this first moment. What they mean by πολιτεία is indicated by the word βασιλεία, kingship.[38] They also point out that their loyalty to tradition has its own rationale: being subjects in a monarchy (βασιλευομένοις) has already granted them the two greatest benefits available to mankind: freedom and rule over others. And thus, the stage is set for the first proper discussion of Rome's constitution.[39]

This reading demonstrates that the dressing of that stage has not been carried out casually. Dionysius makes use of his prehistorical material not just to prove the ethnicity of the Romans, but to work out methodological priorities. He has not done so in an authoritarian, monologic manner. Employing a range of rhetorical and semantic devices, he involves readers in the evaluation of the sources, and the types of historical writing that are

---

[37] Sall. *Iug.* 41.2; see Koestermann 1971 ad loc.; Lintott 1972.
[38] On the term πολιτεία in the *Roman Antiquities*, see also Pelling in the present volume, pp. 204–6.
[39] For which I refer readers to Wiater 2011a, 172–85.

appropriate to the material. To close, I consider what we can conclude about the relationship between these narrative strategies and the political ambitions of Dionysius' history.

Narrative, Nationalism, and Augustan Context

Rome had long encouraged the persistence of *polis*-based organization in the Greek world. That promoted the assimilation in the minds of Greek observers (mostly historians) of Rome's structures to their own, however tricky that process proved in its details.[40] The categories and terminology of Greek historiography produced a way of talking about Rome that fostered a sense of similarity, whilst allowing space for the expression of anxiety about Rome's domination. But beyond his description of Rome, we can see in Dionysius a parallel between Roman rationalizations of their own civilizing mission and Dionysius' view of the Romans as a civilizing influence. It is Rome that is responsible for leading a cultural development where the Greeks can once again live up to the values of their own history, values from which they have become alienated by subsequent political disunity and barbarian influence. The view easily overlaps with the sense of Rome's destiny as a civilizing conqueror, so powerfully expressed by Vergil.[41] That overlap could be read as Dionysius' conformity with the ideology of the conqueror – enfeebled Greeks requiring Rome to take the lead in political renewal. But any negative associations of the complicity of the subaltern need to be balanced against the sense that it is Greek history and culture that set the standard for effective governance and civilized communities. Augustan identity was itself complex, and that complexity is reflected in Dionysius' open handling of conflicting evidence, as much as it is in Varro, or in the multilayered rendering of prehistory in Vergil. Furthermore, it is useful to remember the variety of different ways in which, in visual culture, the Augustans could figure their relationship to an idealized Greek past. The archaizing reliefs of the Palatine, with their figures recalling archaic Greek sculpture, are just as expressive an encapsulation of an Augustan idealization of the Greek past as the more

---

[40] Fundamental is Ando 1999. See too Woolf 1994, 123; Madsen 2006. Millar 1987, 8–10 suggests that the *polis* model, as Polybius conceived of it, fitted Rome's own history particularly well. As Ando 1999, 30 points out, at least by the Augustan period, the term *polis* had become a stand-in for Rome itself.

[41] Dionysius' idea of the Romans redeeming Greek culture is most clearly expressed at *Orat. Vett.* 3.1. See Hidber 1996, 75–81. For the Romans' sense of mission, Woolf 1994, 119–21.

mainstream imagery, probably drawing on Pergamene stylistic models, on the Ara Pacis.[42] Nor can we overlook the trend, described by Spawforth, toward the 're-hellenization' of Greece from the West.[43]

Schwartz's vision of Dionysius as a betrayer of his national heritage, a collaborator in the oppression of his fellow-countrymen, although the product of an anachronistic vision of national identity that has little bearing on the historical relationship between Rome and Hellas, is still worth considering, if only to clarify what it is that we require of Dionysius' textual practice to prove it invalid. The gain, of course, is a better understanding of the terms in which Dionysius dealt with these issues. The evidence from the pre-foundation narrative, with its openness about the problems of the sources, its involvement of the reader in the historian's decision-making, and its measured scepticism about excessive reconstruction, proves a valuable resource. It is this element that I wish to emphasize as a supplement to Wiater's delineation of the Augustan context to Dionysius' handling of national stereotypes.[44] The verbal strategies discussed above demonstrate that beyond the demands of his own political agenda, Dionysius' motivation comes from the perceptual filters through which he views his own world, and which lead him to make sense of the source-material available to him in the way that he does. His work with Rome's prehistory shows him engaging with the same material that the Augustan poets and antiquarians were working on. But his insistence on variant versions, and on stretching reader involvement even to the extent of offering alternative modes of narrative, mean that it is as a historical critic, as well as a historian, that Dionysius expresses his outsider status, rather than as a propagandist, either for Greece or for an uncritical idealization of Rome.

The contrast between Dionysius and the Second Sophistic is instructive. Although in some respects a founder figure for that movement, the variety of voices, and the diversity of genres in which the authors of the Second Sophistic speak, represent a model of cultural dynamics that is not entirely helpful for understanding Dionysius. His position regarding the benefits of the Augustan revolution is less ambiguous, and for him, if we are to extrapolate from his enthusiasm for Romulus' popular monarchy, the experimental aspects of Rome's current political

---

[42] On Greek archaism in Augustan art, Hallett 2012, 86–100. In the substantial bibliography on the *Ara Pacis*, Hölscher 2004, 76–82 is especially useful on classicism. See too Kleiner 1993, Kellum 1993, Turcan 1995.
[43] Spawforth 2012, 12 and *passim*.   [44] Wiater 2011a, 206–22.

development were an inspiration.⁴⁵ Like Polybius, Dionysius seems more alive to the shortcomings of Greek history than to the shortcomings of Roman imperialism, the dynamics of which are so central to the Second Sophistic.⁴⁶ And unlike his successors, Dionysius had no knowledge of the damage caused by the Julio-Claudians or Domitian.

We might interrogate his treatment of colonization and settlement, to find evidence for a sharper inflection of nationalist ideas. There Dionysius is disappointing. There is little sign of the urgency familiar from Vergil: the burgeoning sense of national consciousness, or the strangeness of the confrontation between cultures.⁴⁷ But here we should be aware of our own context, particularly our expectations of how nationalist rhetoric is expressed. Although it is fruitful to read the *Aeneid* as an epic inflected by modern concerns about nationhood and identity, we must bear in mind that the concrete concepts of nationhood that we detect there are postclassical products, dated by most to an origin in the late eighteenth century.⁴⁸ The key contrast between Dionysius and Vergil is Dionysius' failure to grant priority to the Trojan foundation story, even though he does include lengthy, if sceptical, discussion of it. But that lack of priority is itself revealing, as it enables another ethnic polarity to be avoided. The presentation of the waves of immigration which produced Rome, summarized at the start of book 2, is organized to define Rome as the product of a range of settlers, including a small proportion of barbarians. Dionysius' claim, after all, is not that the Romans are the purest of Greeks, but rather that they have

---

⁴⁵ Most obviously in *Orat. Vett*, but also regularly in *Ant. Rom*. Cf. Goldhill 2001, 25: 'The ancient texts (...) discussed here (...) offer examples and models of considerable sophistication and depth for those more generally interested in post-colonial writing, imperial fiction, and the difficulties of how identity is formulated, asserted, contested in a complex social and intellectual context.' Dionysius does not appear in Henderson's reading of Polybius in the same volume, whilst Strabo, briefly, does: Henderson 2001, 31. The explanation is that Dionysius' political agenda is focussed on prehistory (also pre-Polybian). Woolf 1994, 127–35 argues that in the high empire, the stakes in the cultural exchange between Greece and Rome were different.

⁴⁶ Henderson 2001, 47–9 gives a succinct statement of Polybius' vision of Greek decline. Millar 1987, 4–5 notes that it is impossible to establish whether Polybius regarded Roman rule as desirable, or even as inevitable, cf. Ando 1999, 11–12. Champion 2004 and Baronowski 2011 are book-length treatments of that subject.

⁴⁷ Syed 2005, 207: 'Most of the pivotal moments of the plot are marked by references to ethnicity.' She compares Vergil's and Dionysius' versions of Roman ethnicity, 212–14, cf. Wiater 2011a, 213–17.

⁴⁸ So Greenwood 2010, 108: 'the intermingling of Asia and Europe [in the *Aeneid*] (...) destabilizes the idea of a simple cultural and national identity.' Stephens and Vasunia 2010, 4–10 plot the emergence of the Classical tradition against the development of modern nationalism; cf. Syed 2005, 220–3. Interesting corroboration of the eighteenth-century origin of nationalism is Spelman's dissertation on the veracity of Aeneas' landing in Italy, as if Dionysius were not sufficiently explicit: Spelman 1758, vol. 1, 210–19.

lost fewer traces of their Greek origin than some other Greek communities.[49] The manner in which the diversity of the sources is brought forwarded mirrors this view of Rome's makeup. The assemblage of stories and the assemblage of settlers both place the responsibility for a unifying vision on the reader, following prompts from the historian. In spite of the boldness of the claim to show that the Romans were Greeks, any attentive reader of book 1 will see how provisional that ethnic definition is, and how sceptical Dionysius himself is of a crude nationalist polarity between Greek and Roman.

A counterpart to this diffuse idea of ethnicity in determining the national character is that Dionysius' history is almost the opposite of teleological: there is little evidence that it is Rome in the present that represents the real focus of history, and correspondingly little advantage to be gained through the rhetoric of 'from small origins to greater conclusions'.[50] However, this relative absence of teleology does not lead Dionysius into an overconfidence in the details of his depiction – that he saves for the period after Rome's foundation, when the discourse of the inhabitants of the πόλις permits a full identification of Rome with better-documented historical Greece. As the Roman πόλις is evolving, he is careful to suspend judgement, to warn against oversimplification, and to invite readers into a collaborative venture in the face of an enormous mass of conflicting sources. The message emerges that it is the behaviour of the Romans as Greeks once Rome is established that matters, rather than the less certain conclusions that can be drawn about any society from its ethnic origin. Surely the experience of Rome's own multiculturalism, as well as reading Roman history, led him to that position. In examining his account of Rome's prehistory, the desire to appear as a responsible historian takes priority over a polarizing vision of national identity. In the new Augustan world order, with its global scope and increased internationalism, that would make more sense than sustaining an opposition between Greeks and Romans that, at least as a determining factor in history, may well have appeared as rather stale. To end by returning to Polybius: we can see in Dionysius' work with prehistory a different kind of pragmatic historian at work, one whose scepticism, and narrative flexibility, fit the context of Rome as an established world power. Dionysius eschews appeals to any philosophical theory, or deterministic view either of human action, or of

---

[49] *Ant. Rom.* 1.89.4.   [50] Although there are some traces: Pelling 2016.

the cosmic forces underlying it, and he shows little interest in a historical cycle of constitutions. For Dionysius, it is individual moral commitment, including that of the historian, to an international ideal of civil society, rather than impersonal forces – among them ethnic origin – that play the central role in determining the course of history.

PART 3

Dionysius and Augustan Rome

CHAPTER 8

Dionysius on Regime Change

Christopher Pelling

1. Constitutions

Dionysius is not very complimentary about Polybius. He lists him among the authors that no-one manages to read to the end, along with Phylarchus and Hieronymus and several others (*Comp.* 4.30). This is of a piece with his generally dismissive approach to Hellenistic writings, so inferior to the classical models and indeed to the renaissance of his own generation: the introduction to *On Ancient Orators* leaves us in no doubt about that.[1] In the introduction to the *Antiquities*, he aims a sideswipe at Polybius for his casual treatment of Roman ἀρχαιολογία: he was one of those who treated only a few things, did not do so with serious ἀκρίβεια,[2] and just threw it all together 'from any hearsay that came along' (ἐκ τῶν ἐπιτυχόντων ἀκουσμάτων, *Ant. Rom.* 1.6.1).[3] The Thucydidean allusiveness[4] makes the point clear – Polybius falls short of those Thucydidean standards. Dionysius is hitting Polybius where it hurts, on the area of careful research which was Polybius' pride, and also hitting below the belt, as there is no mention of all the history that Polybius did cover in detail. There are further sideswipes as well, some naming Polybius (starting at 1.7.1, where he is among those who have just 'slurred over' Dionysius'

---

[1] Where it becomes clear that his criticisms of 'rhetoric' are not confined to 'oratory' in the narrow sense: *Orat. Vett.* 3 includes the 'many worthwhile histories' written by his own generation and in 4 he promises to move his series of critical analyses on to historians 'if I have the time'. Cf. Wiater 2011a, 121. On *Orat. Vett.*, see Wiater and Yunis in this volume.
[2] Despite all those Polybian professions of concern with ἀκρίβεια: for these see Fantasia 2004, esp. 56–7, 64–5; for those of Dionysius himself, 62–4 and Oakley in this volume.
[3] Except where stated all Dionysius references in this chapter are to *Ant. Rom.* Translations are my own.
[4] Cf. esp. Thuc. 1.22.2, οὐκ ἐκ τοῦ παρατυχόντος πυνθανόμενος ... ἀκριβείᾳ περὶ ἑκάστου ἐπεξελθών. Dionysius' ἐκ τῶν ἐπιτυχόντων ἀκουσμάτων at 1.6.1 echoes 1.1.4 and 1.4.2, where he had distanced his own writing from that sort of material, and at *Thuc.* 6 he uses the same phrase in an even clearer echo of Thuc. 1.22.2: cf. Hunter in this volume, pp. 40–1.

subject, ἐπισεσυρκότων) and some just implicit.⁵ This contentiousness should not be overstated: Polybius was not his target in most of his anti-Hellenistic barbs, and indeed Polybius' own criticisms of his predecessors have something in common with the strictures of *On the Ancient Orators*. In any case, such combative allusiveness is itself a sign of homage as well as dismissiveness, an acknowledgement that, even if this is shadow-boxing, it is Polybius' shadow that is worth taking on. Thucydides' own nods to Herodotus are not wholly different. Still, in both Thucydides and Dionysius the distancing from those models remains very clear.

Polybius' shadow looms larger still, looms indeed over the entire conception of the work. Most obviously, it seems to be envisaged as a prequel: Dionysius' work finishes as Polybius' starts, a mirroring counterpart to the way that Posidonius and Strabo started their histories where Polybius finished. That fits the preoccupation with picking suitable beginnings and ends that is so clear in the theoretical works (*Thuc.* 10-12; *Pomp.* 3.8-10, 4.2). But it also reflects a deeper conceptual difference, one that centres on historical explanation.⁶ Polybius' focus is on those 'fifty-three years' in which Rome grew to dominate the Mediterranean world, and his explanation is in terms of their πολιτεία: not just their 'constitution', though this is very important, but their institutions as well, all those aspects which figure in book 6 – military customs, respect for tradition, funeral speeches for women, and much more. These institutions have taken time to develop, of course, but Polybius' weight falls on the here and now, those institutions as they were for that fifty-three-year surge to greatness. For Dionysius, one has to go back earlier: right back to the beginning, and to the ἀρχαιολογία of Rome, starting '745 years' ago – the precision at 1.3.4 makes a point, contrasting with Polybius' '53'.⁷ In particular, one needs to see how much the Romans have learned from Greece. So criticising Polybius for only grazing the earlier material may be cheap, but Dionysius is not just missing the point when he blames Polybius for something he never intended to do (as, arguably, he does miss his author's point in criticising Thucydides' choice of start and finish, *Thuc.* 10–12 and *Pomp.* 3). For Dionysius, Polybius *should* have intended to do it, because

---

⁵ Thus, *Roman Antiquities* book 1 corrects Polybius' version of the etymology of the Palatine (1.32.1) and rejects his chronology in the dating of Rome's foundation (1.74.3). The resilience of Rome, Dionysius goes on to explain, is not just a matter of *Tyche*, Fortune, 'as some think' (2.17.3–4, echoing 1.4.2 and 1.5.2); the catchword *Tyche* itself points to Polybius, and Dionysius illustrates the point by saying that if it had just been Fortune then Rome would have sunk without trace after Cannae. It was after Cannae that Polybius put his own explanation of Rome's resilience in his book 6. On Dionysius' 'intertextual debate' with Polybius, see esp. Schultze 2000. I say a little more in Pelling 2007, 2016.

⁶ On this cf. Delcourt 2005, 51–3 and esp. Wiater 2011a, 189–98. ⁷ Schultze 2000, 13.

that early history is so crucial. And the *Antiquities* go on to deliver what the prologue promises, spending what might seem a disproportionate time on the earliest history.[8] For Dionysius it is not disproportionate at all: it is the earliest times that mattered most if one was to understand Roman greatness.[9]

That difference between Polybius and Dionysius also extends to their treatment of constitutions, and thus to regime change; and once again it makes sense to see it as a mix of homage and combativeness. Part of Dionysius' programme focuses precisely on constitutions. He will treat not merely all the wars and internal divisions, but also something more:

> I shall also go through all the forms of *politeiai* that they had, both under the kingship and after the end of the monarchy, and explain what was the ordering of each ... (*Ant. Rom.* 1.8.2)

So constitutions do matter, and that is Polybian, but the plural is telling too. It is a matter of all the various constitutions that they had at different stages, not just the one final form to which Polybius gave so much space.

Then we hear more along similar lines at the very end of *Roman Antiquities* book 1, but with one telling difference. He repeats his insistence that the Romans were 'living a Greek life' from the very beginning:

> I have innumerable things to say on this subject, with lots of evidence that I can adduce and supporting statements made by men who deserve belief; but I reserve all this for the account that will be given of their πολιτεία. (*Ant. Rom.* 1.90.2)

'Of their *politeia*': this time, just one of them. He refers back to this passage later on as well (7.70.2), and that makes it clear (what we might otherwise have doubted) that what he means by this 'account' is indeed the rest of the *Antiquities* itself, not some separate, Aristotle-like essay 'On the Constitution of the Romans'.[10]

So: is it one constitution, or several? It is both, and the way it is both is interesting. One reason is simply that breadth of meaning of πολιτεία, once again extending to all sorts of institutions and customs, not just the 'constitution' in a narrow sense.[11] In that passage in book 7 he makes it clear that the 'innumerable' bits of 'evidence' he will give consist in 'ancient

---

[8] Notice Oakley's observation in this volume, p. 128, that Livy 'catches up with' Dionysius: the final books of Dionysius are *shorter* than Livy's equivalent.
[9] For one aspect of this, Rome's readiness from the earliest days to welcome migrants and defeated enemies into its melting pot (2.17.3–4), see Pelling 2016, 171–2; Fromentin 2004, 314.
[10] I.e., the sort of work that he had contrasted with his own history at *Ant. Rom.* 1.8.3.
[11] Schultze 1986, 132–3.

habits and customs and practices' that have lasted to his own day. Things like that are not going to be abandoned just because of a change of 'constitution' in the narrow sense, and the early books are in fact full of such customs that start in the regal period and go on to the late Republic, even though he often also points out that they have *not* quite lasted till his own day, but have fallen into disuse or abuse in the last century of the Republic (below, pp. 216–17, 219–20). But it also points to the way that very often Dionysius is concerned to blur the edges of constitutional changes, stressing elements of continuity across the boundaries. Of course, the change from kingship to Republic matters: that is true in that passage of 1.8.2, 'both under the kings and after the overthrow of the monarchy', and several of those statements of continuity of customs have similar phrasing, typically 'both under the kings and after the institution of yearly magistrates' (*Ant. Rom.* 2.6.1, 16.3, 27.3; 3.62.2). Still, once we get to the overthrow of the last Tarquin, the transition is dealt with in a more nuanced way. We do get the phrase μεταβολὴ τῆς πολιτείας, but not where we might expect. It is not used of Tarquin's overthrow, but of his reign (4.42.5). So it is he, not Brutus and his co-conspirators, who are responsible for regime change: he is the one who changes 'kingship' to 'an acknowledged tyranny' (4.41.2) – an echo perhaps of Polybius, who in his treatment of 'the cycle of the constitutions' (ἀνακύκλωσις) marks it as an important stage when good kingship turns into bad tyranny[12] (though others, including Aristotle as well as Plato, had said similar things);[13] an echo certainly of Plato himself, where the phrase 'acknowledged tyranny' marks a culminating stage in the decline of one-man rule at the end of book 8 of the *Republic* (8.569b), in a passage famous enough to be echoed by Cicero, Appian, and Plutarch too.[14] Tarquin's behaviour in power is then almost a catalogue of the stereotypes of tyrannical behaviour,[15] with several features that are easy to parallel from Plato and from many other places – the bodyguard, the elimination of rivals, the clampdown on free speech, and so on. So it is Tarquin who is the game-changer; in that passage at *Ant. Rom.* 1.8.2, that move from 'the kings' to 'the overthrow of the monarchy' may not be coincidental, as Tarquin may have been a monarch, but he was a tyrant rather than a king.

---

[12] Emphasised already at Polyb. 6.3-4, then esp. 6.7.7-9, with stress on sexual ὕβρις and conspiracy coming from the best of the citizens.
[13] Arist. *Eth. Nic.* 8.1160b7–12; *Pol.* 5.1310b16–31, 1312b39–13a3, 1314a33–7.
[14] Used by Cic. *Att.* 2.17.1 of Pompey, App. *B Civ.* 1.101.473 of Sulla, and Plut. *Caes.* 57.1 of Caesar. I discuss this more fully at Pelling 2011, 424-5.
[15] Cf. Fromentin 2003, 79-81.

Once the Tarquins are thrown out, the emphasis can then fall on the correct, traditional procedure for election: there was an *interrex* and 'the people went to the field *where it was their custom* to elect magistrates' (4.84.5). In fact, these constitutional steps are almost a perfect mirror of what Brutus has just indignantly mapped out as the proper and traditional way of choosing a king, namely decree of the senate, appointment of *interreges*, a vote in the assembly, and proper sacrifices (4.80.2) – all the things that the previous kings had done and that the dreadful Tarquin had not. Once in power, the consuls turn to the restoration of so much that had been abandoned under his reign (5.2.2), and a lot of it goes back to the constitutional proprieties of Servius Tullius.[16] Certainly something big has happened:

> Thus, then, the kingly *politeia* of the Romans was dissolved, for these reasons and at the hands of these men. It had lasted 244 years after Rome's foundation, but in the time of the last king had become a tyranny. It was during the 68th Olympiad, when Ischomachus of Croton won the foot-race, and when Isagoras held the annual archonship at Athens. (*Ant. Rom.* 5.1.1)

So even in those first words of book 5, it is noted that the last holder of the kingship had changed it to tyranny, and the new order is in many ways closer to the old order than the disruptive period that had come in between. It is reassertion of a continuity as much as a break. That is certainly a different emphasis from what we get in Livy, where there is much more of a feeling at the end of book 1 of a firm break with the past, with the early faltering steps of book 2 marking the difficult infancy of liberty.

In a way, too, we have been here before. Some of Dionysius' first audience might certainly feel they have been here before, but in reality, rather than in their reading: there are all the suggestions of that later time when a Brutus had struck a blow for liberty and stood before the Roman people with a sword dripping blood. More on that later (pp. 219–20). But even within the text we have been here before, at Alba Longa: for at the end of book 1 Amulius' tyrannical rule was described as ἀκοσμία (or ἀνομία: there is a textual problem, *Ant. Rom.* 1.85.1), and the usurpation is thought of as recovery. Numitor organised it all back 'into the old way' (εἰς τὸν ἀρχαῖον ἐκόσμει τρόπον, 1.85.1), and Amulius' reign was just a blip on the screen. That is quite important when we come to Romulus' first steps, which can be represented as sticking with the kingship that had served 'us'

---

[16] As is stressed by Wiater 2011a, 179.

so well (2.4.1):[17] so continuity again, across not merely a usurpation but also even a shift of city, and incidentally continuity forwards as well, as Romulus then is the first king to follow much of that constitutional template that Brutus will be proclaiming 250 years later for beginning an office. Uncle Numitor even approved of the Rape of the Sabine Women (2.30.2), so, there too, there is a sort of stamp of approval from the Alban past: it is not at all tyrannical, and – Dionysius characteristically adds – there are lots of Greek precedents too (2.30.5).

2. Individuals

So behaviour is what counts, not constitutions; and the same is true of his treatment of the decemvirate in the middle of the fifth century. It is Livy who treats that as regime change, *iterum mutatur forma ciuitatis* (3.33.1).[18] Dionysius' weight falls instead on the behaviour of the men in power. That fits other aspects of Dionysius' thinking too. When, for instance, he ponders the historical significance of the trial of Coriolanus, he dwells on various aspects: the growing tendency to require a broader populism among the elite, the path that led to the admittance of plebeians to the higher magistracies, and so on. That leads on to the question of the tribunate. Has that, all things considered, been a good thing or a bad thing? Well, he answers, it all depends whether you get good tribunes or bad tribunes ... (7.65). He says something very similar about the dictatorship (5.77.6).[19] One wonders too, as Clemence Schultze has wondered,[20] whether this concentration on *tribunicia potestas* and its good and bad holders within the broad sweep of Roman history might have something of an Augustan tinge about it – perhaps the dictatorship too, even though that was not an Augustan office – and that is another point to which we will come back (p. 218).

This concentration on individuals as individuals, with the capacity to make a big difference either way, may also help to explain the disagreement in Dionysian scholarship whether things started going wrong with Servius Tullius. Was he the one who started the rot? Partly yes, because there were certainly irregularities in the way he took over the throne; partly no, as he

---

[17] Cf. Fox in this volume, p. 191.
[18] Ogilvie 1965, 456 takes him to task for this as a 'distortion of the facts', for this was in fact a legally appointed commission to do some fact-finding and to draw up new laws, which turned out to be the Twelve Tables: and that, indeed, is the way that Dionysius does describe it. It is only at the later, tyrannical stage that there can be talk of restoring 'its old form to the constitution' (*Ant. Rom.* 11.8.2) and 'a change of the *politeia*' (11.22.2); once again the word πολιτεία drifts between its narrow sense of 'constitution' and the wider sense of 'the way things are done'. See also Hogg in this volume.
[19] Cf. Pelling 2016, 168–9.   [20] Schultze 1986, 139–40.

was such a good ruler in power; but he does not fit neatly into any linear scheme, simply because he is an individual.[21] If there is some linearity there, it is as much in the history that does not happen, because Servius was believed to be on course for a peaceful development of the Roman constitution towards democracy (*Ant. Rom.* 4.40.3), again suggesting that it was Tarquin, not Brutus and the others, who was responsible for the real constitutional disruption. There is much more linearity in Livy 1, and not just in its recurrent stress on the various reigns' physical expansion of the city. Livy also develops interpretative lines that thrust forward to the overthrow of the monarchy. Violence comes in with the killing of Ancus Marcius and then steadily grows, with Tarquinius Priscus injecting a new, much more modern and late Republican tone into politics.[22] Every aspiring contender then elbows his way to power, and each usurpation is more violent and bloody than the last, until that final explosion of violence when a Brutus strikes the blow for freedom and inaugurates that new phase of Roman history. In some ways Dionysius' history has more continuities, as we have seen; in others it is more jumpy, as different reigns differ just according to the man in power,[23] and Dionysius' portrayal of Tarquinius Priscus is more positive than Livy's.

Perhaps, though, we should just think of the two authors as 'preparing for' the Republic in rather different ways. In Livy, the whole rhythm of the regal period pre-plays that of the Republic. Just as his Tarquinius Priscus brings that new note of violent, competitive ambition, so centuries later all those late Republican figures will aim for power, and violence will escalate after the Gracchi; but in Livy that cycle has to start sharply afresh with the birth of the Republic – a sort of ἀνακύκλωσις of his own, then, but one not phrased in constitutional terms. In Dionysius, we have a messier pattern whereby features of the Republic gradually take shape, as the city takes over and where necessary remoulds what it had found to be important under the kings.

---

[21] Cf. Delcourt 2005, 322–37, a section entitled 'Les ambiguïtés d'un règne: Servius Tullius'; also Fromentin 2003, 2004, though in her view Dionysius does his best to downplay the irregularities.

[22] Beginning at *Ab urbe condita* 1.33.11, *Romanis conspicuum eum nouitas diuitiaeque faciebant; et ipse fortunam benigno adloquio, comitate inuitandi beneficiisque quos poterat sibi conciliando adiuuabat* ('The freshness of his arrival and his wealth made Romans notice him; and he himself helped his fortune along with the graciousness with which he greeted people, the affability of his entertaining and the generosity with which he wooed everyone he could'). *Nouitas, benignus, adloquium, comitas, inuitare, beneficia, conciliare*: these are the buzzwords of late Republican electioneering.

[23] Cf. esp. Fromentin 2004, 320–3, on the various qualities seen in each king to justify their successive selection as kings. She brings out how important this is to the stress in the early books on elective kingship. Those qualities matter, and not just for their good and bad consequences: they are also the individuals' titles to rule.

3. Logos

So far, then, one could see Dionysius as providing a sort of narrative version of an insight of – Polybius!

> Lycurgus, then, foresaw through some sort of reasoning the cause and character of events as they naturally happen, and therefore put together his πολιτεία without anything harmful (ἀβλαβῶς); the Romans have achieved the same result in the way their state is set up, but have not done so by any reasoning but through many trials and experiences, continually choosing the better course on the basis of what they came to understand in the midst of events. That is how they came to the same conclusion as Lycurgus, and it is the best of the πολιτεῖαι in our time. (Polyb. 6.10.12–14)[24]

For Polybius, then, Rome learns by experience: there is nothing there of the visionary Lycurgus, who could work out λόγῳ τινί what was going to happen and 'combine in it the features of all the best πολιτεῖαι', as he has put it a few sentences earlier, rather than plumping for just one. It is a matter of gradual accumulation, making one choice after another in the middle of trials and hardship (notice that ἀβλαβῶς, typifying the *Spartan* side of the contrast): a matter of 'learning through suffering', in fact, of πάθει μάθος. Dionysius too has the Romans groping their way forward in one crisis after another, and may indeed be echoing Polybius early in book 1 when he speaks of 'κόσμος of the πολιτεία, which they built up on the result of many experiences, drawing something useful from every critical occasion' (*Ant. Rom.* 1.9.4). But there is not the same teleological thrust as Polybius implies (or at least seems to imply, as this part of Polybius is only preserved in summary). Polybius has Rome on track for the best constitution, that 'mixed' constitution that Lycurgus got to by a sort of hole-in-one:[25] in fact an even better version of the mixed constitution than Sparta managed, as Polybius goes on to make clearer when he reverts to Sparta at the end of book 6 (esp. 6.50.5–6). For Dionysius it is a much more up-and-down and hit-and-miss thing, with in particular a perpetual danger there may be miss rather than hit, and things could go badly wrong.

There is a further point. For Polybius, as we saw, it was not a matter of λόγος for Rome as it was for Lycurgus. Walbank is doubtless right,[26] and we should not press this to imply that it was all just automatic reflex and the

---

[24] That apparent similarity does not exclude the possibility of some dialogue with the missing part of book 6 where Polybius himself gave a historical sketch (6.11a with Walbank 1957–79, vol. 1, 663–73; Pelling 2007, 254). On the 'strong teleological design' of Polybius' histories, with Rome's universal dominion as the τέλος in view, see Grethlein 2013, 224–40.
[25] I say a little more about this at Pelling 2016, 159–61, with further comparison of Cicero, *De republica*. On Rome's capacity to learn from experience see now Moore 2017.
[26] Walbank 1957–79, vol. 1, 662.

Romans never thought at all before taking the choices they successively made; but Polybius' emphasis certainly does not fall on the theorising or the reflection, but on the immediate response. For Dionysius, there are most certainly λόγοι: again and again and again. Thus, the regal period begins and ends with speeches considering what sort of constitution to adopt.[27] Once the city is built, Romulus explains that there are lots of constitutions among both Greeks and barbarians, but three especially good ones, even though each has its 'congenital bad fates' to go along with it, κῆρας συμφύτους (probably a Platonic and Polybian echo):[28] monarchy, oligarchy, or shared government by everyone. He is prepared to go along with any of them, either to rule or be ruled (*Ant. Rom.* 2.3.7–8).[29] And the people duly say that the kingship has served them well at Alba: it is therefore important that Amulius' tyrannical reign was only an aberration (above, p. 207). When we reach the end of the monarchy, we have something similar. We have Brutus standing there over the corpse of Lucretia, calling those present to vengeance, and they have just been passing the bloodstained dagger around: now 'let us consider what form of authority over the city we ought to have next, ... and even before that what should be the κόσμος of the πολιτεία to set up after getting rid of the tyrants: for it is best not to leave anything unexamined or undebated' (*Ant. Rom.* 4.72.1). And then there were many λόγοι from many people, some supporting monarchy, some supporting rule by the senate 'as happened in many Greek cities', some preferring democracy as in Athens, with ἰσονομία as its watchword (*Ant. Rom.* 4.72.2–3). At this, Brutus steps back in and suggests that perhaps this is not the time; maybe they ought to get rid of the tyrants first ... – though that does not stop him from giving us several more chapters on the need, if it is to be monarchy, to change the name by which the rulers should be called, and perhaps two would be better than one, just like the Spartans, and limit their rule to a year, just like at Athens, and there ought to be some thought given too to the insignia of office, and there is

---

[27] Cf. Fox 1993, 36, commenting that 'the virtues that Dionysius sees in Roman rule are not simply those things which he observes to have happened; they are the product of the deliberate application of ideas by the early Romans themselves'.

[28] Pl. *Resp.* 10.608e–f, the idea of the soul like everything else having a σύμφυτον κακόν τε καὶ νόσημα; Polyb. 6.10.3–4 (with Walbank's n. ad loc.), the application to constitutions. But notice that Dionysius does not expand on what those 'congenital bad fates' are: the enigmatic quality is eased by the allusiveness – 'for more details, compare Polybius', as it were – but also reflects his narrative technique of allowing the deficiencies to emerge gradually as the narrative progresses. Dionysius uses the phrase again, presumably alluding back to 2.3, in the important passage at the very end of book 5 where he is discussing the dictatorship and how it became unpopular: 5.77.6.

[29] In so saying he is in line with the advice of grandfather Numitor (*Ant. Rom.* 2.3.1, 4.1). That is another sign of the continuity between different regimes and, here, different ancestral cities.

religion too – perhaps have a *rex sacrorum*, again as they do in Athens. But perhaps we really should leave the details till later (*Ant. Rom.* 4.73–5). Precisely, one is inclined to say: for Heaven's sake, do get on with it. There is again a clear contrast with Livy, whose narrative moves rather briskly at this point.[30]

The wordiness is not just a reflection of Dionysius' own taste for speeches, clear though that is both here and in his rhetorical works. It also makes an interpretative point, or rather several. One is that recurrent stress on learning from the Greeks, with all those references to Athens and Sparta.[31] Nino Luraghi suggested that Dionysius' Romans are thoroughly on the chronological ball here, as they are looking across to the Athenian constitution 'in the archonship of Isagoras' (5.1.1, above, p. 207), i.e., the very year that Cleisthenes established many of those features of the democracy that could be described with that catchword ἰσονομία.[32] Perhaps that is so: Dionysius can indeed indulge in chronological metrics when he wants to, for instance a little later when he notes that the battle of Marathon came 16 years after the funeral speech for Brutus (*Ant. Rom.* 5.17.4);[33] but the inference is made shakier by the way that so many Greek models, including Athenian models, are already figuring in the setup of Romulus' constitution as well, when it is hard to think Dionysius knew any more about eighth-century Athens than we do. The same is true when Tullus Hostilius talks of Athenian generosity with the citizenship at *Ant. Rom.* 3.11.4, some time around 670 BC.[34] But it is the general drift that matters, not the details, and Rome is already finding that the best way to get things right is to look to Greece.

There is also the very value of λόγοι, and that is where the different emphasis from Polybius really comes. For it is not just here that the Romans weigh up the possibilities of constitutional change: they do so at the beginnings of the reigns of Numa, Tullus, and Tarquinius Priscus as well (*Ant. Rom.* 2.57.3–4; 3.1.1, 46.1), and when Servius Tullius does not go through this rigmarole at the beginning of his reign, it is marked as irregular and controversial (esp. *Ant. Rom.* 4.8, 10), as the last Tarquin is

---

[30] Cf. Oakley in this volume.
[31] See Schultze 2012, 126-31 on this capacity of Romans to learn from experience, others' as well as their own.
[32] Luraghi 2003, 278. Greek synchronisms seem to have been particularly important in constructing this critical phase of Rome's history: see Griffiths 2013, esp. 85–7.
[33] Schultze 1995 brings out that much of Dionysius' chronology, especially his Greek-Roman synchronism, is more meticulous and thoughtful than has often been thought.
[34] Solon is misdated by at least a generation as well (*Ant. Rom.* 5.65.1, 'in the time of our fathers' for something ninety years earlier).

quick to point out when he questions the king's position so many years later (4.31.2). They have a full-dress debate on this, not without its artificiality: 'I don't think I've been a bad king really.' 'Oh, I think you have' (4.30–36). But again it does underline the way that Romans have always been prepared to talk things out. They will still be doing so in the middle of the Coriolanus panel, with a further constitutional debate (*Ant. Rom.* 7.55, cf. below, p. 216–17). That is a point that Dionysius has already made explicit under Romulus' reign:

> That, then, was the basis for Roman concord, so firmly established by the customs instituted by Romulus that never, in the course of 630 years, did they move against one another in bloodshed and slaughter despite many great political disputes between the people and those in power, just as always tends to happen in every city great or small. No, they dealt with these by a process of persuasion and instruction, sometimes making concessions and sometimes receiving them, and thus they resolved their complaints in a civic and civil way. That lasted until Gaius Gracchus gained power as a tribune and destroyed the concord of the state; and since then they have ceaselessly been killing and driving each other into exile and showing no restraint in extreme measures when in quest of victory. (*Ant. Rom.* 2.11.2–3)

He returns to the theme later, emphasising that, despite all those fierce class-differences in the early Republic, it never came to bloodshed because they always managed to find a solution by talking things through:

> It was like brothers dealing with brothers or children dealing with parents in a well-ordered house: they would talk to one another about fairness and justice, and settle their quarrels through persuasion and talk, and not allow themselves to do anything irreparable or wicked against one another. Contrast what the Corcyreans did during their faction, and the Argives, and the Milesians, and all Sicily, and many other cities. (*Ant. Rom.* 7.66.5)

On the face of it that is an odd emphasis, not least because it comes apropos of the long Coriolanus sequence, and there would seem to be a fair amount of bloodshed when Coriolanus leads the Volscians against his own people. Dionysius dwells too, almost gruesomely, on the amount of blood when Lucretia and then Verginia meet their deaths.[35] But there *is* a point there: it was blood, yes, but not the sort of bloodletting that as he says was so distinctive of Greek στάσις, in Corcyra and elsewhere, when one whole side takes on the other side in arms. For that sort of thing one has to wait for the late Republic, for the Gracchi and beyond, and that too was a point

---

[35] Lucretia: *Ant. Rom.* 4.71.2, 76.3: see Schultze in this volume. Verginia: *Ant. Rom.* 11.37.3, 40.1. The same goes for the killing of Servius Tullius: *Ant. Rom.* 4.38.6.

that Dionysius stressed in the first of those passages, with one of his characteristic glances forward to how things were later to get a whole lot worse. So Dionysius' Romans do have this gift for speechifying, not perhaps for making speeches as stylish as the Greeks could manage, but at least for managing to use speeches to get things done; and it is right to link this with Dionysius' own taste for speeches, especially during the Struggle of the Orders. They may go on a bit; they surely *do* go on a bit; but at least they worked.

4. Experience

So the Romans start by pondering constitutions, and deciding to stick with kingship; they end the regal period by pondering constitutions again, and deciding to move to what Dionysius several times calls ἀριστοκρατία. There are several ways we could make sense of those different decisions. We could see it as a sign of the growth of Rome to political maturity, and that is the way that Daniel Hogg takes it:[36] the Roman people were not yet politically sophisticated enough under Romulus. That may be right, and if so it is a theme that is there in Livy as well, most explicitly at the beginning of book 2: liberty came at the right time, for Rome would not have been able to cope with all those civil disturbances of the early Republic if it had come under any of the earlier kings (Livy 2.1.5–6).[37] Another possibility would be to say that the Romans are simply guided by their experience in both cases.[38] This is how it is summed up in the people's response to Romulus' invitation to consider their options:

> It would make no sense for us to find fault with our system, which under kings has given us the biggest goods that humans know, freedom and rule over others ... not learning through reason any more than through experience. (*Ant. Rom.* 2.4.1–2)

That manages to combine a loud echo of Thucydides' Diodotus, who talks about 'the biggest things, freedom or rule over others' (3.45.6), with, very likely, an echo of the Constitutions Debate in Herodotus, where a similar argument forms the culmination of Darius' speech:

> 'What was the source of our freedom? Who gave it to us? Was it a δῆμος, or was it an oligarchy, or was it a monarch? My proposal then is that, as a single man gave us our freedom, we should continue that same principle; and,

---

[36] Hogg 2008, 69, 77–8, 115–6. [37] For discussion, cf. Fox 1996, 115–39, esp. 127, 137.
[38] Pelling 2007, 254.

besides, that we should not abandon our traditions when they are good ones. For that way lies harm.' (Hdt. 3.82.5)[39]

So experience tells; the same is true in those other debates at the beginning of reigns, as each time the experience of the previous king has not been at all bad. By the time we get to Tarquin, the experience is very bad indeed, and it is time for a change, even if it is a change that also stresses the continuities. Once again, it is the man, and all the man's deficiencies, which make the difference. And once again we can see this as a version of at least part of Polybius' line. Yes, change in Rome is gradual, and is itself the result of painful experiences; but λόγος and λόγοι are more important than Polybius implied, as that was the way in which they came to terms with those experiences.

5. Idealism?

Still, is this not all terribly bland, a rosy picture of 'change without revolution', whereby those wise early Romans exploited the flexibility of the system to manage their city so superbly? If this is Dionysius, is this a Dionysius whose historical insight one can really respect?

I hope that one can, and that there is a little more edge and a little less blandness. Certainly, when Dionysius talks about his own present day and the recent past, there is none of that blandness at all. Time and again, he talks about customs or achievements of the early Romans that have not stood the test of time; that was clear in that comment about the most important aspect of all, that achievement of managing to avoid civil strife through bloodshed (2.11, above, p. 213). There are so many similar reflections too: the men of power are no longer prepared to defer to the senate (*Ant. Rom.* 5.60.2); Sulla was the first and only dictator not to behave well in power, and so the underlying truth that the dictatorship is a sort of tyranny has only recently come out (*Ant. Rom.* 5.77.4–5); there are not many men these days of the sort who led frugal lives and refused monarchy when offered (*Ant. Rom.* 10.17.6) – though one wonders perhaps if there might be one, a certain Augustus Caesar.[40] And Irene Peirano has argued

---

[39] Romulus' οὔτε ἄρχειν ἀπαξιῶ οὔτε ἄρχεσθαι ἀναίνομαι at *Ant. Rom.* 2.3.8 may also echo and reverse Otanes' οὔτε γὰρ ἄρχειν οὔτε ἄρχεσθαι ἐθέλω at Hdt. 3.83.2. We should not be pernickety about chronology here: it is true that neither Herodotus nor Thucydides would be writing for at least three hundred years after Romulus, but the Greek writers can be thought of as encapsulating a timeless wisdom that an insightful statesman might have shared long before their time. Cf. Fox 1993, 42, 46.

[40] Some further cases listed at Luraghi 2003, 273–4; Wiater 2011a, 198-204; Peirano 2010, 46–7. Sordi 1993 observes that these pessimistic allusions to Dionysius' own times are particularly frequent in the

that the first seeds of that decline can already be traced in the fragments of Dionysius' concluding books, describing the war with Pyrrhus.[41] That again marks an interesting relationship with Polybius, whose work carries its own premonitions of a later decline, with its seeds already visible.[42]

But might that make Dionysius not merely bland but a nostalgic bore, a romanticising figure not about the present but about the past? After all, Matthew Fox has argued in detail that Dionysius has an 'idealising' view of the regal period, in the sense both of developing an interpretation according to a preconceived model and of demonstrating the sort of generosity in building that model that suits his idea of a 'good' historian, connected as that is to being a good person (*Pomp.* 3.15).[43] Others have said similar things.[44] But, whatever one says about the regal period, there is not much of the second sort of idealising, the rosy-eyed sort, in Dionysius' history of the early Republic. People just behave so badly. Emilio Gabba has pointed to the importance of Thucydides in the background of, particularly, the Coriolanus sequence by pointing out what does not happen, particularly that internecine bloodshed,[45] but there is also so much of Thucydidean stasis that *does* happen:[46] words changing their meaning, so that partisan rhetoric is often so misleading; bitter feuding, with self-seeking partisanship sometimes bordering on the murderous; wilful blindness to the real social issues; a readiness to put factional over civic interests even when the enemy is at the gate, and to use those threatening outsiders as ways of doing down one's own countrymen.[47] And Dionysius has a clear eye himself for untimely idealism. There is the speech of Manius Valerius, for instance (*Ant. Rom.* 7.54–6), in the middle of the early fifth-century crisis caused by

---

treatment of Romulus' constitution (*Ant. Rom.* 2.6.2–4, 11.3 [above, p. 213], 12.4, 14.3): as each seems more relevant to the late Republic than to the Augustan era, she thinks that they are taken over from an anti-Caesar pamphlet of *c.* 53–48 BC. That need not follow. They are similar to reflections elsewhere in the history (pp. 206, 218–20), and their clustering here can be seen as programmatic, with Romulus setting the tone both for success and for later decline – at least, perhaps, until Augustus stopped the rot?

[41] Peirano 2010, 52–3.
[42] Pelling 2007, 248-9, with further references. Even the mixed constitution shows some signs of coming decline: Walbank 1957–79, vol. 1, 647. The conclusion at Polyb. 6.57 is especially gloomy, looking forward to an inevitable slip towards ochlocracy.
[43] Fox 1993, 1996, esp. 53–63: 'an already defined conception of what regal history was about, of what Rome's early development was leading to . . .' (63).
[44] Thus Delcourt 2005, 46–7, 221–4; Wiater 2011a, 161, 167–8, both focusing especially on the regal period.
[45] Gabba 1991, 81–5.
[46] Pelling 2010, 113 with 117-8, n. 16. More on Thucydidean intertextuality in Fox 1996, 82–92.
[47] Thus Schultze 1986, 130–1, 'Dionysius presents Rome as a sharply divided *polis*' with the terms of the division seen in very Greek, ὀλίγοι vs πολλοί, terms; 'bitter divisions, desperate poverty, exile for the plebeians, intransigence on the part of the rich, potential violence'.

Coriolanus' intransigence. Valerius is a moderate figure and a friend of the plebeians, who successfully urges the senate to consent to the trial of Coriolanus. His argument is that the people will surely respond to such magnanimity in kind, respecting all the good things that they know Coriolanus has done for the state. All well and good – but in fact the tribunes do *not* respond in kind, and everything very swiftly gets worse. Valerius is just too idealistic, and it is interesting that it is his speech that also has one of the clearest and most intelligent versions of the Polybian 'mixed constitution', including a view of ἀνακύκλωσις: every sort of regime has its day and changes for the worse, but this ἀριστοκρατία has not yet had time to impose its own checks upon itself: better to do so now while there is still time .... Fair words, and the senate are for the moment persuaded; but the later narrative, especially but not only within the Coriolanus panel itself, will show how reluctant the elite is to check its own excesses. Not that anyone else is much better; the tribunes have just shown the popular side equally lacking in restraint.

There is a similar exposure of over-idealism when we reach the decemvirate later in the century. The first year of the decemvirate goes very well indeed, so much so that the elite begin to think that this may be the answer to everything, that such a setup can continue and no further magistrates may be needed (*Ant. Rom.* 10.57.3). Yet that dream turns sour too, with the second year revealing decemvirs who are very bad people indeed, and showing once again that one cannot simply rely on good people always to be there to do the steering. One reason why their dream is so over-optimistic is captured by the reason that the aristocrats found that solution so attractive: they wanted to get rid of the tribunate, and that is what was implicit in that 'no further magistrates may be needed'. The absence of tribunes as a check on decemviral excess is soon made explicit, for it gets even worse when the appalling Appius Claudius starts exploiting for his own protection the tribunician rights that (much more clearly in Dionysius than in Livy) have also passed to the decemvirs (*Ant. Rom.* 11.6, 30.4, 39.1). Important as the quality of the individuals may be – once again, that insight that when you have got good tribunes it is good and when you have got bad tribunes you have got bad (above, p. 208) – you need the right institutions too, the institutions to suit the time.

So yes, the Romans did manage to talk themselves out of mass bloodshed, and that matters immensely; but only just. Perhaps that is the best way of looking at those foreglances to the bad days of the late Republic that were to come. It could all so easily have been different, and one indication of that is that one day it *was* going to be very different.[48] The institutions were not so firmly based and reliable that success, perhaps even survival, was guaranteed. We saw earlier that there was not so much teleology in Dionysius as in Polybius. Even if Rome was in fact steered to a happy outcome so often, it could so easily have been different, and experience might have taught different lessons.

6. Augustus

Tyranny, then, did not come at the end; but the principate did. If the late Republic indicated how those early experiences might easily have been worse, does Augustus suggest ways in which they might have been so much better? Might, in fact, Roman history be analogous to the way Dionysius saw Greek culture in *On the Ancient Orators*, with a glorious classical past, a sad decline, and then a contemporary revival (above, p. 203)?

Certainly, many of these themes may seem to have an Augustan ring. Indeed, that whole question of continuity between the regal period and the Republic might seem to be a mirror image of any Augustan claim of *res publica restituta*. If Augustus' one-man rule proved the best way of restoring what was most valuable about the Republic, masked by the right sort of title rather as Dionysius' Brutus demanded nearly 500 years earlier (above, p. 207),[49] Dionysius can be seen as showing the early Republic as the best way of restoring what was most valuable about the monarchy: the monarchy, then, as *res publica praefigurata*. Nor would Augustus have cavilled at the notion that there were lessons of virtue to be learned from the people and traditions of the distant past – rather, indeed, as the virtues of the great classical authors might make them the best models for one's own writing style.[50] That stress on people as much as constitutions can certainly be given an Augustan tweak: getting the right person to do the job is the crucial thing, even if one needs attention to the institutions too. Nor might the great man have minded that stress on the tribunate (above, p. 208), his own *summi fastigii uocabulum* (Tac. *Ann.* 3.56.2) – though he might have been less enthusiastic about that emphasis on the fact that the despicable decemvirs were arrogating the power of the tribunes (above, p. 217). At one point, Dionysius points to a further lesson learned from the Greek world, the way that Greek states had begun with monarchies, then changed to

---

[48] I add some further thoughts along these lines at Pelling 2016, 166–8.
[49] In discussion of De Jonge's paper at the conference in Leiden (June 2012), Joy Connolly drew a thought-provoking parallel between the need for masked literary technique and the way in which the realities of Augustan power also needed to be cloaked.
[50] Cf. Wiater 2011a, 174–5, 223 and in this volume; Delcourt 2005, 367–8.

other forms of government when monarchs abused their power – then found it wise to return to one-man rule when speedy remedies were required for new crises (*Ant. Rom.* 5.74.1–3). What could be more Augustan than that?

There is no room for a full discussion here, and several of the other writers in this volume make important contributions.⁵¹ Many of the 'Augustan' resonances can be taken either way, with hints of reservation or criticism as well as of acclaim; and there are some points where, if we press the Augustan suggestions, we would have to posit a Dionysius who is being almost unbelievably tactless. The nineteen-year-old Octavian had made a great deal of the vultures that appeared to mark his remarkable election as consul, mirroring the twelve that had appeared to eighteen-year-old Romulus at the city's foundation;⁵² Dionysius leaves no doubt that there was something fishy about Romulus' birds (ἀπάτη, *Ant. Rom.* 1.86.3), just as there must have been about Octavian's. Another important case concerns the legal status of the decemvirate when they continued in office without formal ratification. Octavian had done the same as *triumvir* in 37 and 32 BC.⁵³ At several points in Dionysius, this continuation is the first thing that critics of the regime mention, either in murmurs or in full-dress speeches (and that is not true in Livy, even though the issue is also mentioned there); at the end of Dionysius' account, it is this that, Verginius argues, relieves the army of any duty to keep to their oath of allegiance – another theme that had resonance with the late 30s BC (*Ant. Rom.* 11.43.3). In fact, the triumvirs did have something of a legal case, and so – if there is any history here at all – would the decemvirs too; but one would never think that from Dionysius' emphasis, which is wholly unfriendly to the decemvirs.

Still, it is unlikely to be pure coincidence either that there are so many places where we might catch a contemporary whiff – though it may also be significant that they often gesture more to the end of the Republic, the period of worst decline, than to the Augustan era itself (above, pp. 215–16 and n. 40). One of these comes at the biggest moment of regime change, as the first Brutus comes into public, again with the dripping sword, and

---

⁵¹ See Fox, De Jonge, Viidebaum, and Yunis in this volume. For a measured and sophisticated discussion of Dionysius and Augustan ideology, see Wiater 2011a, 206-16.
⁵² Suet. *Aug.* 95 (with Wardle 2014, 534 n. ad loc.); App. *B Civ.* 3.94.388; Dio Cass. 46.46.2; Obs. 69: cf. Syme 1939, 184. For Romulus' age cf. *Ant. Rom.* 2.56.7: 'all who have written about it' agree on eighteen.
⁵³ Pelling 1996, 26–7, 48, 67–8. The rest of this paragraph expands some brief remarks at Pelling 2007, 257; Pelling 2016, 169.

harangues the people with anti-tyrant rhetoric (*Ant. Rom.* 4.77–83): just as the later Brutus was to do on the Ides of March. The first Brutus succeeded; the second Brutus failed. What are we to make of that? Is this the speech that the second Brutus *ought to* have given in 44 BC, in which case we might have had a return to that world where effective rhetoric could save the state from civil bloodletting? But in that case we would never have had vengeance or the second triumvirate or Augustus either. Or is it rather a suggestion that the world had changed, that the better way now to achieve those continuities, to restore the Republic, was to learn that different lesson from the Greek world and go back to one-man rule after all?

Perhaps it is either and both: instead of putting the question in pro-Augustan or anti-Augustan terms, we should think of Dionysius echoing those preoccupations of Augustan political discourse without preaching about them, introducing ideas that meshed with the political propaganda without crudely echoing it or taking sides. The important thing was that *it all still mattered*: we had been here before, the issues were not too different; it was not just that one needed to go back to the beginnings to answer Polybius' questions, one needed to go that far back to understand the present day as well. That too, in itself, might have an Augustan ring, if one thinks about all that projection of himself and his family as the embodiment of ancient habits (how those royal females must have hated all that wool-making). At least thus far, it is not too removed from the historical sensibility of Virgil or of Livy.

Still, we have seen earlier that there were important differences between Livy and Dionysius, and one of those centred on regime change: how much of a break does the end of Livy 1 or Dionysius 4 really make? For Livy, a lot; for Dionysius, rather less. Constitutions do matter. Otherwise Dionysius' players would not spend so much time talking about them. But eventually it was more important who was found to do the job. Those who wanted to find an Augustan resonance there were free to do so.

CHAPTER 9

How Roman Are the Antiquities? *The Decemvirate according to Dionysius*

Daniel Hogg

Introduction

In their introduction to this volume, Casper de Jonge and Richard Hunter identify the complex relationship between Greece and Rome as the main theme of the *Roman Antiquities*, the product of an author who is both 'thoroughly Greek' and 'very Roman'.[1] But how does this play out in practice? The simplest approach, undoubtedly a valid one, is to take the *Roman Antiquities* as Roman insofar as their subject matter and source material is Roman, but their framework and outlook upon the world fundamentally Greek. Dionysius certainly invites (instructs?) us to think that way, and doing so opens up rich interpretative possibilities. In a recent article about the end of the *Roman Antiquities,* Irene Peirano drew attention to the significance of where Dionysius has chosen to end his work, not just in terms of the First Punic War, but also with respect to the possibility that 'the Romans show signs of the same political tendency towards tyranny which eventually caused the decline (and barbarisation) of the Greek world'.[2] The general argument that the *Roman Antiquities* present us with Romans who not only surpass the Greeks in positive measures of Greekness, but also point towards a Greek-style decline towards tyranny is persuasive. Broadly put, in this reading Dionysius is a Greek historian of Rome, providing a Greek interpretation of Roman material. Perhaps this is what we might expect.

Nonetheless, there is rather more to Dionysius than his Greek background alone. Dionysius read widely in Latin as well as Greek, and had close associations with Roman citizens over a period of more than twenty years. Some of these men had substantial political careers, or came from significant political families: Metilius Rufus would become governor of the province of Achaea, and Quintus Aelius Tubero's father was a legate in

[1] See the introduction to this volume, p. 7.   [2] Peirano 2011, 53.

Asia, and his sons both consuls.³ These associations with Romans left a mark: elsewhere in this volume, Clemence Schultze sees resonances of Augustus' moral programme in Dionysius' accounts in the *Roman Antiquities* of the deaths of Lucretia and Horatia, and Casper de Jonge explores in detail the shared themes and ideas of Dionysius' *On Composition* and Horace's *Ars Poetica*.⁴ We can surely then posit that Dionysius was not only a Greek historian of Rome, but was also to some degree a product of first-century Rome. That is to say, we can enrich our view of Dionysius' history by seeing him not only through the prism of a Greek writing a Greek history of Rome, but also by locating him more generally as a historian of Rome writing in first-century Rome, and so influenced by this environment, as well as by the Greek heritage to which modern scholars have, nonetheless rightly, given so much weight.

There are two common ways of interrogating Dionysius' status as a historian in first-century Rome. I will propose a third method. The two commonest ways are (1) by thinking about him as a Greek under Roman rule, and (2) by looking for echoes of Augustus in the *Roman Antiquities*. Should we suggest that Dionysius' choice of subject matter allows him to avoid confronting Roman decline directly, instead allowing him occasional hints at the consequences of Roman conquest?⁵ Are the *Roman Antiquities* a way of reassuring Greeks about their place in the world, while tactfully giving Romans moral advice, as Nino Luraghi has suggested?⁶ Do the *Roman Antiquities* assert the ultimate superiority of Greeks and/or Greekness (brackets classical) while performing a delicate balancing act that also grants the Romans an upper hand?⁷ Is it about, say, in some way, the inevitability of tyranny? How does Augustus fit into all of this, if at all?

Both of these approaches – seeing Dionysius as a Greek responding to Rome, and searching for Augustus – are crucial for understanding the *Roman Antiquities*. Yet if we only ask these questions, we lose sight of one very important point: what were the 'soft' influences on Dionysius? In other words, how far was his writing conditioned by his association over two decades with politically powerful Roman citizens? Put differently, to what extent can Dionysius be seen to be in tune with contemporary Roman opinion? One way to explore this question, in my view under-emphasised, is to examine how the machinery of government operates in

---

³ See the introduction to this volume, p. 8.
⁴ See the chapters by Schultze and De Jonge in this volume.   ⁵ So most recently Peirano 2011, 52.
⁶ Luraghi 2003.   ⁷ As Wiater 2011a, e.g., 218.

the *Roman Antiquities*, and how far this operation might be conditioned by the functioning of government in the first century.

The story of the decemvirate offers especially fruitful terrain for such a study. For one, Dionysius affords it great significance: this single episode covers roughly one book's length, straddling the centre of the *Roman Antiquities*. Embedded within the story is the preface to the second half of the *Antiquities*, giving the story programmatic status. Furthermore, as I will argue, the story is an outstanding example of Dionysius' ability to marry Greek historiographical method and tradition with Roman material, presenting a view of the world which manages to be both Roman and Greek. The story of the decemvirate permits an examination of the internal workings of the Roman state, when it also has many of the elements that look forward to first-century Republican Rome: a ruler, Appius Claudius, rises to prominence within a group, using legal process to try to establish his power; there are proscriptions; the senate bickers and squabbles and is unable to control its magistrates. In amongst all this, Dionysius presents the motif of *metus hostilis* (fear of the enemy) or the interface between Roman internal problems and threats from foreigners; and he captures an image of a chaotic, semi-functioning city that in peacetime can hardly run itself, but can just about contain a tyrant. I will concentrate upon that aspect of the *Roman Antiquities* which is concerned with how the Roman state functions; Dionysius' task is to find an account which (1) shows how the Romans were able to avoid tyranny and civil war for as long as they did, but (2) is not so perfect that it cannot explain Rome's later descent into civil war. The answer lies, I think, not so much in the nature of Rome's potential tyrants, as in that most Roman of things, the nature of the senate.

Situating the Decemvirate

According to the implausible common tradition, the decemvirate was the board that codified Roman law in the Twelve Tables, then turned tyrannical and was expelled in 449 BC. Dionysius' version is as follows (*Ant. Rom.* 10.50–11.44).[8] Romilius proposes sending Roman ambassadors to Athens and the Greek cities in Italy, to bring back laws for the Romans to adopt. The proposal is accepted and the ambassadors depart. When they return in 451 BC, the Romans appoint the decemvirate, a body of ten, to oversee the selection and establishment of these laws. All other magistracies

---

[8] Livy 3.9–64; Cic. *Rep.* 2.54, cf. 2.3; Polyb. 6.11.1; Tac. *Ann.* 1.1.1. See further Hogg 2013. On the decemvirate in Dionysius, see also Pelling and Oakley in this volume.

are suspended while the decemvirs are in power. The decemvirs are headed by Appius Claudius. In their first year the members of the decemvirate discharge their duties admirably, and are chosen to continue in office for a second year. Now power begins to corrupt the decemvirs: they take a secret oath, promising not to oppose each other, starting to disregard the senate and courting only the common people. They start putting citizens to death and confiscating others' estates, using the courts as their tool. When the second year comes to an end, the decemvirs simply continue into a third year without any vote at all. The third year sees the decemvirate become ever more tyrannical (*Ant. Rom.* 10.60.6, 11.2.1–3.1). The best citizens desert the Roman state, and Rome comes under pressure from raids from the neighbouring Sabines and Aequians. The decemvirate tries to raise an army in the senate; they succeed, but they now face open opposition from Valerius and Horatius. The decemvirate control the army through cruelty and executions; the assassination of the plebeian hero Siccius is the final straw for the army that is encamped at Crustumerium and Fidenae. The rest of the army, at Algidum, is tested by Appius' attempt to seize a girl, Verginia, the daughter of the centurion Verginius. These actions provoke rebellion among the soldiers and the people, and the decemvirate are finally overthrown and its members executed or exiled; Appius meets his death in prison before his trial. Order is restored.

The episode has been described as significant within a cluster of events in the middle of the fifth century that together amounted to the end of the formative period of the Roman Republic,[9] along with the lawmaking embassy to Athens in 454 BC and the possible third secession of the plebs in 445 BC. The tradition that Dionysius inherits includes Cicero and stretches back to at least Polybius.[10] This tradition connects the decemvirate via attempted tyranny and sexual hubris back to the last days of the Tarquinii; Dionysius' account recasts these themes to explore the changing nature of political life in the Republican period.

The story of the decemvirate is the central element of the *Antiquities*. In the first place, the story, which runs from *Ant. Rom.* 10.50 to 11.44, straddles the boundaries of the first and the second decades of the *Antiquities*, just as it forms the centrepiece of Livy's first pentad.[11] Furthermore, since it looks forward to late Republican Rome and back to the foundation of the Republic, the story is central to even more than

---

[9] Cf. Cornell 1995, 272, with discussion of the Twelve Tables, 272–5.
[10] Polyb. 6.1.1; Cic. *Rep.* 2.61–3; Cornell 1995, 272; Zetzel 1995, 222. See, e.g., Poma 1984, 79–104 on Polybius' archaeology and its relationship to Cicero's *De Republica*.
[11] Livy 3.33–49; Forsythe 1999, 80.

that.¹² This is not a slant unique to the *Roman Antiquities*, and there are further strong parallels between the accounts of Livy and Dionysius, which have been discussed in detail elsewhere.¹³ These close resemblances make a comparison between Livy's and Dionysius' accounts a rich opportunity to see what is Dionysian about Dionysius' account.

The story of the decemvirate is disrupted by a break between the end of book 10 and the beginning of book 11. This break, occurring before the final year of decemviral rule, is fortified by Dionysius' 'second preface' (*Ant. Rom.* 11.1.1–5): this is the only instance of Dionysius having a programmatic statement and the start of a book coincide after Book 1.¹⁴ That this preface separates the first half of the *Antiquities* from the second is likely to be important.¹⁵ Furthermore, there is a possibility that Dionysius has manipulated the chronology of the period to allow him to start the eleventh book with the dramatic events of the final year of the decemvirate. He says at the beginning of Book 11:¹⁶

> In the eighty-third Olympiad, in which Krison of Himera gained the prize, and Philiscus was archon at Athens, the Romans dissolved the rule of the decemvirate, which had governed the commonwealth for three years. (*Ant. Rom.* 11.1.1)

While there are sources which put the decemviral rule at three years (e.g., Cic. *Rep.* 2.62), it was more common to put it at two (Diod. Sic. 12.23–5; Livy 3.33–54; Tac. *Ann.* 1.1.1).¹⁷ There is precedent for the chronology Dionysius has selected, but we may at least think it possible that he has made strict chronological accuracy subservient to a pleasing arrangement

---

¹² Ungern-Sternberg 2005, 84–5 at 85: 'To an amazing extent ... past and present seem to be indissolubly interlaced in the accounts of the second Decemvirate'.

¹³ Ungern-Sternberg 2005, 85–9 suggests that Livy and Dionysius relied on essentially the same source or sources. One example is that both Livy and Dionysius have speakers in the senatorial debate propose the appointment of an *interrex* (Livy 3.40.7; Dion. Hal. *Ant. Rom.* 11.20.5).

¹⁴ The 'second preface' (11.1.1–5) is cited in Oakley's chapter in this volume, pp. 135–7. Tacitus postpones a traditional introductory motif, the survey of imperial resources, until *Ann.* 4.4, as part of a powerful declaration of a new beginning now that Sejanus has entered the narrative (Martin and Woodman 1989, 14, with thanks to Rhiannon Ash for the idea). Cf. Thuc. 5.26.

¹⁵ 'Middles' frequently contain crucial moments. Pelling 2004, 318–9 has drawn attention to the dramatic function of Caesar crossing the Rubicon at the middle of Plutarch's *Caesar* (34) and of Curio's flight to Caesar in the middle of Cassius Dio's history (40.66.5). Cf. Myres 1953, 62, 81–8, who argues that one of the structural principles of Herodotus' history is pedimental: that is, the work has its climax at the centre. De Jong 2002, 250 rejects this on the ground that the placing of such a 'centre' in Herodotus' work is subjective.

¹⁶ Translations are adapted from Cary 1937–1950.

¹⁷ Schultze 1995, 192–214 acknowledges this third decemviral year but does not discuss it. Gabba 1964, 187 discusses the problem in Dionysius' chronology, and refers to Dionysius' lost work on the subject.

of his history. Paul Martin has argued that Dionysius plays games with his chronology, so it should not be surprising that some episodes fall conveniently within the parameters of the Olympiad/consular dating systems.[18] This would chime well with Simon Northwood's thesis that, for Dionysius, the suitability of material for his argument trumped considerations of historicity.[19]

There is no need for a third decemviral year to make first-century resonances apparent. Chris Pelling and Jürgen von Ungern-Sternberg have pointed out the possible parallel between the decemvirs' illegal retention of power beyond the first year and the Second Triumvirate.[20] It would be tempting here to see Augustus as a target in this; and as Pelling argues in this volume, there is enough in the *Antiquities* for keen readers to see Augustus if they wish to.[21] But it would be wrong to force the point, especially so in this episode, and even more so if we are supposed to be reminded of the Second Triumvirate: while the Second Triumvirate did extend its power beyond the five-year limit twice, Octavian pointedly stopped using the title 'triumvir' after 33, while Antony continued to do so. This would make Antony a better fit with Appius and his followers. But it would also distract attention from the more important focus of the story, which is that the senate was not equipped to stop the tyranny.

As the resonances with contemporary Roman history expand, so Dionysius' target narrows. The second preface is much briefer than the first one (*Ant. Rom.* 1.1–8),[22] and consequently more simplified.[23] Whereas in the first preface, Dionysius had engaged competitively with a dozen or so lesser historians, in the second he concentrates his fire on Herodotus and Thucydides.[24] Referring to the founding principles of history, he says that people are not satisfied with learning only bare facts (*Ant. Rom.* 11.1.2).[25]

---

[18] Martin 1993, 196–8.   [19] Northwood 1998.
[20] Pelling 1996, 26 with note; Ungern-Sternberg 2005, 85–7.
[21] Pelling in this volume, pp. 218–20. See Wiater 2011a, 8–18, 206–16 for a discussion of Dionysius' interaction with Augustan ideology.
[22] This brevity can give the impression of simplification: Porciani 1997, 95 argues that Dionysius' reconstruction of his audience at 11.1 is 'semplificato', reduced to the two categories of philosophers and politicians, when he referred to three types in the first preface, philosophers, politicians and the general public (cf. Porciani 1997, 91).
[23] Porciani 1997, 91, 95.
[24] Compare Livy's second preface at 6.1–3 (Kraus 1994, 83–8; Oakley 1997, 381–6). The break between Livy's fifth and sixth book is much cleaner (and, admittedly, artistically more satisfying) than *Ant. Rom.* 10–11. The end of Livy 5 is downbeat, like *Ant. Rom.* 10.60, the haphazard rebuilding of Rome (Livy 5.55) complementing the end of freedom under the decemvirs. The beginning of Livy 6, like *Ant. Rom.* 11.1, is more optimistic. Dionysius' engagement with his predecessors is more conventional than Livy's, who competes with himself and his own first pentad (Kraus 1994, 83).
[25] Cf. Gabba 1991, 80–1; Porciani 1997, 91–3.

People wish, he says, to know more about the Persian wars than simply that the Persian army was defeated by the Athenians and Lacedaemonians. He rewrites and expands upon Thucydides:[26]

> For most people it is not sufficient to extract only this from history, that, to make the argument on the basis of this example, the Athenians and the Lacedaimonians won the Persian war, prevailing in two sea-battles and one land battle (δυσὶ ναυμαχίαις καὶ πεζομαχίᾳ μιᾷ) against the barbarian, who led three million men, while they themselves with their allies led no more than one hundred and ten thousand, but they also wish to learn from the history the places in which the events occurred, and to hear the reasons why men accomplished these amazing and incredible deeds, and to read who were the leaders of the armies of both the barbarians and the Greeks, and to be ignorant of not a single incident, so to say, that happened in those engagements. (*Ant. Rom.* 11.1.2)

> Of earlier deeds, the greatest done was the Median war, yet this too had a speedy outcome in two sea-battles and two land-battles (δυοῖν ναυμαχίαιν καὶ πεζομαχίαιν). (Thuc. 1.23.1)

Thucydides' summary, which simply mentions the decisive events of the Persian wars, is not enough. Readers of history require that Thucydides' account must be complemented by a fuller narrative of the details of the Persian wars.[27] This is already narrated in Herodotus' history, and indeed the references to causes (τὰς αἰτίας), wonderful events (τὰ θαυμαστά), and the Greek/barbarian axis (τῶν τε βαρβαρικῶν καὶ τῶν Ἑλληνικῶν) all recall the preface to Herodotus' history too. The point is not to disparage Thucydides' coverage,[28] even though in his rhetorical writings Dionysius expressed substantial reservations about Thucydides' choice of the beginning and end of his work (*Thuc.* 10–12; *Pomp.* 3.8–10, 4.2; see also Pelling in this volume). Rather, Dionysius stresses the continuity of history, saying that there exist causes before events, and history must record these causes as well as the events themselves. Dionysius emphasises the point by repeating it. He says that it is not enough to know the end of the Peloponnesian War, but rather the causes behind that end, the debates, the battles, and so forth. In other words, it is not enough that there exist the *Hellenica* of Xenophon and Theopompus, which narrate just the end of the Peloponnesian War. Readers also need to know the causes behind that end; they need to know Thucydides' history (*Ant. Rom.* 11.1.3). So Herodotus is a precondition of

---

[26] For this passage and its rewriting of Thucydides, see also Oakley in this volume, p. 138.
[27] On Dionysius' detailed narration in the *Ant. Rom.*, see Oakley in this volume.
[28] For a different view, see Oakley in this volume, p. 138.

Thucydides, and in his turn, Thucydides is a precondition of Xenophon and Theopompus. This list of continuations gestures towards Dionysius' treatment of Polybius,[29] whom Dionysius accuses of 'slurring' over the earliest part of Roman history (*Ant. Rom.* 1.6.1, 7.1, 54–61; see Pelling in this volume, pp. 203–4), and whose beginning, the First Punic War, marks the end of the *Roman Antiquities*. By emphasising the original causes behind events, Dionysius argues that his history is the necessary precondition of Polybius'. The claim is a big one: on the authorial level, it places Dionysius on a level with *both* Thucydides *and* Herodotus. More importantly, however, in making this point, Dionysius puts the decemvirate, an internal Roman dispute which lasted three years, on a par with both the Peloponnesian and the Persian Wars, totalling one hundred years of Greek history. There is no doubt, then, that Dionysius locates the *Roman Antiquities* firmly within the Greek historiographical tradition, as we would expect from his rhetorical works. He is also clearly addressing in this instance an audience that is acquainted with the long train of Greek historiography. But at the same time the *Antiquities* is shot through with a sensibility that, while it does have ties to Greek historiographical thinking, is nonetheless firmly rooted in first-century Rome.

Metus Hostilis

While Dionysius frames the significance of his story around Thucydides and Herodotus, the content of his narrative includes elements that tie him strongly into a Roman historical narrative of the first century BC. One key element here is Dionysius' use of the idea of *metus hostilis*, or 'fear of the enemy'.[30] This idea is summarised by Livy (2.39) in the phrase *externus timor maximum concordiae vinculum*, loosely translated as 'fear of an external enemy is the greatest bond of harmony between the orders'. This concept, most commonly associated with Sallust but also present strongly in Livy and elsewhere, is seen as identifying the causes of the breakdown of the Republic at Rome in the period after the total destruction in 146 BC of Carthage, Rome's most important rival in the Mediterranean.

Dionysius had presented in the story of Cincinnatus in book 10 the idea that the *metus hostilis* is as much a tool of control wielded by the powerful as

---

[29] Polybius is also in the background when Dionysius discusses the pleasure and utility of history (*Ant. Rom.* 11.1.4; cf. Verdin 1974, 297; Porciani 1997, 95).

[30] For the *metus hostilis* cf. e.g., Earl 1961; Evrigennis 2008; Jacobs 2010; Lintott 1972; Miles 1995, 79.

it is a genuine fear which binds society together. Cincinnatus was famous for being called from his plough to be consul of Rome. In Dionysius' version (and in Livy's too), he is summoned when peace in Rome is threatened by demagogic tribunes; he threatens to use his consular authority to take the entire Roman people out on campaign, forcing the plebeians to observe the military oath that they have sworn. This so terrifies the plebeians that tumult is averted and order is restored in the city.[31] The idea that the threat of a campaign can be used by a leader to enforce order recurs in a similar way in the account of the final year of the decemvirate.[32] The Sabines and the Aequi sense that, owing to civil discord, Rome is weak and vulnerable to attack. The Romans cannot maintain *concordia* (*Ant. Rom.* 11.2.2–3.1), an interesting reversal of *externus timor maximum concordiae vinculum*. The decemvirs call a senate meeting in order to levy an army. They hope that the threat posed by the Sabines and Aequi will force the acquiescence of the senate in this matter, and so *de facto* consolidate their hold on power. This is the thrust of the speech of the decemvir Lucius Cornelius (*Ant. Rom.* 11.16.2–18.4).

Roman historiographical thinking of the first century is thus always in the background of Dionysius' composition. Events of the first century are hinted at too in the reasons for Rome's weakness at this point. Before the senatorial debate, Dionysius says that the rule of the decemvirate has caused the ruling class to leave *en masse* (11.2.3). Livy says the same thing too (3.38.8–13). Ogilvie has pointed out the resonance in first-century Rome, specifically the desolation of Rome in similar circumstances in 49 BC, when Caesar was reluctant to call on the senate before the war against Pompey (cf. Cic. *Att.* 9.6a, 10.4.8–9), and the manipulation of the senate by Carbo and Cinna in the war against Sulla (cf. Livy, *Epit.* 83–4).[33]

Having a notion of the *metus hostilis* and presenting various episodes that bear comparison with events of the first century does not mean that Dionysius is writing through a first-century Roman prism to the extent that, say, Livy is. For example, Livy differentiates repeatedly and explicitly between *optimates* and *populares* (at 3.35.4, 9, 39.9), which Dionysius does not do.[34] The terms *optimates* and *populares*, referring to factions in first-

---

[31] Livy's Cincinnatus invokes Rome's bellicose patron gods at this point (3.19.12): *nescio quo fato magis bellantes quam pacati propitios habemus deos*: 'By I don't know what fate we have more propitious gods when we are at war than when we are at peace'.
[32] Cf. Livy 3.38.8–13.
[33] Ogilvie 1965, 467; see further Cic. *Brut.* 308, who describes the emptiness of Rome at this point in the 80s BC, and Vell. Pat. 2.23 on the flight of the nobles in 86 BC.
[34] Ogilvie 1965, 464; Ungern-Sternberg 2005, 81–4.

century Republican debates, drag the story out of its own context and into first-century affairs.³⁵ Livy's version of the decemvirate therefore makes it a forward-looking device in ways that Dionysius might not be doing: the influence of first-century accounts reinforces the exemplarity of the episode, which will recur repeatedly in Livy's history.³⁶ In Dionysius, the closest we get is some scant reference by Gaius Claudius to the patrician/plebeian axis (*Ant. Rom.* 11.7.2, 9.6; cf. the *concordia ordinum* at 11.3.1). In this instance, this appears to be a rhetorical device designed to describe the whole of the Roman population, rather than something politically motivated. Yet the blandness is expressive too, assuming a unity which we know from the previous six books does not actually exist.

The complexity of the moral impetus underlying the *metus hostilis* in Dionysius, then, should be seen in combination with other elements that Dionysius shares with Roman historians of the same period who write in Latin. Perhaps, indeed, we should be more confident about painting a Dionysius who is not only functioning on a Greek-Roman axis, but is also assessing Roman behaviour on its own terms. Dionysius is certainly a classicising or Atticising Greek rhetorician, whose explicit engagement is with Greek writers of the classical, Hellenistic, and his own periods. But we should not underestimate the presence of Roman influence on what he is saying about Rome. The fact that Dionysius' history is not as Roman as Livy's should not obscure the fact that he is writing in terms dictated by first-century Roman events and historiographical thinking. He is, in other words, not always being a Greek historian of Rome, with capital G and small h; he is also being a historian of Rome who happens to be writing in Greek.

The Debate in the Senate House

It is one thing to present a Roman Dionysius who might arguably only be reflecting his sources. One area, however, where he is undoubtedly his own man is in his speeches. Normally, these are taken as evidence of Dionysius' classicising, rhetorical approach. This is undoubtedly the case. But I will instead present the view that, in the set-piece senatorial debate of the final year of decemviral rule, the arrangement of the speeches shows

---

[35] Forsythe 1999, 82, though his chief interest is in the historicity of particular events. Cf. in this story, Livy 3.35.4, 9; also 4.9.5, 8, 11, 5.24.9. See further Cic. *Sest.* 96, who uses the distinction. Cf. Hellegouarc'h 1972, 500–5 on *optimates*, 518–25 on *populares*.

[36] For example, in Sempronius' speech at 9.34.1; Cincinnatus' speech at 4.15.3–4; Canuleius at 4.3.17, with an interesting note at Chaplin 2000, 159 n. 58.

Dionysius trying to encapsulate behaviour in the senate of the Roman Republic. He does so by reflecting known problems in senatorial discussions; and so it is there where I believe we find Dionysius encapsulating his idea of Romanness.

The senate meeting is called by the decemvirs with the aim of consolidating their hold on Rome in the face of the threats posed by the Sabines and Aequi (*Ant. Rom.* 11.4–21; cf. Livy 3.39.1–41.6). The meeting is tempestuous. The speeches, fairly short by Dionysian standards, reflect the choppy feel; it is difficult, and indeed not the point, to discern clear lines.[37] There is interruption (11.4.3–4, 6.1), unexpected silence (11.4.5–7), forced silence (11.6.2), heated argument (11.21.1–2), and the threat of violence (11.6.1). In between, there are formal speeches by Gaius Claudius, Appius' uncle, who preaches moderation (11.7–14 and the less formal 15.3–5), and Lucius Cornelius, a supporter of the decemvirate (11.16.1–18.4). There is also direct discourse by Appius Claudius (11.4.5, 21.4–5), the decemvir Marcus Cornelius (11.15.1–2), and their opponents Horatius (11.5.2–4) and Valerius (11.19–20).

This tempestuousness is reflected in Dionysius' treatment of various themes. Family provides no clear indication of which side a speaker will favour: while the Cornelii brothers support each other, Appius' uncle Gaius opposes him. Individuals' manner of speaking accords with their experience; otherwise the issue of age is also messy, much more so than it is in Livy, who divides the senate along lines of seniority (Livy 3.41.1, 41.5): in Dionysius, some older senators support the decemvirate, and some oppose it. Marcus Cornelius, a decemvir and apparently senior, says that he is not of an age to be patronised by Gaius Claudius, Appius' uncle (11.15.1). Lucius Cornelius, the brother of Marcus Cornelius, is also an experienced man, being a consular (11.16.1), but he too tries to make an issue of Gaius Claudius' age (11.16.2). He portrays his argument as one of action, speed and decision (11.16.5, 18.2), characteristics which are traditionally the province of young men, though he does not force the distinction. His speech is peppered with vigorous, rapid rhetorical questions (11.18.2; cf. Horatius doing the same at 11.5.3). The rhetorical questions of Gaius Claudius, by contrast, are more drawn-out and convoluted (11.9.5–6),

---

[37] But cf. Burck 1934, 32–3, who argues that Dionysius' presentation is more formally arranged, with two symmetrical pairs of speeches, by Valerius and Horatius on the one hand and Cornelius and Valerius on the other, encasing the central speech by Gaius Claudius. Burck pinpoints one difference: 'Livy strebt nicht eine realistische Wiedergabe der historischen Sitzung an'. Forsythe 1999, 81 expresses his irritation: 'Dionysius once again exhibits his rhetorical incontinence by devoting 18 chapters to a detailed description of this senatorial debate'.

befitting his seniority. Cornelius' speech starts rambunctiously, expressing surprise (θαυμαστόν, 'amazing', 11.16.2), while Gaius Claudius' opens with a more measured subordinate clause (11.7.1). Outside the direct discourse, however, things are less certain. In Livy's account, the younger senators (*iuniores*) support the decemviral faction (3.41.1). Dionysius used the motif of younger men making up a faction in the story of Coriolanus (*Ant. Rom.* 7.21.3), but in the decemvirate, some of the younger speakers support the decemvirs' opponents (11.21.1).

A comparison with Livy shows that Dionysius' account is full of formal conflict and disorder. Just as Dionysius' account of the procedure revels in chaos, so does confusion about procedure dominate the content of the speeches. This is clearest in Appius' attempt to maintain order against the anarchy of the decemvirs' chief opponents, Valerius and Horatius (e.g., *Ant. Rom.* 11.4.5, 6.2–3, 6), an attempt to manage tyrannical-style power through control over procedure. The timing of the division at the end of the meeting creates a moment of conflict. In Livy's account, Valerius and Horatius interrupt during the formal division (3.41.1). In Dionysius, however, there is no clear point at which this division takes place. The senate has changed its mind after every speech (*Ant. Rom.* 11.15.5, 19.1, 21.1), and so each of the factions is ahead at one point:

> When the majority of the opinions had been delivered, and those who sanctioned the war seemed to be much more powerful than the rest... (*Ant. Rom.* 11.19.1)

> It was easy to discern that this opinion delivered by Valerius pleased the majority, so far as one could guess from their voices... (*Ant. Rom.* 11.21.1)

Finally, Valerius' anti-decemviral speech appears to carry the day, but instead he and Cornelius argue about whether the division has already been taken (11.21.1–3). Appius tries to exert control, simply declaring the matter already settled (11.21.4–6). His victory is only partial, and Valerius and Horatius are able to organise some opposition outside the senate house (11.22.1).

For one, the number of competing voices in this debate is consistent with Dionysius' method of developing debate in the *Roman Antiquities*. Debate is one of the chief ways in which Rome has changed since the expulsion of the kings. Then, Brutus acceded to the consulship after one speech to the conspirators and a *contio* (*Ant. Rom.* 4.70–85). During the consulship, he is opposed in direct discourse only by his fellow consul,

Collatinus (5.9.2–3). The intervening books have seen changes in the way people speak. In the long pre-trial hearing of Coriolanus, for example, there is a large number of speakers, but the speakers are separated sometimes by days, and there is no interruption.[38] Violence, too, is a feature of the earlier debate over Volero's bill, when Laetorius is struck by the supporters of the consul Appius, the father of Appius the decemvir (*Ant. Rom.* 9.48.4).[39] Yet there is no debate which is quite so cluttered with voices or violence as this one.[40]

Secondly, it is possible that Dionysius has first-century senatorial debates in mind when constructing this debate. Dionysius has the debate turn several times, with senators routinely agreeing with the speaker who preceded them. Among Augustus' many reforms to the senate during the Principate, Suetonius records that in important debates Augustus would call speakers not in order but as he pleased, so that the senators might advise rather than simply agree with the previous speaker (*ac si censendum magis quam adsentiendum esset*, Suet. *Aug.* 35.4). I wonder whether we are invited here to think of this reform when we read about Dionysius' senators unhelpfully echoing their predecessors' opinion. If so, we might then be able to see the seeds of the failure of Republican Rome in the first century: Dionysius' senate shows tendencies of not being able to manage its affairs, which can explain Rome's decline into civil war in the first century BC, and allow its revival, if the senate can be streamlined. Augustus hovers here in the background also.

Verginia

The weakness of the senate as a body for controlling a tyrant is made even clearer in the story of Verginia, which brings about the dissolution of the decemvirate (*Ant. Rom.* 11.28–44; Livy 3.44–9). Appius, the decemvirate's leader, will be brought down not by the direct actions of the senate, but by the offence he commits against the people. A girl, Verginia, catches his eye; he uses one of his lackeys to try to get hold of the girl, so he can have her for

---

[38] Coriolanus speaks (*Ant. Rom.* 7.22–4, 25.4); then Minucius (7.28–32, 38.3–4), whose speech is paired with Sicinius' (7.33.3–34.5, 36.3–4); then Decius (7.40–6), whose speech is paired with Appius Claudius' (7.48–53); then Manius Valerius (7.54–6); then Coriolanus again (7.57).

[39] The complicated tradition of the Appii Claudii in this period is untangled by Wiseman 1979, 77–8. For present purposes, it is sufficient to note that both Dionysius and Livy differentiate between Appius Claudius, the consul of 471, and Appius Claudius, the decemvir; this differs from the evidence of the Fasti (see Degrassi 1947, 26–7).

[40] Valerius refers to the 'confusion' which Appius has engendered in the state (συγκεχύκατε, *Ant. Rom.* 11.4.7).

himself. But before he can succeed in this, Verginia's father, Verginius, stabs her to death, preserving her honour.[41] The episode outrages the Roman people, and, in a lost section of Dionysius' account, the decemvirs are ultimately forced to resign.

The story of Verginia gives the motifs of tyranny, *libido* and sexual hubris a Republican flavour.[42] The decemvirate had been explicitly figured as a tyranny several times already in the story: the narrator refers to the decemvirate's supporters as 'flatterers of tyrannical power' at *Ant. Rom.* 10.54 and φιλοτύραννοι, 'friends of tyranny', in the preface to the final year of the decemvirate (11.2.2). Earlier, Horatius compared Appius to the tyrannical Tarquinius Superbus (11.5.2), as Verginius does during this trial.[43] C. Claudius' description of the behaviour of the decemvirs recalled stock descriptions of tyrannies, including, crucially, charges of insults to men's wives and licentiousness towards daughters (11.10.3–4).

Roman tyranny means the Tarquinii, and the regal period had been explicitly recalled at the end of the second year of the decemvirate's rule (10.59.5).[44] When the people saw the lictors carrying the *fasces*, their minds were cast back to the days of the kings (Livy has a similar scene at 3.36). This custom had been abolished by Valerius Publicola during his first consulship (*Ant. Rom.* 5.19.2–3), shortly after the death of Brutus. The practice was then still fresh in the collective memory of fifth-century Romans. History returns now with the decemvirate. The *fasces* become important again towards the end of Verginia's hearing.

Livy[45] emphasises the connection between the decemvirate and the regal period, drawing attention to the parallel between Verginia and Lucretia (Livy 3.44.1: see Schultze in this volume). They each encompass the example of *pudicitia*, 'modesty or chastity', bringing out the degeneracy of the tyrants who seek to ruin them;[46] the beauty of the women, important in Dionysius (Lucretia: *Ant. Rom.* 4.64.4; Verginia: 11.28.1–2), is central in Livy too (Lucretia: 1.57.10; Verginia: 3.48.7). As it was with

---

[41] Compare the story of Lucretia, who commits suicide after being raped (*Ant. Rom.* 4.64–76): see Schultze in this volume.
[42] See Briquel 2004, 139–40; Wiseman 1979, 77–81 on the tradition of the tyrannical Appius Claudius.
[43] Livy 3.39.1 has his Horatius use the figure similarly in his account, as he calls the decemvirs 'ten Tarquins'.
[44] See further Briquel 2004, 139–41.
[45] There exist other versions in Diod. Sic. 12.24; Val. Max. 6.1; Cic. *Rep.* 2.63. See Briquel 2004, 143–5 with bibliography on Diodorus; Briquel 2004, 145 on Cicero.
[46] E.g., Bernard 2000, 242, 256–7, who lists *forma, castitas, pudor* and *libido* as common characteristics of the stories of the two women, with further discussion of the typology of women in Livy. See also Kowalski 2002, 152–3.

Sextus Tarquinius, *libido* will indicate Appius' descent into tyranny and be the trigger for his ultimate decline.

Tensions between plebeians and patricians had been present in the episode of the assassination of the plebeian soldier Siccius (*Ant. Rom.* 11.25–7; Livy 3.43),[47] and one fundamental difference between the two women in both Dionysius and Livy is that Lucretia is a patrician, while Verginia is a plebeian. As we saw in the senatorial debate, speech patterns exemplify the changing role of the plebeians since the regal period. At that time, plebeian direct discourse was limited to passing comment on the actions of the main characters. The institution of the tribunate marked the last development in the mode of plebeian speech in the *Roman Antiquities*; since then, the plebeians have consolidated their role in city affairs. Now, in Verginia's trial, the plebeians Marcus Claudius (*Ant. Rom.* 11.29.1–4), Numitorius (11.30.6–7) and Icilius (11.31.4–5) all speak in direct discourse. Afterwards Verginia's father, Verginius, will harangue the troops, also in direct discourse (11.40.5–41.6).

The role of the plebeians is one example of the increasing chaos presented in the *Antiquities*. The trial of Verginia is characterised, as the debate in the senate was characterised before it, by the lack of clarity and the clutter of voices over which Appius tries to be heard. Dionysius stresses the point through the voice of the narrator. At intervals throughout the story, he draws attention to the amount of material he *could* talk about, emphasising how much he needs to keep under control (e.g., *Ant. Rom.* 11.1.6, 24.3–25.1). For example, Livy's balance of the two crimes, one in Rome and one on campaign, *domi militiaeque* (3.43.1), is not so simple in Dionysius. Dionysius tries to balance the competing themes of the army, the people and the senate, but makes the overspill of one into the other clear, as for example:

> The army that was situated at Algidum in the territory of the Aequians, and the whole of the population in the city became hostile to them [the decemvirs] for these reasons. (*Ant. Rom.* 11.28.1)

The difficulty that Dionysius expresses about keeping control of the subject-matter mirrors the difficulty that the decemvirs find in controlling events, for similar reasons: everything is, by now, too chaotic.

In other details, the story is expressively different from the overthrow of Tarquinius Superbus. After Verginius protects his daughter's honour by

---

[47] Briquel 2004, 147 discusses the 'doubling' *(dédoublée)* effect created by the stories of Siccius and Verginia, the one a 'public' crime committed in the military, the other a 'private' crime committed at Rome. Cf. Livy 3.43.1.

stabbing her to death (*Ant. Rom.* 11.37.6), the story moves to the Forum, and so the usurpation seems to begin along the same lines as it had when Brutus proceeded into the forum followed by Lucretia's bier (4.76.3). No time for that now: fighting has spread into the forum before Verginia's bier can be brought in (11.39.2). Valerius and his followers deliver a *contio* over the body, just as Brutus did, but its contents are passed over in just a sentence (11.39.2). If a parallel is to be drawn in detail, then it must be with Verginius' speech to the soldiers at Algidum (11.40.3–41.6), and Verginius makes the link himself:

> Will you not come to a decision worthy of your ancestors, who, on account of the outrage suffered by one woman at the hands of one of the sons of Tarquin ... (*Ant. Rom.* 11.41.2)

But, especially in this story, strict parallels do not work. The rule of the Tarquinii turned out to be uncontrollable, but until the crisis triggered by Lucretia, it had looked like the ruling family could control all too much. In the present story, the confusing ebb and flow, the changes of theatre of action, all contribute to the sense that the rule of the decemvirate has been constantly destabilised. The role of law is an important counterpoint here: the destabilisation of the decemvirate occurred even as Appius, the chief decemvir, tried to exert control through laws and procedures. Let us turn now, then, to the descent of Appius' character into madness as the tyranny progresses.

Tyranny as Figured in the Madness of Appius

Dionysius depicts Appius' tyranny as a descent into madness. There is a difference to be noticed here between Livy's Appius and Dionysius'. Livy's Appius adopts a demagogic attitude in order to get re-elected as decemvir. When elected he will 'throw off the mask', his *aliena persona*, and reveal his tyranny (3.36.1). Dionysius' Appius, on the other hand, maintains the 'best of motives' (*Ant. Rom.* 10.55.1) in the early stages of the decemvirate:

> There came upon Appius a desire (ἐπιθυμία) to adopt an alien magistracy (ξένην ἀρχήν), and to establish laws for the fatherland and to set an example to his fellow citizens of harmony and peace and the recognition by them all of the unity of the commonwealth. Nevertheless, when he had been honoured with this great magistracy (ἀρχῇ κοσμηθεὶς μεγάλῃ), he did not preserve his probity but, corrupted by the greatness of his authority (ὑπὸ μεγέθους ἐξουσίας διαφθαρείς), succumbed to an irresistible passion for

holding office and came very near to running into tyranny; all which I shall relate at the proper time. (*Ant. Rom.* 10.54.7)

While Dionysius gives hints that all is not right with Appius – the desire (ἐπιθυμία) is remarkable, as is the 'alien magistracy' (ξένην ἀρχήν) – Dionysius' Appius *becomes* mad in a way that Livy's does not. Dionysius' Appius draws a line between process and madness: Appius' legitimate power begets madness and leads to tyranny. Appius, who in Livy is described as a 'late Republican *popularis*',[48] provides in Dionysius a more universal warning against the dangers of power. Dionysius therefore perhaps asks his first-century readers to speculate from a universal perspective about connections with Augustus and other first-century Roman dictators.

On its own, criticism of tyranny is harmless enough, but details peppered throughout the story recall events of the Roman first century too. Most clearly, the actions of the decemvirate in their second year of office explicitly recall the proscriptions of Sulla and possibly the Second Triumvirate too. Dionysius says that the decemvirs governed in that year,

> ... becoming themselves both the lawgivers (νομοθέται) and the judges (δικασταί) in all matters, putting many of the citizens to death and stripping others of their estates (τὰς οὐσίας) unjustly (ἀδίκως). (*Ant. Rom.* 10.60.2)

The implication of the proscriptions is stark. More broadly, the interplay between legal process, tradition and sole rule might well have struck a chord with some readers too. In the senate, Appius had been one of a number of decemviral voices trying to keep control over the debate. Now, on the tribunal, Appius' language strikes a placatory tone, responding to the complaints of the crowd even as he tries to secure Verginia for himself (e.g., *Ant. Rom.* 11.31.1–2, 32.3–4). All the while, the madness which grips him at 11.28.3 continues to press upon him (11.33.1, 35.4). The narrator's descriptions become ever more effusive as Appius fails to sate his desire:

> When he left the forum, in anguish and driven mad by his passion ... (*Ant. Rom.* 11.33.1)

> Appius, inasmuch as he was by nature not of sound mind (φύσιν ... οὐ φρενήρης ἀνήρ) and had been corrupted by the size of his power ... (*Ant. Rom.* 11.34.5)

It would be possible to read this passage as dangerously anti-Augustan. Perhaps Appius, who started as one of the decemvirs and is now clearly in

---

[48] Ungern-Sternberg 2005, 83: Appius Claudius 'is described throughout [Livy's account] as a late Republican *popularis*'.

sole charge, is supposed to stand for Augustus, left as the last triumvir standing. The population first realised the tyranny of the decemvirs when they appeared with the *fasces* carried before them (*Ant. Rom.* 10.59.5–60.2); Appius' final sentence in direct discourse is to arrogate the *fasces* to his own person (11.37.3).[49] Appius' madness has escaped his control; it culminates in his final appropriation of tradition. The hint towards the trappings of tradition might point to Augustus too. But if criticism of Augustus were Dionysius' point, this would be extraordinarily crass.[50]

Indeed, Dionysius' method is to locate the *Antiquities* within the Greek tradition as well as the Roman one. To this end, Appius' madness looks backwards as well as forwards. He is described as οὐ φρενήρης, 'not of sound mind' (*Ant. Rom.* 11.35.4). As so often in Dionysius, this phrase looks back both to Herodotus and to an earlier moment in the *Roman Antiquities*. Brutus functions as the hub, a universalising figure against whom other Romans must be compared. The words οὐ φρενήρης point back to Brutus' description of other people's opinions of him when he pretended to be mad (*Ant. Rom.* 4.77.1),[51] reinforcing Brutus' positive characterisation in the early part of his career, and so, by extension, Appius' own early positive characterisation. Now, the reminiscence of Brutus recalls Brutus' concealment of his true intelligence – 'you thought I was mad' – and so triangulates suggestively with Livy's focus upon Appius' concealment under his *aliena persona*. In Dionysius, the sense of concealment works differently. Other Dionysian politicians, such as Romilius, were capable of shifting public personas, but Appius changes more deeply than this: he had, after all, started the story with the 'best of motives'.

If one moves outside the *Antiquities*, Herodotus' story of Cambyses provides a powerful counterpoint to Appius' madness. He too is described as οὐ φρενήρης when he undertakes his campaign against the Fish-eaters (Hdt. 3.25.2).[52] Cambyses' madness is indicated in his disregard for νόμοι, in the Herodotean sense of custom or unwritten law.[53]

---

[49] In Livy, the *fasces* play an important part in the early stages of the decemvirate, when the decemvirs make their first claim to power, and in the speeches in the senatorial debate (3.36, 39.8); Livy's Appius is surrounded by lictors, a magistrate's bodyguard, who carry the *fasces*; and Verginia's fiancé, Icilius, refers to axes and rods (*virgas et secures*, 3.45.7). There are therefore close similarities between the versions, but this specific symbolism is drawn out a little more strongly in Dionysius.
[50] Pelling in this volume, pp. 218–19, makes a similar point.
[51] Ek 1942, 134. On Dionysius' portrayal of Brutus, see Schultze in this volume, pp. 173–4.
[52] Ek 1942, 134–5; Asheri et al. 2007, 424; cf. Hdt. 3.35.4, 5.42.1, 9.55.2; Arr. *Anab.* 3.22.2.
[53] E.g., at Hdt. 3.16.4, 38.1, 38.4; Baragwanath's reading (2008, 115–9) is extremely stimulating. On νόμος in Herodotus, see, e.g., Asheri et al. 2007, 437–8 on Hdt. 3.38.1; Rood 2006, 298–300; Thomas 2006, 69–71.

Cambyses is so far destabilised that νόμος, which one might expect to act as a stabilising force, cannot be used consistently by the reader to measure Cambyses' madness.[54] Νόμοι, in the later sense of written laws, are also central to Appius' madness, since the members of the decemvirate were appointed to establish what turned out to be the Twelve Tables. Appius himself, I have argued, is obsessed with procedure. His failure to exert sufficient dominance through (and over) law might seem to demonstrate the Herodotean and Pindaric principle that νόμος itself is king (Hdt. 3.38.4; Pind. fr. 169 Maehler),[55] but there is more to it than that. Appius is not just a manipulator of νόμος. He is also hamstrung by his responsiveness to the demands of the people, since his first instinct after the hearing was simply to have Verginia taken away by Marcus Claudius (*Ant. Rom.* 11.31.2). Appius' attempts to preserve legality, to placate the people and to satisfy his *libido* create a character torn in a number of directions – including both Greek and Roman – and so in tune with the whole account of the decemvirate, as well as the *Antiquities* as a whole. The decemvirate therefore encapsulates Dionysius' method of drawing Roman and Greek models together.

It is true to say, then, that the Greeks are the framework within which the Romans are judged, even as the Romans surpass them, as they do here. The decemvirate had been appointed in order to oversee the establishment of the laws learned from the Greeks, following the embassy which returned at *Roman Antiquities* 10.55.5. Dionysius recalls the embassy at 11.44.6, upon the resumption after a lacuna, observing that this was the point at which the Roman laws surpassed the Greek:

> But it behoved me neither to make no mention of the Roman laws which I found written on the Twelve Tables, since they are so venerable and so far superior to the codes of the Greeks (οὕτω σεμνῶν ὄντων καὶ τοσαύτην ἐχόντων διαφορὰν παρὰ τὰς Ἑλληνικὰς νομοθεσίας), nor to go on and extend my account of them farther than was necessary. (*Ant. Rom.* 11.44.6)

It is richly ironic that Roman superiority is couched in a period which is full of Roman tyranny, power, popular revolt, madness, and the failure of the senate. Roman constitutional supremacy is a central theme of the *Roman Antiquities*, and so the fact that Rome surpasses Greece should not be unexpected; but coming after the failure of constitutional

---

[54] Baragwanath 2008, 117: 'Cambyses' behaviour cannot be predicted, or in retrospect comprehended, by the dictates of Persian custom; and moreover, his actions are not straightforwardly or inevitably – *predictably* – contrary to such *nomoi*' [original italics].

[55] Asheri et al. 2007, 436–7; Baragwanath 2008, 116.

mechanisms to control or overthrow tyranny, it heralds a two-pronged emphasis for the coming books. Firstly, the Roman supremacy over the Greeks, which had hitherto only existed in distant comparison (e.g., at *Ant. Rom.* 7.66), will occur at their point of contact in Southern Italy. Secondly, Rome is no longer facing its internal problems with the relative bloodlessness it could achieve before.

The point should not be overstated. For all that Rome seems to struggle to avoid tyranny, it does repeatedly manage to do so; the decemvirate is overthrown within two years of displaying tyrannical tendencies. The key however is that constitutional mechanisms can only go so far – the senate is most definitely not effective. This works both ways: Appius tries to exert his tyranny through constitutional means too, and he fails. We might instead see Roman character as surpassing constitutional frailty often enough for Rome to succeed. Polybius may be under fire here too: if Roman success is due to its illustrious men as much as its constitution, where does that leave Dionysius' predecessor, who put such emphasis on the Roman *politeia*, that is, its constitution, institutions, and tradition?

Conclusion

The story of the decemvirate, then, shows us that the *Roman Antiquities* are surely Greek – but they are Roman too, and not only in material and sympathy, but also in the way that Dionysius interprets the world. A stay of more than twenty years in Rome, wide exposure to Latin texts, and association with Romans of significant political status left their mark. Dionysius presents a version of Rome that is not only sprung from Greek origins, and to be interpreted within a Greek context, but is directly influenced by Roman concerns about the nature of Rome in the first century. Dionysius creates a decemviral Rome which fails in the way that first-century Rome fails: an ineffectual senate, proscriptions, dictators with a veneer of legitimacy, popular uproar in the Forum, Roman stability threatened by disharmony between the orders. Civil war is therefore prefigured. But this cannot be a simple narrative of decline; after all, Dionysius has said himself that his history explains and justifies Roman dominion over the whole world (*Ant. Rom.* 1.5.2). However, Dionysius may anticipate the decline of the Republican system of government without risking his central thesis, that Rome deserves its status at the head of the world.

At the heart of the Republican system is the senate. In the *Roman Antiquities*, Dionysius presents the senate as a body that cannot be controlled by a tyrant; but it cannot control a tyrant either. This is the central failure that makes *Roman Antiquities* a product of first-century Rome as much as it is a product of Dionysius' Greek sensibility. This is not to deny Dionysius' Greekness: Greek predecessors provide the frame for the *Antiquities*. Dionysius challenges Polybius. The importance of the decemvirate is made explicit by comparisons to Herodotus and Thucydides; Herodotus' characterisation of Cambyses' struggles with νόμοι forms a foundation for Dionysius' Appius. Tyranny is indeed an eternal question for a Greek historian, and Dionysius sees constitutional forces as so powerful that they can drive people such as Appius mad; perhaps there is a hint towards Augustus, especially in the implication of the proscriptions, and in the use of legal mechanisms to establish single rule. The failure of the senate, however, locates Dionysius even more clearly in first-century Rome. For all that there might be crass or less crass criticisms of Augustus, there is little risk in pointing out the failures of a body that Augustus spent many years trying to reform. Dionysius' Rome, after all, produces no shortage of illustrious men who draw Rome back from the brink. Perhaps Dionysius' Augustus is just one of these.[56]

---

[56] I thank the participants at the Leiden conference, as well as the editors and anonymous referees who suggested a great many improvements to the text. Especial thanks are extended to Casper de Jonge, Richard Hunter and Julietta Steinhauer for their thorough and encouraging comments.

CHAPTER 10

Dionysius and Horace: Composition in Augustan Rome

Casper C. de Jonge

Dionysius' *On Composition* between Greece and Rome

Dionysius' major treatise Περὶ συνθέσεως ὀνομάτων, *On the Arrangement of Words* or simply *On Composition*,[1] is the only extant work from antiquity that is exclusively devoted to the stylistic arrangement of words. Dionysius' systematic exposition on the four means of composition (melody, rhythm, variety, propriety), the two aims of composition (attractiveness, ἡ ἡδονή, and beauty, τὸ καλόν) and the three types of composition or 'harmonies' (ἁρμονίαι) presents itself as a technical handbook for students of rhetoric.[2] But the treatise differs from Dionysius' other rhetorical works in its wide scope. Whereas most of his criticism concentrates on Attic oratory and historiography, this work examines a wide range of passages in Greek literature, covering different genres, periods and dialects. Dionysius' preferred models of stylistic composition include not only prose authors like Demosthenes (presented as the best and most complete orator in *On the Ancient Orators*), but also Euripides, Aristophanes and lyric poets such as Simonides, the 'austere' Pindar and the 'smooth' Sappho.[3] Dionysius' incontestable champion of stylistic composition, however, is Homer: the *Iliad* and the *Odyssey* are generously cited throughout the treatise.

Traditionally, *On Composition* is understood as a characteristic product of the Greek tradition of rhetorical theory and literary criticism.[4] This Hellenocentric perspective is obviously in agreement with Dionysius'

---
[1] Grube 1965, 217: 'our critic's masterpiece'. Important studies on *Comp.* are Roberts 1910, Pohl 1968; Donadi and Marchiori 2014. Translations of Dionysius in this chapter are adapted from Usher 1974–1985. Translations of Horace are adapted from Freudenburg 1993 (*Satires*) and Russell in Russell and Winterbottom 1972 (*Ars Poetica*), with consultation of Fairclough 1926. I wish to thank Richard Hunter for his valuable suggestions on an earlier version of this chapter.
[2] *Comp.* 10–11: the two aims; *Comp.* 12–16: melody; *Comp.* 17–18: rhythm; *Comp.* 19: variety; *Comp.* 20: appropriateness; *Comp.* 21–4: the three harmonies.
[3] See the indexes in Roberts 1910, 353; Aujac and Lebel 1981, 229–30. On Demosthenes as Dionysius' preferred model of oratory, see Yunis in this volume, pp. 84–5.
[4] E.g., Aujac and Lebel 1981, 34–41; De Jonge 2008, 41–8.

presentation of his own project: he writes in Greek, he cites Greek (and no Latin) literature and he places himself in a scholarly tradition that goes back all the way to Plato's *Cratylus*.[5] In his treatise Dionysius explicitly refers to several Greek predecessors who developed theories on language, music, metre and rhetoric, including Aristotle, Theodectes, Theophrastus, Aristoxenus, Aristophanes of Byzantium and Chrysippus of Soli.[6] Hellenistic critics of poetry also influenced Dionysius' thought, although he does not mention them: *On Composition* clearly builds on the theories of the so-called *kritikoi* who are cited in Philodemus' *On Poems* (on which more below). Whereas their debates on sense, sound and composition (σύνθεσις) focused on the quality of good poetry, Dionysius' teaching aims to help students to compose effective and beautiful prose: his principal concern is the genre of πολιτικοὶ λόγοι (public eloquence: *Comp*. 1.3).[7]

While it thus remains important to study Dionysius' work in relation to the views of earlier Greek theorists, this chapter aims to cast new light on the treatise *On Composition* by adopting a synchronic, Roman perspective. Dionysius wrote a Greek treatise about word arrangement in Greek literature; but he published the work in Rome, and he addressed it to a young Roman student called Metilius Rufus.[8] Despite its focus on the literature of archaic and classical Greece, *On Composition* is thus a work with a Roman context and for a Roman audience. We should therefore feel encouraged to ask how this Greek treatise fits into the intellectual environment of Augustan Rome. What could a Roman student like Metilius Rufus learn from it?[9] And did Dionysius' teachings on stylistic writing conform – or perhaps even respond – to the theory and practice of (Greek and) Latin authors in Rome?[10] This chapter will argue that Dionysius' literary criticism can indeed be fruitfully interpreted as participating in the discourse of Roman literature under Augustus. The aim of this contribution is to identify a number of intriguing parallels between the technical language, the aesthetic assumptions and the literary theories of Dionysius and Horace, two contemporary authors in Rome, who were both deeply interested in the nature and

---

[5] *Comp*. 16.4 mentions Plato's *Cratylus* as an authoritative text on etymology.
[6] Cf. De Jonge 2008, 34–41; the index in Aujac and Lebel 1981, 225–8.
[7] On the *kritikoi* known to us from Philodemus, see Porter 1995; Janko 2000, 120–89; on Dionysius and the *kritikoi*: the introduction and Viidebaum in this volume, pp. 22–3 and 114–15.
[8] *Comp*. 1.4. On the identity of Metilius Rufus, see below, p. 247.
[9] Weaire 2012 examines the pedagogical relationship between Dionysius and Metilius Rufus, focusing on the ways in which a Greek teacher of a Roman student establishes his authority.
[10] On Dionysius' knowledge of Latin, see *Ant. Rom*. 1.7.2; cf. De Jonge 2008, 60.

the effects of good writing.[11] *On Composition* was written at the end of the first century BC, roughly in the same period as the *Ars Poetica*, which is dated around 20 or 10 BC and may have been the poet's last work.[12] We do not know which work was published first; in what follows, we will not attempt to trace direct influence from one work to the other, but rather demonstrate that both works participate in the literary discourse of Augustan Rome.

Some scholars have already recognized connections between Horace and Dionysius. Kirk Freudenburg has shown that Dionysius' composition theory casts light on the poetic theory of Horace's *Satires* (as we will see below).[13] Richard Hunter has demonstrated that there are remarkable parallels between Dionysius' literary theory and Horace's *Odes*.[14] Their views on literary imitation (μίμησις), their analogies between writing and painting and their evaluations of Pindar and Sappho all suggest, as Hunter states, that Dionysius and Horace 'are in touch with similar streams of criticism'.[15] He concludes that 'further close attention to Dionysius may reveal that we can know more about the interaction of Augustan criticism and Augustan poetry than is often believed'.[16] Following this suggestion, this chapter will explore the relationship between Horace's *Ars Poetica* and Dionysius' *On Composition*, adopting the style of a Dionysian σύγκρισις.[17] The first part of this chapter will present a general comparison of Dionysius and Horace, their place within Augustan Rome and their literary theories. The second part will concentrate on what may be called the central theme of composition theory in both Dionysius and Horace: the idea that the best and most beautiful style is achieved by a skillful arrangement of common words.

Dionysius and Horace

We should of course not ignore the differences between our two authors and their works. *De compositione verborum* is a technical rhetorical treatise

---

[11] Fuhrer 2003 shows that Horace's poetry can be regarded as a product of the lively debate (in poetry, philosophy and literary criticism) on 'good poetry' in the first century BC; she briefly mentions Dionysius and his views on composition (Fuhrer 2003, 355–6), but concentrates on the (complex) connections between Horace and Philodemus' *On Poems*.

[12] *Comp.* belongs to the middle period of Dionysius' works: see Bonner 1939, 25–38; De Jonge 2008, 20 n. 100; the absolute date is unknown. On the date of *Ars P.*, see Rudd 1989, 19–21; Frischer 1991, 17–49; Reinhardt 2013, 500.

[13] Freudenburg 1993, 109–84. Cf. Fuhrer 2003, 355–6.

[14] Hunter 2009, 124–7 on *Carm.* 4.1–2 and *Comp.* 22–3.   [15] Hunter 2009, 115.

[16] Hunter 2009, 124.   [17] Cf. Dionysius' comparison of Herodotus and Thucydides in *Pomp.* 3.

with a systematic structure, which focuses on one specific aspect of style (composition, not diction or figures). Horace's letter to the Pisones, on the other hand, is a poem with a loose, associative structure, which deals with a great variety of topics related to the composition of poetry, including content, style and the figure of the poet. The genre of *Ars Poetica* remains a matter of dispute: epistle, didactic poem or something else; perhaps even a parody of a Peripatetic treatise.[18]

In his monumental commentary on the *Ars Poetica*, Brink emphasizes the differences between rhetoric and poetics.[19] It has become almost a commonplace to state that the *Ars Poetica*, despite the title used by Quintilian (*Inst.* 8.3.60), is *not* a handbook of literary theory.[20] No reader will deny that Horace's poem is much more than a treatise versified.[21] However, while completely accepting the formal differences between a complex, subtle and ironical Latin poem and a Greek handbook on rhetorical composition, we should not close our eyes to the remarkable correspondences between the *Ars Poetica* and treatises of Greek rhetorical and poetical theory. Various scholars have indeed pointed out parallels between the *Ars Poetica* and contemporary Greek literary theory in Rome. Many readers are now happy to understand the *Ars Poetica* as responding – in a variety of ways – to the teachings of Philodemus' *On Poems*.[22] Doreen Innes has identified structural parallels between the *Ars Poetica* and Longinus' *On the Sublime*.[23] And last but not least, Niall Rudd has noted a close resemblance between one specific section of Horace's poem (119–52) and Dionysius' discussion of the tasks of the historian in the *Letter to Pompeius*.[24]

A comparison between Dionysius and Horace is in fact not so far-fetched as the scarce references to Dionysius in Brink's commentary might suggest. It is true that Dionysius primarily writes for 'all those who aim to become good orators' (*Comp.* 1.3–4), but his examples of pleasant and beautiful composition, as we have seen, are drawn from

---

[18] On the elusive genre of *Ars P.*, see Frischer 1991, 87–100 (and 61 for the 'parody' theory); Hardie 2014, 43.
[19] Brink 1971, 139 on *Ars P.* 47–8.
[20] Rudd 1989, 34; Armstrong 1993, 189. Laird 2007, 135 'resists' referring to the *Ars Poetica* as a 'treatise', but accepts the parallels between Horace and Longinus suggested by Innes 1995, 11–12 (see below).
[21] Cf. Russell 1973, 114.
[22] See, e.g., Armstrong 1993; Fuhrer 2003. Janko 2000, 10 boldly states that 'there should be no doubt that Horace had read and absorbed the *On Poems*'.
[23] Innes 1995, 111–12 compares the structure of Horace's *Ars P.* and Longinus' *Subl.*: both authors 'subvert' a formal superstructure.
[24] Rudd 1989, 22 n. 25 notes that *Pomp.* is 'a work close in time' to the *Ars P.*

poetry as well as prose. Dionysius repeatedly claims that his teachings are valuable for 'prose writers *and* poets', Homer is presented as the champion of word arrangement, and the final chapters of his treatise (*Comp.* 25–6) in particular explore the resemblances between good prose and poetry.[25]

Both Horace and Dionysius were influenced by Aristotelian as well as Hellenistic ideas on poetry. Dionysius builds on the stylistic theories of Aristotle's *Rhetoric* and Theophrastus' *On Style*; the *Ars Poetica* draws on material familiar to us from Aristotle's *Poetics*, even if Horace was probably not familiar with the latter text (nor was Dionysius).[26] The Hellenistic influence on both texts is substantial, though more difficult to assess. In the scholarship on both Horace and Dionysius, one learned Greek man plays a crucial role (although neither of our authors ever mentions him): the Epicurean philosopher, poet, rhetorician and literary critic Philodemus of Gadara (110–35 BC), who studied in Athens and worked in Italy from ca. 55 BC. The fragments of his rich oeuvre have survived in the damaged papyrus scrolls of the Villa dei Papiri at Herculaneum. Philodemus' work *On Poems*, with its critical discussion of the Hellenistic *kritikoi*, will be especially relevant to our comparison of Dionysius and Horace.[27]

The commentator Porphyrio, as is well known, informs us that Horace incorporated 'the most conspicuous precepts' of Neoptolemus of Parium (third century BC).[28] Neoptolemus is one of the critics who are cited in Philodemus' *On Poems*, the fragments of which show significant points of contact with both the *Ars Poetica* and Dionysius' *On Composition*.[29] A direct link between Philodemus and Horace seems to be secured by the fact that Horace addresses his poem to the family of the Pisones: two *iuvenes* and their father, who may be identified either as Lucius Calpurnius Piso Caesoninus, consul in 58 BC, the father-in-law of Julius Caesar, and, more importantly for our purposes, the patron of Philodemus, or as his son, Lucius Calpurnius Piso Pontifex, who was consul in 15 BC, and the

---

[25] For 'poets and prose writers', see, e.g., *Comp.* 3.1. On the relation between prose and poetry in *Comp.* 25–6, see De Jonge 2008, 329–66.
[26] For Peripatetic influence on Dionysius, see Bonner 1938; De Jonge 2008, 34–5; cf. Yunis in this volume, pp. 96–8, and Fox in this volume, pp. 191–3, on Aristotelian recognition in *Ant. Rom.* For Peripatetic influence on Horace, see Brink 1963, 79–134; Reinhardt 2013, 505–8. Both Dionysius and Horace may have been familiar with Aristotle's *On Poets* (now lost).
[27] On Philodemus and Dionysius, see the introduction to this volume, pp. 25–6.
[28] Porphyrio, *Comm. in Hor.* ad *Ars P.* 1, p. 162, 6–7 Holder: *in quem librum congessit praecepta Neoptolemi* τοῦ Παριανοῦ *de arte poetica, non quidem omnia sed eminentissima*. On this much debated testimony, see Brink 1963, 43–78; Russell 1973, 114; Rudd 1989, 23–5; Reinhardt 2013, 504–5.
[29] Neoptolemus is discussed in Phld. *On Poems* 5.

patron of Antipater of Thessalonica.³⁰ A clear connection between Philodemus and Dionysius is less easy to establish; Dionysius dislikes 'the chorus of Epicureans' – which might be one reason for him to be silent about his well-known Greek colleague, who was slightly older and well respected among the Roman elite;³¹ but it is beyond doubt that his theory of σύνθεσις builds on the work of the critics who are discussed in Philodemus' *On Poems*.³²

Just like Horace, Dionysius writes for an influential Roman family: he presents *On Composition* as a birthday present for his student Metilius Rufus, who (as we know) was to become proconsul of Achaea under emperor Augustus.³³ The father of Metilius Rufus, whom Dionysius praises as the 'most esteemed' of his friends, may have acted as his patron (*Comp.* 1.4). In short, both Horace's poem and Dionysius' treatise are firmly embedded in the social, cultural and political context of Augustan Rome. If these two works can be shown to stand partly in the same tradition, Philodemus' *On Poems* might well be regarded as one of their common ancestors.

De Compositione Verborum and *Ars Poetica*

Let us consider a number of common themes that we find in Dionysius' *On Composition* and Horace's *Ars Poetica*. Some of these themes are traditional topics or even commonplaces in Greek and Roman rhetoric and criticism; other parallels reflect special interests of the first century BC, perhaps even the literary tastes of the Augustan Age. We do not need to assume that Horace and Dionysius borrow such themes from specific sources, nor do we have to believe that there was direct influence between the Greek critic and the Roman poet, even if some of the correspondences are indeed suggestive. It is enough for present purposes that Dionysius and Horace participate in the same discourse of poetics and literary criticism in Augustan Rome. Ideas, theories and literary values were exchanged in a great variety of ways, involving many Greek and Roman individuals: on the one hand, there were various contexts that provided opportunities for

---

³⁰ Lucius Calpurnius Piso Caesoninus: Frischer 1991, 52–9; Lucius Calpurnius Piso Pontifex: Rudd 1989, 19; Armstrong 1993, 199–200. On Philodemus and Horace, see Frischer 1991, 64–6; Armstrong 1993, 190–9; Armstrong and Oberhelman 1995, 235–6; Janko 2000, 10 (cited above, n. 22); Fuhrer 2003, 350–64; Armstrong 2004; Laird 2007, 134–5.
³¹ See *Comp.* 24.8. Cf. De Jonge 2008, 37.
³² Dionysius and the *kritikoi* in Philodemus' *On Poems*: Aujac and Lebel 1989, 39–41; Janko 2000, 178; Fuhrer 2003, 256; De Jonge 2008, 44–6, 193–6, 362–5.
³³ On the identity of Metilius Rufus, see Bowersock 1965, 132. Cf. Wiater in this volume, p. 74.

oral exchange, for instance the professional teaching of rhetoricians (e.g., Dionysius himself, or someone like Apollodorus of Pergamon, Augustus' instructor) and literary circles like the groups around Maecenas and Messalla or the network in which Dionysius and his Greek and Roman friends participated – I will return to Dionysius' addressees and colleagues at the end of this chapter.[34] On the other hand, the exchange will also have taken place via written texts of different kinds – private letters, poems, treatises.[35] The *Ars Poetica* and *On Composition* were both stimulants to and products of this literary discourse in Rome: we will see that the two works adopt similar motives, while playing with them in different ways.

The first category of parallels consists of ideas that Horace and Dionysius share with several earlier (and later) writers on rhetoric and poetry; in many cases these parallels can be traced back to Aristotle or the Peripatetic tradition. Such themes include the well-known question about the roles of 'art' and 'nature' (*ars* and *natura* or *ingenium* / φύσις and τέχνη) in the process of composition. Aristotle had already raised this question in connection with Homer.[36] Horace and Dionysius, like most critics, believe that there should be a balance and a fruitful cooperation between art and nature.[37] Another central idea in both writers that is linked with the Peripatetic tradition is the important concept of appropriateness (*aptum, decor* / τὸ πρέπον). Dionysius presents appropriateness as one of the four means of composition, next to melody, rhythm and variation (*Comp.* 20). He focuses on the ways in which stylistic composition (vocal and rhythmical patterns in particular) can properly (i.e., mimetically) express subject matter, as when Homer represents Sisyphus' labors in spondaic rhythms and rough sounds.[38] Dionysius acknowledges that other aspects of τὸ πρέπον are also important: 'appropriateness is that treatment which is fitting for the underlying characters and actions' (τοῖς ὑποκειμένοις προσώποις τε καὶ πράγμασιν); thus different emotions (anger, cheerfulness, lamentation, fear) require different types of word arrangement.[39] In the *Ars Poetica* appropriateness is at least as important a concept. Like Dionysius, Horace states that metrical form should correspond to subject

---

[34] On Dionysius' network, see Hidber 1996, 1–8; De Jonge 2008, 25–34.
[35] Fuhrer 2003, 352 adopts a similar concept of 'poetological discourse' in Rome.
[36] Arist. *Poet.* 8.1451a24.
[37] *Ars P.* 408–11; Dion. Hal. *Dem.* 47.2; cf. *Imit.* fr. 1 (φύσις, μάθησις, ἄσκησις). Longinus, *Subl.* 36.4 favours a 'holding together' (ἀλληλουχία) of art and nature (cf. *Subl.* 2). Cf. Ov. *Tr.* 2.424; for further parallels, see Rudd 1989, 217. On nature and art in Dionysius, see also Yunis and Wiater in this volume, pp. 66, 90.
[38] *Comp.* 20.8–22 on *Od.* 11.593–7.
[39] *Comp.* 20.3–4: ὀργιζόμενοι, χαίροντες, ὀλοφυρόμενοι, φοβούμενοι.

matter (*Ars P.* 73–86, note *aptum* in 81). Elsewhere, he points out that speech should be appropriate to the age of different characters (153–78, note *decor* in 157, *aptis* in 178); and, like Dionysius, Horace thinks that style must properly express emotion: 'sad words suit (*decent*) a mournful countenance, threatening words an angry one; sportive words are for the playful, serious for the grave' (105–7). Solemnity here replaces fear, but the other three emotions (sadness, anger, cheerfulness) are identical to the ones mentioned by Dionysius. The concept of proportion also underlies Horace's views on poetic unity, formulated in the opening passage on the grotesque painting of a creature whose parts do not properly fit together (1–5).

To the same category of 'Peripatetic' correspondences between Horace and Dionysius belong two basic distinctions that are traditional in postclassical rhetoric and poetics. First, there is the division between subject matter and style, which goes back to Aristotle.[40] The distinction is essential to the stylistic treatises of Dionysius, who separates thoughts (νοήματα, ὁ πραγματικὸς τόπος) from words (ὀνόματα, ὁ λεκτικὸς τόπος).[41] This roughly corresponds to Neoptolemus' division between ποίησις (content, plot) and ποίημα (diction, style), which has been thought to underlie the structure of the *Ars Poetica* (with 45–118 treating style, 119–294 content).[42] More important for our purposes are Horace's explicit references to the distinction between *res / materia* and *uerba* (esp. 38–41). Secondly, there is the division between selection of words (or diction) and the arrangement of words (or composition), a distinction that is implicit in Aristotle's *Rhetoric* and was presumably made explicit in Theophrastus' *On Style*.[43] Dionysius' treatise deals with composition (σύνθεσις) alone; we do not know if he ever fulfilled his promise to write the corresponding treatise on the selection of words (ἐκλογὴ ὀνομάτων), which he hoped to present to Metilius Rufus for his next birthday.[44] Horace naturally deals with both diction and composition (see esp. *Ars P.* 45–7, cited below).

When we look at the specific instructions offered on diction and composition, more parallels between Horace and Dionysius can be

---

[40] Arist. *Rh.* 3.1.1403b14-18: see Russell 1973, 114; Yunis in this volume, pp. 88–9.
[41] *Comp.* 1.5. Cf. Yunis in this volume, pp. 88–9.
[42] Russell 1973, 114–15 and Laird 2007, 135–6 are rightly cautious.
[43] Cf. Theophr. fr. 691 Fortenbaugh (= Dion. Hal. *Isoc.* 3). The theory is implicit in Arist. *Rh.* 3.2–6 (diction) and 3.8–9 (composition): see Fortenbaugh 2005, 293. See also *Rh.* 3.2.1404b24-5 (ἐκλέγων συντιθῇ).
[44] See *Comp.* 1.8–10. On diction and composition, see De Jonge 2008, 53–4; Yunis in this volume p. 92.

detected. For instance, both authors pay attention to the formation of new or innovative words, and in that context both authors immediately add that borrowing unusual words from earlier (Greek) writers can be more effective. Horace grants poetic license (*licentia*) to 'the fashioning of words never heard by the kilted Cethegi' (*fingere cinctutis non exaudita Cethegis*), immediately adding that words will win easier acceptance if 'they spring from a Greek fount' (*Ars P.* 50–3). Dionysius states that poets and prose authors look at the subject matter and 'fashion words that suit it and illustrate it' (κατασκευάζουσιν ... οἰκεῖα καὶ δηλωτικὰ τῶν ὑποκειμένων τὰ ὀνόματα); and then adds that 'they also borrow many (such) words from earlier writers' (πολλὰ δὲ καὶ παρὰ τῶν ἔμπροσθεν λαμβάνουσιν, *Comp.* 16.1). The focus is slightly different: Dionysius concentrates on mimetic language, Horace on neologisms; but they both argue that the Greek tradition lends authority to the introduction of unusual expressions.

A second category of parallels between *Ars Poetica* and *On Composition* may be related not so much to a common source or tradition, but rather to the cultural world of the authors and their audiences. Both Dionysius and Horace are ready to draw analogies between writing and the fine arts.[45] They are particularly fond of comparisons with painting, music and metalworking, to the extent that they expect their audience to be familiar with the technicalities of these arts. Even in the details these analogies are remarkably similar. Horace compares the poet who makes mistakes with a harper (*citharoedus*) who is laughed at when 'he always blunders on the same string' (*ridetur chorda qui semper oberrat eadem*, 356). Dionysius reports a similar story: 'I have seen an able and very renowned harpist booed (κιθαριστὴν θορυβηθέντα) by the public because he struck a single false note (χορδὴν ἀσύμφωνον)' (*Comp.* 11.8). If Dionysius really 'saw' this disappointing concert (he uses the word ἰδών), it may well have been somewhere in Rome, where there was indeed a large crowd for musical events; Cicero's *De Oratore* describes a similar scene.[46] Because of their immense popularity, musical performances could helpfully serve as accessible illustrations of the workings of aesthetic experience. Again, there are differences in the details. Horace believes that some faults are forgiven: 'the string (*chorda*) does not always yield the sound (*sonum*) that hand and mind intended' (*Ars P.* 348); Dionysius' harpist, on the other hand, was booed because a single false note spoiled the entire melody.

---

[45] For Dionysius' comparisons of texts with statues and paintings, see Viidebaum in this volume, pp. 112–14.
[46] *De or.* 3.196; see also *Orat.* 173.

Another artistic analogy that connects *Ars Poetica* and *On Composition* is that of metalworking. Both Horace and Dionysius believe that writers should pay attention to the smallest details, and in order to prove their point both critics draw comparisons between writers and engravers, who imitate in bronze human nails and locks of hair:

> The poorest (*imus*) craftsman from the School of Aemilius will reproduce nails and mimic soft hair (*capillos*) in bronze, though he has no luck with the overall effect of his work, because he will not know how to organize the whole. (*Ars P*. 32–5)

Did Dionysius think of the same workshops in Rome when he compared Demosthenes' detailed attention to euphony to the subtle handwork of craftsmen?

> For it appears to me far more appropriate in a man who is composing political speeches, which are to be permanent memorials to his own powers, that he should not ignore even the smallest details, than it is for painters and engravers (ζωγράφων καὶ τορευτῶν παισίν), who display their manual skills and industry upon perishable materials, to exhaust the refinements of their artistry on fine veins, young plumage, the first beard's down (τὰ φλέβια καὶ τὰ πτίλα καὶ τὸν χνοῦν) and minute details of a similar character. (*Comp*. 25.35)[47]

The analogies serve opposite purposes: Horace underlines that for the composition of the whole one needs more than just skill in representing the details; Dionysius, on the other hand, argues that even the greatest artists pay due attention to the smallest details. But the examples (including the representation of human hair) are drawn from the same domain, and both Dionysius and Horace suggest a hierarchical contrast between the 'poor' craftsmen (note *imus*, 'poorest', 'lowest in esteem') and the more honorable class of writers: the Pisones and Metilius Rufus should identify, of course, with the latter group.[48]

This brings us to the third group of parallels between Horace and Dionysius, which can be primarily explained from the didactic character of their works: both authors present themselves as patient but stern professors, who repeatedly stimulate and encourage their students.[49] Dionysius refers to the daily exercises of young Metilius Rufus (*Comp*. 20.23, 26.17); Horace adopts the persona of an instructor – or perhaps, as

---

[47] For similar passages, see *Dem*. 50.4, 51.7.
[48] I follow Rudd 1989, 115 in my interpretation of *imus* (32). For different options, see Brink 1971, 117–18; Bentley reads *unus*.
[49] On the didactic aspects of *Ars P*., see Hardie 2014; for those of *Comp*., Weaire 2012.

Frischer has argued, of a pedantic Peripatetic scholar – who regularly addresses the two younger Pisones.[50] Every teacher wants his students to work. It should therefore be no surprise that Horace's famous *limae labor et mora* ('the toil and tedium of the file', *Ars P.* 291) finds parallels in Dionysius' persistent emphasis on labor: he reminds his student(s) that Isocrates spent ten years on the composition of his *Panegyric*, and that Plato many times rewrote the first sentence of his *Republic*, until he had reached the best result (*Comp.* 25.32–3).

Our final category consists of some remarkable correspondences in the details of Horatian and Dionysian composition theory that cannot easily be paralleled from other extant sources. Hellenistic theories like those of the *kritikoi* may play a role here, and we should always allow for the possibility that such ideas were circulating more widely in Rome. I will mention two of these parallels; the second one will then be further examined in the remaining part of this chapter.

One striking agreement between Horace and Dionysius is their distinction between the aesthetic categories of beauty and attractiveness. Dionysius thinks that composition has two aims, namely τὸ καλόν and ἡ ἡδονή (*Comp.* 10; cf. *Dem.* 47). Horace claims that poems should not just be beautiful but also pleasing:

> non satis est pulchra esse poemata: dulcia sunto
> et quocumque uolent animum auditoris agunto.
>
> It is not enough for poetry to be beautiful; it must also be pleasing and lead the hearer's mind wherever it will. (*Ars P.* 99–100)

Horace is obviously alluding to Greek theory: *animum auditoris agunto*, as many scholars have noted, translates ψυχαγωγεῖν ('to lead the soul'). Commentators have also identified the agreement between Horace and Dionysius concerning the aesthetic aims of beauty and attractiveness. As often, Brink emphasizes the difference between Dionysius' 'technical' discussion and Horace's focus on emotions.[51] But on closer inspection, Dionysius' theory appears to be quite similar to that of Horace. Under beauty (τὸ καλόν) Dionysius lists impressiveness, dignity, solemnity, seriousness, dignity, mellowness and similar qualities; attractiveness (ἡ ἡδονή), on the other hand, appears through freshness, charm, euphony, sweetness and persuasiveness (*Comp.* 11.2). In other words, it is the

---

[50] Frischer 1991, 99. On Horace's didactic persona, see Hardie 2014, 46.
[51] Brink 1971, 183. Immisch 1932, 62–75 is more inclined to accept the similarities between the two passages. Greek ἡδύς and Latin *dulcis* have of course the same connotation of sweetness.

attractiveness (ἡδονή) of a text that affects or carries away the reader, just as Horace's *dulcia* refers to the effect on the reader's soul. The term *pulchra* ('well made', Brink; 'formally correct', Rudd), on the other hand, denotes the intrinsic, formal quality of a poem. Rudd notes that 'a work with this quality alone would be impressive in a rather cold and austere way':[52] this formulation almost sums up Dionysius' description of a work that has beauty, but no attractiveness; the Greek critic specifically mentions the examples of Thucydides and Antiphon, who lack charm; Herodotus, on the other hand, has both beauty and attractiveness.

Finally, there is the idealization of skillful word arrangement, which establishes a close connection between our two authors.[53] Both Dionysius and Horace draw a contrast between ordinary, common words, on the one hand, and artful, 'clever' word arrangement, on the other.[54] In the remaining part of this chapter, I will argue that their emphasis on composition (*iunctura*, σύνθεσις) is indeed, as Donald Russell has observed, 'characteristically Augustan'.[55]

The preceding list of correspondences between Dionysius and Horace is not exhaustive. If we extend our view outside *On Composition* and *Ars Poetica*, parallels can also be found between Horace's *Odes* and *Satires* and Dionysius' other critical essays: these correspondences include traditional topics, such as the virtue of lucidity and the theme of organic unity, views on particular authors to be imitated (including Sappho and Pindar, the poetic models of smooth and austere composition) and more specifically the discourse of the sublime. The list of parallels shows that Dionysius and Horace are indeed, as Hunter has suggested, 'in touch with similar streams of criticism'.[56]

The Artful Arrangement of Common Words: Dionysius

The central message of *On Composition* is that skillful word arrangement (σύνθεσις or ἁρμονία) has more impact than the careful selection (ἐκλογή) of words:[57]

> Many poets and prose-writers, both philosophers and orators, have carefully chosen words (λέξεις) which are very beautiful and suited to their subject-

---

[52] Rudd 1989, 167.   [53] See esp. *Ars P.* 47–8; *Comp.* 4.13 (cited below).
[54] Immisch 1932, 61–2 already noted that this theme is found in various ancient writers, including Horace and Dionysius, but also Philodemus and Longinus. Brink 1971, 139 on the other hand, emphasizes the differences: Horace does not discuss euphony, hiatus and rhythm.
[55] Russell 1973, 117.   [56] Hunter 2009, 115.
[57] This section repeats and reworks some of the ideas that I present in De Jonge 2018.

matter, but have reaped no benefit from their efforts because they have given them a haphazard and unmusical arrangement (ἁρμονίαν); whereas others have taken humble words which might easily be despised (εὐκαταφρόνητα καὶ ταπεινὰ ὀνόματα), and by arranging them in a pleasing and striking manner (συνθέντες δ' αὐτὰ ἡδέως καὶ περιττῶς), have succeeded in investing their discourse with great beauty (πολλὴν τὴν ἀφροδίτην). (*Comp.* 3.2)

Dionysius illustrates his point by citing two beautiful compositions that are (in his view) put together from relatively simple words: the opening lines of *Odyssey* 16 (*Comp.* 3.8) and the well-known story of Gyges and Candaules from Herodotus 1.8–10 (*Comp.* 3.15). In the first passage, Odysseus, disguised as beggar, and Eumaeus are preparing their breakfast in the swineherd's hut, when suddenly Telemachus appears. According to Dionysius, these lines have an enchanting effect on the audience, despite their ordinary vocabulary: more attractive poetry does not exist. In his typical didactic, interactive manner, Dionysius asks his reader to identify the factor that makes the Homeric passage so enchantingly beautiful:[58]

> Wherein lies the persuasiveness (πειθώ) of these lines, and what causes them to be what they are? Is it the selection of words (ἐκλογὴν τῶν ὀνομάτων) or the composition (σύνθεσιν)? No one will say, 'selection', I am sure. For the whole passage is woven together from the most commonplace, humble words (τῶν εὐτελεστάτων καὶ ταπεινοτάτων ὀνομάτων), such as might have come readily to the tongue of a farmer, seaman or artisan, or anyone else who takes no trouble to speak well. If the metre is broken up (λυθέντος τοῦ μέτρου), these same lines will appear banal and without quality. They contain no excellent metaphors or examples of *hypallage* or *catachresis* or any other type of figurative language, nor are there many glosses (γλῶτται) or exotic (ξένα) or newly coined words (πεποιημένα ὀνόματα).[59] What alternative, therefore, is there left but to attribute the beauty of the style (τοῦ κάλλους τῆς ἑρμηνείας) to the composition (σύνθεσιν)? (*Comp.* 3.9–12)

Dionysius here suggests that his favorite tool of *metathesis* (the rearrangement of words) would prove that composition – and not vocabulary – is responsible for the charming quality of the Homeric passage: if one broke up the metre (and thereby destroyed the σύνθεσις), the remaining words would be banal (φαῦλα) and unworthy

---

[58] On the interactive style in Dionysius, see Wiater 2011a, 279–97.
[59] *Hypallage* is metonymy (substitution of one name for another): see Quint. *Inst.* 8.6.23; on the related figure of *catachresis*, see *Inst.* 8.6.35–6.

of admiration (ἄζηλα).⁶⁰ The ordinary vocabulary in the Homeric passage corresponds to the down-to-earth, everyday-like character of the scene: the words used in this passage are those words that the swineherd Eumaeus would perhaps use himself, just like any 'farmer, seaman or artisan'. As Hunter has argued, the critical terminology of social class distinctions in this passage could be traced back to the characterization of Euripides (and his preference for 'everyday things') in Aristophanes' *Frogs*.⁶¹ In *On Demosthenes* Dionysius presents a similar distinction between the language of the elite and that of 'men who work on the land and the sea, and common tradesmen': there, Dionysius recommends the use of a middle style, a mixture of grandeur and simplicity, by which the orator could convince both upper and lower classes in his audience.⁶² In the Eumaeus passage, 'humble words' seem to be words that denote humble things: the passage contains words like 'hut' (κλισίη), 'breakfast' (ἄριστον) and 'vessels' (ἄγγεα).

Dionysius is remarkably fond of Homer's *Odyssey* in *On Composition*: there is no other text from which he cites more passages in this treatise. The final chapter of *On Composition*, for example, cites the opening passage of *Odyssey* 14, in which Odysseus, disguised as a beggar by Athena after his arrival at Ithaca, finds Eumaeus sitting in front of his humble house.⁶³ Dionysius' interest in Homeric passages on swineherds and beggars must be explained precisely by the contrast that he observes between the lowliness of theme and the ordinary words, on the one hand, and the beauty of composition, on the other.⁶⁴ The following table shows some of the passages from the *Odyssey* that Dionysius cites in which beggars and swineherds play a significant role:

---

⁶⁰ On *metathesis*, see Greenberg 1958; De Jonge 2005; 2008, 367–90. Fuhrer 2003, 353–60 compares the method of *metathesis* in Philodemus and Horace. For a different dimension of *metathesis*, see Wiater in this volume, pp. 76–82.
⁶¹ Hunter 2009, 19.   ⁶² *Dem.* 15.2. See Yunis in this volume p. 91 n.19.
⁶³ It is significant that this passage is cited in a discussion of how poetry can be made to resemble prose: this is an example of beautiful poetry that borders on the style of prose, not only because of the variation that the poet adopts in the length and form of the clauses, as Dionysius emphasizes in his discussion, but also (we may add) because of the low character of the theme and the simple language. On Eumaeus in *Comp.*, see De Jonge 2018.
⁶⁴ The remarkable prominence of Eumaeus in Dionysius' treatise might be related to Phld. *On Poems* 1 fr. 159 Janko where Janko 2000, 366–7 has reconstructed the word συφορβός (swineherd), 'an unexpectedly low character for the high genre of epic'. Like Dionysius, some of the Hellenistic critics of poetry seem to have been interested in the beauty of Homeric poetry that deals with low subject matter in simple diction.

Comp. 3.8	*Od.* 16.1–16	Odysseus and Eumaeus in the swineherd's hut
Comp. 4.12	*Od.* 16.273	Eumaeus leads Odysseus as beggar
Comp. 5.8	*Od.* 14.425	Eumaeus kills a boar
Comp. 16.9	*Od.* 6.137	Odysseus looks ugly, 'befouled with brine'
Comp. 26.11	*Od.* 14.1–7	Odysseus approaches the hut of Eumaeus

The disguised Odysseus, whose visit to Eumaeus provides Dionysius with several examples of excellent composition, has in fact a programmatic function in Dionysius' composition theory: Dionysius points out that the technique of σύνθεσις could be compared to the Homeric goddess Athena, who is capable of completely changing the appearance of Odysseus:

> For she (Athena) used to make the same Odysseus appear in different forms at different times, – at one time small, wrinkled and ugly, 'resembling a pitiful aged beggar' (*Od.* 16.273; 17.202, 337), and at another time, by another touch of the same wand, 'she rendered him taller to see, and broader; and she made his wavy hair to fall over his shoulders like the hyacinth flower' (*Od.* 6.230–1; 23.157–8). So also compositions take the same words (ὀνόματα), and make the ideas (νοήματα) that they convey appear misshapen, beggarly and mean, and at another time sublime, rich and beautiful. And this is after all what makes the difference between one poet and another poet, between one orator and another orator: the dexterity with which they arranged their words (τὸ συντιθέναι δεξιῶς τὰ ὀνόματα). (*Comp.* 4.12–13)

A crucial word in the final sentence is δεξιῶς: good poets and orators are recognized by the fact that they combine their words 'skillfully', 'dexterously'. The word δεξιός had been established as a critical term at least since Aristophanes' *Frogs* (1009), where Euripides states that skill (δεξιότης) is one of the two qualities for which a poet should be admired. Dionysius uses the word more than once to characterize skillful composition. Commenting on Herodotus' story of Gyges and Candaules (1.8–10), his second main example of enchanting composition, Dionysius remarks that its charming quality, like that of the passage cited from *Odyssey* 16, is due to skillful word arrangement: the scene itself is 'lowly' (ταπεινόν), 'dangerous' (ἐπικίνδυνον) and 'closer to ugliness than to beauty' (τοῦ αἰσχροῦ μᾶλλον ἢ τοῦ καλοῦ).[65] The words are as lowly as the contents to which they refer: they are 'artless' (ἀνεπιτήδευτα) and 'not carefully

---

[65] On Gyges and Candaules (Hdt. 1.9–13) as an intertextual model in Dionysius' *Roman Antiquities*, see Schultze in this volume pp. 169–70.

chosen' (ἀνέκλεκτα). The story, however, 'has been told with great dexterity' (εἴρηται σφόδρα δεξιῶς, *Comp.* 3.14–16), i.e., the words have been skillfully arranged.

The Artful Arrangement of Common Words: Horace

Let us now turn to Horace, whose fascination with artful composition is already clear from his *Satires*. *Satire* 1.4 is a complex poem, which is full of irony and ambiguous statements. My discussion must be brief and will focus on a passage that resonates with some of the ideas of Dionysius that we have just encountered.[66] Horace draws a contrast between the satiric verses that he and Lucilius write, on the one hand, and the epic poetry of Ennius, on the other: unlike Ennius, whose lines consist of elevated, bombastic language and epic, military themes, the satirist composes verses in simple words (*puris . . . verbis*). The difference between the genres will be seen, Horace says, if you 'break up' (i.e., rearrange) the lines (*si dissoluas*, 55; *si soluas*, 60) and take away the rhythms and metres of these poems. In the case of the satirist, no poetry will remain, whereas in the case of Ennius, the rearranged passage will still contain elevated words and heroic subject matter: here one would still find 'the limbs of a dismembered poet':

> Therefore, it is not enough to write out verse in simple words (*puris . . . uerbis*) that, if you rearrange them (*si dissoluas*), any real-life father could use in raging at his son, just as the father in the play. Now concerning the verses I now write, which Lucilius wrote at one time, if you should take away their fixed rhythms and metres (*eripias si / tempora certa modosque*), making the word earlier in line later and putting last things before first, you would not discover the limbs even of a dismembered poet (*disiecti membra poetae*) as (you would) if you broke down (*si soluas*) 'Once foul Discord had broken back the brazen posts and gates of war' (*postquam Discordia taetra / Belli ferratos postis portasque refregit*, Enn. *Ann.* 225–6 Sk.) (*Sat.* 1.4.53–62)[67]

As Freudenburg has observed, this passage is closely related to the argument of *On Composition* and the method of metathesis that Dionysius frequently applies.[68] In his discussion of the opening of *Odyssey* 16, as we

---

[66] The following interpretation owes much to Freudenburg 1993, 145–50; Armstrong and Oberhelman 1995; Gowers 2012, 166–9.
[67] Translation adapted from Freudenburg 1993, 146.
[68] Freudenburg 1993, 131–2. Fuhrer 2003, 362 n. 15 argues that the position of Horace is different from that of Dionysius: in her interpretation, the Latin poet does not diminish the role of ἐκλογή (diction), but admires Ennius' poetry with its elevated words. But this interpretation seems to miss the irony of the passage: the point is exactly that Horace '*disingenuously* alleges that there is more poetry in an epic line of Ennius than in his or Lucilius' satires' (Gowers 2012, 167; my italics).

have seen, Dionysius points out that 'if the metre is broken up' (λυθέντος τοῦ μέτρου) the Homeric lines will appear banal (φαῦλα) and without quality. Whether the persona of the satirist in *Satire* 1.4 is to be identified with Horace himself or with one of his critics (as Freudenburg suggests), it is clear that he applies the same method of rearrangement: in both passages, low subject matter and simple diction are contrasted with artful composition, including metre and word order, and both critics refer to the procedure of metathesis to prove their point that composition means everything. The complex syntax and word order of lines 53–62 themselves underline the pervasive importance of composition, even if Horace's ironical words might be interpreted as suggesting the opposite (i.e., that Ennius does not need word order to be good poetry). The main difference between the line cited from Ennius and Horace's own lines is that the former has an almost prosaic, straightforward word order, whereas Horace's poetry with its convoluted word order appears to be itself the result of a metathesis, i.e., a highly complex rearrangement of a simple prose text. If one would break up (*si dissoluas*) Horace's lines again, no poetry would remain, as the artful word order has become its main quality and the characteristic of good poetry.[69]

Horace returns to the topic of word arrangement in the *Ars Poetica*. Here is the well-known passage on *callida iunctura* (skillful arrangement):[70]

> in uerbis etiam tenuis cautusque serendis
> dixeris egregie notum si callida uerbum
> reddiderit iunctura nouum.

As to words: if you are delicate and cautious in arranging them, you will give distinction to your style if an ingenious combination makes a familiar word new. (*Ars P.* 46–8)

The crucial words *serendis* and *iunctura* are echoed in a later passage of the *Ars Poetica*, which is part of the discussion of satyr-play and its style:[71]

> ex noto fictum carmen sequar, ut sibi quiuis
> speret idem, sudet multum frustraque laboret
> ausus idem; tantum series iuncturaque pollet,
> tantum de medio sumptis accedit honoris.

---

[69] This line of interpretation follows Armstrong and Oberhelman 1995, 243–4.
[70] Following Rudd 1989, 156, I retain the order of the lines in the manuscripts, because I take *serendis* (46), which anticipates *series* (242), as referring to the arrangement of words. Brink 1971, 134–5 defends Bentley's transposition 46–45.
[71] Cf. Rudd 1989 ad 240: 'By "poetry newly fashioned from familiar elements" H. means style, not content, as is clear from *series iuncturaque*'.

I shall make up my poem of known elements, so that anyone may hope to do the same, but he will sweat and labour to no purpose when he ventures; such is the force of arrangement and combination, such the splendour that commonplace words acquire. (*Ars P.* 240–3)

There has been some debate concerning the relationship between the notions of *iunctura* and σύνθεσις. For Immisch they are the same; Russell suggests a strong connection between the two; Brink, on the other hand, points out that σύνθεσις is largely concerned with euphony (i.e., rhythm and melody), whereas *iunctura* is primarily a syntactic and semantic phenomenon: a smart collocation can give a new meaning to a well-known word or phrase (e.g., *carpe diem*).[72] While agreeing with Brink that the focus of Dionysius' σύνθεσις is different from that of Horace's *iunctura*, I would like to draw attention to some striking correspondences in their discourse and their approach to word arrangement.

There are four aspects of Horace's discussion of *iunctura* that particularly correspond to elements in Dionysius' treatment of σύνθεσις. First, the poet is advised to select commonplace words: 'words taken from the common stock' (*de medio sumpta*, *Ars P.* 243) can be compared with 'contemptible and humble words' (εὐκαταφρόνητα καὶ ταπεινὰ ὀνόματα, *Comp.* 3.3). Horace formulates this rule in his discussion of satyr-play (*Ars P.* 220–50), but we should not suppose that it pertains to that genre exclusively. As scholars have observed, the style praised in this section seems to be the style that Horace adopts in his own poetry:[73] satyr-play is presented as the mean between tragedy and comedy, between the grand and the simple style. Commonplace words (*de medio sumpta*) are similar to the 'plain words' that distinguish Horace's poetry from that of Ennius (*pura uerba*, *Sat.* 1.4.53, above). Elevated or bombastic vocabulary is thus rejected by both Horace and Dionysius, but where the Roman seems to prefer words of the middle style (*de medio sumpta*), Dionysius, as we have seen, supposes that beautiful composition may arise even from the low register, that is, from words that are 'contemptible and humble'. The difference should not be exaggerated: it may be explained by the purposes of Dionysius' argument in the opening chapters of *On Composition*: word arrangement is *so* effective, he argues, that a beautiful passage may emerge *even* from the humble words of a farmer or a seaman. In other passages, Dionysius advocates the use of 'common

---

[72] Immisch 1932 *ad loc.*; Russell 1973, 117; Brink 1971, 139. Cf. Rudd 1989, 157. Pers. 5.14 (*iunctura callidus acri*) famously echoes Horace's expression.
[73] Armstrong 1993, 188.

words', which he calls κύρια ὀνόματα (*Comp.* 4.21). This expression, which has an Aristotelian background, is also found in the *Ars Poetica*: in line 234 Horace refers to *dominantia nomina*, which is a pure calque of κύρια ὀνόματα.[74] 'Dominating names' are familiar words (as opposed to metaphors, glosses, etc.) and roughly correspond to *de medio sumpta*, 'ordinary language'.[75]

Secondly, both authors draw attention to the important idea of skill or cleverness: Dionysius, as we have seen, believes that good orators and poets are recognized by 'the combining of words in a skilful, dexterous way': τὸ συντιθέναι δεξιῶς τὰ ὀνόματα (*Comp.* 4.13). I suggest that this formulation expresses an idea similar to Horace's *callida iunctura* (*Ars P.* 47–8). Just like δεξιός, the word *callidus* has the connotation of 'practical skill': it is the dexterity that one acquires by experience and practice.[76]

Thirdly, both Horace and Dionysius present clever word arrangement in terms of a metamorphosis, although they do so in different ways: for Horace *notum* becomes *nouum* (*Ars P.* 47–8: the 'well-known' becomes 'new'; an idea that is expressed by the ingenious placing of the words in the two lines), while for Dionysius misshapen, humble and beggarly words (ἄμορφα καὶ ταπεινὰ καὶ πτωχά) are – just like Odysseus – transformed into sublime, rich and beautiful ones (ὑψηλὰ καὶ πλούσια καὶ καλά, *Comp.* 4.12).

Finally, there is the theme of distinction. We have seen that for Dionysius dexterous composition is the quality by which 'one poet differs (διαλλάττει) from the other, one orator from the other' (*Comp.* 4.13). Horace makes a similar claim: he proudly announces that *he* will mould poetry from the familiar, so that *other* poets will toil in vain when attempting the same: 'such is the force of arrangement and combination, such the splendour that commonplace words acquire' (240–3).[77]

Dionysius, Horace and the Tradition of Composition Theory

Although the focus of Horace and Dionysius, as we have seen, is slightly different (semantic collocation versus euphonious harmony), they attach the same importance to effective word arrangement (*series, iunctura,*

---

[74] Arist. *Poet.* 21.1457b1. See Brink 1971, 285–6.   [75] See Cic. *De orat.* 3.177; *Or.* 163.
[76] Cf. De Jonge 2012a, 722–4.
[77] Cf. Oliensis 1998, 222: 'In the fashioning of a poem as of a gentleman, it is easy enough to make a silk purse out of silk, harder to achieve the same result with a sow's ear. What distinguishes the poet is the art by which he transforms the familiar and commonplace (*notum, medium*) into something novel and distinguished'.

σύνθεσις, ἁρμονία). The ideal of a skillful arrangement of ordinary words seems to have had a special appeal to writers of the Augustan Age, but it was by no means a new concept.[78] In a brief statement on composition in his *Rhetoric*, Aristotle already recommends selecting words from ordinary language:

κλέπτεται δ' εὖ, ἐάν τις ἐκ τῆς εἰωθυίας διαλέκτου ἐκλέγων συντιθῇ· ὅπερ Εὐριπίδης ποιεῖ καὶ ὑπέδειξε πρῶτος.

Art is cleverly concealed, when one selects his words from ordinary language and puts them together. That is what Euripides does; he was the first to point the way. (Arist. *Rh*. 3.2.1404b24-5)

While the terminology of ἐκλέγειν (ἐκλογή) and συντιθέναι (σύνθεσις) anticipates the parameters of Dionysius' stylistic theory, the words κλέπτεται δ' εὖ seem to hint precisely at the idea of cleverness that Horace expresses with the adjective *callidus* and Dionysius with the adverb δεξιῶς.[79]

The seeds of *synthesis* theory are thus already present in Aristotle. However, it seems that the high moment for composition in critical theory came in the first century BC, in late Republican and Augustan Rome. A good history of ancient composition theory, which remains to be written, should examine the points of contact between a number of Greek and Roman authors, including Philodemus, Cicero, the author of the *Rhetorica ad Herennium*, Horace and Dionysius, who all belong to the first century BC.[80] Since Hellenistic poetic theory appears to be a major influence on both Horace and Dionysius, the emphasis on σύνθεσις in Philodemus' *On Poems* is especially relevant. One passage from that work idealizes the skillful arrangement of commonplace words in a formulation that suggests connections with the Dionysian and Horatian passages cited above. We cannot be sure about the exact context of this fragment, but Janko proposes that Philodemus is here citing the views of Pausimachus, one of the Hellenistic critics:[81]

καί φη[σι τὸ "τιν]ὰς λέγειν ἐκ [καλῶν κ]αὶ ποιητικῶν ὀν[ομάτω]ν τὸ χρηστὸν ἢ [φαῦλον] πόημα, κατὰ [δ' ἄλλους], τὸ πολλάκις [εἰρημέν]ον,

---

[78] See Freudenburg 1993, 128–32 on the 'theoretical precedents' of Dionysius and Horace.
[79] Cf. Grube 1965, 95; Freudenburg 1993, 129–30. Like Aristotle, Longinus, *Subl*. 40.2 picks out Euripides as one of the models of clever composition. Cf. De Jonge 2012a, 718–19. Both Euripides (*Comp*. 11.19, 23.9, 25.22, 26.13) and Aristophanes (*Comp*. 26.14) figure prominently in Dionysius' treatise.
[80] Scaglione 1972 offers useful observations but remains unsatisfactory as a 'historical survey'.
[81] Janko 2000, 244–5. I cite Janko's translation.

φαῦλα γί[νεσθαι ἐ]ξ ἰδιωτικῶν [καὶ ἐξ ε]ὐτελῶν, συ[γ]κει[μένω]ν δὲ καλῶς, χ[ρ]ησ[τά."]

> Some, he says, claim that good or bad verse arises from beautiful and poetic words, but according to others, as has often been said, inferior (verses) arise from commonplace and ordinary (words), but when (such words) are beautifully arranged, good (verses arise). (Phld. *On Poems* I fr. 55)

This critic of poetry uses the same terms as Dionysius in his instructions on rhetorical prose (note καλός, φαῦλος, χρηστός, etc.). That the transition between poetic criticism and rhetorical composition theory in the first century BC was indeed a smooth one is confirmed when we compare Cicero and Horace. In the *Orator* Cicero claims that, in composing speeches, words should not be selected with particular attention to euphony, 'as the poets do' (*ut poetae*), but 'taken from ordinary language' (*sumpta de medio*).[82] Cicero seems to imply that in this respect prose differs from poetry. Just a few decades later, however, Horace applies precisely the same formulation *sumpta de medio* to the language of poetry (*Ars P.* 243, above).

The tradition of composition theory does not end, of course, with Dionysius and Horace. It is tantalizing that Longinus, the author of *On the Sublime*, claims to have composed a separate work Περὶ συνθέσεως in two books.[83] Some idea of what it contained can be deduced from his discussion of σύνθεσις in *On the Sublime* (39–42), which shows many points of contact with Dionysius' *On Composition*. Like Dionysius, Longinus believes that both poets and prose writers can achieve distinction by cleverly combining ordinary words:

> ἀλλὰ μὴν ὅτι γε πολλοὶ καὶ συγγραφέων καὶ ποιητῶν οὐκ ὄντες ὑψηλοὶ φύσει, μήποτε δὲ καὶ ἀμεγέθεις, ὅμως κοινοῖς καὶ δημώδεσι τοῖς ὀνόμασι καὶ οὐδὲν ἐπαγομένοις περιττὸν ὡς τὰ πολλὰ συγχρώμενοι, διὰ μόνου τοῦ συνθεῖναι καὶ ἁρμόσαι ταῦτα † δ' ὅμως † ὄγκον καὶ διάστημα καὶ τὸ μὴ ταπεινοὶ δοκεῖν εἶναι περιεβάλοντο, . . .

> Many writers both in prose and poetry, who are not by nature sublime, perhaps even the very opposite, while using for the most part current vulgar words, which suggest nothing out of the ordinary, yet by the mere arrangement and fitting together of these . . . have achieved dignity and distinction and a reputation for grandeur, . . . (Longinus, *Subl.* 40.2)[84]

---

[82] *Orat.* 163: Cicero here deals with 'sound' (*sonus*) and 'rhythm' (*numerus*): compare Dionysius' μέλος and ῥυθμός (*Comp.* 11.15–26).
[83] Longinus, *Subl.* 39.1.
[84] Translation adapted from Fyfe and Russell in Halliwell, Fyfe and Russell, and Innes 1995.

Even if we do not adopt either δολίως (deceitfully) or δεξιῶς (dexterously) as an emendation for the corrupt † δ' ὅμως †, it is clear that Longinus' discussion seamlessly fits into the pattern that we have established between Dionysius and Horace:[85] for Longinus, common words and artful composition lead not only to distinction (διάστημα), but even to the sublime.

An Augustan Taste: Dionysius, Augustus and Virgil

Our discussion has revealed a remarkable agreement between the approaches to stylistic composition in the works of Dionysius and Horace. I have argued that their views must be understood as participating in the literary discourse that connects various Greek and Roman poets and critics in Rome: we have identified traces of similar ideas in the fragments and works of Pausimachus, Philodemus, Cicero and Longinus. It is not possible to reconstruct the precise connections among all these individual authors; as I have pointed out above, such connections may have involved both oral exchange and written communication.

In the case of Dionysius, the various members of his literary circle should of course be taken into account. He may well have made connections with Roman intellectuals via the father of his student Metilius Rufus, to whose birthday we owe the existence of *On Composition*. The Metilii are interestingly included in the *Roman Antiquities* (3.29.7), suggesting that there may have been a relationship of patronage between this family and the Greek critic. But Dionysius also exchanged ideas with the prominent lawyer and historian Quintus Aelius Tubero, the addressee of his *On Thucydides*; Cicero had been a friend of his father Lucius Aelius Tubero.[86] Dionysius also had ample opportunities for exchange with other Greek rhetoricians: let us here just be reminded of Dionysius' friend Caecilius of Caleacte (*Pomp.* 3.20), who is the target of Longinus' *On the Sublime*. Finally, who knows what mediating role Dionysius' other addressees may have played in Augustan Rome: learned men like Ammaeus, Demetrius and Gnaeus Pompeius Geminus.[87]

The ideal of a skillful arrangement of ordinary words seems to have a special relevance to the stylistic writing of the Augustan Age: many of the theorists of composition mentioned above belong to this period. That there are links between Philodemus and the Augustan poets is now

---

[85] Immisch 1925, 26–7 has proposed δολίως: see also Immisch 1932, 80–1. De Jonge 2012a proposes δεξιῶς on the basis of *Comp.* 4.13 (above). For further connections between Dionysius and Longinus, see De Jonge 2012b.
[86] See Cic. *Lig.* 5.12.   [87] See De Jonge 2008, 27–8.

commonly accepted;[88] Horace and Dionysius were fully engaged in the cultural life of Augustan Rome; Longinus' date remains uncertain, but claims for an Augustan context have indeed been made.[89] Could we in fact speak of an Augustan stylistic taste, that is, a taste shared by various Greek and Roman writers, critics, rhetoricians and poets? To conclude this chapter, I would like to indicate two ways in which the stylistic doctrine of both Dionysius and Horace ties in with the rhetorical and literary culture of Augustan Rome: first, the preferences of Augustus himself, and second, the poetic style of Virgil.

Suetonius tells us that Augustus' style of speaking was 'elegant and chaste' (*elegans et temperatum*).[90] The *princeps*, being a student of the Greek rhetorician Apollodorus of Pergamon, detested 'the foulness of far-fetched words' (*reconditorum uerborum fetor*). His own style was extremely clear and moderate, as Suetonius tells us, holding the middle between two faulty extremes: on the one hand, Augustus avoided the archaisms of Tiberius, whom he criticized for his 'obsolete and pedantic expressions' (*exoletas ... et reconditas uoces*); on the other hand, he objected to the decadent style of Maecenas with its 'unguent-dripping curls' (*myrobrechis cincinnos*). Augustus also accused Mark Antony for his stylistic inconsistency, as he was switching between archaic and Asianic registers. In other words, Octavian objected to those orators and politicians who used unusual, difficult and obscure words (either old-fashioned or innovative), whereas he himself adopted a clear style consisting of common words. It is in this stylistic preference that Augustus' Atticism coincides with Dionysius' Atticism. When Dionysius expresses his gratitude to Rome by observing that its leaders are εὐπαίδευτοι (well educated) and γενναῖοι τὰς κρίσεις (excellent in their judgment, *Orat. Vett.* 3.1), it is therefore tempting to conclude that Dionysius is (also) thinking of the eloquence of Augustus himself.[91] The comeback of the Attic muse in the world of Rome was made possible first of all by the administrative power of Rome, Dionysius claims; but he must also have appreciated the fact that the Roman emperor himself was trained in the Greek tradition, and that he shared his preference for clear and common vocabulary.

Let us finally turn from prose once more to poetry, this time not to Horace but to the greatest poet of the Augustan Age. In his own time, the secret of Virgil's poetic style was already recognized and analyzed in terms

---

[88] See esp. Armstrong, Fish, Johnston and Skinner 2004.
[89] Mazzucchi 2010 and De Jonge 2012b offer arguments for a date in the Augustan period.
[90] Suet. *Aug.* 86. My translations of Suetonius are based on Rolfe 1998.
[91] *Orat. Vett.* 3.1–3 is cited by Wiater in this volume, pp. 72–3. Cf. Yunis in this volume, pp. 85–88.

that echo the ideals of Dionysius and Horace. In a much debated testimony, Marcus Vipsanius Agrippa accused Virgil of being the 'inventor of a new kind of stylistic affectation (*cacozelia*), neither extravagant nor affectedly simple, but based on common words (*ex communibus uerbis*) and for that reason not at once perceived'.[92] As Görler has pointed out, Agrippa must here be alluding to Virgil's remarkable arrangement of unpretentious words.[93] Virgil's *uerba communia* may be compared to Horace's *de medio sumpta*. Gian Biagio Conte explains Virgil's style as a sublime style, which makes use of artful syntax and the unexpected transposition of linguistic elements.[94] The secret of Virgil's poetry, not unlike that of Horace's *Odes*, is to be sought in the surprising and powerful collocation and juxtaposition of words rather than in the vocabulary itself, which consists, as Conte remarks elsewhere, of 'terms not conspicuously poetic, "neutral" words, so to speak, employed in prose and the language of everyday usage'.[95]

It would be interesting to explore further points of contact between Dionysius and the Roman poets of his time, and I conclude with a brief suggestion. We have seen that Dionysius shows a remarkable preference for examples from the *Odyssey*. In *On Composition* he cites various passages featuring the swineherd Eumaeus, depicting scenes from everyday life, such as the morning meal with pots and vessels in the swineherd's hut (*Odyssey* 16), which Dionysius cites in order to demonstrate the enchanting effect of σύνθεσις. Various parallels for this pastoral scene could be adduced from Virgil's *Eclogues* and *Georgics*, but the closest parallel is perhaps book 8 of the *Aeneid*, where Evander entertains Aeneas in his humble house on the Palatine.[96] It has been pointed out that Evander's house on the Palatine anticipates Augustus' modest dwelling on the same hill.[97] Suetonius considers the (relatively) small proportions of Augustus' residence as typical for his temperate lifestyle, and he admires the 'simplicity of his furniture and household goods'.[98] If it is true that Virgil's imitation of the Homeric scene also alludes to Augustus, this might add a further dimension to Dionysius' emphasis on Eumaeus' dwelling (in various parts of his treatise

---

[92] Donat. *Vit. Verg.* 44. Translation adapted from Camps 1969, 120.
[93] Görler 1979, 179–80. On the meaning of the difficult passage, see also Jocelyn 1979 (who defends the manuscript reading Vipranius); Horsfall 1995, 225–6.
[94] Conte 2007, 63–7 examines the connections between Virgil's style and the composition theory of Dionysius and Longinus.
[95] Conte 1994, 282. On Virgil's vocabulary, word order and style, see O'Hara 1997; Horsfall 1995, 217–48; Dainotti 2015 with further bibliography.
[96] On the connections between Eumaeus and Evander, see Knauer 1964, 252–4; Gransden 1976, 25–6.
[97] E.g., Gransden 1976, 30. [98] Suet. *Aug.* 72–3.

On Composition). It is the simplicity of a modest house, then, in which Greek criticism, Latin poetry, and the self-fashioning of Augustus come together.[99] Such suggestive parallels should stimulate us to explore further the fascinating connections between Greek literary theory and Latin literature in Augustan Rome.

[99] I further explore this idea in De Jonge 2018.

Envoi: Migrancy

Joy Connolly

> An authentically migrant perspective would, perhaps, be based on an intuition that the opposition between here and there is itself a cultural construction, a consequence of thinking in terms of fixed entities and defining them oppositionally. It might begin by regarding movement, not as an awkward interval between fixed points of departure and arrival, but as a mode of being in the world. The question would be, then, not how to arrive, but how to move, how to identify convergent and divergent movements; and the challenge would be how to notate such events, how to give them a historical and social value.[1]

Acts of scholarship do not typically demand a public accounting. Classicists may protest especially loudly that the distance between their sources and contemporary experience makes such an accounting irrelevant or foolish. But in the regular course of research into classical texts, topics do arise that resonate powerfully with public concerns – what we may usefully think of as 'wicked problems', complex, difficult problems composed of interdependent elements, that have no definitive formulation and no immediate or ultimate optimal solution, where the people involved hold radically different views and may not agree on the nature of the problem in the first place. Hannah Arendt argued that even in the darkest times, filled with such problems, we can expect illumination to come 'less from theories and concepts than from the uncertain, flickering, and often weak light that some men and women, in their lives and their works, will kindle under almost all circumstances and shed over the time and space that was given them on earth'.[2] At the root of Arendt's lifelong commitment to reading Greek and Roman authors lay her belief that some of this humanity-preserving light was to be found there: in Plato, Virgil, Cicero, and Augustine.

---

[1] Carter 1992, 101, cited in Chambers 1994, 48. [2] Arendt, 1968, ix.

Dionysius of Halicarnassus may strike us as an unlikely candidate to join Arendt's light-bearers. But the chapters in this volume have convinced me that his remarkable effort to speak 'between cultures and between genres', as editors Casper de Jonge and Richard Hunter put it in their introduction, places him among them. This makes him a useful example for us to study now. In citing utility as my criterion, I am following Dionysius himself, who explained that his study of Roman history was driven by his conviction that scholars should choose topics that are 'outstanding' and have 'utility' (μεγαλοπρεπεῖς ... ὠφέλειαν, *Ant. Rom.* 1.1.2). Arriving in Rome around 30 BC, a year or so after the battle of Actium, probably before he turned thirty, Dionysius joined many others of his generation who travelled from the Greek-speaking parts of the empire to live and work at its core: Strabo of Amasia, Nicolaus of Damascus, Caecilius of Caleacte, Timagenes of Alexandria. Like Hannah Arendt, Jacques Derrida, Édouard Glissant, Edward Said, Gayatri Spivak, Homi Bhabha, and others working in the Americas and Europe in the modern era, all these Greeks were migrant thinkers.

Global migration is one of the wicked problems of the twenty-first century. More than a million migrants entered Europe from Africa alone in 2015. Migration on this scale presents severe challenges not only to national and multinational economies, social systems, and the environment, but also to the internal cohesiveness of the states that absorb migrants in large numbers. By introducing unfamiliar languages of speech, posture, and gesture, different histories, and new assumptions about how the world works and should work, migrants remind the inhabitants of the nations they enter that there are alternatives to native or traditional meanings – alternatives that may unsettle or undermine the conventions of the migrants' new 'home'. Understanding the impact of migration demands close attention to its psychology, or rather psychologies, since there is never a univocal account of the motivations, experience, and effects of migrancy. Migrants' intellectual and artistic contributions – as powerfully felt among elites and in popular culture in late Republican and early Imperial Rome as they are in the contemporary world – are key to prompting fresh thinking about how to keep societies coherent and secure without aiming for undesirable ideals of homogeneity and conformity.

Modern migrants have spoken eloquently about their distinctive position in society and history. When Hannah Arendt reads the *Aeneid*, one hears her, a Jewish thinker exiled from Germany, thinking in the positions of both Virgil and Aeneas, *auctor* and *actor*. Migrants, Homi Bhabha points out, gather on the edge of cultures that gradually but never totally lose their foreignness for them. Constantly aware of their outsider status, they retain a specially sharpened sensitivity to the ways communities form themselves, the costs and benefits of that formation, and the psychological processes involved in self-translation and embedment, as far as it is allowed, in the new environment. Movement between places, languages, and cultures creates a doubleness in migrant writing that reveals the complex, dynamic intersections of memory, values, and fantasy always at work in the formation of communal identity.[3]

These intersections are the central object of study throughout the series in which this book appears, *Greek Culture in the Roman World*. Examining a rich variety of cultural artifacts, from religious rituals, athletics, political debate, jurisprudence, novels, histories, and scientific texts to family tombstones and public inscriptions, the series' volumes reveal the complex interplay of local, translocal, and imperial reference points in Greeks' and Romans' negotiation of the new social and political possibilities that emerged in the Mediterranean under Roman rule. As editors De Jonge and Hunter note in their review of the debate over Dionysius' readership at the end of their introduction, we must think carefully about how different our distinction between 'Greeks' and 'Romans' is from those that were made by inhabitants of the empire, where Greek speakers adopted Roman citizenship and Roman names and well-off Romans sought cultural capital through the acquisition of Greek learning. The lines blur – not least because writers in each language strive to make it so.

In this brief envoi, I comment on Dionysius' work in light of his migrant status. In doing so, I seek to shed light on the orientation and thought not only of Dionysius alone or even all his Greek compatriots writing in Augustan Rome, but a much larger group: the writers in Latin we call 'Roman'. These Greeks and Romans are linked by experiences of migrancy and imitation, repeated over and over again throughout their histories. Harvey Yunis points out that for Dionysius, when he writes as a critic, imitation is 'the ruling concept of rhetorical study and practice; it ties the study of the exemplary past to the creation of the new'. Nicolas Wiater and Clemence Schultze observe that when he writes as a historian, Dionysius presents his task in conventional terms as holding up *exempla* for readers to avoid or imitate. Now, every student of Roman literary history knows two things. Roman literature is produced almost entirely by Latin speakers who are born elsewhere than at Rome, who migrate to the city. And every

---

[3] Bhabha 1994, 122–7. Even as I use it, I want to draw attention to the limits of identity as a term: see the trenchant critique of the term in Brubaker and Cooper 2001.

literary genre self-consciously imitates a Greek one – even satire, which Quintilian calls 'our own' (10.1.93) but whose practitioners allude to Greek forebears in lyric and comedy. Set this against the broader Roman habit of imitating Greek philosophy and religion and ways of counting time and organizing social life, and Roman culture emerges as thoroughly extraordinary in human history.[4]

Whether they write in a language that was only one of the languages they grew up with, like Ennius, or in a language that belonged to a faraway imperial metropolis, like Catullus or Virgil or the elder Seneca, most writers in Latin do and re-do and re-do again the translational labor of Dionysius: the labor of exploring another community in depth, its memories and aspirations and styles of expression – and not just any community, but the one whose history was conquest and domination. The recent experience is one Dionysius shares with Republican and Imperial Latin writers, for whom Roman conquest was typically not more than a century old. Like Dionysius, the poet Horace also came as an outsider to Rome, born as he was in the Samnite south of Italy: this parallel adds another dimension to the comparative examination of these two authors undertaken by Casper de Jonge. Recent research by Laurens Tacoma and others paints the broader picture of Rome under the principate, where migrants constituted up to a third of the population, perhaps half of them enslaved.[5] As migrants entered the urban core from the provinces, Romans of different classes and professions migrated around the empire: senators and their entourage on assignment in the provinces, traders, soldiers, entertainers, and migrant laborers. To better understand Dionysius, then, is to gain insight into the dynamics that shape Roman literature of the late Republic and early Empire.

As Latin authors became a part of and an accessory to Roman literature by imitating it, they joined a culture that was from its earliest imperial foundation imitative of another. These authors, in short, imitated cultural rules and gestures that we should be wary of calling simply 'Roman' in the first place, but that always blurred the lines between 'Roman' and something else, usually something Hellenic. Largely thanks to the self-conscious effort of the Latin poets to summon up that spectral presence, no line of Latin poetry can be read without the ghost of its Greek forebear making its influence felt. The fact that every single Roman treatment of political, epistemological, moral, and aesthetic concepts grows up from ground

---

[4] Feeney 2016 insists on (and makes a solid case for) the extraordinary nature of Roman culture.
[5] Tacoma 2016.

established by Greek thinkers means that Roman thinkers are always already engaged in a dialogue with someone else, with another text. By virtue of its ongoing close engagement with Greek language, thought, and writing, Roman literary writing (if not Roman culture) chooses for itself a doubleness that possesses or mimicks (this is itself a complex problem) the characteristics of migrancy. The effect persists long into Roman Imperial history.

It is true that linguistic and ethnic binaries were deployed in Rome's aggressive consolidation of political and social order within its empire. Not Etruscan or Oscan but Latin was the exclusive language of public inscriptions up and down the Italian peninsula. But the historical realities and phenomenological experience of the imitative system of Roman culture should make us pause to question our continued use of the binary classifications of 'Greek', 'Italic', and 'Etruscan' versus 'Roman' when we study Roman literature. As far as 'identity' goes (and where does it stop?) Latin writers' constant evocation of Greek ancestry and influence places Latin literary writing in a space of permanent ambiguity.

I have argued elsewhere that the unusual imitative turn of Roman literature demands more thought and study, as regards both its aesthetics and its ethics, and that we should understand Roman writing as fundamentally, eternally, and inescapably engaged in exploring the condition of human relationality.[6] That Dionysius is engaged in the same project is clear from the start of this volume. The act of speaking between – between rhetoric and history, Athens and Rome, Greek and Latin, fiction and accuracy, detail and abstraction, past and present, continuity and disruption – is the governing theme of the editors' introduction to Dionysius of Halicarnassus. In his habit of writing across, as a Greek writing about Roman history and dedicating books on Greek style to Roman friends, all the while underscoring the role of Roman power in sustaining Greek cultural influence, Dionysius is a useful guide to Roman literature, specifically, its peculiarly other-oriented ethical disposition.

I will gesture here to just three of the many rich themes the collection draws our attention to: Dionysius' claim that the Romans spring from Greek ancestry; his implicit claim that individual action is the driver of human history; and his treatment of the paradoxically learnable

---

[6] Connolly, forthcoming 2018a, 2018b. See further Glissant 1997, 34–5, who provocatively describes the relational tensions in Caribbean literature as 'the violent sign of their consentual, not imposed, sharing ... the main themes of such a poetics [are] the dialectics between the oral and the written, the thought of multilingualism, the balance between the present moment and duration, the questioning of literary genres, the power of the baroque, the nonprojectile imaginary construct'.

unreasonability of taste. These three ideas about history and aesthetics are closely intertwined – the intertwining itself a phenomenon that Jacques Rancière has done much to explore that is also worth considering here, not least in his analysis of Tacitus' description of Percennius.[7]

In his chapter on the *Roman Antiquities*, Matthew Fox argues that through his claim that the Romans originated as ethnic Greeks, Dionysius draws a parallel between Roman rationalizations of their own civilizing mission and his own view of the Romans as a civilizing influence. 'But any negative associations of the complicity of the subaltern', Fox comments, 'need to be balanced against the sense that it is Greek history and culture that set the standard for effective governance and civilized communities'. Furthermore, Fox shows how Dionysius cultivates the habit of telling several versions of the same story. As I read Fox's reading, Dionysius' startling rewriting of Roman history emerges as the quintessential work of hybridity: an act of cultural rebranding that, through its bold reclamation of the trope of biological kinship and its embrace of narrative variety, undermines the notion of the essentialism of a prior originary culture.

Édouard Glissant cites the image of the rhizome from the work of Deleuze and Guattari in his argument that identity must no longer be understood as existing completely within the roots that it claims for itself, but rather as existing in a network of relations to others. Where 'the intolerant violence of filiation was formerly buried in the sacred mystery of the root', as Glissant argues, Dionysius undoes that mystery by claiming Greece as Rome's own.[8] If you believe you can opt in, then you can believe that all forms of culture are continually in flux, continually changing, in a state of hybridity. To Dionysius, then, the engine of history cannot be reduced to the activity of any single ethnic collective. Rome is always Greek/Roman, the one eliding into the other. Further, and more radically, it appears that Dionysius views the fate of collectives not as a matter of national character or destiny, but action on the level of the individual or the small group. Fox tracks how the *Roman Antiquities* places individual historical agents at the forefront. They are the ones who take the initiative and perform definable action: an old man, a god, a small community. 'For Dionysius', he concludes, 'it is individual moral commitment, including that of the historian, to an international ideal of civil society, rather than impersonal forces – among them ethnic origin – that take the central role in determining the course of history'.

---

[7] See especially Rancière 1994, 24–41; Rancière 2010.   [8] Glissant 1997, 18, 61.

Christopher Pelling also sees deep significance in Dionysius' interest in individual action and character. To Dionysius, Pelling argues, constitutions matter very little, if at all; individual men and their actions do. In his analysis, Dionysius' history of Rome advocates for learning by doing and learning by suffering. (In fact, Pelling argues, Dionysius is imitating Polybius' emphasis on learning by doing; but I will leave the puzzle of Greeks imitating Greeks writing about Romans for another day.) As arbitrary as they may seem, men's individual choices are the key to understanding the past, and presumably the present and future. Like Arendt, who argues against the claim of Hegel and Marx that history is made by supra-human forces and structures, Dionysius chooses to underline the unexpected, contingent, and indeterminate, leaving open a space for human action.

The most important human action the Romans undertake is speech. This makes their politics and their growth to empire possible. But it is a particular kind of speech, as Pelling shows: the Romans cultivate the habit of working things out through public exchange. Referring to the episode in which Romulus establishes Rome as a monarchy with popular consent (*Ant. Rom.* 2.11.2–3), Pelling comments: 'That, then, was the basis for Roman concord, so firmly established by Romulus . . . . They dealt with [ongoing conflict] by a process of persuasion and instruction, sometimes making concessions and sometimes receiving them, and thus they resolved their complaints in a civic and civil way', until Gaius Gracchus arrived on the scene (see also 7.66.5). So the 'wordiness' of Dionysius' history, a central concern in the chapter of Stephen Oakley, does not simply reflect his personal taste for speeches. Rome's monarchic and then its Republican regime emerges from popular deliberation. He allots to the people the capacity for judgment and a voice: 'We do not at all desire a new form of government' (*Ant. Rom.* 2.4.1).[9]

What could be more Greek than popular deliberation? In Dionysius' Rome, the habit of talking things through makes Rome a copy of Athens. History, politics, cultural sensibility, taste, and rhetorical skill blend together under the emblem of imitating Greeks. As Pelling asks: 'Might, in fact, Roman history be analogous to the way Dionysius saw Greek culture in *On the Ancient Orators*, with a glorious classical past, a sad decline, and then a contemporary revival?'

---

[9] Even Dionysius' text participates on a meta-level: as the exchange of speech creates ὁμοφροσύνη, which according to Romulus binds the city together, providing its best defense (*Ant. Rom.* 2.3.1), the variety and multiplicity of Dionysius' own narrative creates a tension with the theme of unity.

Several of the chapters here develop the historical analysis of Fox and Pelling, who present the Romans developing over time, and track it through Dionysius' rhetorical writings. By becoming their best ruling selves, which is to say by becoming Greek, the Romans (as represented by Dionysius imitating Polybius) learn in a particular way: by experience and suffering, πάθει μάθος. In talking their way through problems, they also follow a curriculum that is unmistakably Greek: rhetoric, the art of effective communication. In his account of the Decemvirate, Daniel Hogg shows that Dionysius presents speeches and (senatorial) debate as central characteristics of the Roman Republic. From the insights of Richard Hunter, Stephen Oakley, Laura Viidebaum, Harvey Yunis, and Nicolas Wiater, it becomes clear why Dionysius marries his history of Rome with critical essays on rhetoric. If what passes for knowledge emerges within language, then critical knowledge must involve the exploration of language itself. To turn it around, rhetoric is an exploration of what passes for knowledge – how knowledge and beliefs take shape in the framework of social power: who can speak, when, and in what style.

Richard Hunter's chapter on the critic points out how, according to Dionysius, one can gradually learn good judgment. Recalling Dionysius' representation of historical agency as a matter of individual action, we are in a position to understand the importance of individual taste in Dionysius' critical essays. That is, we can now understand his emphasis on irrationality and indeterminacy in his account of critical judgment not as a result of subjective uncertainty, but as a key part of his moral and political project. Just as the characters in his tale of Rome's past make history, so his readers will make Rome's present and future by their good judgments of rhetoric and literature. They learn to judge by looking backward to past judgments, imitating them, and observing and moderating their own reactions.

The feedback loop, as Wiater compellingly shows, rests on a complex psychological interplay of unfulfillable desire. His chapter, along with Viidebaum's and Yunis', illuminates Dionysius' acknowledgment of the irrationality of aesthetic perception, ἄλογος αἴσθησις. Χάρις, Viidebaum shows, is indeterminate in Dionysius as in Cicero: it is impossible for the critic to pin down. Is this because Dionysius has run up against the ineffable indescribability of poetic language – 'the process called poetic invention that mingles breath and sense in a way that no one has explained and no one ever will?'[10] Not at all. As Hunter and Yunis agree, the

[10] Coetzee 2003, 98.

acquisition of good taste is a matter of individual agency: and taste is a moral as well as an aesthetic judgment. 'Yet because concepts and perceptions of beauty can be shared over the generations', Yunis remarks, the proper styles of imitation also require 'a moral seriousness that is common to both the historical models and present-day practitioners'. The critic's powers end where the reader's or listener's moral responsibility begins. Dionysius frequently invokes the concept of a 'natural' style, as Yunis and De Jonge point out, to bolster his claims for the ethical significance of speech.

In his brilliant essay 'Feeling Classical: Classicism and Ancient Literary Criticism', which provides the scaffolding for Wiater's essay, James Porter explores the 'realm of pleasures' that comes with the practices of classicism, focusing on the pleasure of following the rules of Attic speech to that of recognizing at an instant the sound of Demosthenes or the look of a Polyclitus – 'immediate, sensuous, and ultimately ideological'.[11] Porter's concern is the relationship between euphony and literary criticism, and then by extension the ideological functions of literary criticism in the ancient Mediterranean world. Wiater's interest here, and mine, is on how 'feeling classical' is a way of 'feeling Roman' that is simultaneously a way of 'feeling Greek' – a phenomenological experience that illuminates how the expression of speech, aesthetic judgment, emotion, and identity become entangled in everyday life to create powerful emotional identifications.

As Porter recognizes in his essay on classicism, voice is a compelling but uncertain carrier of culture. It is immensely useful in conveying a style of self. It is the marker of humanity. But as Aristotle points out (*Politics* 1253a10-15), the voice (φωνή) is merely the vehicle for λόγος, not identical to it. 'Man is the only animal whom [nature] has endowed with the gift of speech (λόγος)' (1253a9-10). Aristotle draws a distinction here between 'mere voice' (φωνή) and λόγος, the vehicle of human intellect and ethics. The theorist Mladen Dolar captures this idea in his comment that '[t]he logos is wrapped in voice'.[12] As he notes, the voice rests in a 'peculiar and paradoxical' position of what we might call 'extimacy'. It lives at its core of λόγος, making the communication of thought possible; but the limits and failures of the voice also constantly haunt us, reminding us of the impossibility of perfectly embodying and conveying thought. Hence the overdetermined need for rules to constrain the formation and expression of voice – even as the critic acknowledges the limits of his ability to describe their effects.

---

[11] Porter 2006b, 310.   [12] Dolar 2006, 105.

There is pleasure here too, in managing the voice and one's train of thought according to the rules of Atticism. We can hear in Dionysius' comments echoes of the previous generation, and especially Cicero. Near the beginning of his treatise *Orator*, Cicero praises men 'who adapt themselves to the refined and scrupulous ears of an Athenian audience' as those 'who deserve to be considered as speaking in an Attic manner'. What is Attic? As Viidebaum and Wiater show, it is everything, in a way: 'brusque and fierce, provided that [the speaker] uses elegant and well-turned expressions' – something simple but not neat, that is not over-heavy but acts like 'thunder and lightning' (*Orat.* 9).

While Dionysius acknowledges the limits of his critical discourse, he has much to say about the powers of speech to move us, to alert us to the beliefs and commitments of others, past and present, in historical writing as well as rhetorical discourse. I see in Oakley's analysis of his attention to sensation and detail, combined with his concern for speech and style explored in several other papers in the volume, especially De Jonge and Viidebaum, another trace of Dionysius' migrant status. Migrants, Iain Chambers points out, are acutely sensitive to the ghosts that shadow every discourse, the estrangement that potentially exists within us all, to 'the presence that persists, that cannot be effaced, that draws me out of myself toward another'.[13] Like Cicero, an outsider of a different type, Dionysius sets himself to categorize the ways carefully composed and arranged words, in both text and delivery, connect human beings to one another.

Drawing on the contributors' arguments, I have suggested that in Dionysius, ethnic identity is not determinative. To be Roman is to be a member of a community of actors, whose virtue rests in individual agency, in choice. This explains Dionysius' interest in taste and his acknowledgment of the uncategorizable and indescribable in critical discourse. As his rhetorical essays fix the Roman empire as the site of discriminating and authoritative judgment in the ineffable matter of speech, his histories authorize the individual decisions that create empire – and encompass their arbitrary nature.

Édouard Glissant writes insightfully about the great founding books of communities all over the globe – the Hebrew Scriptures, the *Odyssey*, the *Aeneid*, the *chansons de geste*, Icelandic sagas, African epics. All deal with exile and errantry, figures he uses to illustrate his account of migrancy. These are 'books about the birth of collective consciousness, but they also introduce the unrest and suspense that allow *the individual to discover*

---

[13] Chambers 1994, 6.

himself there (my italics)'.¹⁴ Glissant's underscoring of self-discovery picks up on Dionysius' preoccupation with individual agency and choice.

Dionysius is a founder of what we are accustomed to calling the 'western' tradition – a canon-builder, portable handbook-writer, synthesizer of Roman history for readers outside Rome. But consider him instead in light of recent claims by Anthony Appiah, for instance, that there is no 'western culture'; on the contrary, individual agents over time seize ideals and values and make them their own.¹⁵ Seen from this perspective, Dionysius emerges as one of the earliest exempla of cultural appropriation. He is not a receiver but an active creator of culture, a migrant who has travelled across borders and now writes across borders, intent on the project of purposive conservation, the planned management of a resource to prevent destruction.

---

¹⁴ Glissant 1997, 15.   ¹⁵ Appiah 2016.

Bibliography

Abbenes, J.G.J., Slings, S.R., and Sluiter, I. eds. 1995. *Greek Literary Theory after Aristotle. A Collection of Papers in Honour of D.M. Schenkeveld*. Amsterdam.
Ando, C. 1999. 'Was Rome a polis?' *Classical Antiquity* 18: 5–34.
Andrén, A. 1960. 'Dionysius of Halicarnassus on Roman monuments.' In *Hommages à Léon Herrmann*. Collection Latomus 44. Brussels. 88–104.
Appiah, A.K. 2016. 'There Is No Such Thing as Western Civilization.' *The Guardian*. 6 November.
Arendt, H. 1968. *Men in Dark Times*. New York.
Armstrong, D. 1993. 'The Addressees of the *Ars Poetica*: Herculaneum, the Pisones, and Epicurean Protreptic.' *Materiali e Discussioni* 31: 185–230.
Armstrong, D. 1995. 'The Impossibility of Metathesis: Philodemus and Lucretius on Form and Content in Poetry.' In Obbink 1995: 210–32.
Armstrong, D. 2004. 'Horace's Epistles 1 and Philodemus.' In Armstrong-Fish-Johnston-Skinner 2004: 267–98.
Armstrong, D. and Oberhelman, S. 1995. 'Satire as Poetry and the Impossibility of Metathesis in Horace's Satires.' In Obbink 1995: 233–54.
Armstrong, D., Fish, J., Johnston, P.A., and Skinner, M.B. eds. 2004. *Vergil, Philodemus, and the Augustans*. Austin.
Asheri, D., Lloyd, A., and Corcella, A. 2007. *A Commentary on Herodotus Books I-IV*. Oxford.
Aujac, G. 1978. *Denys d'Halicarnasse: Opuscules rhétoriques*. Tome 1. Paris.
Aujac, G. 1988. *Denys d'Halicarnasse: Opuscules rhétoriques*. Tome 2. Paris.
Aujac, G. 1991. *Denys d'Halicarnasse: Opuscules rhétoriques*. Tome 4. Paris.
Aujac, G. 1992. *Denys d'Halicarnasse: Opuscules rhétoriques*. Tome 5. Paris.
Aujac, G. and Lebel, M. 1981. *Denys d'Halicarnasse: Opuscules rhétoriques*. Tome 3. Paris.
Avenarius, G. 1956. *Lukians Schrift zur Geschichtschreibung*. Meisenheim am Glan.
Badian, E. 1966. 'The Early Historians.' In *Latin Historians*, ed. T.A. Dorey. London. 1–38.
Baragwanath, E. 2008. *Motivation and Narrative in Herodotus*. Oxford.
Baraz, J. 2012. *A Written Republic: Cicero's Philosophical Politics*. Princeton.
Barchiesi, A. 2009. 'Roman Perspectives on the Greeks.' In *The Oxford Handbook of Hellenic Studies*, ed. G. Boys-Stones, B. Graziosi, and Ph. Vasunia. Oxford. 98–113.

Baronowski, D.W. 2011. *Polybius and Roman Imperialism*. London.
Battisti, D.G. 1997. *Dionigi di Alicarnasso: Sull'imitazione*. Pisa.
Batstone, W.W. 2009. 'Postmodern Historiographical Theory and the Roman Historians.' In *The Cambridge Companion to the Roman Historians*, ed. A. Feldherr. Cambridge. 24–40.
Bauman, R.A. 1993. 'The Rape of Lucretia, "Quod metus causa" and the Criminal Law.' *Latomus* 52: 550–66.
Beard, M., North, J., and Price S. eds. 1998. *Religions of Rome*. 2 vols. Cambridge.
Bencivenni, A. 2014. 'The King's Words: Hellenistic Royal Letters in Inscriptions.' In *State Correspondence in the Ancient World: From New Kingdom Egypt to the Roman Empire*, ed. K. Radner. Oxford. 141–71.
Benediktson, D.T. 2000. *Literature and the Visual Arts in Ancient Greece and Rome*. Norman.
Bhabha, H. 1994. *The Location of Culture*. London.
Bishop, C. 2015. 'How to Make a Roman Demosthenes: Self-Fashioning in Cicero's *Brutus* and *Orator*.' *Classical Journal* 111: 167–92.
Bocksch, O. 1895. 'De fontibus librorum v et vi Antiquitatum Romanarum Dionysii Halicarnassensis quaestiones variae.' *Leipziger Studien zur classischen Philologie* 17: 165–274.
Bonner, S.F. 1938. 'Dionysius of Halicarnassus and the Peripatetic Mean of Style.' *Classical Philology* 33: 257–66.
Bonner, S.F. 1939. *The Literary Treatises of Dionysius of Halicarnassus. A Study in the Development of Critical Method*. Cambridge.
Bowersock, G.W. 1965. *Augustus and the Greek World*. Oxford.
Bowersock, G.W. 1979. 'Historical Problems in Late Republican and Augustan Classicism.' In Flashar 1979a: 57–78.
Bremmer, J. 1997. 'Why did Medea Kill her Brother Apsyrtus?' In *Medea: Essays on Medea in Myth, Literature, Philosophy, and Art*, ed. J.J. Clauss and S.I. Johnston. Princeton. 83–100.
Brink, C.O. 1963. *Horace on Poetry. Prolegomena to the Literary Epistles*. Cambridge.
Brink, C.O. 1971. *Horace on Poetry. The 'Ars Poetica.'* Cambridge.
Briquel, D. 1984. *Les Pélasges en Italie*. Rome.
Briquel, D. 1993. *Les Tyrrhènes, peuple des Tours*. Rome.
Briquel, D. 2004. 'La chute des décemvirs: aux origines d'un récit.' In *Images d'Origines. Origines d'une Image. Hommages à Jacques Poucet*, ed. P.-A. Deproost and A. Meurant. Leuven. 139–56.
Brubaker, R. and Cooper, F. 2009. 'Beyond "identity".' *Theory and Society* 29: 1–47.
Bruns I. 1896. *Das literarische Porträt der Griechen im fünften und vierten Jahrhundert vor Christi Geburt*. Berlin.
Büchler, O. 1936. *Die Unterscheidung der redenden Personen bei Lysias: eine stilistische Untersuchung der διήγησις*. Heidelberg.
Bundrick S.D. 2008. 'The Fabric of the City: Imaging Textile Production in Classical Athens.' *Hesperia* 77: 283–334.
Burck, E. 1964². *Die Erzählungskunst des T. Livius*. Berlin. [first edition 1934]

Bux, E. 1915. *Das Probouleuma bei Dionys von Halikarnaß.* Dissertation. Leipzig.
Calboli, G. 1987. 'Asianesimo e Atticismo: retorica, letteratura e linguistica.' In *Studi di retorica oggi in Italia*. Bologna. 31–53.
Camps, W.A. 1969. *An Introduction to Virgil's Aeneid*. London.
Canfora, L. 2006. 'Thucydides in Rome and Late Antiquity.' In *Brill's Companion to Thucydides*, ed. A. Rengakos and A. Tsakmakis. Leiden. 721–53.
Cantarella E. 1991. 'Homicides of Honor. The Development of Italian Adultery Law over Two Millennia.' In *The Family in Italy from Antiquity to the Present*, ed. D.I. Kertzer and R.P. Saller. New Haven. 229–44.
Carter, P. 1992. *Living in a New Country: History, Travelling, and Language.* London.
Cary, E. 1937. *The Roman Antiquities of Dionysius of Halicarnassus.* Vol. 1. Cambridge, MA. 1937.
Cary, E. 1939. *The Roman Antiquities of Dionysius of Halicarnassus.* Vol. 2. Cambridge, MA.
Cary, E. 1940. *The Roman Antiquities of Dionysius of Halicarnassus.* Vol. 3. Cambridge, MA.
Cary, E. 1943. *The Roman Antiquities of Dionysius of Halicarnassus.* Vol. 4. Cambridge, MA.
Cary, E. 1945. *The Roman Antiquities of Dionysius of Halicarnassus.* Vol. 5. Cambridge, MA.
Cary, E. 1947. *The Roman Antiquities of Dionysius of Halicarnassus.* Vol. 6. Cambridge, MA.
Cary, E. 1950. *The Roman Antiquities of Dionysius of Halicarnassus.* Vol. 7. Cambridge, MA.
Chambers, I. 1994. *Migrancy, Culture, Identity.* London.
Champion, C.B. 2004. *Cultural Politics in Polybius's Histories*. Berkeley.
Chaniotis, A. 2016. 'History as an Argument in Hellenistic Oratory: The Evidence of Hellenistic Decrees.' In *La Rhétorique du Pouvoir. Une exploration de l'art oratoire délibératif grec*. Entretiens sur l'antiquité classique 62, ed. M. Edwards. Vandoevres. 129–74.
Chiron, P. 1993. *Démétrios:* Du style. Paris.
Chaplin, J.D. 2000. *Livy's Exemplary History*. Oxford.
Chiron, P. 2010. 'Les noms du style chez Démétrios (Ps.-Démétrios de Phalère): collection ou système?' In Chiron-Lévy 2010: 71–85.
Chiron, P. and Lévy, C. ed. 2010. *Les noms du style dans l'antiquité Gréco-Latin.* Louvain.
Closterman, W.E. 2014. 'Women as Gift Givers and Gift Producers in Ancient Athenian Funerary Ritual.' In *Approaching the Ancient Artifact: Representation, Narrative, and Function. A Festschrift in Honor of H. Alan Shapiro*, ed. A. Avramidou and D. Demetriou. Berlin. 161–74.
Coetzee, J.M. 2003. *Elizabeth Costello.* New York.
Cohen, D. 1991a. 'The Augustan Law on Adultery: The Social and Cultural Context.' In *The Family in Italy from Antiquity to the Present*, ed. D.I. Kertzer and R.P. Saller. New Haven. 109–26.

Cohen, D. 1991b. 'Sexuality, Violence, and the Athenian Law of Hubris.' *Greece and Rome* 38: 171–88.
Connolly, J. 2007. 'Being Greek / Being Roman: Hellenism and Assimilation in the Roman Empire.' *Millennium Jahrbuch zu Kultur und Geschichte des ersten Jahrtausends n. Chr.* 4: 21–42.
Connolly, J. 2018a. 'The Space between Subjects.' In *Marginality, Canonicity, Passion*, ed. M. Formisano and C.S. Kraus. Oxford. 313–28.
Connolly, J. 2018b. 'The Promise of the Classical Canon: Hannah Arendt and the Romans.' *Classical Philology* 113: 6-19.
Conte, G.B. 1994. *Latin Literature. A History*. Baltimore.
Conte, G.B. 2007. *The Poetry of Pathos. Studies in Virgilian Epic*. Oxford.
Cornell, T.J. 1995. *The Beginnings of Rome: Italy and Rome from the Bronze Age to the Punic Wars*. London.
Cornell, T.J. ed. 2013. *The Fragments of the Roman Historians*. Oxford.
Dainotti, P. 2015. *Word Order and Expressiveness in the 'Aeneid.'* Berlin.
Damon, C. 1991. 'Aesthetic Response and Technical Analysis in the Rhetorical Writings of Dionysius of Halicarnassus.' *Museum Helveticum* 48: 33–58.
Degrassi, A. 1947. *Inscriptiones Italiae. Volumen XIII – Fasti et elogia. Fasciculus I – Fasti consulares et triumphales*. Rome.
Delcourt, A. 2005. *Lecture des* Antiquités Romaines *de Denys d'Halicarnasse. Un historien entre deux mondes*. Brussels.
Dewald, C. 1987. 'Narrative Surface and Authorial Voice in Herodotus' *Histories*.' In *Herodotus and the Invention of History*, ed. D. Boedeker and J. Peradotto. *Arethusa* 20: 147–70.
Dewald, C. 2002. '"I Didn't Give My Own Genealogy": Herodotus and the Authorial Persona.' In *Brill's Companion to Herodotus*, ed. E.J. Bakker, I.J.F. Jong, and H. Wees. Leiden. 267–89.
Dixon, S. 2001. 'Women's Work: Perceptions of Public and Private.' In *Reading Roman Women*. London. 113–32.
Dolar, M. 2006. *A Voice and Nothing More*. Cambridge.
Donadi, F. 1986. 'Il "bello" e il "piacere" (osservazioni sul *De compositione verborum* di Dionigi d' Alicarnasso).' *Studi Italiani di Filologia Classica* 4: 42–63.
Donadi, F. and Marchiori, A. 2014. *Dionigi d'Alicarnasso. La composizione stilistica*. Trieste.
Drerup, E. 1923. *Demosthenes im Urteile des Altertums*. Würzburg.
Drossaart Lulofs, H.J. 1965. *Nicolaus Damascenus on the Philosophy of Aristotle. Fragments of the First Five Books Translated from the Syriac with an Introduction and Commentary*. Leiden.
Dueck, D. 2000. *Strabo of Amasia: A Greek Man of Letters in Augustan Rome*. London.
Earl, D.C. 1961. *The Political Thought of Sallust*. Cambridge.
Eden, K. 1986. *Poetic and Legal Fiction in the Aristotelian Tradition*. Princeton.
Edwards, C. 1993. *The Politics of Immorality in Ancient Rome*. Cambridge.

Edwards, M.J. 2013a. '*Hypokrites* in Action: Delivery in Greek Rhetoric.' In *Profession and Performance: Aspects of Oratory in the Greco-Roman World*, ed. C. Kremmydas, J. Powell, and L. Rubinstein. London. 15–25.
Edwards, M.J. 2013b. 'Dionysius and Isaeus.' In Kremmydas-Tempest 2013: 43–9.
Egger, M. 1902. *Denys d'Halicarnasse: Essai sur la critique littéraire et la rhétorique chez les Grecs du siècle d'Auguste*. Paris.
Ek, S. 1942. *Herodotismen in der Archäologie des Dionys von Halikarnass. Ein Beitrag zur Beleuchtung des beginnenden Klassizismus*. Lund.
Eliot, T.S. 1923. 'The Function of Criticism.' *Criterion* 1: 31–42.
Elsner, J. 2007. *Roman Eyes. Visuality and Subjectivity in Art and Text*. Princeton.
Erker, D.S. 2009. 'Women's Tears in Ancient Roman Ritual.' In *Tears in the Graeco-Roman World*, ed. T. Fögen. Berlin. 135–60.
Evrigennis, I.D. 2008. *Fear of Enemies and Collective Action*. Cambridge.
Fairclough, H.R. 1926. *Horace:* Satires, Epistles *and* Ars Poetica. Cambridge, MA.
Fantasia, U. 2004. 'ἀκρίβεια.' In *Lexicon Historiographicum Graecum et Latinum I*, ed. C. Ampolo, U. Fantasia, and L. Porciani. Pisa. 36–66.
Fantham, E. 1991. '*Stuprum*: Public Attitudes and Penalties for Sexual Offences in Republican Rome.' *Échos du Monde Classique* 35: 267–91.
Fantham, E. 1997. 'The Contexts and Occasions of Roman Public Rhetoric.' In *Roman Eloquence*, ed. W.J. Dominik. London. 91–105.
Feeney, D. 2016. *Beyond Greek: The Beginnings of Latin Literature*. Cambridge.
Feldherr, A. 1997. 'Livy's Revolution: Civic Identity and the Creation of the *res publica*.' In *The Roman Cultural Revolution*, ed. T. Habinek and A. Schiesaro. Cambridge. 136–57.
Feldherr, A. 1998. *Spectacle and Society in Livy's* History. Berkeley.
Ferrari, G. 2002. *Figures of Speech: Men and Maidens in Ancient Greece*. Chicago.
Fisher, N.R.E. 1992. *Hybris: A Study in the Values of Honour and Shame in Ancient Greece*. Warminster.
Flashar, H. ed. 1979a. *Le classicisme à Rome aux 1ers siècles avant et après J.-C.* Entretiens sur l'antiquité classique 25. Vandoeuvres-Geneva.
Flashar, H. 1979b. 'Die klassizistische Theorie der Mimesis.' In Flashar 1979a: 79–111.
Fornara, C.W. 1983. *The Nature of History in Ancient Greece and Rome*. Berkeley.
Fornaro, S. 1997. *Dionisio di Alicarnasso:* Epistola a Pompeo Gemino. *Introduzione e commento*. Stuttgart.
Forsythe, G. 1999. *Livy and Early Rome: A Study in Historical Method and Judgement*. Historia Einzelschriften 132. Stuttgart.
Fortenbaugh, W.W. 2005. *Theophrastus of Eresus. Sources for His Life, Writings, Thought and Influence. Commentary Volume 8. Sources on Rhetoric and Poetics (Texts 666–713)*. Leiden.
Foster, E. and Lateiner, D. eds. 2012. 'Introduction.' In *Herodotus and Thucydides*. Oxford. 1–8.
Fox, M. 1993. 'History and Rhetoric in Dionysius of Halicarnassus.' *Journal of Roman Studies* 83: 31–47.
Fox, M. 1996. *Roman Historical Myths: The Regal Period in Augustan Literature*. Oxford.

Fox, M. 2001. 'Dionysius, Lucian, and the Prejudice against Rhetoric in History.' *Journal of Roman Studies* 91: 76–93.
Fox, M. 2011. 'The Style of the Past: Dionysius of Halicarnassus in Context.' In Schmitz-Wiater 2011a: 93–114.
Fox, M. and Livingstone, N. 2010. 'Rhetoric and Historiography.' In *A Companion to Greek Rhetoric*, ed. I Worthington. Malden, MA. 542–61.
Freudenburg, K. 1993. *The Walking Muse. Horace on the Theory of Satire*. Princeton.
Frischer, B. 1991. *Shifting Paradigms. New Approaches to Horace's* Ars Poetica. Atlanta.
Fromentin, V. 1993. 'La définition de l'histoire comme "mélange" dans le prologue des *Antiquités Romaines* de Denys d'Halicarnasse.' *Pallas* 39: 177–92.
Fromentin, V. 1998. *Denys d'Halicarnasse:* Antiquités Romaines. Tome I. Paris.
Fromentin, V. 2003. 'Fondements et crises de la royauté à Rome: les règnes de Servius Tullius et de Tarquin le Superbe chez Tite-Live et Denys d'Halicarnasse.' In *Fondements et crises du pouvoir*, ed. S. Franchet d'Espèrey, V. Fromentin, S. Gotteland, and J.-M. Roddaz. Pessac. 69–82.
Fromentin, V. 2004. 'Choisir le meilleur: la royauté élective à Rome selon Denys d'Halicarnasse.' *Ktèma* 29: 312–23.
Fromentin, V. 2006. 'Denys d'Halicarnasse et Hérodote III, 80–82 ou Comment choisir la meilleure constitution pour politique Rome?' *Pallas* 72: 229–42.
Fuhrer, Th. 2003. 'Was ist gute Dichtung? Horaz und der poetologische Diskurs seiner Zeit.' *Rheinisches Museum* 146: 346–64.
Gabba, E. 1979. 'Eduard Schwartz e la storiografia greca dell'età imperiale.' *Annali della Scuola Normale di Pisa* 9: 1033–49.
Gabba, E. 1991. *Dionysius and* The History of Archaic Rome. Berkeley.
Gabba. E. 1994. 'Per Dionigi d'Alicarnasso.' *Athenaeum* 82: 496–7.
Gaida, E. 1934. *Die Schlachtschilderung in den* Antiquitates Romanae *des Dionys von Halikarnass*. Dissertation. Breslau.
Galinsky, K. 1996. *Augustan Culture: An Interpretive Introduction*. Princeton.
Galinsky, K. 2005a. *The Cambridge Companion to the Age of Augustus*. Cambridge.
Galinsky, K. 2005b. 'Vergil's Aeneid and Ovid's Metamorphoses as World Literature.' In Galinsky 2005a: 340–60.
Gantz, T. 1975. 'The Tarquin Dynasty.' *Historia* 24: 539–54.
Garland, R. 1985. *The Greek Way of Death*. Ithaca.
Gaughan, J.E. 2012. *Murder Was Not a Crime: Homicide and Power in the Roman Republic*. Austin.
Geigenmueller, P. 1908. *Quaestiones Dionysianae de vocabulis artis criticae*. Dissertation. Leipzig.
Gelzer, Th. 1975. 'Klassik und Klassizismus.' *Gymnasium* 82: 147–73.
Gelzer, Th. 1979. 'Klassizismus, Attizismus und Asianismus.' In Flashar 1979a: 1–55.
Gerber, D.E. 1982. *Pindar's* Olympian *One: A Commentary*. Toronto.

Gildenhard, I. 2007. *Paideia Romana: Cicero's Tusculan Disputations.* Cambridge Philological Society Supplements 30. Cambridge.
Glissant, E. 1997. *Poetics of Relation.* Ann Arbor.
Glucker, J. 1978. *Antiochus and the Late Academy.* Hypomnemata 56. Göttingen.
Görler, W. 1979. '"Ex Verbis Communibus ΚΑΚΟΖΗΛΙΑ". Die augusteischen "Klassiker" und die griechischen Theoretiker des Klassisizmus.' In Flashar 1979a: 175–211.
Goldhill, S. ed. 2001. *Being Greek Under Rome. Cultural Identity, the Second Sophistic and the Development of Empire.* Cambridge.
Goudriaan, K. 1989. *Over classicisme. Dionysius van Halicarnassus en zijn program van welsprekendheid, cultuur en politiek.* Dissertation. Free University Amsterdam.
Gow, A.S.F. and Page, D.L. 1968. *The Greek Anthology. The Garland of Philip and Some Contemporary Epigrams.* 2 vols. Cambridge.
Gowers, E. 2012. *Horace: Satires, Book I.* Cambridge.
Gozzoli, S. 1976. 'Polibio e Dionigi d'Alicarnasso.' *Studi Classici e Orientali* 25: 149–76.
Gransden, K.W. 1976. *Virgil: Aeneid, Book VIII.* Cambridge.
Greenwood, E. 2010. 'Mimicry and Classical Allusion in V.S. Naipaul's *The Mimic Men.*' In *Classics and National Cultures*, ed. S.A. Stephens and Ph. Vasunia. Oxford. 100–20.
Greenberg, N.A. 1958. 'Metathesis as an Instrument in the Criticism of Poetry.' *Transactions of the American Philological Association* 89: 262–70.
Grethlein, J. 2013. *Experience and Teleology in Ancient Historiography: 'Futures Past' from Herodotus to Augustine.* Cambridge.
Griffin, M.T. 1989. 'Philosophy, Politics, and Politicians.' In *Philosophia Togata: Essays on Philosophy and Roman Society 1*, ed. M.T. Griffin and J. Barnes. Oxford. 1–37.
Griffiths, A.H. 2013. 'Where Did Early Roman History Come From?' *Bulletin of the Institute of Classical Studies* 56: 79–87.
Grube, G.M.A. 1950. 'Dionysius of Halicarnassus on Thucydides.' *Phoenix* 4: 95–110.
Grube, G.M.A. 1961. *A Greek Critic: Demetrius On Style.* Toronto.
Grube, G.M.A. 1965. *The Greek and Roman Critics.* London.
Halbfas, F. 1910. *Theorie und Praxis in der Geschichtsschreibung bei Dionys von Halikarnass.* Dissertation. Münster.
Hall, J. 2007. 'Oratorical Delivery and the Emotions: Theory and Practice.' In *A Companion to Roman Rhetoric*, ed. W.J. Dominik. Malden, MA. 218–34.
Hallett, C.M. 2012. 'The Archaic Style in Sculpture in the Eyes of Ancient and Modern Viewers.' In *Making Sense of Greek Art*, ed. V. Coltman. Exeter. 70–100.
Halliwell, S. 2002. *The Aesthetics of Mimesis: Ancient Texts and Modern Problems.* Princeton.

Halliwell, S. 2011. *Between Ecstasy and Truth. Interpretations of Greek Poetics from Homer to Longinus.* Oxford.
Halliwell, S., Fyfe, W.H., Russell, D.A., and Innes, D.C. eds. 1995. *Aristotle, Poetics. Longinus,* On the Sublime. *Demetrius,* On Style. Cambridge, MA.
Hansen, M.H. and Nielsen, T.H. eds. 2004. *An Inventory of Archaic and Classical Poleis.* Oxford.
Hardie, P. 2014. 'The *Ars Poetica* and the Poetics of Didactic.' *Materiali e Discussioni* 72: 43–54.
Harris, W.V. 1986. 'The Roman Father's Power of Life and Death.' In *Studies in Roman Law in Memory of A. Arthur Schiller,* ed. R.S. Bagnall and W.V. Harris. Leiden. 81–95.
Harrison, J.R. 2003. *Paul's Language of Grace in Its Graeco-Roman Context.* Tübingen.
Hartog, F. 1991. 'Rome et la Grèce.' In *ΕΛΛΗΝΙΣΜΟΣ: Quelques jalons pour une histoire de l'identité grecque,* ed. S. Saïd. Leiden. 149–67.
Heath, J. 2005. *The Talking Greeks: Speech, Animals, and the Other in Homer, Aeschylus, and Plato.* Cambridge.
Heath, M. 1989. *Unity in Greek Poetics.* Oxford.
Heldmann, K. 1982. *Antike Theorien über Entwicklung und Verfall der Redekunst.* Munich.
Hellegouarc'h, J. 1972. *Le Vocabulaire latin des relations et des partis politiques sous la République.* Paris.
Hemelrijk, E.A. 2004. 'Masculinity and Femininity in the *Laudatio Turiae.*' *Classical Quarterly* 54: 185–97.
Henderson, J. 2001. 'From Megalopolis to Cosmopolis.' In Goldhill 2001: 29–49.
Hendrickson, G.L. 1905. 'The Origin and Meaning of the Ancient Characters of Style.' *American Journal of Philology* 26: 249–90.
Henrichs, A. 1978. 'Greek Maenadism from Olympias to Messalina.' *Harvard Studies in Classical Philology* 82: 121–60.
Hidber, Th. 1996. *Das klassizistische Manifest des Dionys von Halikarnass.* Stuttgart.
Hidber, Th. 2011. 'Impacts of Writing in Rome: Greek Authors and Their Roman Environment in the First Century BCE.' In Schmitz-Wiater 2011a: 115–23.
Hill, H. 1961. 'Dionysius of Halicarnassus and the Origins of Rome.' *Journal of Roman Studies* 51: 88–93.
Hölscher, T. 2004. *The Language of Images in Roman Art.* Cambridge.
Hogg, D. 2008. *Speech and Action in the* Antiquitates Romanae *of Dionysius of Halicarnassus: The Question of Historical Change.* DPhil thesis. Oxford (open access https://ora.ox.ac.uk/objects/uuid%3A30012af0-0ba8-46cd-a9d8-d53d8d3f73c1).
Hogg, D. 2013. 'The Decemvirate.' In *The Encyclopaedia of Ancient History,* ed. R.S. Bagnall, K. Broderson, C. Champion, A. Erskine and S. Hübner. Vol. 4. Malden, MA. 1947–8.
Holder, A. 1967. *Pomponi Porfyrionis Commentum in Horatium Flaccum.* Hildesheim.
Hornblower, S. 1987. *Thucydides.* London.

Hornblower, S. 2008. *A Commentary on Thucydides. Vol. III.* Oxford.
Horsfall, N. 1995. *A Companion to the Study of Virgil.* Leiden.
Hunter, R. 2003. 'Reflecting on Writing and Culture: Theocritus and the Style of Cultural Change.' In *Written Texts and the Rise of Literate Culture in Ancient Greece*, ed. H. Yunis. Cambridge. 213–34 (= Hunter 2008: vol. 1, 434–56).
Hunter, R. 2007. 'Sappho and Latin Poetry.' In *I papiri di Saffo e di Alceo: atti del convegno internazionale di studi, Firenze, 8–9 giugno 2006*, ed. G. Bastianini and A. Casanova. Florence. 213–25.
Hunter, R. 2008. *On Coming After: Studies in Post-Classical Greek Literature and Its Reception.* Berlin.
Hunter, R. 2009. *Critical Moments in Classical Literature. Studies in the Ancient View of Literature and Its Uses.* Cambridge.
Hunter, R. 2012. *Plato and the Traditions of Ancient Literature: The Silent Stream.* Cambridge.
Hunter, R. 2014. 'Attic Comedy in the Rhetorical and Moralizing Traditions.' In *The Cambridge Companion to Greek Comedy*, ed. M. Revermann. Cambridge. 373–86.
Hurst, A. 1982. 'Un critique grec dans la Rome d'Auguste: Denys d'Halicarnasse.' In *Aufstieg und Niedergang der römischen Welt* 2.30.1: 839–65.
Immisch, O. 1925. *Bemerkungen zur Schrift vom Erhabenen.* Heidelberg.
Immisch, O. 1932. *Horazens Epistel über die Dichtkunst.* Leipzig.
Innes, D.C. 1985. 'Theophrastus and the Theory of Style.' In *Theophrastus of Eresus: On His Life and Work*, ed. W.W. Fortenbaugh, P.M. Huby, and A.A. Long. New Brunswick. 251–67.
Innes, D.C. 1995. 'Longinus: Structure and Unity.' In Abbenes-Slings-Sluiter 1995: 111–24.
Innes, D.C. 2002. 'Longinus and Caecilius: Models of the Sublime.' *Mnemosyne* 55: 259–84.
Jacobs, J. 2010. 'From Sallust to Silius Italicus: *Metus hostilis* and the Fall of Rome in the *Punica*.' In *Latin Historiography and Poetry in the Early Empire*, ed. J.F. Miller and A.J. Woodman. Leiden. 123–40.
Jahn, O. and Kroll, W. 1964. *Cicero,* Brutus. 7th edn. rev. by B. Kytzler. Berlin.
Janko, R. 2000. *Philodemus:* On Poems*, Book 1.* Oxford.
Jocelyn, H.D. 1979. '*Vergilius cacozelus* (Donatus, *Vita Vergilii* 44).' *Papers of the Liverpool Latin Seminar* 2: 67–142.
de Jong, I.J.F. 2002. 'Narrative Unity and Units.' In *Brill's Companion to Herodotus*, ed. E.J. Bakker, I.J.F. de Jong, and H. van Wees. Leiden. 245–66.
de Jonge, C.C. 2005. 'Dionysius of Halicarnassus and the Method of Metathesis.' *Classical Quarterly* 55: 463–80.
de Jonge, C.C. 2008. *Between Grammar and Rhetoric. Dionysius of Halicarnassus on Language, Linguistics and Literature.* Leiden.
de Jonge, C.C. 2011. 'Dionysius of Halicarnassus and the Scholia on Thucydides' Syntax.' In *Ancient Scholarship and Grammar. Archetypes, Concepts and Contexts*, ed. S. Matthaios, F. Montanari, and A. Rengakos. Berlin. 459–86.

de Jonge, C.C. 2012a. 'Clever Composition. A Textual Note on Longinus, *On the Sublime* 40.2.' *Mnemosyne* 65: 717–25.
de Jonge, C.C. 2012b. 'Longinus and Dionysius on the Sublime. Rhetoric and Religious Language.' *American Journal of Philology* 133: 271–300.
de Jonge, C.C. 2014a. 'The Attic Muse and the Asian Harlot: Classicizing Allegories in Dionysius and Longinus.' In *Valuing the Past in the Greco-Roman World*, ed. J. Ker and C. Pieper. Leiden. 388–409.
de Jonge, C.C. 2014b. 'Ancient Theories of Style (léxis).' In *Encyclopedia of Ancient Greek Language and Linguistics*, ed. G.K. Giannakis. Leiden. 3.326–31.
de Jonge, C.C. 2017. 'Dionysius of Halicarnassus on Thucydides.' In *The Oxford Handbook of Thucydides*, ed. R. Balot, S. Forsdyke, and E. Foster. Oxford. 641–58.
de Jonge, C.C. 2018. 'Eumaeus, Evander, and Augustus. Dionysius and Virgil on Noble Simplicity.' In *Homer and the Good Ruler*, ed. B. van den Berg and J.J.H. Klooster. Leiden. 157–81.
de Jonge, C.C. forthcoming. 'Linguistic Naturalism and Natural Style. From Varro and Cicero to Dionysius.' In *Language and Nature in Classical Rome*, ed. G. Pezzini and B. Taylor. Cambridge.
Joshel, S.R. 2002. 'The Body Female and the Body Politic: Livy's Lucretia and Verginia.' In *Sexuality and Gender in the Classical World: Readings and Sources*, ed. K. McClure. Oxford. 163–87.
Jost, K. 1936. *Das Beispiel und Vorbild der Vorfahren bei den attischen Rednern und Geschichtsschreibern bis Demosthenes*. Paderborn.
Kaster, R.A. 2005. *Emotion, Restraint, and Community in Ancient Rome*. Oxford.
Kellum, B. 2003. 'Sculptural Programs and Propaganda in Augustan Rome: The Temple of Apollo on the Palatine.' In *Roman Art in Context*, ed. E. D'Ambra. Englewood Cliffs. 75–83.
Kennedy, G. 1972. *The Art of Rhetoric in the Roman World*. Princeton.
Kierdorf, W. 1980. *Laudatio funebris. Interpretationen und Untersuchungen zur Entwicklung der römischen Leichenrede*. Meisenheim am Glan.
Kim, L. 2014. 'Archaizing and Classicism in the Literary Historical Thinking of Dionysius of Halicarnassus.' In *Valuing the Past in the Greco-Roman World*, ed. J. Ker and C. Pieper. Leiden. 357–87.
Kirchner, R. 2005. 'Die Mysterien der Rhetorik. Zur Mysterienmetapher in rhetoriktheoretischen Schriften.' *Rheinisches Museum* 148: 165–80.
Kleiner, D.E.E. 1993. 'The Great Friezes of the Ara Pacis Augustae. Greek Sources, Roman Derivatives, Augustan Social Policy.' In *Roman Art in Context*, ed. E. D'Ambra. Englewood Cliffs. 27–52.
Klotz, A. 1938. 'Zu den Quellen der Archaeologia des Dionysios von Halikarnassos.' *Rheinisches Museum* 87: 32–50.
Knauer, G.N. 1964. *Die* Aeneis *und Homer: Studien zur poetischen Technik Vergils mit Listen der Homerzitate in der Aeneis*. Göttingen.
Koestermann, E. 1971. *C. Sallustius Crispus:* Bellum Iugurthinum. Heidelberg.
Kraus, C.S. 1995. *Livy:* Ab Urbe Condita, *Book VI*. Cambridge.

Kremmydas, C. and Tempest, K. eds. 2013. *Hellenistic Oratory: Continuity and Change.* Oxford.
Kurtz, D. 1970. *ΑΚΡΙΒΕΙΑ: Das Ideal der Exactheit bei den Griechen bis Aristoteles.* Göppinger Akademische Beiträge 8. Göppingen.
Laird, A. 2007. 'The *Ars Poetica.*' In *The Cambridge Companion to Horace,* ed. S. Harrison. Cambridge. 132–43.
Lamp, K.S. 2013. *A City of Marble: The Rhetoric of Augustan Rome.* Columbia.
Langlands, R. 2006. *Sexual Morality in Ancient Rome.* Cambridge.
Langlands, R. 2014. 'Exemplary Influences and Augustus' Pernicious Moral Legacy.' In *Suetonius the Biographer,* ed. T. Power and R.K. Gibson. Oxford. 111–29.
Larsson Lovén, L. 1998. 'LANAM FECIT. Woolworking and Female Virtue.' In *Aspects of Women in Antiquity. Proceedings of the first Nordic Symposium on Women's Lives in Antiquity,* ed. L. Larsson Lovén and A. Strömberg. Jonsered. 88–95.
Latacz, J. 1966. *Zum Wortfeld 'Freude' in der Sprache Homers.* Heidelberg.
Lausberg, H. 1960. *Handbuch der literarischen Rhetorik.* Munich.
Lendle, O. 1992. *Einführung in die griechische Geschichtsschreibung.* Darmstadt.
Lesky, A. 1971. *Geschichte der griechischen Literatur.* Bern.
Levene, D. 1997. 'Pity, Fear and the Historical Audience: Tacitus on the Fall of Vitellius.' In *The Passions in Roman Thought and Literature,* ed. S.M. Braund and C. Gill. Cambridge. 128–49.
Lintott, A.W. 1972. 'Imperial Expansion and Moral Decline in the Roman Republic.' *Historia* 21: 626–38.
Lucarini, C.M. 2015. 'I due stili asiani (Cic. Br. 325; P.Artemid.) e l'origine dell'atticismo letterario.' *Zeitschrift für Papyrologie und Epigraphik* 193: 11–24.
Luce, T.J. 1965. 'The Dating of Livy's First Decade.' *Transactions of the American Philological Association* 96: 209–40.
Luraghi, N. 2003. 'Dionysios von Halikarnassos zwischen Griechen und Römern.' In *Formen römischer Geschichtsschreibung von den Anfängen bis Livius: Gattungen – Autoren – Kontexte,* ed. U. Eigler, U. Gotter, N. Luraghi, and U. Walter. Darmstadt. 268–86.
MacFarlane, R. 2007. *Original Copy. Plagiarism and Originality in Nineteenth-Century Literature.* Oxford.
MacLachlan, B. 1993. *The Age of Grace: Charis in Early Greek Poetry.* Princeton.
McEwen, I.K. 2003. *Vitruvius: Writing the Body of Architecture.* Cambridge MA.
McGinn, T.A.J. 1998. *Prostitution, Sexuality, and the Law in Ancient Rome.* Oxford.
McHardy, F. 2008. *Revenge in Athenian Culture.* London.
McNeil, L. 'Bridal Cloths, Cover-ups, and Kharis: The "Carpet Scene" in Aeschylus' *Agamemnon.*' *Greece and Rome* 52: 1–17.
Marin, D. 1956. 'L'opposizione sotto Augusto e la datazione del *Saggio sul sublime.*' In *Studi in onore di Aristide Calderini e Roberto Paribeni.* Milan. 1.157–85.
Marin, D. 1969. 'Dionisio di Alicarnasso e il latino.' In *Hommages à Marcel Renard,* ed. J. Bibauw. Brussels. 595–607.

Marincola, J. 1997. *Authority and Tradition in Ancient Historiography*. Cambridge.
Marincola, J. 2007. 'Speeches in Classical Historiography.' In *A Companion to Greek and Roman Historiography*, ed. J. Marincola. Oxford. 118–32.
Marincola, J. 2013. 'Polybius, Phylarchus, and "Tragic History": A Reconsideration.' In *Polybius and his World: Essays in Memory of F.W. Walbank*, ed. B. Gibson and T. Harrison. Oxford. 73–90.
Martin, P.M. 1993. 'De l'universel à l'éternel: la liste des hégémonies dans la préface des A. R.' *Pallas* 39: 193–214.
Martin, R.H. and Woodman, A.J. eds. 1989. *Tacitus:* Annals*, Book IV*. Cambridge.
Martinho, M. 2010. 'Caractérisation et noms du style moyen selon Denys d'Halicarnasse.' In Chiron-Lévy 2010: 201–20.
Masden, J.M. 2006. 'Intellectual Resistance to Roman Hegemony and Its Representativity.' In *Rome and the Black Sea Region: Domination, Romanisation, Resistance*, ed. T. Bekker-Nielsen. Aarhus. 63–82.
Mazzucchi, C.M. 2010. *Dionisio Longino, Del sublime*. Milan.
Miles, G.B. 1995. *Reconstructing Early Rome*. Ithaca.
Millar, F.G.B. 1987. 'Polybius between Greece and Rome.' In *Greek Connections: Essays on Culture and Diplomacy*, ed. J.T.A. Koumoulides. Notre Dame. 1–18.
Milnor, K. 2005. *Gender, Domesticity, and the Age of Augustus: Inventing Private Life*. Oxford.
Momigliano, A. 1990. 'The Herodotean and the Thucydidean Tradition.' In *The Classical Foundations of Modern Historiography*. Berkeley. 29–53.
Moore, D. W. 2017. 'Learning from experience: Polybius and the progress of Rome.' Classic Qusterly 67, 132–48.
Mora, F. 1995. *Il pensiero storico-religioso antico. Autori greci e Roma I: Dionigi d'Alicarnasso*. Rome.
Moussy, C. 1966. *Gratia et sa famille*. Paris.
Myres, J.L. 1953. *Herodotus: The Father of History*. Oxford.
Nesselrath, H.-G. 2013. 'Latein in der griechischen Bildung? Eine Spurensuche vom 2. Jh. v. Chr. bis zum Ende des 3. Jh.s n. Chr.' In Schubert-Ducrey-Derron 2013: 281–319.
Nichols, M.F. 2009. *Vitruvius and the Rhetoric of Display: Wall Painting, Domestic Architecture and Roman Self-Fashioning*. Dissertation. Cambridge.
Noè, E. 1979. 'Ricerche su Dionigi d'Alicarnasso: la prima stasis a Roma e l'episodio di Coriolano.' In *Ricerche di storiografia greca di età romana*. Pisa. 21–116.
Norden, E. 1909. *Die antike Kunstprosa vom VI. Jahrhundert v. Chr. bis in die Zeit der Renaissance*. 2 vols. 2nd ed. Leipzig. [First Edition 1898.]
Northwood, S.J. 1998. *Four Studies in the Historiography of Early Rome*. Dissertation. Manchester.
Oakley, S. P. 1997–2005. *A Commentary on Livy, Books vi–x*. Oxford.
Oakley, S.P. 2010. 'Dionysius of Halicarnassus and Livy on the Horatii and the Curiatii.' In *Ancient Historiography and its Contexts: Studies in Honour of A.J. Woodman*, ed. C.S. Kraus, J. Marincola, and C. Pelling. Oxford. 118–38.

Obbink, D. ed. 1995. *Philodemus and Poetry. Poetic Theory and Practice in Lucretius, Philodemus and Horace*. Oxford.
Ober, J. 1989. *Mass and Elite in Democratic Athens. Rhetoric, Ideology, and the Power of the People*. Princeton.
Ober, J. 1998. *Political Dissent in Democratic Athens: Intellectual Critics of Popular Rule*. Princeton.
Ogilvie, R.M. 1965. *A Commentary on Livy Books 1–5*. Oxford.
O'Hara, J.J. 1997. 'Virgil's Style.' In *The Cambridge Companion to Virgil*, ed. C. Martindale. Cambridge. 241–58.
Oliensis, E. 1998. *Horace and the Rhetoric of Authority*. Cambridge.
Olson, K. 2008. *Dress and the Roman Woman: Self-Presentation and Society*. Abingdon.
Ooms, S. and de Jonge, C.C. 2013. 'The Semantics of ΕΝΑΓΩΝΙΟΣ in Greek Literary Criticism.' *Classical Philology* 108: 95–110.
Pailler, J.-M. 1988. *Bacchanalia. La répression de 186 av. J.-C. à Rome et en Italie*. Rome.
Parmentier, E. and Barone, F.P. 2011. *Nicolas de Damas. Histoires, Recueil de coutumes, Vie d'Auguste, Autobiographie*. Paris.
Pausch, D. 2011. 'Augustus chlamydatus. Greek Identity and the *bios Kaisaros* by Nicolaus of Damascus.' In Schmitz-Wiater 2011a: 143–62.
Pavano, G. 1936. 'Dionisio d'Alicarnasso, critico di Tucidide.' *Memorie della R. Accademia delle Scienze di Torino* 68: 251–91.
Pavano, G. 1958. *Dionisio d'Alicarnasso: Saggio su Tucidide*. Palermo.
Peirano, I. 2010. 'Hellenized Romans and Barbarized Greeks: Reading the End of Dionysius of Halicarnassus' Antiquitates Romanae.' *Journal of Roman Studies* 100: 32–53.
Pelling, C. 1996. 'The Triumviral Period.' In *The Cambridge Ancient History x²: The Augustan Empire, 43 B.C.–A.D. 69*, ed. A.K. Bowman, E. Champlin, and A. Lintott. Cambridge. 1–69.
Pelling C. 2004. 'Plutarch on the Outbreak of the Roman Civil War.' In *Festschrift für Gerhard Dobesch zum fünfundsechzigsten Geburtstag am 15. September 2004*, ed. H. Heftner and K. Tomaschitz. Vienna. 317–27.
Pelling, C. 2007. 'The Greek Historians of Rome.' In *A Companion to Greek and Roman Historiography*, ed. J. Marincola. Malden, MA. 244–58.
Pelling, C. 2010. '"Learning from that Violent Schoolmaster": Intertextuality and Some Greek Views of Roman Civil War.' In *Citizens of Discord: Rome and its Civil Wars*, ed. B.W. Breed, C. Damon, and A. Rossi. Oxford. 105–18.
Pelling, C. 2011. *Plutarch: Caesar*. Oxford.
Pelling, C. 2016. 'Preparing for Posterity: Dionysius and Polybius.' In *Knowing Future Time in and through Greek Historiography*, ed. A. Lianeri. Berlin. 155–73.
Pernot, L. 2006. *L'ombre du tigre. Recherches sur la réception de Démosthène*. Naples.
Pernot, L. 2015. *Epideictic Rhetoric: Questioning the Stakes of Ancient Praise*. Austin.
Pohl, K. 1968. *Die Lehre von den drei Wortfügungsarten. Untersuchungen zu Dionysios von Halikarnaß, De compositione verborum*. Tübingen.
Pollitt, J.J. 1965. *The Art of Ancient Greece: Sources and Documents*. Cambridge.

Pollitt, J.J. 1974. *The Ancient View of Greek Art: Criticism, History, and Terminology*. New Haven.
Poma, G. 1984. *Tra Legislatori e tiranni: problemi storici e storiografici sull'età delle XII Tavole*. Bologna.
Porciani, L. 1997. *La Forma proemiale*. Pisa.
Porter, J.I. 1995. 'Οἱ κριτικοί: A Reassessment.' In Abbenes-Slings-Sluiter 1995: 83–109.
Porter, J.I. 2006a. 'Introduction: What Is "Classical" about Classical Antiquity?' In *Classical Pasts. The Classical Traditions of Greece and Rome*, ed. J.I. Porter. Princeton. 1–65.
Porter, J.I. 2006b. 'Feeling Classical: Classicism and Ancient Literary Criticism.' In *Classical Pasts. The Classical Traditions of Greece and Rome*, ed. J.I. Porter. Princeton. 301–52.
Porter, J.I. 2011. 'Against λεπτότης: Rethinking Hellenistic Aesthetics.' In *Creating a Hellenistic World*, ed. A. Erskine and L. Llewellyn-Jones. Swansea. 271–312.
Porter, J.I. 2016. *The Sublime in Antiquity*. Cambridge.
Pritchett, W.K. 1975. *Dionysius of Halicarnassus: On Thucydides*. Berkeley.
Quadlbauer, F. 1958. 'Die *genera dicendi* bis Plinius dem Jüngeren.' *Wiener Studien* 71: 55–111.
Rancière, J. 1994. *The Names of History*. Minneapolis.
Rancière, J. 2010. *Dissensus: On Politics and Aesthetics*. New York.
Rawson, E. 1989. 'Roman Rulers and the Philosophical Adviser.' In *Philosophia Togata: Essays on Philosophy and Roman Society*, ed. M.T. Griffin and J. Barnes. Oxford. 233–57.
Redfield, J. 1982. 'Notes on the Greek Wedding.' *Arethusa* 15: 181–201.
Rehm, R. *Marriage to Death: The Conflation of Wedding and Funeral Rituals in Greek Tragedy*. Princeton.
Reinhardt, T. 2013. 'The *Ars Poetica*.' In *Brill's Companion to Horace*, ed. H.-Ch. Günther. Leiden. 499–526.
Richard, J.-C. 1993. 'Sur deux discours programmes: à propos d' A.R. 3,10,3–11,11.' *Pallas* 39: 125–41.
Roberts, W.R. 1900. 'The Literary Circle of Dionysius of Halicarnassus.' *Classical Review* 14: 439–42.
Roberts, W.R. 1901. *Dionysius of Halicarnassus. The Three Literary Letters*. Cambridge.
Roberts, W.R. 1910. *Dionysius of Halicarnassus. On Literary Composition*. London.
Robling, F.-H. and Adamietz, J. 1992. 'Asianismus.' In *Historisches Wörterbuch der Rhetorik*, ed. G. Ueding. Tübingen. 1.1114–21.
Rochette, B. 1997. *Le Latin dans le monde grec. Recherches sur la diffusion de la langue et des lettres latines dans les provinces hellénophones de l'Empire romain*. Collection Latomus 233. Brussels.
Rolfe, J.C. 1998. *Suetonius*. Volume 1. Cambridge, MA.

Rudd, N. 1989. *Horace:* Epistles, *Book II and* Epistle to the Pisones *('Ars Poetica')*. Cambridge.
Russell, D.A. 1964. 'Longinus', *On the Sublime*. Oxford.
Russell, D.A. 1973. *'Ars Poetica.'* In *Horace*, ed. C.D.N. Costa. London. 113–34.
Russell, D.A. 1979. *'De Imitatione.'* In *Creative Imitation and Latin Literature*, ed. D. West and T. Woodman. Cambridge. 1–16.
Russell, D.A. 1981. *Criticism in Antiquity*. London.
Russell, D.A. 1998. 'The Panegyrists and Their Teachers.' In *The Propaganda of Power: The Role of Panegyric in Late Antiquity*, ed. M. Whitby. Leiden. 17–50.
Russell, D.A. and Winterbottom, M. 1972. *Ancient Literary Criticism. The Principal Texts in New Translations*. Oxford.
Rutherford, R.B. 2012. *Greek Tragic Style: Form, Language and Interpretation*. Cambridge.
Rutledge, S.H. 2007. 'Oratory and Politics in the Empire.' In *A Companion to Roman Rhetoric*, ed. W.J. Dominik and J. Hall. London. 109–21.
Sacks, K.S. 1983. 'Historiography in the Rhetorical Works of Dionysius of Halicarnassus.' *Athenaeum* 61: 65–87.
Sacks, K.S. 1986. 'Rhetoric and Speeches in Hellenistic Historiography.' *Athenaeum* 64: 383–95.
Saxonhouse, A.W. 2006. *Free Speech and Democracy in Ancient Athens*. Cambridge.
Scaglione, A. 1972. *The Classical Theory of Composition from its Origins to the Present. A Historical Survey*. Chapel Hill.
Scheller, P. 1911. *De Hellenistica historiae conscribendae arte*. Dissertation. Leipzig.
Schenkeveld, D.M. 1964. *Studies in Demetrius* On Style. Amsterdam.
Schenkeveld, D.M. 1975. 'Theories of Evaluation in the Rhetorical Treatises of Dionysius of Halicarnassus.' *Museum Philologum Londiniense* 1: 93–107.
Schenkeveld, D.M. 1988. '*Iudicia vulgi*: Cicero, De oratore 3.195ff. and Brutus 183ff.' *Rhetorica* 6: 291–305.
Schenkeveld, D.M. 2000. 'The Intended Public of Demetrius's *On Style*: The Place of the Treatise in the Hellenistic Educational System.' *Rhetorica* 18: 29–48.
Schlikker, F.W. 1940. *Hellenistische Vorstellungen von der Schönheit des Bauwerks nach Vitruv*. Berlin.
Schmitz, T.A. 2011. 'The Image of Athens in Diodorus Siculus.' In Schmitz-Wiater 2011a: 234–51.
Schmitz, T.A. and Wiater, N. eds. 2011a. *The Struggle for Identity. Greeks and their Past in the First Century BCE*. Stuttgart.
Schmitz, T.A. and Wiater, N. 2011b. 'Introduction: Approaching Greek Identity.' In Schmitz-Wiater 2011a: 15–45.
Scholz, B.I. 1992. *Untersuchungen zur Tracht der römischen Matrona*. Cologne.
Schubert, P., Ducrey, P., and Derron, P. eds. 2013. *Les Grecs héritiers des Romains: huit exposés suivis de discussions*. Entretiens sur l'antiquité classique 59. Vandoeuvres / Geneva.

Schubert, W. 1991. 'Herodot, Livius und die Gestalt des Collatinus in der Lucretia-Geschichte.' *Rheinisches Museum* 134: 80–96.
Schütrumpf, E. 2011. '"As I thought that the speakers most likely might have spoken…" Thucydides *Hist.* 1.22.1 on composing speeches.' *Philologus* 155: 229–56.
Schultze, C.E. 1986. 'Dionysius of Halicarnassus and his Audience.' In *Past Perspectives: Studies in Greek and Roman Historical Writing*, ed. I.S. Moxon, J.D. Smart, and A.J. Woodman. Cambridge. 121–41.
Schultze, C.E. 1995. 'Dionysius of Halicarnassus and Roman Chronology.' *Proceedings of the Cambridge Philological Society* 41: 192–214.
Schultze, C.E. 2000. 'Authority, Originality, and Competence in the Roman Archaeology of Dionysius of Halicarnassus.' *Histos* 4: 6–49. (http://research.ncl.ac.uk/histos/Histos_BackIssues2000.html)
Schultze, C.E. 2011. '"The Sole Glory of Death": Dying and Commemoration in Dionysius of Halicarnassus.' In *Memory and Mourning: Studies on Roman Death*, ed. V.M. Hope and J. Huskinson. Oxford. 78–92.
Schultze, C.E. 2012. 'Negotiating the Plupast: Dionysius of Halicarnassus and Roman Self-Definition.' In *Time and Narrative in Ancient Historiography: The 'Plupast' from Herodotus to Appian*, ed. J. Grethlein and C. Krebs. Cambridge. 113–38.
Schwartz, E. 1903. 'Dionysius von Halikarnassos.' *Paulys Realencyclopädie der classischen Altertumsiwssenschaft* V.1: 934–61. [Reprinted: Schwartz, E. 1957. 'Dionysios von Halikarnassos.' In *Griechische Geschichtschreiber*. Leipzig. 319–60.]
Sebesta, J.L. 1998. 'Women's Costume and Feminine Civic Morality in Augustan Rome.' In *Gender and the Body in the Ancient Mediterranean*, ed. M. Wyke. Oxford. 105–17.
Sharrock, A.R. 1991. 'Womanufacture.' *Journal of Roman Studies* 81: 36–49.
Small, J.P. 1976. 'The Death of Lucretia.' *American Journal of Archaeology* 80: 349–60.
Solodow, J.B. 1979. 'Livy and the Story of Horatius, 1.24–26.' *Transactions of the American Philological Association* 109: 251–68.
Spawforth, A. 2012. *Greece and the Augustan Cultural Revolution*. Cambridge.
Spelman, E. 1758. The Roman Antiquities *of Dionysius Halicarnassensis, translated into English with Notes and Dissertations*. London.
Stephens, S.A. and Vasunia, Ph. eds. 2010. *Classics and National Cultures*. Oxford.
Swain, S. 1996. *Hellenism and Empire. Language, Classicism, and Power in the Greek World AD 50–250*. Oxford.
Syed, Y. 2005. *Vergil's* Aeneid *and the Roman Self.* Ann Arbor.
Syme, R. 1939. *The Roman Revolution*. Oxford.
Tacoma, L. 2016. *Moving Romans: Migration to Rome in the Principate*. Oxford.
Takács, S.A. 2000. 'Politics and Religion in the Bacchanalian Affair of 186 BCE.' *Harvard Studies in Classical Philology* 100: 301–10.
Tanner, J. 2006. *The Invention of Art History in Ancient Greece: Religion, Society and Artistic Rationalisation*. Cambridge.

Thomas, Y. 1984. '*Vitae necisque potestas*: Le père, la cité, la mort.' In *Du châtiment dans la cité: supplices corporels et peine de mort dans le monde antique. Table ronde organisée par l'École française de Rome*. Rome. 499–548.
Too, Y.L. 1995. *The Rhetoric of Identity in Isocrates: Text, Power, Pedagogy*. Cambridge.
Treggiari, S. 1991. *Roman Marriage. Iusti Coniuges from the Time of Cicero to the Time of Ulpian*. Oxford.
Turcan, R. 1995. 'Le Classicisme Augustéen.' In *L'Art Romain dans L'Histoire*. Paris. 83–105.
Ungern-Sternberg, J. von. 2005. 'The Formation of the "Annalistic Tradition": The Example of the Decemvirate.' In *Social Struggles in Ancient Rome*, ed. K.A. Raaflaub. Oxford. 75–97.
Usher, S. 1965. 'Individual Characterization.' *Eranos* 63: 99–119.
Usher, S. 1974. *Dionysius of Halicarnassus: The Critical Essays in Two Volumes*. Vol. 1. Cambridge, MA.
Usher, S. 1982. 'The Style of Dionysius of Halicarnassus in the *Antiquitates Romanae*.' *Aufstieg und Niedergang der Römischen Welt* 2.30.1: 817–38.
Usher, S. 1985. *Dionysius of Halicarnassus: The Critical Essays in Two Volumes*. Vol. 2. Cambridge, MA.
Vandiver, E. 1999. 'The Founding Mothers of Livy's Rome: The Sabine Women and Lucretia.' In *The Eye Expanded: Life and the Arts in Greco-Roman Antiquity*, ed. F.B. Titchener and R.F. Moorton. Berkeley. 206–32.
Verdin, H. 1974. 'La fonction de l'histoire selon Denys d'Halicarnasse.' *Ancient Society* 5: 289–307.
Wagner-Hasel, B. 2012. '*Tria himatia*. Vêtement et mariage en Grèce ancienne.' In *Vêtements antiques: s' habiller, se déshabiller dans les mondes antiques*, ed. F. Gherchanoc and V. Huet. Arles. 39–46.
Walbank, F.W. 1957–79. *A Historical Commentary on Polybius*. 3 vols. Oxford.
Walker, A.D. 1993. '*Enargeia* and the Spectator in Greek Historiography.' *Transactions of the American Philological Association* 123: 353–77.
Wallace-Hadrill, A. 2008. *Rome's Cultural Revolution*. Cambridge.
Walt, S. 1997. *Der Historiker C. Licinius Macer*. Stuttgart.
Wardle, D. 2014. *Suetonius*: Life of Augustus. Oxford.
Weaire, G. 2002. 'The Relationship between Dionysius of Halicarnassus' *De Imitatione* and *Epistula ad Pompeium*.' *Classical Philology* 97: 351–9.
Weaire, G. 2005. 'Dionysius of Halicarnassus' Professional Situation and the *De Thucydide*.' *Phoenix* 59: 246–66.
Weaire, G. 2012. 'How to Talk to a Roman Student: The Teacher's Authority in Dionysius of Halicarnassus' *De compositione uerborum*.' *Illinois Classical Studies* 35–36:46–67.
Weissenberger, M. 2003. 'Lysias 1905–2000.' *Lustrum* 45: 7–166.
Welles, C.B. 1934. *Royal Correspondence in the Hellenistic Period: A Study in Greek Epigraphy*. New Haven.
White, H. 1973. *Metahistory: The Historical Imagination in 19th-Century Europe*. Baltimore.

White, H. 1978. 'Interpretation in History.' In *Tropics of Discourse*. Baltimore. 51–80.
Whitmarsh, T. 2001. *Greek Literature and the Roman Empire. The Politics of Imitation*. Oxford.
Whitmarsh, T. 2009. 'Greece and Rome.' In *The Oxford Handbook of Hellenic Studies*, ed. G. Boys-Stones, B. Graziosi, and Ph. Vasunia. Oxford. 114–28.
Whitmarsh, T. 2011. 'Greek Poets and Roman Patrons in the Late Republic and Early Empire.' In Schmitz-Wiater 2011a: 197–212.
Whitmarsh, T. 2013. *Beyond the Second Sophistic. Adventures in Greek Postclassicism*. Berkeley.
Whitmarsh, T. 2016. *Battling the Gods. Atheism in the Ancient World*. London.
Wiater, N. 2011a. *The Ideology of Classicism. Language, History, and Identity in Dionysius of Halicarnassus*. Berlin.
Wiater, N. 2011b. 'Writing Roman History – Shaping Greek Identity: The Ideology of Historiography in Dionysius of Halicarnassus.' In Schmitz-Wiater 2011a: 61–91.
Wiater, N. 2014. *Dionysius von Halikarnass: Römische Frühgeschichte Band 1: Bücher 1 bis 3*. Stuttgart.
Wiater, N. 2018a. 'Getting Over Athens: Re-writing Hellenicity in the Early Roman History of Dionysius of Halicarnassus.' In The Hellenistic Reception of Classical Athenian Democracy and Political Thought, ed. B. Gray and M. Canevaro. Oxford. 209–35.
Wiater, N. 2018b. *Dionysius von Halikarnass: Römische Frühgeschichte Band 2: Bücher 4 bis 6*. Stuttgart.
Wilamowitz-Moellendorff, U. von 1900. 'Asianismus und Atticismus.' *Hermes* 35: 1–52.
Williams, R. and Orrom, M. 1954. *A Preface to Film*. London.
Williams, R. 1977. *Marxism and Literature*. Oxford.
Williams, R. 2005. *Culture and Materialism: Selected Essays*. London.
Wiseman, T.P. 1979. *Clio's Cosmetics*. Leicester.
Wiseman, T.P. 2002. 'History, Poetry, and Annales.' In *Clio and the Poets: Augustan Poetry and the Traditions of Ancient Historiography*, ed. D.S. Levene and D.P. Nelis. Leiden. 331–62.
Wiseman, T.P. 2008a. *Unwritten Rome*. Exeter.
Wiseman, T.P. 2008b. 'The Legend of Lucius Brutus.' In Wiseman 2008a: 292–305.
Wiseman, T.P. 2008c. 'Roman Republic, Year One.' In Wiseman 2008a: 306–19.
Wisse, J. 1995. 'Greeks, Romans, and the Rise of Atticism.' In Abbenes-Slings-Sluiter 1995: 65–82.
Woerther, F. 2013. *Apollodore de Pergame. Théodore de Gadara. Fragments et témoignages*. Paris.
Woerther, F. 2015. *Caecilius de Calè-Actè. Fragments et témoignages*. Paris.
Woodman, A.J. 1988. *Rhetoric in Classical Historiography. Four Studies*. London and Sydney.

Woolf, G. 1994. 'Becoming Roman, Staying Greek.' *Proceedings of the Cambridge Philological Society* 40: 116–35.
Wooten, C.W. 1975. 'Le développement du style asiatique pendant l'époque hellénistique.' *Revue des études grecques* 88: 94–104.
Wooten, C.W. 1987. *Hermogenes:* On Types of Style. Chapel Hill.
Wooten, C.W. 1989. 'Dionysius of Halicarnassus and Hermogenes on the Style of Demosthenes.' *American Journal of Philology* 110: 576–88.
Worman, N. 2015. *Landscape and the Spaces of Metaphor in Ancient Literary Theory and Criticism*. Cambridge.
Wysłucha, K. 2012. 'The Role of Music in Ancient Rhetoric.' *Papers on Rhetoric* 11: 224–36.
Yunis, H. 1996. *Taming Democracy: Models of Political Rhetoric in Classical Athens*. Ithaca.
Zanker, P. 1987. *Augustus und die Macht der Bilder*. Munich.
Zetzel, J.E.G. 1995. *Cicero:* De Re Publica, *Selections*. Cambridge.
Zizek, S. 1997. *The Plague of Fantasies*. London.

Index of Passages Discussed

Aristotle
Rhetoric 3.1404b24-5 261

Dionysius of Halicarnassus
Roman Antiquities 1.1–8 130–2, 137–40, 143
1.3.1–2 61
1.5.3 4
1.6.4 4
1.8.2 205
1.16 183
1.20–1 183–4
1.31 16–17, 188–9
1.45 187–8, 189–90
1.54 187
1.70.4 14
1.74 190–1
1.83–4 192
1.86.3 219
1.89.1 9–10
1.90.2 205
2.3.5 194–5
2.4.1–2 195, 214–15
2.11.2–3 213
2.12.4 15
3.21–2 162–8, 175–6, 177, 178
4.64–84 169–74, 176, 177, 178, 179, 183
4.72–5 75
5.1.1 207
5.1–13 144–8
5.52–7 148–52
5.56.1 132–3, 137–40, 149
5.66–8 76
7.54–6 216–17
7.66.1–5 133–4, 137–40, 213
8.64–5 156–60
10.54.7 236–7
10.60.2 237
11.1.1–5 135–40, 225–6
11.1.2 226–8
11.4–21 230–3
11.28.1 235
11.41.2 236
11.44.6 239–40
14.6.3 61–2
On Composition 1.5 89
3.2 253–4
3.8–12 254–5
4.8–11 80–2
4.12–13 256–7, 260
4.14 20
6.8–9 101
11.2 252–3
11.8 250
21.1–2 94
25.35 251
On Demosthenes 1–8 97
10.3 103–4
15.2 255
19.1 95
22.2–5 68–70
51.2–4 102
54.8 121
On Dinarchus 7.5 66–7
On Isaeus 11.1 78–9
11.4 79–80
On Isocrates 5.1 6
17.1 60–1, 62–3
On Lysias 8.5–6 110
11.3–4 47
12.2–9 119
On the Ancient Orators (Preface) 5, 9, 14, 64, 72–3, 85–6, 87–8, 104, 122–3, 264
On Thucydides 1.1–2 38–40
2.3–4 44–5
4.1–3 45–8
13–17 129–30
24.12 38–9
25.1–2 37–8, 40–2
34.7 49
35.1 45
37–41 58
45.3–6 52–4

Dionysius of Halicarnassus (cont.)
  55.3–4 42–3
  55.5 43
  First Letter to Ammaeus 11.4
    58–9
  Letter to Pompeius 3 182
  6.7 140

Horace
  Ars Poetica 32–5 251
  38–41 39
  46–8 258–9, 260
  99–100 252–3
  234 260
  240–3 258–60, 262
  291 252
  356 250
  Satires 1.4.53–62 257–8

Longinus, *On the sublime* 40.2 262–3

Plato, *Phaedrus* 264 c 99
  278d 101
Polybius 6.10.12–14 210–11

Thucydides 1.22.1 52–3
  1.22.4 40–1
  7.14.4 43

General Index

Aeschines 103
ἀκρίβεια, 'accuracy' 141–2, 154, 159, 203
Ammaeus 8, 33, 263
Antipater of Thessalonica 7, 12–13, 247
Antony, Mark 226, 264
Apelles 113
Apollodorus of Pergamon 25, 248, 264
Apollonius Molon 24
Arendt, Hannah 267–8, 273
Aristophanes 242; *Frogs* 22, 46, 255, 256
Aristophanes of Byzantium 243
Aristotle 7, 22, 44, 58–9, 89, 95, 96–7, 98, 99, 109, 193, 206, 243, 246, 248, 249, 275
Aristoxenus 7, 24, 243
Asianism 5, 19–20, 72–3, 82, 85, 86, 87–8, 109, 123, 264
Atticism 5, 19–20, 85, 86, 87–8, 104, 109, 264, 276
Augustine 267
Augustus *passim*; Dion. Hal.'s attitude to 13–16, 104; on style 19–20, 264

Bacchylides 111

Caecilius of Caleacte 7, 8, 13, 25, 263, 268
Caesar, Julius 229
Callimachus 48
Calpurnius Piso 153
Calvus, C. Licinius 19
χάρις, 'charm' 47, 66, 110–24
Chrysippus 7, 20, 24, 243
Cicero 18–19, 25, 28, 42, 85, 86, 93, 122, 224, 261, 262, 263, 276
Claudius Quadrigarius 154
Crates of Mallos 22

Demetrius, *On style* 23, 96, 98, 120–1
Demosthenes 15, 19, 45, 48, 58–9, 65, 68–70, 83–105, 121, 242

Dio Chrysostom 6
Diodorus Siculus 169
Dionysius of Halicarnassus life 1–2, 7–9;
  On composition 74, 95, 242–66;
  On Demosthenes 83–105, 117; *On imitation* 4, 84; *On Lysias* 106–24; *On Thucydides* 37–54, 58;
  First Letter to Ammaeus 95; *Letter to Pompeius* 50–2, 108; *Roman Antiquities*, speeches in 75–6, 142, 143, 147–8, 165–6, 174, 211–14, 230–3

Ennius 257–8, 259
Euripides 242
Eusebius 142

Fabius Pictor 24, 152, 153, 168, 192, 193

Gellius, Cn. 153–5
Geminus, C. Pompeius 8, 33, 263

Hegesias 19, 80–2
Hermogenes 93–4, 96
Herodotus 24, 29, 41, 75, 80–2, 169–70, 173, 177, 178, 182, 214, 226, 227, 238–9, 241, 256
Hesiod 111
Hieronymus 153, 203
Homer 248, 254–7, 265–6
Horace 22, 26, 31, 39–40; *Ars Poetica* 243–66; *Sat.* 1.4 257–8
Hyperides 19, 21, 85

imitation see *mimesis*
'irrational criterion' 47–8, 100, 115, 116–20, 122, 124
Isaeus 78–80, 120
Isocrates 5, 19, 41, 44, 51, 59–64, 66, 90, 93, 97, 101, 102, 103, 107, 109, 120, 122

kritikoi, the 22–3, 37, 100, 114–15, 116, 243, 247, 252

299

Licinius Macer 154
Livy 11, 28–9, 127–8, 146, 148, 152, 153–4, 155–6, 159, 162, 166, 168, 169, 171, 207, 208, 209, 212, 214, 220, 224, 226, 228, 229–30, 232, 234–5, 238
Longinus, *On the sublime* 14, 25, 41, 51, 101, 245, 262–3
Lucian 6
Lysias 19, 54, 65, 78–9, 85, 90, 91, 93, 94, 97, 101, 106–24, 142

Maecenas 264
Menander 53, 54–5
metathesis 57, 76–82, 90–1, 254, 257–8
mimesis 4–5, 41, 53, 77, 79, 83–4

Neoptolemus of Parium 246
Nicolaus of Damascus 7, 11–12, 13, 268

Ovid 39, 78

Pandora 111
Pausimachus 115, 116, 261
Pericles 52–4
Peripatetics 108, 109, 246, 248, 249
Philodemus 22–3, 25–6, 114, 245, 246–7, 261–2
Philostratus 6
Phylarchus 203
Pindar 7, 21, 23, 111, 239, 242
Piso, L. Calpurnius 12, 153, 246
Plato 7, 21, 22, 44, 51, 52, 76, 88, 93, 97, 99, 102, 103, 206, 211, 243
Plutarch 6, 49, 55
Polybius 24, 74, 153, 181, 193, 195, 198, 199, 203–5, 206, 210–11, 212, 215, 216, 217, 218, 220, 224, 228
Polyclitus 7, 275
Posidonius 195
prepon 91, 98, 99–100, 248–9

Quintilian 25, 54, 93, 95

Rhetorica ad Herennium 93, 261
Rufus, Metilius 5, 8, 10, 74, 221, 243, 247, 263

Sallust 195, 228
Sappho 21, 23, 242
Second Sophistic, the 197–8
Similes 164
Simonides 242
Socrates 44
Stoics, the 99
Strabo 7, 11, 13, 268
styles, classification of 93–8
Sulla 237

Theodectes 243
Theodorus of Gadara 25, 74
Theophrastus 24, 96, 107, 243, 249
Theopompus 137, 139, 140, 178, 227
Thrasymachus 97
Thucydides 4, 20, 37–54, 58, 59, 60–3, 80–1, 91, 93, 94, 97, 98, 102, 103, 122, 129–30, 138, 141, 177, 178, 182, 203, 204, 214, 216, 226–8, 241
Tiberius 264
Timaeus 153
Timagenes of Alexandria 7, 13, 268
Tubero, Q. Aelius 8, 28, 33, 48, 74, 154, 221, 263

Valerius Antias 154
Varro 7, 28, 196
Virgil 186, 188, 190–1, 192, 196, 198, 220, 264–6
Vitruvius 112

White, Hayden 3, 181
wool-working 164

Xenophon 141, 177, 178, 227

For EU product safety concerns, contact us at Calle de José Abascal, 56–1°, 28003 Madrid, Spain or eugpsr@cambridge.org.